# THE MOST VICIOUS KILLERS EVER CAUGHT!

The simple act of murder is not enough for some heinous killers. Their insane bloodlust can only be satisfied by torturing their victims — with everything from acid to red-hot knives to electric shocks — exacting tremendous pain before they snuff out their lives forever.

Now, from the authentic files of *True Detective* magazine, read the horrifying true crime accounts of murderers whose perversion shocked the country: TORTURE KILLERS like Philadelphian Gary Heidnik, who kept women as "sex slaves" shackled in his basement, raping and torturing them daily; Antonio Dorsett of Florida, who knifed his victims dozens of times and then poured salt in their wounds to increase their agony; and Westley Allan Dodd, Washington state's infamous child killer, who kept a diary listing all the ways he planned to kill little boys!

## TORTURE KILLERS II

**PINNACLE BOOKS AND *TRUE DETECTIVE* MAGAZINE
TEAM UP TO BRING YOU THE
MOST HORRIFIC TRUE CRIME STORIES!**

FROM THE FILES OF <u>TRUE DETECTIVE</u> MAGAZINE

# TORTURE KILLERS II

Edited by
Rose G. Mandelsberg

PINNACLE BOOKS
WINDSOR PUBLISHING CORP.

*The editor wishes to express her heartfelt thanks and appreciation to Stan Munro whose relentless efforts made this book possible.*

*A special mention to Chris whose torture techniques are legendary.*

PINNACLE BOOKS are published by

Windsor Publishing Corp.
475 Park Avenue South
New York, NY 10016

The P logo Reg U.S. Pat & TM off. Pinnacle is a trademark of Windsor Publishing Corp.

First Printing: February, 1994

Printed in the United States of America

# TABLE OF CONTENTS

# "A FIRE POKER PIERCED HIS BRAIN!"

## by Bruce Gibney

In the blistering Las Vegas heat the crowd assembled. Old friends coming to wish the man a last goodbye, they arrived in polished new Mercedes and rusted, aging Chevys. They wore everything from silk suits with designer labels stitched into the collars to simple church clothes displaying their mothers' sewing skills.

They formed a spectrum of Las Vegas society, from entertainers whose names lit up the giant casino marquees to working stiffs who cleaned the cafeterias and drove the cabs. They were young and old, black and white, and every shade in between. They numbered about 500—a good crowd by Las Vegas standards.

Winston would have liked that. He always did like a good crowd.

Winston DeWitt Hemsley was a star. He worked and partied with the likes of Sammy Davis, Ben Vereen, and Gregory Hines. It was difficult to find a person who worked in the Vegas entertainment industry who did not know the handsome, quiet-spoken choreographer or seen his work.

Hemsley had danced on Broadway, as well as Vegas. He was a star performer and choreographer with the shows *Jubilee!* and *Hallelujah, Hollywood* at the Ballys Hotel-

7

Casino and with the *Lido de Paris* show in Paris and Las Vegas. Over the years, he had provided joyous entertainment for hundreds of thousands of customers.

Hemsley was born in New York's South Bronx. It was a tough neighborhood, a place where kids grew up fast and died young. Hemsley wanted no part of it. Some kids used their fists to escape the South Bronx. But Hemsley used his talent. A gifted dancer, he auditioned and was accepted at the New York School of Performing Arts, immortalized in the movie and TV series *Fame* as an avenue for kids with talent into the world of the arts.

Hemsley spent four years at Performing Arts. After graduation, he and a buddy hoofed it to Broadway to see if they could get work. For two years Winston knocked on doors. Then one afternoon, he heard they were casting the chorus line of a new musical at the Shubert, a musical called *Hello, Dolly.*

Hemsley caught the eye of the producer and was signed to the chorus line. Just 20 years old, Winston Hemsley was already in the big time.

Hemsley moved to Las Vegas in 1972. By then, he had made a name for himself as both a dancer and a choreographer. His first big show was *Jubilee!* at the old MGM Grand. It was a big show, with lavish production numbers and dance numbers that brought the boozy, gambling crowd to its feet. The first show sold out; for the next 18 years, it remained one of the hottest tickets in town.

Hemsley had rolled the dice and come up a winner. But he was betting on his talent, and that was a sure thing.

Hemsley's next show was *Hallelujah Hollywood,* followed by another huge hit, *Les Girls.* These shows had all the Hemsley earmarks: great dance numbers set to great songs and presented with plenty of show-biz glitter.

Over the next decade, Winston Hemsley, compiled a listed of credits as thick as the Vegas phone book. He hung out with Vegas elite, but he also remained the pleasant, soft-voiced youngster who had escaped from the

South Bronx. He was modest about his achievements and large with his praise. "Good dancers always make you look good," he once said. "Heck, I am getting applause for other people's work."

Hemsley was once asked, if he could do it all over again, what he would change. For once, the slender, happy choreographer was at a loss for words. Finally, he admitted that he probably wouldn't change a thing. "All I've ever wanted to do is dance, and that is what I am doing. My whole life is dance and dancing. Not many can say they are doing exactly what they always wanted to do."

On April 27, 1989, Hemsley performed as a guest artist with the Opus Dance Company in the Tropicana Hotel showroom. Typically, patrons packed the legendary night-spot to see their favorite dancer. Hemsley did not disappoint them. A newspaper critic later said it was one of the best dance shows he had seen in his 20 years of reviewing.

At the time, no one realized it would be Winston Hemsley's last show.

May 9, 1989, fell on a Tuesday. At 2:30 p.m., Las Vegas police received a frantic call about a possible murder at the 2800 block of Castlewood Drive.

A patrol officer snaking along Tropicana Boulevard took the call. When he pulled up in front of the condominium complex, he saw a car parked in the driveway and a man standing nearby.

"Did you call?" the officer asked.

"Yes," the man answered, trembling. Pointing to a ground-floor condo with the door ajar, he said, "In there."

The officer went up the winding cement walkway and through the open door. "Jesus Christ, look at all the blood!" the officer said from inside. He walked out of the complex back to the patrol car. Lifting the dash mike to his lips, he requested that a homicide team be dispatched to the scene.

Metro Investigators Norm Ziola and Mike Geary, under the direction of Sergeant Bill Keeton, responded. They were followed by more patrol officers and criminalists Margie Holland and Dan Connell.

Entering the plush condo, the detectives saw a slim, middle-aged man sprawled face down on a thick rug in the living room. Blood welled out from beneath his face and chest, staining the thick shag rug. The victim's abdomen was enlarged, suggesting he had been dead several days.

While the criminalists donned rubber gloves and prepared to process the crime scene, Detectives Ziola and Geary walked to the front of the house. The first patrol officer on the scene told them what he knew.

The man who had been standing in front of the condominium when the police first arrived was sitting in the back of the cruiser. A compact man in his mid 30s, Weldon James told police in a shaky voice, "I can't believe this."

James told detectives that he had known the victim, Winston Hemsley, since 1973. The two friends had one lived together and remained close after James left. "We were family," he said sadly. "Like brothers."

James said he left town May 7th on business and returned that afternoon. On his answering machine he found calls from several persons trying to get in touch with Winston. He said he called Hemsley's home but got no response. He drove out to the condo and found the front door ajar. He opened the door and found his longtime friend dead on the living-room floor.

"I can't believe this," James said repeatedly. "You aren't going to find anyone nicer than Winston."

Nice or not, Winston Hemsley certainly didn't deserve the gruesome fate that befell him.

Detectives Ziola and Geary went back into the house. Marjorie Holland was examining a blood splotch on the living-room wall. Dan Connell was in the bedroom. A photographer was bent over the bloated body of the famed Vegas dancer, taking pictures that Winston's public — except possibly a jury — would never see. Las Vegas Metro was hard at work.

Ziola and Geary were seasoned cops. They spent a good part of their working lives in tragic surroundings. The sight of mayhem and death no longer surprised. But even in their grim world, this was something different.

Winston Hemsley had died a violent, bloody death. The quantity of blood was astounding. It was everywhere the detectives looked: on the floor, the walls — even sprayed on the cathedral ceiling that rose 14 feet above them. It was a mess, one of the bloodiest spectacles Detective Ziola had seen in his 20 years of police work.

Moving forward, Detectives Ziola and Geary crouched by the body. They noted that Hemsley's slim body was bloated and marked by lividity, indicating he had been dead at least 24 hours. He had also apparently suffered stab wounds to the chest and been beaten. The beating had been unusually ferocious; Ziola saw a small amount of brain matter oozing from the skull.

What a waste, the veteran cop thought. What a pointless waste.

The investigation spread out into the neighborhood. Winston Hemsley had been in show business, but his neighborhood was simply squaresville — a modest, middle-class enclave that might have been plucked from a suburb anywhere in the country and dropped down in the midst of the Vegas glitz.

Neighbors were a bit surprised to find detectives knocking on their doors. A few knew Hemsley; they described him as a nice guy who always said hello. They didn't really know him that well, they said. A couple of neighbors in the same condo complex were aware that Hemsley was in show business. They said he kept late hours and had friends over at all hours of the night. They were quick to point out that the visitors were polite and never made a ruckus. No one had apparently seen Hemsley in the last few days. No one had heard or seen anything that suggested their neighbor had been in trouble or was the victim of foul play.

Detectives Ziola and Geary returned to the victim's condo. The neighborhood canvass had not provided sleuths with any hard leads, but they had better luck inside the apartment. Criminalists Holland and Connell had examined the condo, room by room. They found one blood trail that led from the body through the condo to a sliding glass door, and then another from the kitchen into the master bedroom.

On the floor in the master bedroom, the probers found a fireplace poker, a pair of scissors, and a clawhammer, wrapped in bloodied sheets and clothes. The poker had a black, cast-iron hook with a spear-type head. The scissors were the type used to cut fabric with. The clawhammer had a blue plastic handle.

All the items were bloodied and were apparently used in the murder. Additionally, the handles of both the hammer and the poker each had fingerprints on them in the victim's blood. The criminalists had also discovered bloody prints on a lightswitch plate and on the glass door leading out of the house. The prints looked good enough to identify the person who'd left them.

The bloodied instruments of death were bagged as evidence. They would be sent to lab technicians who would try to lift the prints.

Ziola and Geary felt confident when they left the condo. They didn't have an eyewitness or a suspect description. But they had something potentially better—the killer's prints in the victim's blood.

Winston Hemsley's murder was big news, and Las Vegas television gave it celebrity coverage. Reporters had no trouble getting quotes.

"Last night was not a good night in town for the shows," said Winston's manager. "So many dancers had

12

studied or performed with Winston. I don't think a curtain went up on time and I don't think anybody did a good show. They were that upset by his death."

Hemsley had been working on plans for a show based on his own life story. It was a rags-to-riches sort of thing, an upbeat saga with lots of dance and good times. The show, nearing production stage, was shelved. The good times, at least for a while, were over.

Hemsley had been a Buddhist — as such, he strived for world peace and reached out to people through entertainment. But there had been no peace in his death. It had been brutal, bloody, and pointless.

The autopsy was performed by Dr. Giles Sheldon Green on May 10, 1989. According to the report, Hemsley had suffered one penetration wound of the left inside of the chest and five penetrating stab-type wounds in the back. Internally, the former dancer had suffered extensive destruction to the left side of the skull. Bone fragments had been driven deep into the cranial cavity. The brain, Dr. Green noted, was badly decomposed. There were 30 lacerations on the scalp, massive depressed skull fractures on the left side, and brain tissue oozing out of the lacerations. Some, the skilled pathologist noted, had a definite pattern.

Green discovered two linear marks with a skipped area between them — a horrible wound that seemed to match the pattern of a clawhammer blow.

"The body was badly decomposed, which somewhat limited my ability to perform the autopsy," Green noted. "My guess is he was dead four to five days before the discovery."

During the autopsy, Dr. Green discovered a chunk of iron about the size of a human nipple embedded in the brain. The tip was later matched to the fire poker discovered in the victim's master bedroom.

The three-page autopsy report supported in cold black print what the detectives had seen that grim Tuesday afternoon. Winston Hemsley had been gruesomely beaten and stabbed to death with a ferocity that shocked even veteran lawmen.

What, detectives wondered, had motivated such a craven act? What could have prompted the killer to strike with such violence that the blood of the Buddha-worshipping victim had ended up sprayed on the cathedral ceiling 14 feet above his broken head?

Robbery, apparently, was part of it. In a search of the master bedroom, criminalist Connell had discovered a cable coupling that had apparently been connected to a VCR on top of the portable television. The VCR was gone. Also missing was personal jewelry and a much-prized Longine watch purchased after the *Jubilee!* show opened at the old MGM Grand.

The biggest item missing, however, was from Hemsley's garage—his white '64 Buick Electra. The buffed and much-cared-for classic was gone—as were Hemsley's keys.

A BOLO was issued. Police were playing catch-up, but they knew that if they could retrieve the car, it might go a long way toward solving the case.

Police were still searching for the prized car on May 15th, when 500 persons gathered at a Buddhist ceremony in honor of Winston Hemsley. It was an odd, touching ceremony. Incense burned as Winston's friends and family remembered the good times with laughter and tears.

A family member recalled how Winston had worked hard to save money for dance school and how quickly he progressed from the High School of the Performing Arts to Broadway. "He lived his life to the fullest with dance," she told mourners. "He did what he wanted to do. His spirit will be with all of us."

A friend of the old South Bronx days said he envied Winston because "he did everything he wanted to do. He was a star all over the world. People are dancing his steps everywhere you look. He lived out his life dream. He became what he always dreamed of becoming."

Hemsley was remembered as a man who was generous to a fault. He had never forgotten what it was like to be poor and as a result, he had gone out of his way to help those who were less fortunate.

Hemsley adopted strangers. He fed them and let them stay weeks at a time at his house until they got on their feet. Friends told police that this side of their friend worried them. Taking strangers into your house was dangerous; you never knew what might happen.

Winston didn't listen, though. He believed that Buddha would look after him. But sleuths knew that even Buddha wasn't much good against a guy who was swinging a fire poker.

The identity of the poker swinger was still a mystery and police had few clues.

Police learned that Hemsley, who was artistic co-director of the Simba Dance Studio and who taught dance at Backstage Dance Studio, left the latter studio on Saturday afternoon with a couple of friends and went to his residence. The friends told police that Hemsley wanted them to have a few drinks and unwind. About nine o'clock a stranger came to the door and said he was a friend of "Sam's." Hemsley let him in.

The guests said they had never seen the man before. The stranger said hello and then said little for the rest of the evening. Around midnight, the two guests rose to leave. "We asked the guy if he needed a lift home. He said he didn't," one guest told police.

The two guests went home. Three days later Hemsley was dead on the living-room floor.

The guests said they didn't know who "Sam" was. Nor did they know what interest Hemsley had in the stranger. He might have been a drifter. That figured since Winston was known as a soft touch.

The guests said the stranger was in his early 20s, stood 5-foot-10 and weighed about 250 pounds. He had a massive face with a scar on his forehead and wore a thin mustache and his hair in thin braids.

Police looked through the victim's address book and questioned several people. Their efforts didn't lead anywhere; the man remained a stranger.

The other lead came from a lab. Detectives Ziola and Geary had hopes that the criminalists might produce something. The killer had been sloppy in his attack on Hemsley and sloppy when he lurched around the apartment, overturning furniture and leaving behind plenty of bloody fingerprints. Ziola and Geary had hoped that this sloppiness might lead to something. It finally did.

Criminalist Marjorie Holland had examined the murder weapons at the crime lab and attempted to lift prints off the rubber handle of the clawhammer. The blood, however, was too dry to get a good lift. But she did get a good set of prints off the lightswitch plate in the living room. That was solid evidence; match the prints to a suspect, the sleuths thought, and you had your killer.

The prints were put through the AFIS, the Automated Fingerprint Identification System, with a repository of 200,000 fingerprints maintained by the department. The AFIS was a highly prized crime-fighting tool. It could do in a few minutes what it would have taken several fingerprint experts weeks to do. It scanned thousands of prints in seconds. Although it had just recently come on line, the AFIS packed a punch and had already put a few crooks behind bars.

The prints found in Hemsley's condo were entered into the machine. Detectives waited patiently at their coffee-stained desks for the results.

They got a result, all right, but it wasn't good. According to the AFIS operator, the prints had not matched up with any of those on file in the print repository. That meant the suspect did not have a criminal record in the state, did not work for the casinos or hotels, or was not listed with any state or federal agencies.

To police, he was a nobody, an invisible man who, like

thousands of other invisible men, drift through Las Vegas like a high desert wind.

Detective Ziola felt like the western marshal who had suddenly run out of bullets. He had fingerprints — but no suspects and no leads.

On October 8th, when newsmen asked how the case was progressing, Ziola told them it wasn't. "We're just plodding along," he said. He urged anyone with information about Hemsley's death to contact him at homicide. But that seemed as likely to work as feeding peanuts to an elephant to get it to sing.

Officially, the Hemsley murder investigation was at a standstill. Detectives Ziola and Geary closed the folders and returned them to the case file marked "Unsolved."

The story disappeared from the newspapers. Newsmen went on to other stories, Hemsley's friends got on with their lives, Vegas got on to being Vegas. And Ziola and Geary got on to being cops.

The murder case, which had so traumatized and tantalized Las Vegas, appeared to have come to an end with no final act. For a performer, that was no way to go. And Winston Hemsley had been one hell of a performer.

In April 1991, police finally got the break in the case they were looking for. It came from the AFIS fingerprinting system. Although the crime-scene prints had originally come back from the AFIS without a match, departmental policy dictated that all unmatched prints be run periodically in case any matching prints suddenly came on file. When the unknown prints in the Hemsley case were run again 11 months after the murder, the operators found a match.

Robert Jerrod Mayfield, 20, of North Las Vegas was entered into the AFIS after a 1988 arrest for burglary and grand theft. He had been arrested after stealing a woman's purse with $300 in it. Since the burglary had occurred almost a year before the Hemsley murder, Mayfield's name was on record and the computer should have matched his prints. It hadn't however. Call it computer error.

Mayfield lived in a rundown neighborhood in North Las Vegas. His jail booking sheet showed him to be a black man, 5 feet, 10 inches tall, 250 pounds, with a rose tatoo on his upper right arm. His size and weight, Detective Ziola noted, fit descriptions of the burly stranger who had visited the nimble dancer on the last night he was seen alive.

After his arrest on burglary charges, Mayfield had been placed on probation. His probation officer told detectives that Mayfield had been AWOL in September and October 1989 and February 1990.

According to the probation report, the parolee's residential pattern was unstable, and he moved often without advising his probation officer. He was considered unsupervisable due to lack of cooperation and poor attitude.

Mayfield's work habits fit his lifestyle: employed at a hotel as a bus person, terminated; employed at a restaurant as a dishwasher, self-terminated; employed at a McDonald's restaurant, terminated; employed at another hotel as a kitchen runner, terminated; employed at Montgomery Ward Department Store as a maintenance person, relocated; employed at a landscaping firm as a treetrimmer, terminated.

The report was revealing but not damning. It reflected a troubled man who couldn't keep a job too long, but one who, with the right attitude and a couple of breaks, could straighten himself out.

Mayfield had a bad attitude, sleuths learned. He got a break when the computer failed to turn up his name at first. But now his luck was about to change.

Police checked Mayfield's old addresses on his probation sheet. They finally located him holed up with relatives in North Las Vegas. Police swarmed into the area, and Mayfield was arrested. His relatives were stunned. They had no idea that Bobby was in trouble again. Bobby

18

was in trouble, all right — big-time trouble.

Detective Ziola took one look at the eye-bulging, 250-pound purse snatcher and knew he had the right man.

Mayfield was taken to an interrogation room. His statement was brief: "I don't know nothing about no murder." End of interrogation.

Mayfield was booked into the Clark County Jail, charged with murder. He pled not guilty at his brief September 12th arraignment.

The case against Mayfield was airtight. Witnesses were prepared to testify that Mayfield had been at the Hemsley home on the night of May 7, 1989, the last night Hemsley was seen alive.

Police had also recovered jewelry and a VCR, believed to be Hemsley's, which Mayfield had given a girlfriend days after the murder.

And most incriminating were Mayfield's fingerprints in Hemsley's blood that were lifted from the lightswitch.

Mayfield's goose was cooked and he knew it. On February 13, 1991, one day before jury selection was to begin, Mayfield pled guilty to murder and was sentenced to two consecutive life sentences, plus 18 years.

Before sentencing by Judge Joseph Bonaventure, Mayfield apologized to the court, saying he was not a killer by nature and acted in self-defense. He said that after the guests left, he and Hemsley stayed at the house and talked. He said he was having a good time when he turned his back for a moment. When he turned around, Hemsley was coming at him with a fire poker.

Although outweighing his host by almost 100 pounds, Mayfield said he was terrified of Hemsley. He said he snatched the poker away from his host, then beat him to death on the living-room floor. Not knowing what to do, he dragged the body through the house. He then scooped up the VCR and jewelry and got out of there quickly.

He said he didn't report the crime to police because he was an ex-con on parole and thought that the authorities wouldn't believe him.

He was right; they didn't.

Robert Mayfield is currently serving two life terms plus 18 years in the state prison at Carson City.

EDITOR'S NOTE:

*Weldon Jones and Sam are not the real names of the persons so named in the foregoing story. Fictitious names have been used because there is no reason for public interest in the identities of these persons.*

# "ALIVE AND THRASHING AS THEY CUT OFF HER HEAD!"

## by Bill G. Cox

Early on Friday, December 11, 1987, two workers driving to their jobs at a large meat-packing plant northeast of Amarillo, Texas, were glad they had a heater in their vehicle. Shortly before 5:30 a.m., the temperature was 38 degrees, and the wind was blowing from the north at 29 miles per hour. As the men sped along Folsom Road in the darkness of predawn, the headlights of their car flashed across something white in the ditch between the pavement and a barbed-wire fence.

"My God, that looked like a woman's body!" exclaimed the man on the passenger side.

The driver slammed on his brakes and backed up his car to get another look. What they saw was a horrible sight: Lying face down and wearing only a pair of white panties was the body of a woman without her head! The two witnesses didn't even get out of the car but sped on to the meat plant. There they notified a plant security officer who phoned the Potter County Sheriff's Department in Amarillo about the grisly discovery.

Sheriff's dispatcher Lisa Rexroat radioed shift supervisor Corporal James Bartlett to contact the office by public phone. Patrolling in his unit, Bartlett instructed the dispatcher to call him at a designated number. The dispatcher informed Bartlett that a security officer at the meat plant had reported a headless body on Folsom Road a short distance outside the city limits. (She called by phone to prevent any journalists monitoring the police frequency from rushing to the scene and possibly destroying evidence.)

After telling the dispatcher to radio Deputy Dennis Mc-Manaman to head for the site, the shift supervisor sped to the location. Deputy Jerry Brinkley also joined his colleagues at the scene.

Exiting their units, the deputies saw the body of a young woman lying face down with her legs spread. She was clad only in white nylon panties. One arm was stretched upward.

The women had been decapitated. Only the stub of her neck remained. It was a gaping, bloody sight that sickened the officers. The missing head was nowhere to be found, and the body and ground were relatively clean of blood. The victim had apparently not been decapitated at the scene.

After a brief examination, Corporal Bartlett got on the radio again to his office, giving orders for the dispatcher to notify Sheriff's Lieutenant Shelby Vitatoe and the Potter-Randall Counties Special Crimes Unit (SCU). The crime unit is a special force comprising officers from the Amarillo Police Department and the Potter and Randall Counties Sheriff's Departments. The city of Amarillo lies within both counties. The crack investigative unit is assigned all homicides in the geographical area. The unit has received national recognition and has a remarkable case clearance rate of 94 percent.

Workdays can start at any one of the 24 hours in a day and night for Special Crimes investigators. Lieutenant Jimmy Stevens, then coordinator of the unit, received the call at his home shortly before 6:00 a.m. He hung up and called Sergeant Sandy Morris, the assistant coordinator who was in charge of field investigations. Morris picked up Stevens, and they drove to the crime scene about one half-mile north of Northeast 24th Avenue on Folsom Road. Other SCU agents were also called out.

It was still dark when Stevens and Morris viewed the body, illuminated by spotlights and flashlight beams.

As they checked the body, the deputies briefed the investigators on how the body was found. Morris noticed vehicle tracks visible in the grass and weeds in the ditch, showing that the vehicle had pulled off the road. The body was lying across the tire tracks.

"She must have been killed someplace else and then dumped here," Sergeant Morris speculated to the other officers. That the blood, the head, and the victim's clothing were all missing supported his theory. Also, the corpse sprawled over the tire impressions indicated it had been dumped from the back of the vehicle, the investigators noted.

"Probably carried here in a car trunk or a pickup bed," another officer added.

On the chance that the killer or killers would have disposed of the head, clothing, and other evidence at points distant from the body, Sergeant Morris gave instructions for the city sanitation department to keep a lookout for the items at the city's waste collection central site and also the city landfill west of town where sanitation trucks dumped their loads.

As deputies spread out to check roads and fields for the victim's head and clothing, Sergeant Modeina Holmes, who is now assistant coordinator of the Special Crimes Unit, began recording the crime scene, filming it on video and taking still color photos.

Sergeant Greg Soltis, an SCU crime scene technician and investigator, assisted Holmes with measurements and diagrams at the body site. As the crime scene processing continued, a large truck pulled close to where Deputy Cindy Thomas was seated in her unit. The driver got out and gave his name to the deputy.

23

He said he heard on the radio news that a body had been found. The trucker reported that he drove a route in the general area daily. Driving along State Highway 136, he had noticed a white, bloodstained glove on the roadway and some other litter beneath the underpass at State 136 and Loop 335. The items had not been there the day before, he added.

The deputy contacted Corporal Bartlett by radio and relayed the information and location of the items. Bartlett drove to the underpass, where he observed the "litter." On closer inspection, he saw that the articles included a white, bloodstained blanket at the road's edge, a white plastic bag containing some clothing, and a bloodstained pair of high-top tennis shoes. About five feet away he observed another plastic bag wrapped around a semi-round object that he realized could be a human head.

When Bartlett radioed his findings, Sergeant Holmes and other investigators at the body scene drove to the new location. It was shortly before 9:00 a.m.

Sergeant Joe Allen, one of the crime unit's ID experts, was the first to join Corporal Bartlett. After viewing the scattered items, he concentrated on the plastic garbage bag pulled tightly around the large, egg-shaped object. To see inside, Allen, wearing surgical gloves to prevent damaging possible fingerprints, carefully slit a seam in the bottom of the bag. He was then able to see the gruesome contents that would give him nightmares for weeks after the investigation.

In the supplemental report he wrote later, Sergeant Allen said, "I could see dark-colored hair, the chin and mouth of the head, and it appeared to be that of a white female." It was a horrible death mask that Allen would never forget for the rest of his life.

Meanwhile, Corporal Bartlett, driving along State 136 to look for more evidence, came upon the trucker who had talked earlier to Deputy Thomas. The truck driver directed the officer to the white, bloodstained glove. After

24

Bartlett asked for an ID technician by radio, Allen arrived to photograph and process the site. As it turned out, two pairs of bloody gloves, the kind used by meat plant workers, were discovered. After collecting the evidence, Allen returned to assist Sergeant Holmes in taking pictures and examining the bloodstained clothing and shoes found near the wrapped head.

The technician-investigators saw that one gray-and-white, high-top tennis shoe, a sock, and a red comb had spilled from the clothing bag. Near the mouth of the bag was a light-colored bloodstained towel.

The plastic bag with the woman's head inside was placed in a box lid and then put into Sergeant Holmes' unit to be transferred to an SCU crime lab, where the body would be scrutinized under a laser light for foreign matter on the skin surfaces.

Next, carefully lifting the bag of clothing and placing it on another plastic bag inside her car, Sergeant Holmes, along with Sergeant Allen, examined the contents for clues to the headless victim's identification. They were in luck. Discovered inside the left-foot tennis shoe along with two rings was a Texas driver's license bearing the name of Jeanette Sue Fain, whose date of birth was listed as August 15, 1961. The description on the license listed Fain's hair as brown. An Amarillo address was also on the license.

Holmes turned over the license to Texas Ranger Larry Gilbreath, who had joined the murder probe. Holmes requested that Gilbreath take it to the Special Crimes Unit office downtown so that a check could be made with police records to possibly confirm the victim's identification.

In the meantime, Sergeant Soltis made preparations to transport the decapitated body to the laser laboratory at Texas State Technical Institute (TSTI), a nearby vocational college.

Soltis and two ambulance attendants, all wearing surgical gloves, gingerly lifted the body onto two clean white sheets placed atop a body bag so that any trace evidence on the corpse wouldn't be disturbed. With the body transferred to a laser lab table at TSTI, the fundamentals of identification began amid the highly technical equipment. From the instep of her foot to the top of the shoulder, the headless body measured 4 feet, 3 inches; with the head, it was estimated the woman had been 5 feet, 2 inches tall. The slightly muscular victim was thought to weigh between 120 and 140 pounds. The examination revealed the head had been severed just below the hairline. Long, brown hair protruded from the hairline at the decapitation point.

Assisting in the search for trace evidence was a TSTI laboratory expert. It appeared that the victim's shoulders and arms had been covered with blood, which had been wiped away. Some writing in blue ink on the back of the left hand was illegible. The examiners found defensive wounds on the left hand; the middle finger was almost severed by a slashing wound.

Sergeant Soltis collected foreign hairs and fibers from the body. A pathologist made swabs of the victim's vagina, anus, and mouth for evidence of sexual assault. The crime scene technicians removed the head, which was in a brown grocery sack inside the white plastic bag, and examined and photographed it.

After the trace evidence search, the body was examined by Lieutenant Tom Bevel (now a captain) of the Oklahoma City Police Department, who came to Amarillo after being contacted by crime unit officers. Bevel is a physical evidence specialist and an expert in the processing of human bodies for blood latent fingerprints.

The body was sprayed with a fine mist containing the chemical orthotoludine. A visual exam had revealed bloody areas on the ankles where the killer might have handled the body. Also, the chemical brought out an area on the right thigh where it appeared that three fingers had touched the skin.

However, after a thorough analysis of the marks, Lieutenant Bevel said it was his opinion that the killer or killers who touched the body had worn gloves or some other covering on their hands. No fingerprints were found.

Meanwhile, the driver's license issued to Jeanette Sue Fain was taken to the records division of the Amarillo Police Department by Corporal Wayne Randolph of the SCU to see if the woman's prints were on record. She did have a file, a minor record involving driving under the influence of alcohol and also a disturbance. Randolph took the police fingerprint card to the TSTI laser lab for comparison with prints from the dead woman made by Soltis.

When the prints were compared, Sergeant Soltis found that they matched. He phoned Lieutenant Stevens at the SCU office to report that the identity of the murder victim was confirmed as Jeanette Sue Fain, 26.

The pathologist performed an autopsy on the body after the evidence examination. It revealed that a minimum of seven slashings or incisions were made to cut off the head. The knife-wielder had slashed the victim's neck from left to right. According to the pathologist, the victim was alive and thrashing about when the wounds were made. Other slash and stab wounds of a minor nature were found on the victim's shoulders and abdomen. Both hands bore defensive wounds.

Of special interest to the investigators was a round contusion on the right forearm, which the pathologist thought was a human bite mark. There was no evidence of strangulation, but contusions found on the head indicated the woman had been struck one or two times, blows that may have knocked her temporarily unconscious, the pathologist said.

Death was attributed to massive loss of blood.

Meanwhile, the SCU investigators entered Jeanette Fain's name into the record division computers to lift out

27

any reports involving the woman. One that surfaced was the minor disturbance report involving Jeannette and another woman. Addresses were given for both women on the report.

Lieutenant Morris and Ranger Gilbreath checked out the addresses but found no one home at either place.

Jeanette's address turned out to be a mobile home park, where the manager recalled that she had lived with a close relative. But neither Jeanette nor the female relative were current residents. The manager recalled that Jeanette's relative was employed by the city of Amarillo.

Acting on this information, the investigators returned to the other address to make a neighborhood canvass to find out if anyone knew Jeannette Fain or her family. While they were doing this, a car pulled up in the driveway. The man at the wheel introduced himself and said he lived at the address with Jeanette's female relative. He said the relative drove a sanitation department truck for the city.

The man added that he hadn't seen Jeanette recently but thought the relative had talked to her by phone on Thursday evening, December 10th. Morris phoned the sanitation office, and it was arranged to have Jeanette's relative meet the officers there.

After informing the woman of her kin's death, they quizzed the relative for possible leads. Keeping her emotions under control—something Lieutenant Morris noted later in his report—the relative said that Jeanette had a drinking problem and was "lovable and overfriendly, would go along with anyone," when imbibing. She recalled she had talked to Jeanette on the phone on Thursday, having called her at a bar Jeanette was known to frequent. Jeanette hadn't seemed upset or talked about anything out of the ordinary, the relative recalled.

Jeanette's husband was a truck driver and was in Los Angeles, California, at the time, the witness said. After the interview, Morris and Gilbreath drove back to the

SCU office, across from the court building in the downtown section, to plan their next move and compare field reports with other investigators.

A startling new development awaited them at the office. SCU Investigator Sergeant Janice Whisenhunt had been taking phone calls from the public after a news release was sent to the local media seeking information about the victim's identity and leads to her slayers. A child welfare worker for the Department of Human Services told Whisenhunt about a bizarre call she received from the principal of an elementary school in northeast Amarillo.

The school official was concerned about three small Laotian children who told their teachers they had seen a man kill an American woman at the house where they lived. Sergeant Whisenhunt phoned the principal and confirmed the story. She and Deputy Bob Lorenc sped to the school to talk with the youngsters and their teachers.

After hearing the weird story, Whisenhunt asked the principal to contact the children's mother and have her come to the school as soon as possible. When the Laotian woman arrived, a Laotian teacher served as interpreter between the investigators and the mother, who did not speak English. The officers brought the mother, children, and interpreter to the SCU office.

In an interview with Sergeant Whisenhunt, through the interpreter, the 37-year-old mother said that she and the children had been in an apartment on Northeast Ninth when an Anglo woman was killed. The woman, who was an employee of the meat-packing plant northeast of the city, said she had left the children with four Laotian men at the address while she worked her evening shift. The killing had occurred after she returned from work. She and the youngsters had been in another room, but they had heard a woman crying, had seen the bloody woman on the floor, and fled from the residence to their own home.

The 7-year-old girl related that she had seen the woman's body taken from the house and placed in a car.

The mother, who apparently had been fearful for her and her children's safety, hadn't reported the horrifying episode. The language difference had also hampered her telling anyone. But now, confronted with the story that the children had told at school, she identified the man who had slain the woman by "cutting her neck" as a Laotian whose first name was Somxay. She said he worked at a Chinese restaurant on the west side of the city. The woman related that she knew only the first names of the three other men at the apartment: Ouy, Vath, and Phet.

After listening to the woman's story, Sergeant Morris and Deputy Lorenc drove to the Chinese restaurant and asked to talk with Somxay. When he was brought to them, the officers said they wanted to talk to him about a murder.

The man instantly extended both arms, and the sleuths handcuffed him. He gave his full name as Somxay Pankham and said he was 26 years old. When the three men arrived at the SCU office, the suspect was advised fully of his legal rights, and the cuffs were removed. The Laotian told the officers that he had been in America for seven years. He said he understood and spoke English well, having learned it in a school in Minnesota.

The suspect readily admitted that he had been in his apartment on Thursday night with three of his friends, but he denied any knowledge of a murder or that there had been an American girl in the residence. He claimed that he knew only the nicknames of his friends, which he gave as Ouy, Vath, and Phet.

While Somxay was being grilled, two assistant district attorneys started processing a search warrant for the suspect's apartment. Somxay consented to have investigators take blood, hair, and saliva samples from him. After this was done, he was booked into jail for investigation of murder.

Meanwhile, Sergeant Morris asked the Laotian mother

for the precise location of Somxay Panekham's apartment. While they awaited the search warrant, the officers began efforts to identify and locate the other men who had been with Somxay.

The Laotian woman told detectives that the man known as "Vath" worked at the meat-packing plant where she also worked. She agreed to accompany Morris there and see if she could find out Vath's full name. After explaining their need to the woman's supervisor and plant security officials, the identification badges of employees who might fit the description and nickname were pulled and shown to the woman.

She identified the badge photo of 27-year-old Sisavath Signavong as an associate of Somxay's and one of the men who had been present when Jeanette Fain was slain. He was not at work and could not be located immediately. The search for him and for the full identities of the others continued.

The apartment where Jeanette was said to have been killed was kept under surveillance by Sergeants Holmes and Allen while the search warrant was obtained. At 10:00 p.m., Morris, Whisenhunt, and Geries arrived at the apartment with the warrant. Holmes and Geries covered the rear door. Morris forced open the front door and he, Allen, and Whisenhunt entered. When a search showed no one was inside, the others were admitted at the back door.

The officers noticed immediately a strong odor of chlorine bleach and the putrid smell of human vomit. With the apartment secured, it was left to Sergeants Holmes and Allen for processing for evidence. They took overall photos of the apartment and vacuumed the rooms for possible trace evidence.

The apartment, one of several in an apartment complex, had two bedrooms, a bath, a living room, and a kitchen. A check with the manager of the complex showed it to be rented to Somxay Panekham, the man in

31

custody. Working throughout the night and going over the apartment foot by foot, Holmes and Allen gathered evidence that disclosed in graphic detail the grisly fate of Jeanette.

In the living room, Sergeant Holmes rolled aside a green-and-white straw mat that appeared awkwardly placed on the floor. The mat was jammed against the wall beneath a large area that obviously had been scrubbed and scraped so hard that the paint had come off the sheet rock. Beneath the mat, Holmes saw a large bleached area on the floor. The spot was still wet and smelled of bleach and vomit.

The investigators surmised that the intensive cleanup work had been done to remove massive bloodstains after the woman's decapitation. Continuing the search, Sergeant Allen found what looked like a large amount of brown hair stuck to the underside of one of three cushions on a sofa. Also discovered under the cushion was a gold earring of the type that attaches to a pierced ear with a wire hook.

"It matches the one that was in the plastic bag of her clothing," Holmes said.

The bag of clothing had been brought to the SCU office where the victim's clothing—a blue satin jacket, blue denim jeans, a white bra cut from the back, a blue-and-white print blouse cut up the back and through the collar, three socks, and a black canvas belt—had been removed and hung up to dry.

Blood had run from the bra and the jacket when they were hung up. When the articles and the bag were later packed for mailing to the FBI lab, a gold earring that had been lodged in a clot of dried blood in the bag's bottom was found by Sergeant Holmes. The earring under the sofa cushion was a perfect match, she noted.

Further evidence of the violent attack on the young woman was a bone chip that Sergeant Holmes picked up near the bleached spot on the floor. Carefully, the well-trained investigator cut out the bleached part of the carpet and placed it in a sack for analysis. She saw that the jute backing underneath the carpet was blood-soaked, and the floor was bloodstained.

In the kitchen, the investigators picked up two knives from a dish drainer on the sink. One, a carving knife, had a wooden handle and the tip of the blade was broken. A substance thought to be blood was on the knife hilt.

Turning to the bathroom, the crime scene technicians found three plastic pans in the bathtub filled with brownish-colored water and items of men's clothing. One pan contained a pair of white gloves identical to the ones found earlier on the highway.

In their search for the other suspects, investigators contacted prominent leaders of Amarillo's Laotian community and were promised their ready cooperation. In the past several years, a large community of Laotian and Vietnamese people had sprung up in the Texas Panhandle city. And, contrary to an old saying, the twain did seem to meet in the blending of Western and Eastern cultures in the Americanized lives of the "boat people," as they sometimes were called.

On Saturday, the biting cold weather of Friday was threatening to become a winter storm, with weather forecasters predicting up to four inches of snow by Sunday. It wasn't a bright outlook for the SCU investigators, who knew their work was just beginning, whatever the weather conditions.

But on Saturday afternoon, they got another break. One of the suspects being sought, the "Ouy" whose first name was all the sleuths had, walked into the Amarillo Police Station and gave himself up. The 24-year-old Laotian was transferred to the crime unit office two blocks away. Identified as Ouy Vongkhamphra, the suspect was grilled by detectives after two Laotian interpreters were summoned and he was warned of his rights in that language.

33

The subsequent confession by the short, thin suspect with shoulder-length black hair was filmed and recorded on videotape. The sleuths couldn't help but notice that among Ouy's tattoos, including ones of a peacock and a dragon, was one depicting a headless tiger!

Ouy made his statement to Sergeants Whisenhunt and Morris through the interpreters. His story, including details of a more complete statement, was this:

He, Somxay, and the man known as Phet went to a bar on Thursday night to play pool and drink beer. They met the American girl there.

Sometime after 11:00 p.m., the three men and the woman, who was in fact Jeanette Fain, were given a ride by a friend to Somxay's apartment. The man nicknamed Vath was watching TV in the living room when the foursome arrived. The friend left after dropping off the others.

With all the lights off except the TV, Somxay and the woman first sat on the sofa talking. Ouy said he didn't pay attention to them, but when he heard the woman crying, he saw that she was lying flat and face up on the floor and Somxay was beside her. Somxay was having trouble getting his tight pants off, and Ouy helped him. Again he turned away. He heard the woman talking louder and louder and said Somxay walked away. Trying to quiet the upset woman, Ouy related that he sat by her and told her he "liked her a lot." She replied she liked him, too, but only as a friend.

When Somxay returned to the woman, Ouy went to use the bathroom, he said. He had been there about five minutes when he heard the weeping woman scream. Coming out of the bathroom, Ouy saw Somxay sitting on the woman and "cutting her neck with a knife." Ouy said he saw blood all over Somxay's hands and arms and the floor.

Ouy said he ran to the bedroom where Vath and Phet were and told them that Somxay had killed the American girl. The Laotian woman who had left her three children at Somxay's apartment while she worked had finished her shift at the meat plant and was with her children in the bedroom. After seeing the bloody woman on the floor, Ouy said, the mother and her youngsters ran out the back door, as did Vath and Phet.

Somxay told Ouy to get him another knife. In the kitchen he picked up a larger knife with a longer blade and gave it to him. He stood and watched as Somxay cut the woman's neck again, this time severing the head from the body.

Somxay then took off the woman's clothes and asked Ouy to cut open her blouse and take it off so they could dispose of the body. Telling Ouy to check her clothing for any identification, Somxay then fetched some plastic bags. Holding up the garbage bags, Somxay told Ouy to put the victim's head, clothing, and identification, which included her driver's license, inside.

The two men then wrapped the bloody body in a blanket and carried it and the bagged head and clothing out to a blue car and put them in the trunk. They drove to the rural road near the freeway and tossed the headless body in the ditch. They then drove to another site under the underpass and dumped the wrapped head and clothing there.

Both men wore the meat-packing gloves and threw them out the car window as they drove. Back at the apartment, they used bleach and detergent to clean up the large amount of blood. Ouy took the two knives used in the decapitation to the kitchen, washed them, and put them in the dish drainer.

Then they went to bed and slept a while. Later, Somxay got up and went to work at the restaurant. Ouy went to a friend's house, where Vath and Phet had fled the night before, and talked to his frightened friends.

Ouy related that Phet walked back with him to the murder scene, got the blue car, and took it to the home of

35

the Laotian woman. Phet said the woman then returned the car to the owner. Ouy concluded that he heard police were looking for him, so he decided to surrender voluntarily. He also said he didn't know what prompted Somxay to kill the woman.

After blood, hair, and saliva samples were taken, Ouy Vongkhamphra was booked into jail on a murder charge.

SCU investigators next contacted the Laotian woman to ask her about her involvement with the car that had been used to dump the body. She told officers that the car originally had been bought by her husband, but after he died about two weeks before, she had been unable to make the payments. However, since she needed transportation for business relating to her husband's death, and because she didn't drive, Somxay had driven for her on her errands. She still had the car on the night of the slaying.

After she fled upon learning a woman had been killed, Somxay came to her apartment. He demanded the keys to the car, and she gave them to him because she thought he might kill her, too, if she refused. That was the last she had seen of Somxay or the car, until it had been returned on Friday. She and Phet then took the car back to the original owner from whom her husband had bought it. The woman did not know the car owner's exact address, although she thought it was in northeast Amarillo.

On Monday, Sergeant Morris picked up one of the Laotian interpreters to translate during the arraignment of Somxay and Ouy in district court on murder charges. After the arraignment, the interpreter told Morris that the man nicknamed Vath, whose full name was Sisavath Signavong, had heard he was wanted by police for questioning. Vath had phoned the interpreter to say he would be at work at the meat plant and officers could come there if they wanted to talk to him.

Sergeants Morris and Allen and the interpreter located Vath on the job. He agreed to accompany them to the

36

SCU office for questioning. On the way, the officers and suspect stopped at an address where the other still-missing suspect was thought to live. No one was home, but while the investigators were canvassing the neighborhood, the man nicknamed Phet drove up in a pickup. He was identified as 30-year-old Somxath Prasathay. He agreed to accompany the officers to the SCU office for questioning.

With the interpreter present and the video camera again recording the suspects' statements, the two men admitted having been at the apartment on the murder night. But they denied any involvement whatsoever in the attack or slaying of Jeanette Fain. They maintained they had been asleep in another bedroom until Ouy ran in and said Somxay had killed the girl. They had run from the apartment to another residence, where they stayed the night.

After the body samples were taken, the two men were booked on witness attachments, pending further investigation of their roles as either witnesses or possible participants in the murder.

On Tuesday, December 16th, the SCU officers got another tip from the Laotian interpreter. He thought he had located the owner of the car used in the disposal of the victim's body. Sergeants Morris and Whisenhunt and Assistant District Attorney Abe Lopez drove out to the address and spotted a 1986 blue Colt sitting in the parking area at a duplex. While another officer was left to watch the car, Lopez returned to his office to get a search warrant from a judge.

Morris drove to the meat plant, where the car owner worked, and asked his permission to search the car. He gave written consent and handed over the keys. He said it would be all right to take the vehicle to the police garage for the processing after Sergeant Morris pointed out that inclement weather would prevent proper examination for fingerprints.

The owner told the officers that he had washed the vehicle when it was returned to him on December 11th because it was muddy. In answer to the detectives' questions, he said he had seen no signs of bloodstains on the car. He was unaware how it had been used until told by the investigators, he said.

The language barrier encountered by the detectives was making the probe increasingly difficult. Sergeant Holmes suggested that the assistance of a Laotian officer who spoke the language would help immensely. Holmes advised an FBI agent of the situation.

The agent reported back to the crime unit that there was a Laotian-born officer available who was a member of the Minneapolis, Minnesota, Police Department. The agent supplied the name of Sergeant Mike Quinn, the Laotian officer's supervisor. Sergeant Whisenhunt placed a call to Quinn and explained the Amarillo crime unit's predicament. Quinn agreed to have Officer Cha Shoua put on special assignment with the Amarillo force. Shoua's expenses would be paid by the Amarillo authorities.

Sergeant Morris drove out to the Amarillo International Airport on December 19th to meet Officer Shoua. He brought him to the SCU office, where the Laotian-born investigator was thoroughly briefed on the Jeanette Fain murder. He was shown all reports, photos, and videos.

Prior to Shoua's arrival in Amarillo, the four suspects in custody had been indicted by a grand jury on charges of murder. Officer Shoua's role in the probe would be a key factor in the later reindictment of the suspects on capital murder charges, a death penalty offense in Texas.

Officer Shoua interviewed the suspects and witnesses in their own language and added greatly to the store of information on the case.

Shoua, Morris, and Whisenhunt drove to the county correction center. Officer Shoua wanted to talk first with Ouy Vongkhamphra. While he did this, Morris and Whisenhunt quizzed another inmate who had been lodged for a time in the same cell with Somxay Panekham, who, wit-

38

nesses said, had cut off Jeanette Fain's head.

The inmate told the officers that Somxay had bragged to him how he killed the American girl. The prisoner gave an affidavit saying that he was told by Somxay that all four of the Laotian men held down Jeanette and forced her to have sex with them. In the affidavit, the witness said:

"He [Somxay] told his friends, 'We're fixing to have some fun.' The girl didn't want to do this, and she was fighting them. Then two dudes started holding her down. The long-haired dude [Ouy], went first, then he [Somxay] got on her. She got loose from one of the dudes that was holding her and pulled his hair. That made him mad, so he got up and went into the kitchen, got a butcher knife, came back and cut her throat.

"He wanted to do it doggie-style, and she didn't. She told him she didn't like crazy sex and didn't want to. When he got the knife, he put on a pair of gloves. The two holding her down knew what he was gonna do. They watched him kill her. He told me, 'We had a dead f—-.' The two that held her ran off . . . He told me he was gonna walk because there wasn't any evidence. He laughed the entire time he was telling me this."

The affidavit was in the inmate's own handwriting and bore his signature.

Another inmate also gave an affidavit in which he quoted the "long-haired Laotian" as saying that Jeanette protested the sexual advances of the men but that "We all took it."

The inmate added that the Laotian told him, "They were all laughing while she was being killed."

Lieutenant Stevens, coordinator of the Special Crimes Unit, credited the work of Minneapolis' Officer Shoua for breaking down language barriers and gaining information that nailed down murder charges against the two suspects, Sisavath Signavong and Somxath Prosathay, who at first had been held as material witnesses.

"We would like to acknowledge District Attorney Danny Hill's office for bringing Shoua here and paying all of his expenses," the lieutenant said.

Before the personable 29-year-old officer returned to Minneapolis, the investigators in SCU chipped in and bought him a pair of cowboy boots, the traditional footwear of the Texas Panhandle.

On June 7, 1989, in a plea-bargain agreement, Somxay Panekham and Ouy Vongkhamphra pleaded guilty to charges of murder in 251st District Court in Amarillo and admitted cutting off the head of Jeanette Fain. They were sentenced to life in prison for the heinous crime. They must serve at least 15 years of their sentences before being eligible for parole. Even if they are paroled, prosecutors said they would initiate legal action to have the two deported from the United States.

District Attorney Hill said the two defendants were allowed to plead on the lesser charge of murder instead of capital murder because of several factors, not the least of which was a predicted trial cost that would have been out of sight. The D.A. estimated the cost might have gone as high as $2 million for each defendant because of translators' salaries, venue changes owing to extensive pre-trial publicity, and the expense of translating the trial transcripts in case of appeals.

There was one final wrapping up of evidence in the murder: Dental impressions taken from all four murder suspects and compared by a human bite expert with the photo of the bite mark on the victim's arm disclosed it had been done by Ouy, SCU investigators said.

The other two defendants entered guilty pleas to a lesser charge in the murder case. On November 29, 1990, Somxath Prasathay pleaded guilty in 47th District Court to a charge of attempted sexual assault in the attack on Jeanette Fain and was sentenced to 10 years in prison.

On December 19, 1990, Sisavath Signavong pleaded guilty to the same charge in 47th District Court and was assessed the same sentence of 10 years by the judge.

All four defendants chose not to appeal their sentences and are confined in the Texas Department of Corrections serving their sentences at this time.

# "GRUESOME FOURSOME PRESCRIBED DEATH FOR 41"

## by Philip Westwood

Julia Drapal had been quite something in her day. As an actress and singer, she had appeared in all of Europe's top theaters. Packed houses greeted her every performance with an enthusiasm reserved for only the very finest of artistes.

But it was in the world of ballet that Julia found her greatest success. As prima ballerina of the Vienna Royal Ballet, it had been Julia's privilege to dance before kings, queens, and heads of state from all over the world. And those dignitaries were equally privileged to have been present when she performed. In her native Austria, Julia Drapal had been a legend.

The public, and particularly the Viennese public, adored Julia. But public adulation is fickle, as transitory as a snowball in August, as thoughtless as a wayward child. Yes, Julia Drapal had been quite something in her day. But that day was back in the 1950s.

By February 1989, life for Julia Drapal had changed beyond all recognition. Gone were the chauffeur-driven limousines that would take her through streets lined with cheering crowds. Gone were the intimate conversations with crowned heads of Europe. Gone were the best suites in the best hotels, where Julia's every wish was granted, her every whim entertained.

Gone, too, was Julia's art. The problem was that Julia's slim, willowy body was not strong enough to take the constant pounding to which her chosen profession subjected it. Ill health forced Julia to retire from the stage. And, as the years passed, her general condition declined. Eventually, it became so bad that her devoted husband could no longer look after her. Doctors decided that Julia needed constant medical attention of the kind that only a hospital and its staff could provide.

And so, as 1988 gave way to 1989, an ambulance collected Julia Drapal from her home in one of Vienna's more fashionable suburbs, and ferried her across the city to an altogether less appealing place. Julia's destination was the Lainz General Hospital.

There was no tangible reason for it, but people tended to quicken their step as they walked by the Lainz General Hospital. Maybe it was the stillness of the grounds. The trees didn't seem to move, even if the wind was blowing. No birds sang. In fact, there were no signs of life to be seen anywhere. No patients sat out on the lawns. No visitors strolled in the gardens with their loved ones. There was nothing, nothing at all to indicate that this was a place that was, in fact, full of people.

But perhaps it was the look of the place, with its long driveway leading to the crumbling, ivy-covered facade, that stirred in passersby some memory of an old horror movie they'd seen and been frightened by long ago. The building certainly gave the impression that it would look just right with lightning playing around its turrets while, inside, dark figures prowled the dingy corridors, perpetrating acts of unspeakable evil. Anyone who picked up on that impression would have been partially correct. Nocturnal thunderstorms were rare. But inside the Lainz General Hospital, the evil prowlers were a terrifying reality.

The place had been constructed 150 years earlier by a

43

wealthy businessman who was eager to show his neighbors the measure of his success. At the time, it had indeed been a splendid place. It was richly decorated, with large, gothic-style windows, ornate pillars on either side of the huge front door, and six gargoyles over the iron gate guarding the entrance to the driveway.

But one and a half centuries of neglect had changed the original conception of the place. The now blackened windows gave it a sinister and forbidding air, the crumbling stonework of the pillars betrayed it as a building unloved, and the weather-beaten gargoyles looked simply hideous.

When it passed out of private ownership, the building had been converted into the Lainz General Hospital. One of the wings of the hospital—known as "Pavilion 5"—was reserved for elderly patients with severe physical problems. All of the patients in Pavilion 5 were over 70 years of age, and it was to one of the wing's three wards—Ward D—that Julia Drapal was brought.

Julia was a difficult patient. Although she no longer enjoyed the lifestyle that her stage career had brought her, she had not managed to shake off the attitude of a temperamental star. She expected the nursing staff to do everything her way and to do as she told them, no matter how impractical that might be. If she didn't get her own way, Julia could be extremely abusive and insulting.

With most of the nursing staff, Julia's attitude cut no ice whatsoever. They had seen it all before. Some old people could be very difficult if they were made to do something in a way they weren't used to. But allowances had to be made. The staff knew it must be difficult to adapt to a new routine after so many years of following the old one.

But the four nurses who worked the night shift in Ward D were not so understanding. As far as they were concerned, the patients had to do things their way. If the patients played along and were not too demanding, then chances were they'd be all right. But any of the elderly inmates who dared to cause any trouble of any kind, or who became so ill that they impinged rather too much on the night nurses' valuable time, received some very special treatment, resulting in what the neatly uniformed quartet casually referred to as "a free trip to God." Over the 10 years that they had worked Ward D, the four nurses had issued literally dozens of "tickets to heaven."

The problem at the Lainz General Hospital was that nobody really cared. The doctors had long ago grown tired of the long hours that they were expected to work, and so they had stopped doing them. Most left promptly at 5:00 p.m., just as they would have done if they'd had an office or a factory job. On weekends, they weren't there at all. The nights and weekends were left in the care of the most junior medical practitioners, doctors so recently qualified that the ink on their degrees was barely dry.

The doctors' attitude had permeated through to the nursing staff. If the doctors didn't work nights and weekends, the nurses argued, why should they? So they, too, restricted themselves to a day-time routine and left the more unsociable hours to their junior colleagues. That meant, at nights and on weekends, the hospital was left in the care of auxiliary nurses, men and women who wanted to be nurses, but who had either failed to take the nursing examinations or had taken them and failed to pass them. Either way, auxiliary nurses, however dedicated they might be, were lacking the formal qualifications of their chosen profession.

The quartet of auxiliaries who comprised the night staff of Ward D had not only failed to gain the formal nursing qualifications, they were also a bit short in the field of vocational calling and dedication. They did the job purely for the money—and the power and authority that it gave them over others less fortunate than themselves. In the outside world, they had no power and authority over anything. But once they put on those crisply starched uniforms and stepped into the quiet confines of Ward D, they were queens of all they surveyed. It was, for them, a powerful feeling.

Waltraud Wagner was the undoubted leader of the quartet. The bespectacled 30-year-old with a good figure and a bad temper exerted over her colleagues a dominance that they accepted with unquestioning obedience. It was not that she barked out orders to them or threatened them. She didn't have to.

Waltraud had that air of authority that made subordinates or equals do as she bade without even thinking about it. Waltraud's uniform helped. She liked uniforms. They were the outward symbol of her power.

She also liked killing. Waltraud could snuff out the life of one of her troublesome patients with no more concern than if she had been swatting a fly. There was, however, one difference. She felt nothing about killing a fly, but she actually *enjoyed* killing her elderly patients.

Waltraud's partners in the deadly atmosphere of Ward D were an unlikely bunch. Second in command was attractive 27-year-old Irene Leidolf. Waltraud liked Irene because she was quiet and rather shy. She also had a large family to support, and that, coupled with her introverted personality, meant that she was the least likely of the quartet to open her mouth, or do anything but simply follow orders.

The eldest of the four, 51-year-old Stefanija Mayer, had been reluctant to join in at first. But with two marriages and two divorces behind her, and with no prospect of a third husband coming along, Stefanija soon realized that she had to look after herself. If she didn't, no one else would. And if that meant helping to bump off a few of the patients in her care, and keeping her mouth shut afterward, then so be it.

The final member of the quartet was the youngest, 25-year-old Marie Gruber. Maria was a plain, thickset young woman whose grim expression suggested that she rather

46

enjoyed the work that Waltraud had marked out for her. But, like Stefanija Mayer, Maria had been extremely reluctant to get drawn in at first. Then, also like Stefanija, she came to realize that she had to look out for herself. Maria had a young child to support and no husband or boyfriend to help her. Eventually, all three got so used to helping Waltraud in her nefarious activities that it became second nature to them. Like Waltraud, they killed without thought, without compassion, and without any regard for the consequences.

Initially, Irene, Stefanija, and Maria all had twinges of conscience over what they were doing. Waltraud had no such problems. In a perverse way, she believed she was doing the elderly patients a favor. Sending them to meet their Maker, reuniting them with their loved ones who had gone on before — it was what the old folk, in her heart of hearts, really wanted, Waltraud told her colleagues. After all, Waltraud said, they were dealing with sick old people, people whose lives were past peak, people who had had their day. Did it really matter if they passed on a couple of months, or a couple of years, before they were supposed to? Waltraud asked. Would anyone miss them? Would anyone express surprise, or suspicion, at their passing? No, Waltraud rationalized, of course they wouldn't.

"Come along, Julia, it's time for your mouthwash," said Waltraud Wagner as she moved with a firm, but unhurried step, toward the bed where Julia Drapal lay half asleep. It was fast approaching 1:00 a.m. on a cold night in the early part of February 1989. Julia had been at the hospital for about four weeks, but her irascible behavior had marked her down for the "special treatment" almost from day one. Her fate had been sealed a few nights earlier when she had resisted Waltraud's attempts to administer a perfectly legitimate medication.

"Get away from me, you common slut!" Julia had yelled to Waltraud.

Poor Julia. She didn't know that you couldn't talk to Waltraud Wagner like that and get away with it. Many patients had died for far less, so many that Waltraud had lost count.

"I don't want it!" Julia snapped, pushing away the dirty glass containing the clear liquid that Waltraud was trying to force into her mouth. "Take it away!"

Patients in several of the beds that lined each side of Ward D turned and looked at the scene around Julia's bed. They knew that Waltraud was not going to take the glass away and that Julia was going to have the mouth-wash no matter what. They didn't know why she had to have it, but they knew that taking it would be the last thing Julia ever did. She would be dead before the morning. It was always the same when someone had the mouthwash. They always died.

The patients also knew that if they appeared to be taking too great an interest in what was going on with Julia, then it would probably be their turn next to take the deadly mouthwash. So they turned over and tried to go to sleep.

"Irene! Get over here! This one's going to be difficult!" Waltraud's rasping voice cut through the stillness of the ward, searing into the brains of the helpless and terrified patients. Irene Leidolf moved quickly when she heard the instruction. It was best not to keep Waltraud waiting, especially when she was trying to administer the mouth-wash.

"Hold her down and keep her still," Waltraud ordered as Irene arrived at Julia's bedside. Irene leaned over the one-time ballerina and pinned her arms to the bed so that she could not move, then looked away and stared intently at the floor. That way, she avoided any contact with Julia's terrified eyes or with the detached, heartlessness in the eyes of her colleague.

With Julia suitably restrained, Waltraud once again raised the glass to the old woman's lips. Julia closed her mouth tight and turned her head away, but Waltraud was ready. They all tried that. It was instinctive, but it was easily overcome, especially for someone so practiced in the art of death as Waltraud.

With her free hand, the nurse simply reached out and placed her thumb and forefinger around the end of Julia's nose. With her air supply cut off, Julia was forced to open her mouth in order to breathe. And as soon as Julia's lips were parted, Waltraud pounced. The speed with which she had the glass wedged into Julia's opened mouth was the result of reflexes perfected over so many years, and on so many patients.

Waltraud tipped the glass upwards, and the liquid it contained spilled down Julia's throat. Julia tried to cough it back out again, but it was a hopeless battle.

The liquid that the glass held was nothing more sinister than plain, ordinary water. But its purpose was anything but innocent. By filling Julia's throat with water, and keeping it filled, Waltraud intended most of the liquid, instead of passing into Julia's stomach, to take an alternative course down her windpipe and into her lungs. Eventually, the old woman's lungs would fill with water and she would drown.

And that is exactly what happened. It took several minutes to accomplish, but that did not cause Waltraud any concern. It was always like that. Julia's "treatment" had been no different in its execution than the dozens of others that Waltraud had carried out.

"All right, you can let go now," Waltraud said to Irene as the last drop of water left the glass and made its way into Julia's bursting lungs. "It's finished."

The two nurses made their way back to the little room at the end of the ward that served as their office. Irene was quiet, as she always was on such occasions. But Waltraud was exhilarated. "That's another one on her way to heaven," she remarked with satisfaction. "She'll soon be with God. We'll check on her in a little while."

Three hours later, Waltraud was back at Julia Drapal's bedside. One look was enough to tell the experienced nurse that the former ballerina was dead. But the agony that Julia had suffered in the hour or so that it took her to die was not so apparent. Still, that did not concern Waltraud. The important thing was that the job had been done.

Back in her office, Waltraud picked up the telephone and called the duty doctor. "One of the patients appears to be dead," she said casually.

"O.K.," the doctor replied with a detached indifference. "I'll be there as soon as I can."

A half hour later, the doctor appeared and was directed to Julia Drapal's bed, which Waltraud had respectfully curtained off from the view of the other patients. The doctor made a brief examination of the stiffening corpse, muttered something about "natural causes," and drawing the curtains behind him, walked briskly to Waltraud's office.

"Make the arrangements to get the body moved to the morgue," he ordered Waltraud as he pulled a bunch of forms from one of the desk drawers. He sighed deeply as he thumbed through the sheaf of papers and thought about the amount of paperwork that he would now have to complete. It was a real nuisance. He had far better things to do. "What was her name?" he asked with more than a hint of frustration.

"Drapal," Waltraud replied calmly as she picked up the telephone and punched the well-worn numbers that would connect her with the morgue. "Julia Drapal."

The autopsy carried out on Julia was a routine affair. It revealed that her lungs were full of water. But this was no great surprise. Water in the lungs is one of the factors present in the perfectly innocent deaths of many old people. The death certificate was filled out: Julia Drapal had officially died from natural causes.

"I told you everything would be all right," Waltraud

50

warned Irene. "You worry too much."

It was the beginning of the weekend. For the four dispensers of death, it was a rare two days off. The same could be said for the patients in their charge. Waltraud had decided that the quartet needed a good night out. And as her idea of a good night out was a few hours in the raucous, boozy atmosphere of one of Vienna's beer cellars, that was where they were. Waltraud always made the decisions — on everything.

"Aren't you happy with what we're doing?" she asked her companions. The steady intake of alcohol over the previous two hours had caused the volume of her voice to rise to a point where it was in danger of becoming embarrassing. "We're doing the old fools a favor. What have they got to live for? They're decrepit, bedridden, can't do anything for themselves. All they've got left are the memories of when they were young and strong. Just think what it must be like to have to lie in bed all day, unable to wash yourself, and having to have all of your bodily needs attended to by strangers like us. And all the time you're lying there, you're remembering how it used to be. The fun you used to have, the plans you made, the dreams of what you were going to do with your life. And then you look around you at how it all turned out. I tell you, we're doing them a favor."

"I wonder if someone will do that kind of a favor for us one day," Stefanija Mayer mused, staring absentmindedly into her beer. Realizing what she had said, Stefanija looked up and saw Waltraud glaring at her. She saw the look in Waltraud's eyes and she got the message. Slowly, Stefanija lowered her head and went back to studying the contents of her glass.

"Can we please change the subject?" Maria Gruber cut in. "Someone might hear us."

"No one will hear us," retorted Waltraud. "Nobody's listening. They're not interested in us. They've all got their own little problems."

For once, Waltraud Wagner was wrong. Somebody was listening, and they were taking an interest in Waltraud and her companions that went beyond mere curiosity.

At a nearby table, Ludwig Schotz brought all of his concentration to bear on the conversation between the four nurses. It was not easy to hear above the din, but he had heard enough to take him off his beer and ruin what, up to that point, had been a perfectly good evening. It was only natural that Schotz should be more shocked than the average beer cellar customer by what he had heard. After all, he was the Lainz General Hospital's chief medical consultant.

"It's preposterous!" said the officer whom Dr. Schotz saw at the Vienna Bureau of Detectives the following morning. "You must have misheard."

"I'm perfectly certain of what I heard," insisted Schotz. "They were talking about killing off the elderly patients on their ward." The doctor went on to say that, before calling in at the police station, he had taken a cursory look through the records of Ward D. He had found that the death rate among the ward's patients was far higher than that of the other two wards on Pavilion 5. "I am convinced that something is terribly wrong on that ward," Schotz concluded.

"All right," the officer finally agreed. "It merits some further investigation. I'll put a man on to it right away."

"He looks a little on the young side for this place," Waltraud Wagner remarked to Irene Leidolf as she looked at the man dozing peacefully in the bed midway along the ward. It was Sunday evening, and the quartet's weekend off was rapidly becoming little more than a memory. "He can't be much more than fifty," Waltraud continued, as a feeling of puzzlement, mingled with suspicion, started to grow inside of her. "What do we know about him?"

Irene didn't know anything about the new arrival. "Apparently, he was admitted last night," she said. "According to his notes, any medication is to be administered by a

52

doctor. We're to give him nothing. If there's a problem, we're to call one of the doctors on this list."

Irene produced a piece of paper from the pocket of her uniform and handed it to Waltraud. Waltraud scanned the names on the list and breathed in so sharply that a strange whistling sound emitted from her lips. All of the names on the list were those of the hospital's most senior doctors. And the name at the top of the list was Dr. Ludwig Schotz.

"What is it?" asked Irene as she heard Waltraud's whistle.

"Either this patient is a very important man," explained Waltraud, "or else the top brass are getting suspicious. And if he were important, he wouldn't be on this ward."

"You mean that they're on to us?" Irene was starting to panic.

"Calm down!" ordered Waltraud. "They can't prove anything. If they could, we wouldn't be here now. And neither would he," she concluded, nodding her head in the direction of the still-dozing newcomer.

"Who is he?" Irene wanted to know.

"A cop," Waltraud replied with a note of exasperation. Didn't Irene understand anything?

"What are we going to do?" Irene asked as her forehead creased.

"Absolutely nothing," Waltraud responded. She looked at Irene. "If we do nothing, then they can do nothing."

Waltraud Wagner was not worried. In fact, she was rather enjoying the battle of wits and wills between her, a lowly auxiliary nurse, and the best brains the hospital and the authorities could muster. Top doctors, experienced policemen — what chance did they stand against a woman like Waltraud Wagner? There was no question in her mind who would win this particular contest.

Day after day, the detective languished in his hospital bed. As each day passed, he became more and more depressed. It was the worst assignment of his career. He was strong and healthy, but he was forced to spend all of his time lying in bed surrounded by sick and disabled old people.

But at least the patients were happier. The mortality rate among them had fallen off dramatically since the detective's arrival. Waltraud knew better than to try anything while he was there.

It was six weeks before the detective was released from his mind-numbing task. "You can't pull him out!" Schotz protested to senior officers at the bureau when he discovered that the detective had been taken off the case.

"We can't do anything else," the doctor was told. "Nothing's happening at the hospital and we can't spare that officer any longer. We have more pressing matters to attend to."

Waltraud Wagner was really proud of what she saw as her victory over the forces of authority. She boasted of it to her three companions. "They'll never catch us," she said in her most superior tone. Yes, Waltraud was full of confidence in her ability to beat the authorities. In fact, she was overconfident to the point of recklessness.

As soon as the police had lost interest in the affairs of Ward D, Waltraud was back to her old ways. She had been deprived of her nights of death dealing for six weeks and she had really missed them. She was anxious to get started again as quickly as possible. The chance to do so presented itself only a couple of nights after the undercover detective had left. It was a chance that Waltraud seized eagerly.

One of Waltraud's elderly female patients, unable to sleep because of a particularly severe headache, had asked the auxiliary for a painkiller.

The patient had never caused Waltraud any trouble. She wasn't always questioning the treatment she was given or complaining about any one of a hundred different things, as Julia Drapal had done. On the contrary, she was quite submissive—a weak, fragile, rather frightened

54

old woman.

But to Waltraud, that was just as bad as being difficult. She couldn't stand those patients who cowered under their bedsheets whenever she approached. They were pathetic and certainly not deserving of any sympathy or compassion.

Since the woman wanted a painkiller for her nasty headache, Waltraud gave her one. And it would be so effective that the old woman would never have a headache or any other kind of pain, ever again. But she had to be a little clever about it.

Back in the early days, when she was just getting started in the art of killing, Waltraud had sent her victims on their one-way journey to paradise by means of a massive dose of insulin injected directly into the vein of an arm. But insulin had its disadvantages. It was fairly slow acting—it didn't work as quickly as Waltraud would have liked—and it was detectable. So Waltraud had developed the "mouthwash." She was proud of her mouthwash, which was cheap, efficient, and virtually undetectable. Its only drawback was that Waltraud needed an assistant to hold the victim down while she administered it.

Although the police had gone, Waltraud couldn't be sure that they had not made contingency plans. Perhaps their withdrawal was just a ruse to lull her into a false sense of security, and they were really still there disguised as nurses, or orderlies, or even doctors. Perhaps they had really left, but had recruited members of the staff as spies with instructions to keep a close watch on her. Perhaps Waltraud was simply getting paranoid.

In any event, she had to be careful. If anyone was keeping a watch on Ward D, their attention was more likely to be drawn to two nurses around a patient's bed administering treatment than it was to one nurse giving a patient an injection. It took several minutes to get the mouthwash into the victim. An injection took only a few seconds.

That settled it. The mouthwash was out. It was back to

the insulin.

Waltraud thought she had covered everything, but she hadn't. In all of her careful planning and sizing up of the situation, there was something that she had completely forgotten. There had recently been a directive issued to all hospital staff that only a qualified doctor was allowed to administer an injection to a patient in the hospital's care.

"Has this patient been given an injection recently?" asked the duty doctor who responded to Waltraud's report that an elderly female patient on her ward appeared to be dead.

Waltraud looked the young doctor up and down. He was new, or, at least, she had never seen him before. "No," she replied. "No injection."

But the young doctor was not only new to the hospital, he was also conscientious. He had not been there long enough for apathy and disenchantment to set in. In his report, the doctor detailed his suspicions that the old woman had been given an injection contrary to the hospital's rules, that the injection had contributed significantly to her death, and that Waltraud Wagner had lied to him. And the autopsy confirmed the doctor's suspicions.

"We've got to stop them!" Dr. Schotz said, slamming his fist down on the desk of the bureau's senior detective. "God knows how many patients they've murdered over the years or how many more will die if we don't do something right now."

The detective finished reading the autopsy report on Waltraud's latest victim and lay the file gently on his desk. "I'm sending in a team of investigators straight away," he announced. "We'll want to go through the records of every patient on that ward who has died during the time that these four nurses have been working the night shift."

"Thank you," said Schotz, overcome with a feeling of relief that, at last, something was going to be done.

The four nurses were placed under arrest while the investigation proceeded. Waltraud Wagner, realizing that it was the end of the road, made a statement admitting what she had done and naming her three partners in crime. But she couldn't remember exactly how many patients had died at her hands over the years. She had simply lost count.

In April 1989, the killer quartet stood trial in Vienna before Judge Birgit Kail. They faced 42 counts of murder, though many people agreed with Dr. Schotz when he said, "I fear that this is only the tip of the iceberg."

For three weeks, the jury of two men and six women listened intently as an array of evidence against the four nurses was presented. At the end of it all, it took them 12 hours to reach their verdicts.

Irene Leidolf was convicted on five counts of murder, and two counts of attempted murder. She was jailed for life.

Maria Gruber was convicted on two counts of attempted murder. She was sentenced to 15 years in jail.

Stefanija Mayer was convicted on one count of manslaughter and seven counts of attempted murder. She was sentenced to 20 years. Upon hearing her sentence, Stefanija fainted and had to be carried from the dock on a stretcher.

And what of Waltraud Wagner, the undisputed leader of the gruesome little gang? Waltraud was convicted on 15 counts of murder, 17 counts of attempted murder, and two counts of inflicting grievous bodily harm. She collapsed on the dock as Judge Kail sentenced her to life imprisonment.

Throughout the trial, Waltraud's unerring belief that she was "doing the old fools a favor" never faltered. "I was only trying to relieve their pain and suffering," she remarked at one point in the proceedings.

Judge Kail looked hard and long at Waltraud. "Some of these patients languished in indescribable agony for many hours after you had administered your 'treatment,' " the judge said sternly. "Do you call that the relief of pain and suffering?"

Waltraud looked at the judge, and then at the floor. She made no reply.

EDITOR'S NOTE:
*Dr. Ludwig Schotz is not the real name of the person so named in the foregoing story. A fictitious name has been used because there is no reason for public interest in the identity of this person.*

# "GARY HEIDNIK'S HOUSE OF HORRORS . . . HIS SEX SLAVES WERE SHACKLED, NUDE AND FED DOG FOOD!"

## by Barry Bowe

North Philadelphia is a rough neighborhood, an inner-city slum seething with poverty, drugs, and every type of criminal depravity. When the graveyard shift at the police station at North Sixth Street and Montgomery Avenue started its tour of duty at midnight on Wednesday, March 25, 1987, however, everything seemed to be routine—a mugging here, a couple of assaults there. Then the phone rang, and a frantic woman's voice began telling a horror story to make even a veteran cop's skin crawl. Moments later, Officers John Cannon and Dave Savage were dispatched to verify the complaint.

The investigation that followed would reveal details that inspired Thomas Harris' best-selling novel and the Academy Award winning film it spawned, *The Silence of the Lambs*. The events that fueled the plot had begun four months prior to that phone call.

**November 20, 1986:** Around 5:30 p.m., just two days before Thanksgiving, Carol Baxter told her boyfriend she was going shopping. Carol was 26 years old and the mother of three infant children. She was also a hooker. Her boyfriend, Tyrone Richards, was an unemployed ex-con, and November 20th was his 30th birthday. They lived together in a third-floor apartment in the 1500 block of

North Sixth.

"I remember the day exactly," Tyrone Richards would say later. "She gave me fifty dollars as a birthday present, and we were talking about where we would spend Thanksgiving—my mother's house, or what."

But Carol didn't go shopping. Instead, she went to the corner of Third Street and Girard Avenue and spent the evening hustling tricks. Around 11 o'clock, Carol's head turned when a shiny Cadillac drove up to the curb. The driver, a bearded man somewhat older than Carol, was white, wore glasses, and had a reddish-brown beard.

The man was tall and square-shouldered. His clothes were casual but nice—dark trousers, sports shirt, and a buckskin jacket with long fringes.

Carol thought the man seemed nice enough, for a john. When they agreed on a price, Carol got in the Caddy and they drove to the man's house, a two-story rowhouse in the 3500 block of North Marshall Street.

Once inside the house, the man asked Carol if she wanted to watch some pornographic films. Carol said, no, she didn't have enough time to watch movies.

"We went upstairs and had sex," Carol would later tell police. "Afterward, he grabbed me around the throat, tightly, and he started choking me." When Carol regained consciousness, her wrists were handcuffed to the bed frame. "Then he took me to the basement and shackled my ankles to a sewer pipe with muffler clamps."

When Carol failed to return home that night or the next morning, Tyrone Richards became concerned. He phoned Carol's girlfriends and her parents. But no one had seen her, and no one could imagine where she was.

**November 24, 1986:** Because she needed Midol, 24-year-old Sandra Lindsay walked to a store near her home in West Philadelphia. Mildly retarded, Sandra slurred her speech. She had trouble pronouncing her name and often called herself by her middle name, Elaine, but family members knew her as Sandy.

A 1980 graduate of West Philadelphia High School, Sandy worked at a sheltered workshop at the Elwyn Institute, a nonprofit agency for the mentally retarded. She hung out with a group of young women she'd met at work. To her family's dismay, Sandy's circle of friends frequented the house of a red-bearded man on North Marshall Street.

"Terrible things went on in that house," one family would later tell police. "Drugs, alcohol, and sex. Anytime they wanted to get drunk, they could get drunk. They just sat over there getting high. And the man that lived there, he was everything to them and everybody had to look up to him. Everyone had sex with him.

"He had a van and took the whole group, four or five of them, to Great Adventure and other parks. They thought they were having fun."

Sandy Lindsay never made it back from the store that day. In the three months that followed, her family members often drove by the house on North Marshall Street hoping to catch a glimpse of her. But they never saw Sandy again.

**December 22, 1986:** Gail Midley was 19 years old and unemployed. She'd dropped out of Edison High School two years earlier after becoming pregnant. When her child was born, she went on welfare. Gail remembered that she had left a pair of gloves at a friend's house. She decided to walk over to reclaim her gloves. She was walking along Lehigh Avenue when a car stopped next to her and the driver initiated a conversation.

"He asked me if I wanted to make some money," Gail would later recall. "I said, 'No, I'm no prostitute.' But I liked his car, a Cadillac, 'eighty-seven.

"So he said, did I want to come with him? I said, 'No, I'm just walking to my girlfriend's house.' So he said, do I want him to take me to my girlfriend's house? I said, 'No, that's okay, it's only around the corner.'

"He said, 'I'm not going to harm you,' " Gail continued. "So I got in his car and he took me to my girlfriend's house and parked his car. Then he took me to TGIFs on City Avenue for dinner and drinks and then he says he wants to take me to Atlantic City the next day.

"So I say, 'Well, I would really like to go but I don't have nothing to wear.' So he gave me a fifty-dollar bill and he took me to Sears and Roebuck. He says, 'Spend up to fifty dollars.' So I bought two pairs of jeans and two tops. After that, he asked me, could he put them on me. I said, sure.

"When I went to his house," Gail continued, "I sat in the kitchen and I was drinking a cooler. When I went in the living room, he brought me a beer. But then he got up and grabbed my neck and shook me. He almost killed me half to death.

"I said, 'Wait a minute, I'll do whatever you want.' So he let me go. He said, 'You be cooperative and nothing will happen to you.' I said, 'Okay,' so he got handcuffs and put them behind my back.

"Then he took me down the cellar, and I seen all these bags. I thought they were body parts in there. So I said, 'It's body parts in these bags, isn't it?' He said, 'No.'

"I said, 'You're going to kill me. You want to kill me.' He said, 'No, I'm not going to kill you. Trust me, I'm not going to kill you.' So he handcuffed me to a pipe with muffler clamps. There was a big hole and he said, 'I'm going to introduce you to my two friends down here.'

"I said, 'They dead down there, aren't they? They dead.' He said, 'No, just trust me. Shut up or I'll hurt you.' And I shut up.

"And when he took the lid off the hole, I seen two girls coming out of there."

**January 19, 1987:** Debbie Dudley was 23 years old, a high school dropout, unemployed. She was one of 11 children and lived with a relative in the 4100 block of North Seventh Street. Friends described Debbie as wildly energetic. They said she drank hard and was quick-tempered.

"I wouldn't want to mess with her," said a teenager from her neighborhood. "She was powerful. I remember when she beat some kid up after he stole ten dollars from her."

"She was nice," recalled another neighbor. "She was good to people here on this block. She wasn't the grouchy type. She was a friendly person, the type of person who went out and turned cartwheels in the rain. But sometimes she drank too much beer and wound up sleeping on somebody's porch."

"She wasn't about no crowd," recalled a family member. "She was by herself mostly. She liked to go off on her own."

On this midwinter day, Debbie Dudley went off on her own—and never came back.

**January 28, 1987:** Tammy Kramer, 18, disappeared from her family's home in the 700 block of South Mole Street.

"I've known Tammy a long time," said one neighbor, "and she wasn't the type that would even call a man, let alone get into a car with one. She went to parties with young people but she didn't go to bars."

"I've known her since we were kids," said another neighbor. "She is a good person and there wasn't anything wrong with her mentally. She was in the Job Corps and I was dating her cousin. I remember she would sit in the park and watch me play ball. I considered her a friend."

**March 20, 1987:** On a Friday night, Patty Conrad pulled up to her family's home in the 1200 block of North Fourth Street in an '87 Cadillac. She was 24 years old and had spent the second half of her life coming and going as she pleased. At the age of 12, Patty had dropped out of school. At 16, she was doing part-time custodial work at City Hall.

"Patty was a quiet little girl," a family member would recall, "but she changed, started hanging around with new friends."

"Go to school and run away," another relative remembered, "go to school and run away. Nobody could hold her. Twelve years old, she's in the street all the time. She's tough, like fire, and she don't take nobody's bull.

"I talk to her. I say, 'You can stay here. You find a nice man, marry the man. I'll give you a home.' "

Out of the blue on March 20th, Patty walked into the house and said, "We're going to Atlantic City."

The relative looked outside and saw a car waiting at the curb. Inside the car were a bearded white man, a young black man, and two black women.

"I can't go no place," the relative told Patty. "I'm too sick."

"We don't have any money for gas."

"You have a Cadillac and you don't have any money?"

He gave Patty two dollars and the Cadillac drove away. Patty Conrad had found a man, but it wasn't the man of her dreams. Rather, he became her worst nightmare.


The bearded man had moved into the house on North Marshall Street two years earlier in 1985. It sat back off the street enclosed by a chain-link fence. The front yard was littered with an assortment of discarded tires and trash. The house itself was a ramshackle affair with bars on the windows and sexually explicit graffiti spray-painted on the front door. A sign above the door proclaimed *UNITED CHURCH OF THE MINISTERS OF GOD.* What made the house stick out like a swollen thumb were the cars parked in the driveway—a Rolls Royce, a 1987 Cadillac, a Lincoln Continental, a customized van, and a Dodge Dart.

"He was quiet at first," the next-door neighbor would recall, "except for the work he was doing on his house. You'd hear him over there banging on the walls and fixing the place up. He was putting in new bathroom fixtures and other things."

And he was digging a dungeon in the basement.

"After about three months," the neighbor continued, "he brought in some stereos and began playing music so loud that my walls shook. I went to him about it and he turned it down. After that, I just banged on the walls to get him to lower the sound. But there were women coming in and out of that house. We didn't know what was going on over there."

The neighbor never dreamed that the loud music was drowning out the sounds of torture sessions.

The air in that neighborhood was often heavy with the stink of decaying garbage, clogged toilets, and backed-up sewer lines. But one night, the next-door neighbor smelled a rotten stench that made her believe that the bearded man had killed himself and his body had started to decompose.

"It smelled terrible," she would later tell police, "like someone left a big piece of steak in the fire. I called the police and an officer came over.

"The music was playing but he didn't answer the door, so we looked in the windows. The policeman and I were standing on the sidewalk in front of the place when he walked out. I said, 'We thought you were dead or something.' "

"No, I'm all right," the man said. "Hey, what do I smell? . . . I just burned a piece of meat, that's all."

"So the policeman said, 'All right, as long as you're okay.' And he left."

A month later, Tyrone Richards was rudely awoken from a deep sleep by a fit of wild screaming, knocking, and a doorbell that wouldn't quit ringing. Richards jumped into his pants and ran down to a second-floor window and looked out. There he saw Carol Baxter for the first time since she'd disappeared four months earlier.

"She was crying and shaking," Tyrone recalled.

"You've got to help me!" Carol screamed. "You're the only one who can help me. He got three girls down in the

65

basement. He got arms and things in the refrigerator!"

"I didn't believe her," Tyrone admitted, but he kept listening to Carol's bizarre story. Half an hour later, he changed his mind.

"We're going down there," Tyrone told Carol, "and we're going to mess this dude up." Then he grabbed a hammer and the two of them raced out of the house. But a block later, Tyrone had a better idea. He stopped at a pay phone and dialed 911.

A few minutes later, Officers Cannon and Savage arrived in a police van. John Cannon was a seasoned veteran—since retired—and Dave Savage was bucking for detective—since promoted. Between them, they heard wild stories almost every night on that beat—most of them drug- or alcohol-induced fantasies. But this was one of the wildest they'd ever heard—torture, sexual abuse, and murder all rolled into one. They had a difficult time believing Carol Baxter but they smelled smoke. Experience told them that a fire was burning somewhere.

"Where do you think we could find this bearded man?" Officer Cannon asked Carol.

"He's probably right around the corner sitting in the car waiting for me to come back," Carol answered.

Officer Savage told Carol and Tyrone to get in the van, and they drove to an all-night gas station/minimart around the corner to look for the bearded man. As unbelievable as it seemed to the officers, a bearded man *was* sitting in a Cadillac.

In a soft voice, he identified himself as 43-year-old Gary Heidnik and he didn't appear to be under the influence of alcohol or drugs. When Officers Cannon and Savage asked him why he thought he was being detained, he spoke calmly. With a vacant gleam in his eyes, he said it must have something to do with neglected child support payments. Both Cannon and Savage had seen that same type of look before—in photos of Charles Manson.

The two policemen transported everyone to the sex

crimes unit at police headquarters, the Roundhouse, at Eighth and Market Streets. Somebody there would get to the bottom of things.

For four hours, teams of detectives interviewed Gary Heidnik and Carol Baxter in separate rooms. She looked sober and didn't appear to be strung out on drugs. Still, the detectives wondered how much of her rapidly delivered, 27-page statement was actually true.

For four months, Carol told the detectives, she'd been chained, raped, and thrust into a big hole in the basement of Gary Heidnik's North Philadelphia house. At first, the hole was small. Carol had to make herself into a ball to fit inside, and a board was put on top to cover the hole. Later, Heidnik dug the hole out and made it big enough for three women.

Right after Thanksgiving, Heidnik brought Sandra Lindsay home. He told Carol and Sandra that the world was full of "impure" people. He wanted Carol and Sandra to bear his children and help him begin a "purified" family. He chained Sandra's feet to a beam with "her legs in the air, her back on the floor."

Then, one by one, Heidnik brought more women home. He chained them all and stripped them nude. He "played one girl against the other" to see who would obey his commands and who wouldn't, who would "rat" on the others and who wouldn't. He turned on the music and pretended to leave the house. Then he listened to see if any of them screamed for help. If so, he cranked up the music and tortured them. He'd gag them to stifle their screams, then stuck screwdrivers into their ears until blood spurted out. Sometimes, he hooked live wires to their metal shackles. Always, there was sex.

Heidnik raped Carol every day in the beginning, she said. As he gathered more "girlfriends," he took turns on all of the women. He wanted them all to produce his "pure" babies.

One day in early February, Sandra Lindsay misbehaved.

For punishment, Heidnik chained her arms to a beam and let her hang for eight hours. She started vomiting, then she lost consciousness. When he unchained Sandra, she fell and hit her head on the floor. When he carried her body upstairs, Carol didn't know if Sandra was dead or alive.

For the next few hours, a power saw buzzed over the music and a horrible smell filled the house for three or four days. Whenever Heidnik came down to the basement to have sex with the women during that period, Carol smelled the same rotten odor on him.

Then, just days before, Debbie Dudley refused to cooperate with Heidnik any longer. For her punishment, she went into the pit. He filled it with water and attached wires to her chains. Then he plugged the cord into an outlet and electrocuted her.

At first, Heidnik stored Debbie's body in a freezer in the basement. But just a few days before with Carol along to help, he drove to New Jersey and dumped the body in the woods.

As time went on, Carol gained the killer's confidence. Occasionally, he allowed her freedom from her bondage, but she had always been too terrified to try to escape—until that night.

"I feared for my safety and the safety of the other girls," Carol Baxter told the detectives. "Gary said he'd kill me if I left or if I didn't help him." But lately, Carol had started to fear for her own life. Shortly before midnight, her opportunity for escape had materialized.

To placate him, Carol said she'd help Heidnik find a new girlfriend to replace Debbie Dudley. For hours, they cruised the streets on the north side of town, looking. When they arrived at the 24-hour minimart at Sixth and Girard, Carol told him to stop the car and let her out. This was where she'd find the new girlfriend for him. He hesitated. He almost drove away. Finally, he agreed, warning Carol that he'd kill her if she tried anything funny.

That was how she'd duped him and sneaked away to her boyfriend Tyrone's apartment.

By 4:00 a.m., the search warrants arrived. Minutes later, Detectives Jim Hansen, Lamont Anderson, and Cliff Lowery broke down the front door to Gary Heidnik's North Marshall Street house. Inside, it was dark — and spooky.

"This is like something out of a Poe story," commented one of the detectives. As they approached the cellar stairway, it was ominously quiet below. The only sounds were their footsteps, creaking on the rickety wooden stairway as they slowly descended toward the torture chamber. But there were no cries for help as their flashlight beams pierced the pitch blackness below. They began to doubt Carol Baxter's story. But to their utter shock, their doubt was short-lived.

The officers found Gail Midley and Tammy Kramer chained to the sewer pipes with muffler clamps and handcuffs. Patty Conrad was chained inside the four-foot dungeon. Two mattresses were thrown on the floor and a portable toilet stood in one corner.

"When we heard the banging," Gail Midley would say later, "we kept quiet because he usually tested us to see if we would scream or holler, so he could beat the s--- out of us.

"When we seen the flashlights and all the cops and stuff coming and they said, 'Everything is all right, y'all free now,' then we knew we were safe."

The women told the officers that they'd been raped and tortured. Gail Midley said she'd lost 40-50 pounds because all she'd eaten for the past three months had been bread, water, dog food, and dog biscuits. All three women appeared to be dehydrated and Gail Midley and Tammy Kramer looked malnourished. Soon, an ambulance was rushing the three hostages to Episcopal Hospital for medical treatment.

By then, evidence technicians, medical examiners, po-

69

lice officers, and investigators were converging on the scene. They started in the kitchen and within minutes realized that Carol Baxter had not been exaggerating. This truly was a "house of horrors."

Two handless forearms, one upper arm, and pieces of a thigh—24 pounds in all—were found in the freezer, wrapped inside plastic bags. Smaller chunks of cooked body parts were found in pots on the stove top and inside the oven. Charred bone fragments were also found in the oven.

Upstairs in a bedroom that was wall-papered with $1 and $5 bills, the detectives found Gary Heidnik's Merrill-Lynch financial statement. To their surprise, it listed assets of more than $500,000. Who in hell were they dealing with, they wondered, Charles Manson or Michael Milken?

All day long, bulldozers plowed up the front yard and backhoes dug up the back, looking for human remains. With forensic technicians sifting through every bit of dirt, curiosity-seekers were drawn to the scene like vultures to a jackal kill.

"Those ain't no dog bones," a voice in the crowd announced when an investigator dropped a large object into a plastic bag. But, officially, the Philadelphia Police Department was playing it close to the vest.

"The investigation is just commencing," Captain Robert Grasso told the flock of reporters who'd gotten wind of the gruesome findings on North Marshall Street. "There are too many aspects about which we know too little." But the media circus had already begun. Television shows were interrupted and news flashes were broadcast over the radio all day long, forcing District Attorney Ron Castillo to call a press conference sooner than he would have wanted.

"You don't run into many cases like this," he understated. "It's something you think you'd see in a movie. Residue of human flesh was found in the house, but there were no indications of any cannibalism." Other than saying that two men were being detained for questioning, the D.A. offered very little information.

At the time, Carol Baxter was across the Delaware River in New Jersey, leading a pack of bloodhounds sniffing through woods, searching for Sandra Lindsay's corpse. In the city itself, lab technicians were attempting to classify and identify the various body parts found at the scene.

Reporters interviewed a woman Gary Heidnik had dated every Wednesday for the past 15 years.

"We always went out to dinner, shows, and concerts," Mindy Lawrence told the press. "He liked to go out. We went to the Presidential, the Bellevue Stratford, and the Academy of Music. He had a nice smile and he made you laugh. He was a silly, jokey kind of man."

Lawrence, 45, told sleuths she'd met Gary Heidnik when they were both working as private-duty LPNs for the same patient. They started dating. In time, he asked her to have his baby—he wanted a son. But Mindy Lawrence refused. She already had three children and thought three were sufficient.

"I happened to have the TV on," she continued, "and my mother called and said, 'Did you hear this—is that your Gary?'

"I said, 'Yes, it certainly is.' But he never hurt me. It shook me to my wits. I guess he just went off. It's a sad, shocking thing, and it's a puzzle. He was gentle and sweet and he treated me well.

"All he wanted was extra girlfriends. I knew two of the women and he liked them both—in a nice way, too. I can't understand it. Why would he hurt his friends?"

By dinner time, the bearded man from North Marshall Street was no longer anonymous. His life story was playing on almost every newscast across the country.

Gary Heidnik had been born on November 22, 1943, in Eastlake, Ohio, a suburb of Cleveland. His father was a machinist, his mother a beautician, but his parents divorced when Gary was two. At first, he and his younger brother lived with the mother, but the boys moved back in with the father three years later.

As a boy, Gary played baseball and delivered newspapers. He was a Boy Scout.

"He was very studious," a family member recalled. "He liked to read, school work mostly. He got good grades in school and he was always telling me he was going to be a millionaire, that he was going to make a lot of money. But he never said how he was going to get it."

Young Gary had a fascination for the military. In 1959, he dropped out of school after the ninth grade and talked his family into enrolling him at Staunton Academy, a prestigious military school in Virginia that boasted Barry Goldwater and John Dean as alumni. Gary attended Staunton for two years, where he was described as a "pretty good student." After returning to Eastlake, Gary quit school a month later on October 4, 1961.

"You take a kid, eighteen or nineteen, they get big ideas," a relative said. "He wanted to follow through, so he left town. He told me he was going out on his own, that he was going to make his own way. I said, 'If you want to go, go.' "

That was the last time the family member ever saw Gary.

"At first, it bothered me," Gary's relative said, "but after a while, after so many years, you give up. I didn't even recognize him until they mentioned his name on the six o'clock news. I said, 'Oh, my God.' But what the hell could I do? I just watched, surprised as hell. Surprised and sick.

"I haven't seen him in years. If he did what they say he did, I don't care what they do to him. They can go hang him and, if they want, I'll go and pull the rope."

Less than two months after he left home, Gary Heidnik enlisted in the Army. The date was November 29, 1961.

After boot camp, he was sent to Fort Sam Houston in San Antonio, Texas, where he received medical training. In May 1962, he was assigned to the 46th Surgical Hospital in Landstuhl, Germany, as a medic.

Then something peculiar happened.

Five months later, the Army shipped Gary Heidnik to the Valley Forge Hospital outside of Philadelphia. On January 30, 1963, Army doctors honorably discharged him with a 100% medical disability. He was only 18 years old and had served only 14 months of his scheduled three-year enlistment. As part of his discharge—which was ruled to be a psychiatric problem resulting from his Army service—Gary Heidnik would receive $1,355 per month for the rest of his life. Prior to entering the service, he had no history of any mental problems whatsoever.

After discharge, Gary Heidnik graduated from a practical nursing program in Philadelphia. Trained in the basics of anatomy and physiology, pediatrics and obstetrics, he started working double shifts at the University of Pennsylvania Hospital and picked up private-duty assignments on the side. He saved his money and bought a home in the University City section in 1967.

In 1971, he established the United Church of the Ministers of God and ordained himself as a bishop. At its peak, membership in his "church" reached eight. At this same time, Heidnik opened an account at Merrill-Lynch with $35,000 in cash and started buying and selling stock, focusing on blue chip issues.

Heidnik also acquired a live-in girlfriend. She could neither read, write, nor tell the difference between a nickel, dime, or quarter. But they had a daughter on March 22, 1978. Six weeks later, on May 7th, the couple visited the girlfriend's 34-year-old sister, a mental patient with an IQ of 30, at a state hospital 35 miles north of Harrisburg. They told the hospital officials that they were taking the sister on a day-trip. Instead, they transported

73

her back to Philadelphia.

Ten days later, state officials found the sister locked in a closet at Gary Heidnik's home. On June 6th, he was charged with kidnapping, rape, deviate sexual intercourse, interference with the custody of a committed person, reckless endangerment, and unlawful restraint. In August, Gary Heidnik entered Coatesville Veterans Hospital for psychiatric treatment. He was still a patient there when his trial began in November. When he took the stand, the defendant testified that he was suffering from a form of schizophrenia and was taking three drugs—Thorazine, Cogentin, and Inderal.

"One of the drugs," Gary Heidnik told the court, "is supposed to stop my head from shaking. I mean, I have problems, you know." With his attorney arguing for psychiatric care rather than incarceration, Judge Charles Mirarchi sentenced Gary Heidnik to serve three to seven years in prison.

On January 29, 1979, Gary Heidnik entered the State Correctional Institute at Graterford as inmate F-9748. At first, he caused no problems, but after six months behind bars, he started to withdraw. Psychotic episodes followed, and prison officials shuttled him back and forth between the prison and psychiatric facilities in the area for the balance of his jail term.

In April 1983, his sentence fulfilled, Gary Heidnik returned to Philadelphia and moved into a trailer near 44th and Sansom Streets. A short while later, he bought the home on North Marshall Street. In the interim, he met Dan Mason, whom he called "my best friend" and started corresponding with a young woman in the Philippine Islands.

On September 30, 1985—two years after the letters started—the Filipino woman arrived in Philadelphia. Three days later, the couple married in Elkton, Maryland. But in less than six months, the mail-order bride was unhappy. On March 6, 1986, she penned a letter to the Philippine Consulate in New York City.

"My husband is *diperensiya sa utak*," she wrote in her native Tagalog—in English, she meant he was crazy. The letter continued:

"Since the very start of our marriage, I have encountered a lot of problems from my husband. He always brings girls in the house and I can see what they are doing inside the bedroom. Week after week, he brings girls and sometimes there are three that he is using at the same time.

"The worst part is, he is even hurting me if I do not obey what he tells me to do. He will make me stand in the corner for twelve hours. And he makes me sleep on the dirty floor.

"I cannot stand the condition I am in now and I am three months pregnant. I do not know any friends that I can turn to . . . I need the help of my countrymen and I am waiting your response.

"My husband is mentally ill and this is what I am really afraid of."

The Philippine Consulate referred the woman to a family in Cherry Hill, New Jersey, where she found emotional support and shelter. In time, she filed charges against her husband for spousal rape, indecent assault, and simple assault but dropped the charges when he apologized to her. She had the baby, but never returned to Gary Heidnik or the home on North Marshall Street.

Dan Mason was another story. Mason worked at the Elwyn Institute workshop with Sandra Lindsay. In fact, he dated Sandra Lindsay and lived off-and-on with Gary Heidnik in the North Marshall Street home and served as Gary's driver, shuttling women back and forth in Gary's van. That afternoon, police picked up Dan Mason for questioning.

By nightfall, the bloodhounds had found a corpse in the New Jersey pine barrens.

George Kerns, a spokesman for the Camden County

Prosecutor's Office, announced that a nude female body had been recovered from a shallow grave, covered with leaves and sticks, in Wharton State Park in Waterford Township, about three miles from the White Horse Pike. The county medical examiner identified the body as Debbie Dudley and determined the cause of death as electrocution.

Detective Edward Rocks of the Philadelphia Homicide Squad's Special Investigations Unit (SIU) went out to the pine barrens along with crime scene technicians to process the scene and search for evidence. Rocks conducted a search scene but found nothing of evidentiary value. Detective Rocks would subsequently interview each survivor, as well as Heidnik himself.

When Rocks interviewed him, Heidnik was being held in the Philadelphia detention center. Rocks came prepared. Armed with a search warrant, Rocks asked the suspect if he could take blood from him. Heidnik complied and was very cooperative although he had little choice in the matter since the sleuth had a warrant with him.

With that development, Gary Heidnik was held without bail.

Gary Heidnik's documented past psychiatric problems left little doubt that his defense strategy would include an insanity plea. And with his vast financial resources, there was little doubt who would defend him: A. Charles Peruto Jr.—often called Junior—one half of the state's best father-son law team.

"He's bonkers," Peruto said after his client's hearing on April 23rd. "I seemed to hear evidence in there that Mister Heidnik was saying that he wanted to make these girls pregnant and raise a family in the basement. Now if you're going to tell me that's the sayings of a sane man, then I should get out of this business."

In addition, Peruto did little to dispel the rumors that Gary Heidnik had been used as a human guinea pig to secretly test LSD while in the Army. Although the Pentagon denied the allegations, lights flashed and buzzers buzzed when a computer operator tried to access Gary Heidnik's military records.

"He mentioned a few things," Peruto told the press, referring to the alleged secret LSD testing, "but I won't tell you what it was. I can only say that I don't want to answer any questions along those lines because they may be extremely important at some later date."

When the case came to trial in July 1988 in a sixth-floor courtroom in city hall, there was little doubt but that Gary Heidnik had committed the crimes for which he stood accused.

"My client is not innocent," Charles Peruto Jr. told the court. "We are not relying on that presumption. He is very guilty. This is not a whodunit. This is a case of why it was done. He is relying on a defense of mental infirmity. His criminal acts will show him to be insane."

The jury had been empaneled in Pittsburgh, 300 miles to the west of Philadelphia, because the defense attorney claimed it would be impossible to find 12 impartial jurors in Philadelphia. As the trial began, Assistant District Attorney Charles Gallagher argued for the death penalty.

"This man is legally sane," the A.D.A. told the jury. "He knew what he was doing and he did it with torture. He kept [his victims] chained and he repeatedly beat them and eventually killed two of them. The evidence will come from the four survivors. You will see how Gary Heidnik took advantage of underprivileged people."

In the end, the jury rejected the insanity plea and found Gary Heidnik guilty on all counts. On March 2, 1989, Judge Lynne Abraham sentenced Gary Heidnik to two death sentences. He is currently sitting on Pennsylvania's death row pending automatic reviews of the cases by the state's Supreme Court. While awaiting his fate, Gary Heidnik has attempted suicide more than once.

EDITOR'S NOTE:

*Carol Baxter, Tyrone Richards, Tammy Kramer, Gail Midley, Patty Conrad, Dan Mason, and Mindy Lawrence are not the real names of the persons so named in the foregoing story. Fictitious names have been used because there is no reason for public interest in the identities of these persons.*

# "UNNATURAL ACTS WITH A RED-HOT KNIFE!"

## by Tom Basinski

Even though the van was called "undercover," it didn't fool anyone. Small children in the neighborhood knew as well as dope dealers and hookers whenever the Flint, Michigan, police were driving about or staking out a house.

The burgundy van, occupied by three Flint narcotics officers, was slowly moving down the 300 block of Mary Street about 9:30 p.m. on January 17, 1990. Lieutenant Jerome Koger was driving, Officer Felicia Smith was riding "shotgun," and Officer Johnny "Be Good" Goodman was in the back. The three were on their way to take license numbers and see if they recognized anyone frequenting a crack house a few blocks away.

As they drove past 329 Mary Street, the officers could see smoke coming out the front door. The smoke wasn't too hard to miss since the house didn't have a front door, or even windows, for that matter.

No one knew the history of this house, but it wasn't difficult to put together the scenario: The owner had worked at the Buick or Chevrolet plant. After being laid off, he tried to sell the house, but couldn't do it. There were no buyers in Flint, so the owner moved to Houston or another Sun Belt city in search of work, and the house was left abandoned. This was a common story in Flint.

When Lieutenant Koger got to the doorway, he was unable to enter because of the smoke. The fire department had been called by police dispatchers, and the officers had to wait. Engine Company Seven from Station Two rolled up minutes later and "knocked down" the fire in a matter of seconds. Fire Lieutenant Larry Edgecomb explained to Lieutenant Koger that the job was easy because the only thing really burning in the house was a body.

Koger radioed for an arson team and the on-call homicide team. Sergeants Norm Day and Mark Smith from homicide arrived within the hour. Sergeants Graham Whipple and Ladale Woods arrived from the arson squad soon thereafter.

Lawmen knew there was no sense in getting a search warrant for the house. No one could, or would, claim a right to privacy there. It was a two-story, single-family dwelling with gray siding. All of the windows were broken out. Trash was strewn about the front porch and driveway.

. The inside revealed two couches overturned along with some end tables. The metal furniture in the kitchen was also overturned. Food had been thrown against the walls, and a dark red substance had been smeared along the west wall of the living room. Someone had spray-painted slogans on the walls that the officers did not understand, words and numbers like "60s" and "Six Oh Boys."

The body was in the basement. "The victim was obviously dead," as the police report put it. It was a male in his late teens or early 20s. He was on his face with his hands tied behind his back. He was wearing expensive, but old, black tennis shoes and black sweatpants. He had been beaten about the head so severely that his head appeared to be almost twice its normal size. His face was so swollen that his eyes were mere slits, his lips bulging and distended. Much of his skin was charred.

Sergeant Day noted the odor of gasoline in the air.

That smell, along with the odor of burned skin, made Day glad he would be retiring soon.

Sergeant Day was impressed with the quick response of the Flint Fire Department. They had not only arrived quickly, they also put out the blaze quickly and without destroying much evidence.

Sergeant Ron Mossman, a 24-year veteran with 13 years in homicide, would be the detective in charge of this case. Mossman was tired, to be sure. He had seen so much death, nearly all of it unnecessary and foolish, during his tenure in homicide.

Yet Mossman geared up for each case as if it were his first one. The victims' pasts did not matter. Mossman handled each case with professional detachment. He did not shed tears for his victims, but there were enough killers in Jackson State Prison who thought Mossman came after them like they had killed one of Mossman's relatives. That is just the way he did it.

Sergeant Mossman made his walk-through of the house, taking notes as he went. The crime lab arrived and began photographing every room. Blood samples were taken from the deceased by lab technician Wendy Pippins.

Samples of liquid, believed to be gasoline, were collected near the body. A large concrete block with blood on one edge was collected and logged in as evidence. Sergeant Mark Smith told Mossman that he believed the block had been dropped on the head of the deceased. Sergeant Mossman shook his head in disgust, but he said nothing.

The body was removed to the morgue at 4:30 a.m. The crime scene work continued for another hour. Mossman looked at his watch. It was time for him to get up, and he had already been working for nine hours.

Lieutenant Joe DeKatch, Mossman's boss, arrived and needed to be briefed. Mossman decided to bring Sergeants Day and Smith and talk with the lieutenant over breakfast. It was going to be a long day. They might as well get something decent in their stomachs before they started.

The detectives would first check the missing person files to see if any young males had been reported missing. Mossman said he wanted to have Sergeant Charlie Middleton of the gang detail look at the writings on the wall at the crime scene.

Mossman had read somewhere that the graffiti at crime scenes was usually related to gang activity. Flint was just starting to feel the waves of gang violence that had started in California. Young boys were getting killed for expensive basketball shoes or professional sports jackets worn by all of the gangs. Life meant nothing to them. For that matter, life in prison meant nothing to them, either.

The autopsy was held at 10:00 a.m. and was conducted by Dr. Willys Mueller. A full set of fingerprints was taken from the corpse. The autopsy told the story of a tragic and violent death.

Dr. Mueller estimated the victim's age to be only 17 to 19. He had been beaten and burned, to be sure. There was also evidence of burn marks not associated with the gasoline torching on his buttocks. The burns were sharply distinct in shape, indicating that some kind of hot metal object, like a heated knife blade, had been applied to the victim's skin.

The burn marks were on both legs, both buttocks, and the anus. They were also near the knees and insides of the victim's legs. Similar marks were found on the sole, instep, and ankle of each foot. Dr. Mueller said, "It looks like this guy was tortured, too. As if beating him half to death wasn't enough."

The body was not burned on the chest because the victim had been lying on his stomach and chest when ignited. Ligature marks on both wrists indicated that he had been tied up tightly.

The victim's face and head revealed the most thorough and brutal beating the pathologist had seen in his long career of dealing with gore. There was not one centimeter of the head that had not suffered damage. Although there was no skull fracture, there was evidence of bleeding inside the skull.

The lips and gums were pulverized. The eyes were swollen and blackened. The face and chest had drag marks, probably from a concrete floor. Death had finally been a blessing for this victim.

Samples of urine, blood, and bile were taken as part of the regular protocol of the autopsy procedure. Dr. Mueller said the cause of death was "diffuse blood trauma to the head." There was no single blow to the head that had caused death but, rather, "cumulative injuries."

Also, as part of protocol, fingerprints were sent to the state crime laboratory in Lansing for computerized comparison.

Later that day as Sergeant Mossman sat recording reports, Sergeant Charlie Middleton poked his head into Mossman's office and said, "Hey Moss, I just went by that Mary Street address. In Los Angeles most of the street gangs are determined by where they live. That Sixties and Six-Oh stuff is from a gang in Los Angeles called the 'Rolling Sixties.' They live around 60th Street. I called a guy I met at a seminar. They're a big gang. Sell drugs and stuff like that. They have automatic weapons and generally play rough.

"Since they didn't write any nicknames on the wall, or didn't do anything else," Middleton continued, "he thinks this stuff is the work of pretenders or wannabees. I told him we might have some of these guys here, but I didn't know. The way people are moving out of Flint these days, it isn't likely someone is going to move here from Los Angeles."

Sergeant Mossman thanked Middleton and went back to work on this case—and several other cases he was working on. Mossman was retiring in late 1992, and he found himself more and more thinking about that day in the tantalizingly near-but-far future.

Nothing happened for several weeks on this case. The body lay unidentified in the morgue with a case number and a "John Doe" tag wired around the corpse's left big toe. Mossman periodically checked the missing persons reports, but he never found anything close.

The body fluid results came back negative for alcohol and drug use. Mossman was not surprised. It looked like the victim had been battered around for a few days. That was plenty of time for the body to absorb any drugs.

Meanwhile, more people were being killed in Flint. Mossman drew his share of these cases. He worked them while he worked this one.

On February 20, 1990, over a month later, Flint police finally learned that the John Doe was Lawrence White, a 19-year old unemployed resident of Flint's north side. White lived about three miles from where he was found dead. White's fingerprints were on file for numerous arrests for theft and narcotics charges. White's family was notified, and they began making arrangements for his funeral.

Sergeants Mossman and Day went to White's home to interview surviving family members. One relative told them that he had been across the street at Willie Murray's house about a week before and Willie had told him that he heard Lawrence was dead. The officers thought this odd since Lawrence had only been identified the day before.

The homicide detectives asked White's family if it ever occurred to them to report Lawrence as missing. One relative said he thought about it, but never did anything about it. He figured Lawrence was probably coming down from a long crack cocaine binge and was sleeping it off somewhere.

In the meantime, Sergeant Middleton had come up with 13 names of men who claimed they belonged to the famous "Rolling 60s" gang from L.A. Since these markings were found around Lawrence White's body, the officers decided to round up the entire gang and see what they had to say.

Preparations for the roundup were extensive. The group members had to be identified, along with addresses and locations where they usually hung out. Pictures were located and distributed, if available.

Deputy Police Chief Jerry Dickenson was briefed on the situation. Dickenson was one of the youngest detectives ever promoted to the rank in the history of the Flint Police Department. He had moved up the ranks and was now in an administrative position.

Dickenson made more money as a deputy chief but did not have as much fun as the working cops. He often met with them informally at the Torch Lounge to be briefed on the progress of current cases. Dickenson was a "cop's cop," revered by all the troops.

All 13 gang members were arrested simultaneously in a combined effort of the entire homicide division along with criminal intelligence—and whatever spare detectives Mossman and Middleton could grab.

The detectives were briefed on the specifics of the Lawrence White case. Middleton learned that White's nickname was "Pie Shark." No one ever learned what that meant. But the sleuths knew that if they asked a Rolling 60s gang member about Lawrence White, the gang members wouldn't know. If they asked about the death of "Pie Shark," they might get a better answer.

The arrests went off with precision. Two hours after the last Rolling 60s member was brought in, the detectives adjourned for a short progress meeting with Sergeant Mossman. Each cop said independently, "These guys don't know anything about this homicide."

The gang members were interviewed for about an hour regarding general criminal activity in Flint. Then they were driven back to where they had been first contacted.

The detectives had gathered intelligence about some

85

robberies that a rival gang had been pulling, along with the location of some stolen semiautomatic weapons. Not surprisingly, the weapons were now in the possession of a rival gang.

Sergeant Mossman was not happy. He knew it was time to go back to Lawrence White's neighborhood and find out why a neighbor knew Lawrence was dead a week before the police had announced it.

The neighbors was LeRon Dodds. He told sleuths he'd heard about Lawrence's death from his friend, Willie Murray. Sergeant Mossman ran the names of Dodds and Murray in the crime computer.

Dodds's name revealed a blank page with the message: "Search Completed." This meant that LeRon Dodds had not had any encounters with the police.

Murray's name, however, almost caused the printer to run out of ink. Apparently, Willie Murray had arrests and detentions for almost every offense imaginable. He was heavily involved in the trafficking and use of crack cocaine. Sergeant Louis Weller of the narcotics division knew Murray well.

As he thumbed through the color photographs of Lawrence White's crime scene, Weller told Mossman, "When Willie is on the stuff, he is certainly capable of doing this."

It did not take long to find someone to do a controlled buy of cocaine from Willie Murray. The officers followed the buy-up with a search warrant for Murray's house.

On February 22, 1990, Sergeant Weller and some local DEA agent, along with the regular Flint narcotics crew, served the warrant. They found a moderate quantity of cocaine along with an AK-47 assault rifle and $7,000 in cash.

Sergeant Mossman interviewed Murray about Lawrence White's death. Murray was not high on crack at the time and gave a rather reasonable interview. He was adamant that he did not know anything about Lawrence's death.

He said Lawrence was like a brother to him. He did not know anything about any Rolling 60s gang either.

On March 13, 1990, two months after Lawrence White's brutal death, Sergeant Mossman was sitting at his desk on the second floor of Flint's aging police station. He was looking out the window at the brown-gray landscape. As much as Mossman liked the seasons in Michigan, these few months of "gray days" were enough to make anyone want to move. The trees were bare and skeleton-like. The grass was brown, and there were still piles of gray, dirt-stained snow waiting to melt along the driveways.

Just then the phone rang. Mossman did not feel like briefing another relative of a homicide victim about the progress of their loved one's case. But he picked up the phone anyway.

The caller, Arthur Crafton, said he had information on Lawrence White's death. After a short period of interrogation, Mossman picked up Crafton outside a local restaurant and drove him to an empty church parking lot.

Crafton said Lawrence White had been killed because he had been given some crack cocaine to sell by Willie Murray and several other guys. Lawrence was also given a gun to protect himself.

When Murray went to collect his share of money, Lawrence told him that some guy had ripped him off for the dope and the gun. Murray did not believe this for a second, so Murray and some friends kidnapped Lawrence, beat him, burned him, and killed him with a cement block.

Mossman thought he was onto something since he had managed to keep the cement block information from the press. No one was supposed to know about it. Mossman also thought about Murray's statement to him that Lawrence White was "like a brother to me."

Mossman tempered his enthusiasm and cautiously asked, "How do you know about all this, Arthur?"

Crafton replied, "Y'see officer, they kidnapped my lady too. They done some awful things to her."

Mossman started to grimace. He had visions of another body out there somewhere. Mossman asked, "What do you mean? What lady?"

Crafton said, "Here's what happened. I don't want to tell you my girl's name. Don't worry. She's still alive. I don't think she's going to want to talk to you, though.

"She and Lawrence was selling some crack for Willie. Lawrence used most of it up himself. She used some, too, I guess. Lawrence sold the gun Willie gave him.

"When Willie come by for the money, they told him they was ripped off. Willie came back with a bunch of guys and got my girl. They drove her to a house where Lawrence already was. I guess they snagged him before her.

"Pie Shark was beat nearly to death. His head looked like an elephant's. Them guys did all kinds of things to my girl and Lawrence, trying to get them to tell about the dope."

Mossman asked what they did.

Crafton replied, "Well, they stripped down Lawrence and tied up his hands. They smacked him around soundly with their hands and kicked him a lot.

"Then, they heated up knives from the stove and burned his ass and whatnot."

To Mossman, this explained the sharply configured burn marks on the victim. This was another detail that had not been released to the press. Mossman was on a roll.

Crafton explained that the gang changed locations a few times. They would put Lawrence in the trunk of a car and drive him to another place where they would beat him and burn him some more.

The five guys took turns having sex with Crafton's girlfriend and made Lawrence have sex with her in front of them.

Finally, Mossman built up enough trust with Crafton to have him tell Mossman the name of his girlfriend, Irene Wilson.

Mossman was happy to learn her name. He would not press Crafton for an in-person meeting just yet. Mossman was curious why Irene was spared death at the hands of these killers who were so brutal to Lawrence White.

Crafton said, "Y'see, officer, one of the guys, Tracy Turner, was boyfriend with Irene's sister. Tracy was the only one who wouldn't have sex with Irene. He felt real bad about what they was doin' to Irene.

"The guys left Tracy to guard Lawrence and Irene. Tracy loosened her ropes when they had her tied to a chair and she escaped. I guess he loosened Lawrence's too, but he was just about dead."

Sergeant Mossman learned that there were six men involved altogether. They were Terry "Terrible" Ferguson, 24, Antonio Hudson, 19, Tracy Turner, 20, Jermaine "Tank" Hammond, 17, Willie "Goob" Murray, 24, and Lystra "Monk" Moore, 18.

It took nine days for Irene Wilson to agree to meet with Sergeant Mossman. She did not trust the police, and for good reason. She was a dealer of crack cocaine and not a good citizen herself. To top it off, she was deathly, hysterically, and justifiably afraid of the six killers.

Mossman enlisted the help of Sergeant Theresa Green, also of the homicide division. Green had her own bundle of cases to work on. However, the other detectives knew that if they needed help on any matter, Theresa Green would help them.

When Irene started talking with Mossman and Sergeant Green, it was evident that the ordeal had angered and sickened her. Irene recounted how two members of the group had stuck a broomstick inside White's rectum. They had also applied the red-hot knife blade to White's anus.

Irene would talk for a while, then cry a little. She

would get stronger and angrier, then she would continue. Mossman was impressed with her resolve.

That evening Mossman sat down and wrote out the strengths and weaknesses of his case. The strengths were obvious: He had an eyewitness to two days of brutal beatings and torture inflicted on Lawrence White.

The weaknesses was that Irene Wilson could, and might, disappear before court. She could flee, or friends of the dope dealers could arrange for her disappearance.

Also, Lawrence White was not dead when Irene last saw him. Some different people could have come in and finished him off. It was not likely, but in the world of courts and defense attorneys, any scenario might surface.

Sergeant Mossman no longer had a mystery on his hands. But he had a case which he knew needed a lot of work done before it was ready to be taken before a jury.

The next day, they decided to start bringing in the principal characters of this brutal drama. Chief Dickenson and Sergeants Mossman and Day decided to start with the youngest player, Jermaine "Tank" Hammond.

The officers arrested Hammond and transported him to police headquarters. Hammond spoke freely about the torture. He appeared to be a willing informant, providing details that only someone present at the scene would know. The detectives noted the young man said he himself did not actually do anything to Lawrence White. They did not believe everything Hammond said, however.

Hammond did tell them details that were consistent with the autopsy. White had been brutally beaten over a period of days. At the end, a large concrete block had been dropped on White's head. He was also doused with gasoline and ignited.

Hammond said that Lystra "Monk" Moore had been the one who dropped the block on White's head. Hammond implicated the same perpetrators Irene Wilson had. Hammond denied doing any harm to White, while Irene Wilson said Hammond was there getting his licks in like

90

the others.

The roundup continued with all of the other players being arrested. The interviews were surprisingly easy. The would-be gangsters admitted what they had done. In a kind of perverse code of conduct, they said Lawrence White had used drugs entrusted to him to sell. Therefore, he had to be punished. He deserved it.

Mossman thought that if you viewed life in such a twisted way, then their actions were at least explainable. The criminal justice system did not view life that way, however.

All of the statements given by the gangsters showed that Jermaine Hammond had been an active participant in White's killing, which was not consistent with his statements to the police.

Mossman, Green, and Day delivered Hammond back to the Flint Police Department to Sergeant McIntyre, the department's polygraph operator.

After the preliminary interview, Hammond was asked if he dropped a block on White's head, if he started the fire that burned Lawrence White, and if he poured any of the gas at 329 Mary Street. To each of these questions Hammond answered, "No."

In his gentle, but bearlike way, Sergeant McIntyre told Hammond he was not being truthful. Surprisingly enough, Hammond changed his answers on the spot. He had no remorse or emotion about it.

"Oh yeah, I did drop that cement block on Pie Shark's noggin. I forgot," Hammond said calmly.

The case was presented to the Genesee County Prosecutor's Office and given to Deputy Prosecutor Randy Petrides. He sorted through the details of sex, blood, and gore and charged Terry "Terrible" Ferguson, Willie "Goob" Murray, and Lystra "Monk" Moore with first-degree murder, two counts of kidnapping, and two counts of criminal sexual conduct. He charged Jermaine Hammond with murder and kidnapping. He charged Tracy

Turner with kidnapping and assault with intent to commit great bodily harm. Antonio Hudson was charged with criminal sexual conduct and assault with intent to commit murder.

In October of 1990, three separate juries were seated for Ferguson, Murray, and Moore. On November 16, 1990, the three juries found all guilty as charged. On January 5, 1991, Judge Thomas Yeotis sentenced the trio to life in prison without the possibility of parole.

Antonio Hudson stood trial in November 1990. He was found guilty as charged and sentenced to life in prison, with parole, plus 10 years. This sentence was handed down on February 3, 1991.

Jermaine Hammond was sentenced to the juvenile detention facility where he will be evaluated in 10 years.

On February 3, 1991, Tracy Turner received 20 years for his crimes.

All of the participants are serving their sentences in the Michigan penal system.

EDITOR'S NOTE:
*LeRon Dodds, Arthur Crafton, and Irene Wilson are not the real names of the persons so named in the foregoing story. Fictitious names have been used because there is no reason for public interest in the identities of these persons.*

# "BEATEN, TORTURED, DEGRADED: A TEN-YEAR-OLD'S ORDEAL!"

## by George Stimson, Jr.

**CINCINNATI, OHIO**
**MAY 11, 1992**

Cincinnati, Ohio, is like many of the nation's other mid-sized cities. With a 1990 population of 364,040, it has its share of lawbreakers. Unlike many other U.S. towns, however, Cincinnati has not followed the national trend of rampant youth gang activity. Thus, the Queen City has avoided the seemingly wholesale murder rate spawned by the gang-turf wars that plague other towns. Still, it does have enough killing to keep the Cincinnati Police Department's Violent Crimes Unit busy.

Most of these homicides do not make front-page headlines. They are sparked by arguments over money, drugs, or sex.

Occasionally, though, a murder is committed that stands out from the others. Something about the victim, the killer, or the method of death makes the entire city sit up and take notice. One such murder occurred in the spring of 1992. The crime was so perverse, violent, senseless, and tragic that the whole town followed the painful developments of the case. Far from rating only a few lines of mention in the newspapers, the case became one of the top local stories of the year.

The neighborhood of Lower Price Hill is located on Cincinnati's west side. It is bordered on one flank by railroad tracks and Mill Creek, on the other by the rising slope that becomes Price Hill proper. As such, it doesn't merge with any of the surrounding neighborhoods. Rather, it's a distinct, if somewhat isolated, community.

Lower Price Hill is mostly residential, except for a bar, a coffee shop, and a few other small businesses near the intersection of West Eighth and State Streets. The area has many old, run-down houses. Some of the buildings are even abandoned and boarded up. It is definitely a working-class neighborhood, though many of its residents are, in fact, unemployed. Not only do most of the residents know one another, but many of them are also related. It is truly a close-knit community.

Monday, May 11, 1992, was a pleasant spring day in the Queen City. Clear and mild, it was a perfect day for children to escape the confines of their homes and play outdoors. In Lower Price Hill, playing outdoors means playing in the streets. Many of the children also like to play in the area's abandoned, boarded-up buildings.

But one child who did not like to play in those old buildings was 10-year-old Aaron Raines. The youngest of the six children in the Raines family, he was a fourth-grader at the Oyler Elementary School up the hill in Price Hill.

The previous summer, Aaron had been struck by a car, an experience that left him shy and insecure. Whenever he played outside, the youngster never wandered far from the family home in the 700 block of Neave Street. Moreover, he had recently dropped a weight on his foot and broken it. Now he wore a partial cast on the affected leg, causing him to hobble around and further restricting the range of his playtime activities.

Nevertheless, Aaron was like most children and loved to play. On the evening of May 11th, a relative gave Aaron a cheese sandwich for dinner and then allowed him to go outside and play tag with his friends until it got dark. The relative looked out into the street every 15 minutes to check on the boy. Everything was normal and fine until around 9:00 p.m., when darkness began falling. Aaron should have returned home by then, but he never appeared.

Alarmed by his unexplainable absence, Aaron's family began searching the neighborhood for him. They checked the streets and other areas where he was known to play, with no success. None of his playmates could say what had happened to him. A dark, ominous feeling took hold of the family members. "I knew something was wrong," one would later say.

After searching for over two hours without results, Aaron's family called the Cincinnati PD at about 11:30 p.m. to report the boy missing.

The police responded immediately, initiating their own search. They, too, checked all the likely areas where Aaron might have gone and questioned children and adults who might have seen anything out of the ordinary. Unfortunately, nobody had seen anything.

Having no luck with the specific areas frequented by the boy, the police decided to search every inch of the neighborhood. This search included several abandoned buildings in the 2900 block of Eighth Street near where it intersected State.

Those buildings were more than 100 years old. They had been two-story, red-brick houses with businesses on the ground floor and apartments above. Although slated for redevelopment, they had been abandoned in 1988 and condemned a year later. The structures had been boarded up, but neighborhood children had removed some of the boards and routinely used the crumbling ruins as a play area. The shy and cautious Aaron Raines was an exception, however. He was not known to play in the buildings. Still, police knew it was necessary to check them out.

About 6:30 p.m. on Tuesday, May 12th, Police Officer Terry Pierana entered one of the Eighth Street buildings. It was just a few blocks from Aaron Raines' home on Neave Street. The interior was almost completely gutted. The officer went up to the second floor, but found nothing of interest there. Back on the first floor, he came across a baseball cap that would later be identified as Aaron's. Then Officer Pierana turned his attention to the basement. As he descended the steep, rickety staircase that led into the cellar, he noticed what appeared to be blood on the railings, and a sickening feeling came over him. Not touching the railings, Pierana made his way down the stairs, shining his flashlight around in the gloomy darkness.

A few seconds later, the search for 10-year-old Aaron Raines came to a tragic end.

The boy was lying on his back in a corner of the trash-strewn cellar. From what Pierana could see, it was immediately apparent to him that the child was dead, probably as a result of major traumas to the body. Officer Pierana immediately reported his grisly find and, minutes later, the building was cordoned off as other uniformed police and detectives converged on the location. After crime scene photographs were taken, Aaron's body was removed and sent to the Hamilton County Coroner's Office for an autopsy.

The next day, the coroner released his report. He said that Aaron Raines had died as a result of a blunt trauma to the head. The coroner further ruled that the death was no accident — it was definitely a homicide.

If the residents of Lower Price Hill were shocked and saddened by the death of Aaron Raines, they were also outraged. Many felt that the abandoned building itself had contributed to the tragedy because it had been left standing even after being condemned. These residents declared that the buildings were unsafe, that they attracted drug dealers, prostitutes, and vagrants. But municipal officials pointed out that there were some 550 abandoned buildings in the city, and no funds were available to tear them all down.

The day after Aaron's body was found, more than 100 residents of Lower Price Hill marched the three miles from where his body was found to Cincinnati's City Hall. There they loudly demanded action from the assembled city council. Although some preservationists argued in favor of saving the structures, the emotions tied to the death of the little boy weighed heavier on the council's civic conscience.

"This building may not have killed this child," said Vice-Mayor Peter Strauss, "but the fact is, he was found in [it]. The community and this council want something done."

And something *was* done. As the Lower Price Hill residents cheered, the city officials announced that they would spend the $30,000 needed to raze the building as soon as the police completed their investigation of the slaying.

The Cincinnati PD homicide squad had been on the job since the moment Aaron Raines' body was discovered. They had been painstakingly combing the dilapidated building for clues, but were keeping quiet about whatever they found.

The sleuths also interviewed friends and family of the victim, as well as other residents of the close-knit neighborhood. These interviews produced some interesting angles and leads in the case.

First of all, the probers discovered that even though the building was boarded up, it was still accessible to neighborhood children, who managed to get inside to explore and play. This fact notwithstanding, Aaron, due to his cautious nature, had not been one of these children. One relative told the investigators that Aaron was afraid of the vacant building and had said that he never played there. "He never played over there in that area that I know of," the relative said. But if he had, she went on, "he had to have somebody with him."

This statement summed up a feeling of the detectives who were working on the case. Aaron's body was found in a place he was known to avoid. If he had gone there willingly, then he had to have done so with someone he knew and trusted. Therefore, the victim must have gone to the building willingly, the police felt, because it was unlikely that a stranger could have coaxed or forcibly taken the child into the building without being noticed — and probably confronted — by someone in the close-knit community.

"Aaron would never have gone off with a stranger," his relative stressed. "If he had been seen with a stranger, the whole neighborhood would have known."

If the boy had gone to the place of his death with someone he knew, then that person had to be known to the rest of the neighborhood. But who was that individual?

"I've been going over it and over it in my mind, trying to figure a person who would want to hurt him," said a relative. "That's just it. Nothing adds up."

The detectives went door to door in the neighborhood and questioned everyone. If the killer was known to any of them, then someone, perhaps inadvertently, would have to know something about the crime. All of the citizens were eager to help. They wanted not only to bring the killer to justice, but to make the city government start taking their lives and needs more seriously.

"We shouldn't be dumped on the way we have for the last thirty years," one resident declared. "We're tired of being treated like we don't count. Our children count . . . Aaron counted and, by God, it's a shame!"

As the investigation into Aaron Raines' murder continued, the police looked into the activities of three brothers who were accused of strangling a young mother to death across the Ohio River in Covington, Kentucky. They finally decided that the two crimes were unrelated.

Weeks went by. The character of Lower Price Hill began to change dramatically. No longer were children permitted to play outside without supervision. Otherwise friendly neighbors became suspicious of one another, aware that the killer might well be a member of the community. They called the police with their ideas and tips. As a result of these tips, police interviewed 145 possible suspects in connection with the Raines murder.

Then, more than two months after the killing, there was a major development in the case. On Monday, July 27th, about 40 neighborhood residents watched as three police officers led a fourth individual into the abandoned building on West Eighth Street. The fourth man was handcuffed and had a trenchcoat pulled over his head to conceal his identity. After about half an hour inside the building, the quartet left. Later that day, police officials called the Raines family to tell them that an arrest had been made in the case. Because of an effective neighborhood grapevine, a group of supporters was already gathered at Aaron Raines' house when the call came in.

The suspect taken into custody was Darryl "Junior" Gumm, a 26-year-old resident of Germantown, Kentucky. Germantown is about 45 miles southeast of Cincinnati. As the investigators had surmised, the suspect was no stranger to the Lower Price Hill area. A relative of Aaron's described the suspect as "an acquaintance" of the Raines family for over 10 years.

The police did not immediately say what had steered the investigation in Darryl Gumm's direction or what the motive for the crime might have been.

Neighbors of the victim's family had mixed reactions to Gumm's arrest. "If he's guilty, I think they should hang him," one of them declared. "But I don't think the boy's guilty. He's been around . . . kids all his life and he's been around my kids, my grandbabies. He's never hurt a child in his life. I think they're using him for a scapegoat."

Others had more mixed opinions of Gumm, likening him to a Dr. Jekyll and Mr. Hyde who was kind and diligent when sober, but dangerous and unpredictable when drunk.

Gumm had worked as a tobacco cutter for two seasons at a farm in Bracken County, Kentucky. The police had arrested him at that farm. "He was a good person," said his supervisor there. "He was very polite and mannerly . . . and he was trustworthy. We would leave the house open when we went somewhere, and we never missed a thing. But when we saw him on the TV, we were shocked. It was, like—this isn't the Junior we know!"

But there were other people who knew Gumm better—they were the ones who had pointed the police in his direction. A female relative of his stated that Gumm had called her from Kentucky on Memorial Day to tell her that he had been in Cincinnati on the day Aaron Raines had disappeared. He had not contacted his relative when he had been in town.

"When I heard he was here and didn't come see me, I thought it wasn't right," the woman later said. Gumm's behavior made her suspicious enough to call the Cincinnati PD's Crime Stoppers program and name him as a suspect in Aaron's death. Word of Gumm's possible involvement had quickly filtered down to the streets of Lower Price Hill, and soon almost everyone there knew that the police were looking for him.

Gumm's criminal record in Hamilton County was limited to a few misdemeanor arrests stemming from his frequent abuse of alcohol. Now, however, he was being held on a $100,000 cash bond in the jail at the Hamilton County Justice Center on a charge of aggravated murder.

On Tuesday, July 28th, the police arrested a second man in connection with the Raines murder. This second arrest came as a result of information supplied by Darryl Gumm. The other man taken into custody was Michael Alvin Bies. The 20-year-old Bies had offered no resistance

100

when officers took him into custody outside a house in Hazard, Kentucky, about 200 miles southeast of Cincinnati. He waived extradition and was immediately transported to Hamilton County. On Thursday, July 30th, Bies was arraigned on a charge of aggravated murder and, like Darryl Gumm, he was held on a $100,000 bond.

Bies was described as a friend of Darryl Gumm's. The pair had met when they had been working together as migrant workers in the tobacco-growing regions of Kentucky.

With the arrests of the two suspects, the police now revealed more details about the murder of Aaron Raines. The new information shocked the entire community . . .

According to the sleuths, Gumm and Bies had lured Aaron into the abandoned building "with the intent to rape him," and they beat him to death when he resisted them. "We believe he was forced into the building, taken into various rooms, and then killed in the basement," said Lieutenant Greg Snider. However, Snider added, the intended rape had never been carried out.

The police said that much evidence had been retrieved from the dilapidated building where Aaron had died, including a board, a concrete block, and a metal pipe. These items, along with a pair of shoes taken from one of the arrested men, were alleged to be the murder weapons.

On Friday, August 7, 1992, Darryl "Junior" Gumm and Michael Alvin Bies appeared in separate Hamilton County Common Pleas courtrooms, where they pleaded not guilty to the charge of beating Aaron Raines to death. The aggravated murder charge against each man included death-penalty specifications, since it was alleged that the killing had occurred during a kidnapping and attempted rape. Trial dates were set for October 5th for Michael Bies and November 2nd for Darryl Gumm.

On Monday, October 5th, jury selection began in the trial of Michael Bies. By the next day, a panel had been chosen. The jury's first task was to tour the building in which the heinous crime had been committed. As they did, a crowd of neighbors observed the scene. They were still bitter about the fact that the building was still standing. "Every time we look at that house, we think about that boy," said one of the onlookers. "Everybody's hoping they tear it down."

Back in the courtroom, the prosecution began with a harrowing opening statement that left some jurors shifting nervously in their seats. Prosecutor Joe Deters vividly described the panic-filled last moments of the dead boy as he was held down and beaten to death in the dark basement. Family members of the victim wept as they heard those grim details.

The prosecutor went on to emphasize the utter depravity of the crime. "This crime is not simply about kidnapping Aaron Raines to rape him and kill him to escape detection," Deters went on. "After Aaron was lying in that basement dead, or near dead, [the defendants] were not satisfied. Michael Bies beat him with his ferocity. [And] with Aaron Raines' blood still on their hands, they then performed oral sex on each other."

As Prosecutor Deters described the crime, Michael Bies sat at the defense table and drew cartoons on a legal pad.

In their opening statement, the defense lawyers asked the jury to keep an open mind. They also said that their client would testify on his own behalf.

One of the first witnesses called by the state was the relative who was babysitting Aaron Raines on the evening he disappeared. The relative described Aaron as a cautious little boy who would never have entered the old building of his own volition. "He wouldn't go in them," the relative said about the abandoned houses. "He's scared of the dark. We used to have to sleep with the light on or the TV on because he was afraid of the dark."

Officer Terry Pierana testified that he discovered Aaron's body on May 12th. He said he entered the building, noticed a bloody palm print on the railing of the basement steps, then walked down the steps and discovered the dead boy. He described the body as lying face up in a corner of the basement. A length of twine was wrapped around the dead boy's neck. Shoe prints were visible on the body. Nearby were the blood-soaked implements which the authorities alleged were used to bludgeon the boy to death.

Another witness testified that she had given Bies and Gumm a ride from Kentucky to Cincinnati on May 11th, and that later that day, she had seen the two men sitting together on a bench in Lower Price Hill.

On Thursday, October 8th, a former deputy coroner testified about the direct cause of Aaron Raines' death. She accompanied her testimony with graphic slides that amply illustrated the ferocity of the attack. "The entire left side of his face had been flattened and the boy's skull was exposed," the former coroner explained to the jury. "There were so many tears to the scalp that they almost became one wound. His skin was broken and the bones underneath the jaw were broken, as were his ribs."

The witness went on to describe how four of Aaron's ribs had been pushed into his chest cavity, puncturing his lung. Gym-shoe prints were visible on the body. Death was caused by multiple injuries to the head, neck, chest, and abdomen.

Adding to the horror was the revelation that even with all these injuries, Aaron's death had probably been slow and agonizing.

Another member of the coroner's office said that Aaron's hair was found on the bloody concrete block and the metal pipe found lying near his body.

That same day, an inmate from the Hamilton County Jail testified that while waiting for trial, Michael Bies had spoken candidly and enthusiastically about the killing. "I asked him how he could feel good about killing a little boy," the inmate recalled. "He said it gave him a great feeling inside — a god-like power. He said, 'Because I have the power to take life and give life.' "

Bies silently shook his head as the jailhouse informant testified.

The prosecutors' next move was to play the tapes made of Bies after his arrest. One was a videotape in which the defendant took officers on a tour of the death house. On two audiotapes, Bies at first denied any knowledge of the crime before he finally offered a version of the crime that put most of the responsibility on Gumm. After the rape attempt, Bies said on the tape, "Junior picked [Aaron] up and carried him downstairs and struck him with a board. I hit him with the pipe three or four times, but Junior did, too. [After the attack], I checked to see if he was breathing, which he was — barely. I wanted to make sure he was all right."

After playing these tapes, the prosecutors rested their case.

The next day, the defense attorneys rested their case, too. In contradiction to what they had promised in their opening statement, they did not call the defendant to testify.

That weekend included the Columbus Day holiday, observed on Monday, so the closing arguments were given on Tuesday, October 13th.

In their closing argument, the prosecutors reminded the jury of the terror and pain inflicted on the young victim. Prosecutor Deters said that the little boy had been dragged around the building by the length of twine wrapped around his neck. "He was probably fighting as hard as a ten-year-old, eighty-five-pound boy can fight against two grown men," Deters said. He showed the jurors the grisly photos of the dead boy. "Think of the absolute terror this boy must have gone through to cause these injuries."

In their turn, the defense lawyers told the jury that though the evidence in the case was certainly horrific, it did not necessarily mean that their client had committed the crime. "Why don't we have more physical evidence linking Michael Bies to this case?" one of the defense attorneys demanded. "There is no doubt that the sympathy for Aaron Raines is very great. We all feel very, very sorry for his death. But you've got to put that aside."

After deliberating for seven hours over a period of two days, the jury returned with their verdict. They found Michael Bies guilty of the aggravated murder of Aaron Raines. They also found him guilty of kidnapping and attempted rape.

The convicted man was immediately escorted from the courtroom. "I have nothing to say," Bies was heard to say.

The next day, all the principals gathered for the penalty phase of Bies' trial. His defense lawyers argued for his life, claiming as a mitigating factor that the defendant was mentally handicapped and had an I.Q. of just 68. "The question is, what are you achieving if you give Michael Bies the death penalty?" one of the lawyers said. "He's a sick, three-year-old man. He's a three-year-old, and we cannot execute a child."

Prosecutor Deters disagreed, contending that Bies was "a parent's worst nightmare. He's a powder keg. This isn't just one incident. This is how he's acted his entire life."

The jury deliberated for about nine hours before agreeing with the prosecution. Many of the jurors shed tears as the death recommendation was read aloud. Michael Bies buried his face in his hands, then hung his head as he was led back to his cell.

"The jury had a very difficult decision to make," Prosecutor Deters said, "and I think they made the right one. I could see the pain in their decision. My sympathy goes to Aaron Raines and his family and not Michael Bies. Michael Bies is the reason for the death penalty in Ohio."

After the death sentence was recommended, Michael Bies was interviewed in the Hamilton County Jail. "The judgment was wrong," the convicted child-killer said. "That's all I can say about it. I didn't do nothing." He emphasized his supposed lack of intelligence. "I'm not big on I.Q. — I ain't much of a reader. I was always put in special classes."

Bies also lashed out at the justice system: "They're playing with my life. The people of Cincinnati already got what they want. They all come out for the trial, and all the reporters were there. What good does it do for me to talk? What would it benefit me to tell the public what I think? Nothing. I'm not afraid to die. The way I see it, God has a chart made up, and when your number comes up, you go. I don't want to die, but I have no reason to be afraid of it."

Regarding the Raines family's grief over Aaron's "number coming up," Bies said, "I feel sorry for them. I've got three kids of my own and I would hate to lose one of them."

Bies' jurors were visibly more shaken than he was. "People who haven't been on a jury don't realize what you go through," one of the panel members said. "If I had to do it all over again, I wouldn't even show up for the pre-trial interview."

Another juror said, "My shoulders feel as though they're up around my ears. My nerves are raw. I can't unwind. Other problems in my life have intensified."

Six of the jurors reportedly went into counseling sessions as a result of their public service.

On Friday, October 30th, Common Pleas Judge J. Howard Sunderman followed the recommendation of the jury and sentenced Michael Alvin Bies to death in Ohio's electric chair. He also meted out to Bies sentences of 10 to 25 years for attempted rape and 10 to 25 years for kidnapping.

Commenting on the sentencing, a relative of the murdered boy said, "It makes you feel better — but it's only half over."

Indeed, there were some developments in the other half of the case that same day. In a ruling in another courtroom, a judge said that the jurors in the upcoming trial of Darryl Gumm would be allowed to hear the incriminating statements given to police by the defendant after his arrest. His defense attorneys were not pleased with the ruling, commenting that Gumm had "talked himself into the electric chair."

Darryl Gumm's murder trial began as scheduled on Monday, November 2, 1992. His trial proved to be more revealing than Michael Bies', shedding more light on both the character of the accused and the methods used by the police to find and arrest him.

After two days, a jury was selected. As it had been with the jurors in the Bies trial, these jurors' first order of business was to visit the house where Aaron Raines had died.

Back in court, Assistant Chief Hamilton County Prosecutor Mark Piepmeier made the opening statement for the state. He said that the defendant told the police about having lured young Aaron Raines into the building by promising to give him $10 to help Gumm remove some copper wiring to be sold for scrap.

"To a little kid like Aaron, the opportunity to make ten dollars is like Christmas morning to him," the prosecutor pointed out. "And even though he was afraid of the building, that was enough to get him in there. The young boy trusted an older man whom he knew. It was the misplacing of his trust that led to his death."

In an echo of the Bies trial, the defense attorneys claimed that Gumm was mentally retarded and unable to perceive reality. They argued, too, that there was not enough evidence to convict him.

On Wednesday, November 4th, a prosecution witness gave the jury a glimpse into the psyche of Darryl Gumm. The witness, a former landlady of his, testified that earlier in 1992, she had evicted Gumm after he claimed to have spoken to her horse and to have had sexual relations with the animal. She added that the defendant was "a violent and brutal man when intoxicated."

A female relative of Gumm's testified that he was a frequent and hostile drunk. She had been the one to alert the police about Gumm, phoning her tip to the Crime Stoppers hotline. She explained that she had done so because she knew that Gumm had spent considerable time inside the building on West Eighth Street looking for copper wire to salvage.

The next day, the prosecutors played a videotaped statement made by Darryl Gumm after his arrest. On the tape, he admitted to being in the house when Aaron Raines was killed, but he blamed the death on his partner-in-crime, even as Michael Bies had done for him.

"I didn't touch the kid," Gumm declared. Michael Bies, he said, "had gone berserk. I couldn't stop him. He wouldn't stop. I was hollering [to Aaron], 'Are you all right?' He wouldn't talk."

But a state witness disputed Gumm's claim that he "didn't touch the kid." A former Hamilton County deputy coroner said that the dead child had no defensive wounds, indicating that he was probably held down by one person while being struck by the other.

Both the prosecution and the defense completed presenting their cases by November 9th. In their closing statements, the prosecutors maintained that Gumm had a long history of violence against both animals and children. While conceding the defendant's limited intelligence, Chief Assistant Prosecutor Thomas Longano said, "Gumm knows right from wrong." Regarding Gumm's depravity, Longano said, "Sex is a hobby, and he liked to have it every day—sex with women, sex with men . . . and sex with a little boy."

"This went beyond purposeful killing," said another of the prosecutors. "This was a mutilation of that boy's body even after he was dead." The prosecutors repeated their contention that Darryl Gumm and Michael Bies had sex with each other before leaving the scene of their ghastly crime.

In their closing, the defense attorneys argued that their client was mentally handicapped, that he had only confessed after being badgered by the police for more than eight hours. "By the time they were done with him, he would have confessed to the assassination of Abraham Lincoln," one of the lawyers asserted. "Nothing that happened in that building can be traced to my client. Somebody should pay for this [crime], but it shouldn't be him."

Despite the defense arguments, the jury decided that Darryl Gumm should pay for the crime. On Tuesday, November 10th, they voted to convict him of aggravated murder, kidnapping, and attempted rape.

Three days later, the same jury recommended that Darryl Gumm be executed for his crime. Prosecutor Longano applauded the jury's decision. "In my twenty years as a prosecutor," he said, "I've never seen a case where the aggravating circumstances were as weighty as in this case. I've never seen an adult or child beaten as badly as Aaron Raines. Every bone in his body was affected in some way. We're pleased with [the jury's decision]. This is what we asked for all along and in the Bies case."

On Wednesday, November 25, 1992, Hamilton County Common Pleas Court Judge Robert Ruehlman agreed with the jury and set May 11, 1993—the one-year anniversary of Aaron Raines' disappearance—as Gumm's execution date. (Automatic appeals will probably delay that date.)

"This defendant was involved in a cold-blooded, calculated plan to kidnap, rape, and kill a defenseless ten-year-old boy," said the judge. "This child knew you, Mr. Gumm, and you lured him to his death."

Family members of the dead boy wept as the trial wound down.

"I ain't guilty," Gumm declared.

As Darryl Gumm was led away to his cell on Ohio's

death row at Lucasville, a relative of his victim commented on the tragic irony of the timid Aaron Raines being killed by someone he knew and trusted. Gumm, said the relative, had been almost like family. "I've known him all my life—at least, I thought I did." The relative added that the death penalty was something of a hollow victory, but a victory nonetheless. "It won't bring [Aaron] back, but it's a relief. It won't be over until both of them pay with their lives."

On Monday, January 25, 1993, a wrecking crew fulfilled the promise made by Cincinnati's city council and began to demolish the building in which Aaron Raines died. A neighbor watching the demolition echoed the sentiments of many local residents when she said, "It should have been torn down a long time ago. It should have been gone before the boy got killed."

# "PEDOPHILE TROLLED FOR YOUNG BOYS . . . HE USED 3 AS EXPERIMENTS IN TORTURE!"

## by Gary C. King

He wasn't a bona fide serial killer by FBI standards, which hold in part that, for a killer to be classified a serial murderer, he must claim three or more victims in at least three separate "incidents."

But for all intents and purposes, he was a serial killer, all right. He claimed two victims in one incident, another in a second, and would have committed his fourth murder in a third if he hadn't been stopped in the process of carrying out the crime.

Although he didn't strike until late summer 1989—at least not as far as authorities in Oregon and Washington State knew—it would later become clear that he was in an extended fantasy state during this period and had been trolling for victims for at least several months prior to that time, working up his nerve to begin the atrocities he eventually committed.

Powerless in his closest relationships, he had begun searching for someone—not just anyone, but someone special—to play his ultimate power trip on. He was lurking in the shadows and waiting until just the right moment to strike.

In many ways, he was like the monsters who came before him—killers like Ted Bundy, Jerome Brudos, Dayton LeRoy Rogers, the Green River killer, and a seemingly endless slew of others. He, like they, sought out strangers as his victims. But instead of women, the victims of choice for most such murderers, this cowardly killer sought out helpless children, young boys whose trust he managed to gain with promises of friendship, money, candy, and toys. When it was all over, few could dispute that his malignant deeds, perhaps because children were involved, proved more savage and emotionally painful in the eyes of lawmen and the disbelieving public than those of his more notorious predecessors.

If it can be said that anything good came out of this case, it is only that this sexual psychopath, this monster hiding inside a human shell, was stopped before he could put his nightmarish fantasy into full play and snuff out more young lives. Before his activities were thwarted, however, he would commit murder with calculated cold-bloodedness, terrorize entire communities, and virtually turn the populace of two states inside-out.

There are few crimes that have instilled such a high degree of public fear as those committed by this killer, mainly because he struck at pure innocents and left everyone wondering who and where he would strike next. No one's children were safe as long as the murderer continued to roam the region's streets and stake out its parks and playgrounds.

The reign of terror that sickened the Pacific Northwest began on Monday, September 4, 1989, Labor Day, in Vancouver, Washington. A few minutes before 7:00 p.m.,

Dave Miller was walking along Northwest Andresen Road, a busy thoroughfare that runs north and south adjacent to the west side of David Douglas Park, when he spotted a mortally wounded child.

The boy appeared to be of Asian or Indian descent. He lay motionless in a ditch that runs along a dirt-bicycle trail in a heavily wooded area of the park. The area, accessible only by foot or bike, is not clearly visible from the park's more public areas. But Miller had been able to see the boy from the side of the road, and he rushed over to see if he could help.

Miller noticed right away that there was a lot of blood on the youngster's upper torso. Miller's first impression was that the boy had been struck by a car. The child, who appeared to be no more than 9 or 10 years old, was unconscious but still breathing, which gave Miller hope that he could be saved. Without moving the boy, Miller ran as fast as he could to a store about three blocks north of the park and called 911.

When officers from the Vancouver Police Department arrived, they could immediately tell that the child was a victim, but certainly not an accident victim. It was obvious to them that he had been stabbed repeatedly in the upper chest!

Because the boy was still alive, attending paramedics felt a glimmer of hope that he could be saved. Without wasting a precious minute, they summoned the Life Flight helicopter from Emanuel Hospital, located just across the Columbia River in Portland, Oregon. The paramedics did what they could for the child at the scene. They then transported him to Fort Vancouver High School, the nearest site where the aircraft could safely land. He was picked up at the school's large parking area a few minutes later by the helicopter.

The boy was barely breathing as a nurse and paramedic feverishly treated his wounds during the short flight to Portland. However, despite their heroic efforts, there was

113

just no way to save him. His injuries were too extensive and he had lost far too much blood. The child, who had no identification on him, was pronounced dead on arrival at the hospital at 7:37 p.m.

Duane Bigoni, a deputy Oregon state medical examiner, was assigned to the case because the child had died in Oregon, even though the attack was believed to have occurred in Washington State. Bigoni concurred with the investigators' opinion that the child had died from fatal stab wounds to the chest and abdomen, but added that a definitive autopsy would still have to be done to determine the exact cause of death and whether or not there were secondary wounds or signs of sexual attack.

"We have very little information on this one," said Bigoni, shaking his head in disbelief. "We don't have an ID on the kid. We're hoping someone will miss him and that way we can get a name."

Meanwhile, a few minutes shy of 8:00 p.m., a worried father began searching the neighborhood adjacent to David Douglas Park for his two young sons who had not yet returned home for dinner from a bicycle ride.

Earlier that day, at about 4:00 p.m., 10-year-old William Neer and his 11-year-old brother, Cole, had informed their father that they were going on one of their rides to a nearby driving range. They planned to scavenge for lost golf balls, for which they were regularly paid one cent each by the golf course's manager. The two boys usually spent their money on baseball cards, model cars and planes, and candy. They had promised their father that they would be home by 6:30 p.m., but they had not yet returned.

Around 9:00 p.m., following a frantic street-by-street search that yielded no trace of the boys or their bikes, and after being unable to find anyone who had seen them, the boys' alarmed father called the Vancouver Police Department to report his two children missing.

When word of the missing boys filtered down to the lawmen investigating the David Douglas Park homicide, about a dozen police officers, firefighters, and members of the Silver Star Search and Rescue Team remained at the scene where the boy's body had been found. They planned to spend the night there.

Fearing that curious onlookers might interfere with their search efforts, police cordoned off the area. They also closed down the northbound lanes of Andresen Road later that evening, according to Vancouver Police Lieutenant Roy Brown.

As the park search continued, the sleuths tried to determine if the victim was one of the Neer brothers. The lawmen moved carefully in their questioning of the distraught father. They didn't want to unduly alarm or distress him further by making irresponsible statements about the boy found in the park. After all, the victim might not be the man's son. Sleuths made every effort to obtain as much information about the man's sons as they could, such as physical descriptions, the clothing they were wearing when they left home, and the types of bikes they were riding.

Meanwhile, at the park, one group of searchers armed with flashlights and lanterns proceeded carefully along the trails while another group beat the bushes in search of evidence and, possibly, another victim. It was slow going under the conditions of night but, a short time later, searchers found not one, but *two* children's BMX bicycles near the trail, about 45 yards south from where the stabbing victim was found. Lieutenant Brown told reporters that investigators did not yet know for certain if one of the bikes belonged to the dead boy, but he added that both bikes fit the description given to police by the Neer boys' father. Fearing that the unnerving discovery meant there might be another victim somewhere, the lawmen decided to call in extra help and expand the search.

"We have no idea at this time who the [dead] boy is,

who the bicycles belong to, or if there are any other victims," said Lieutenant Brown, not wanting to jump to any premature conclusions. He added that he hoped a positive identification would be made soon. "We are going under the assumption that there may be more victims," he said, his statement obviously based on the report filed by the worried father.

Some seven hours later, at about 2:00 a.m., a volunteer from the Silver Star Search and Rescue Team found what all those concerned hoped they wouldn't — another victim. Like the first, it was a little boy. This one was dead at the scene. Appearing to be no more than 10 or 11 years old, his body was lying in heavy brush about 25 yards east of where the bicycles were found earlier in the evening.

Like the first body, the second victim had been stabbed numerous times in the chest and abdomen. Both boys had defensive wounds on their hands and legs, indications that they had attempted to fight off their attacker before succumbing to his violence.

A short time later, there was no longer any doubt who the boys were. Both were identified as William and Cole Neer. William had been found first, police said, and both boys had likely been attacked about the same time, between 6:15 and 6:45 p.m. There was no apparent motive for the murders, which had occurred less than a mile from their home.

"What kind of motive does someone have for killing a ten- and eleven-year-old boy?" asked Vancouver Police Captain Ray Anderson. "There are only so many possible motives in something like this. With adults, there's always the anger motive. People get mad at each other and fight. But when it's a couple of young boys cut up for no apparent reason . . . you just don't know.

"This kind of thing just never happens in Vancouver," continued Captain Anderson. "We can go a whole year without a homicide. These are just two brothers — spitting images of each other — out riding their BMX bikes, and they come across an assailant. We're talking about the kinds of things that happen to other people in other places, but hopefully not to you."

Captain Anderson said both boys were fully clothed when found but cautioned that that did not necessarily mean they had not been sexually assaulted. He said detectives were awaiting tests to determine whether or not the victims, in fact, had been.

"If we find out they were [sexually assaulted], it's something else again," he added.

Investigators sent the victims' clothes and other evidence from the crime scene to the Washington State Crime Laboratory in Kelso, Washington, for analysis, hoping for any kind of break that would lead them at least one step closer to the killer. However, little of significance was learned, dashing sleuths' hopes that the case could be quickly solved.

The case took on a marked intensity like none that Vancouver had seen before. "Homicide cases involving children are always more intense," said Captain Bob Kanekoa of the Vancouver PD. "It strikes you harder than anything when juveniles are involved," he said.

The intensity was evident throughout the next day as the sleuths combed the park with metal detectors in their search for evidence. At one point a knife was found, but it was not considered to be the murder weapon. It was covered with mud and rust, apparently from having been at the location for a considerable time prior to the murders.

Police officials warned area residents to take extra precautions in the David Douglas Park neighborhood, and advised people, especially children, not to go to the park alone. They urged residents to report any suspicious characters or activities in any of the Vancouver neighborhoods, especially those near parks.

Uneasiness and anxiety were virtually pandemic among area residents. Mothers and fathers were seen in areas near David Douglas Park after school the day after the murders. Sentry-like, they positioned themselves about 50 yards apart, lining the paths that schoolchildren normally took to their homes.

"I'm a little jumpy, a little worried," said one area resident after learning about the grim murders. The mother of a third-grader who lived only a few blocks from the park said she began driving her child to school instead of allowing him to ride his bike. "I know the park has had its problems . . . [but] I didn't think anything bad would happen."

Police confirmed that the park had previously been a trouble spot for the department, with late-night teenage drinking parties and occasional fights. But nothing ever came close to matching the senseless violence that claimed the Neer brothers' lives.

Parents weren't the only ones who were jumpy in the aftermath of the Neer murders. The Vancouver School District took the precaution of increasing adult supervision on playgrounds and at student crossing zones. The school also sent letters home, cautioning students not to wander into secluded or wooded areas and to walk or bicycle in groups.

In their efforts to better understand every aspect of the tragedy, detectives began looking at the Neer family's background. Investigators learned that the family had moved to the Vancouver area in 1986 from North Dakota, settling in the suburb of Hazel Dell. Because of employment difficulties, however, the family was forced to move in July 1989 into public housing in the McLoughlin Heights area of Vancouver.

Neighbors told detectives that the Neer family was quiet. They kept to themselves, but were generally well liked. It was common for neighbors to see William and Cole tearing down the streets of the usually quiet neighborhood on their BMX bikes.

"Those boys were always so good," recalled one friend

118

and neighbor. "And they were always together, every time they went out bike riding."

"They were just babies," said a tearful relative of the victims. "I can't imagine anyone doing this to them."

In the meantime, while making arrangements to take the victims' bodies back to their native North Dakota for burial, the boys' father told the Associated Press that he was also making plans to take his only surviving child to Hillsboro, Oregon, where they would live with a relative.

"As soon as I step outside that door," said the father, "I'm gone. I'm not going to lose my last son to this crap." He said he didn't plan to ever set foot in Vancouver, Washington, again, not even to drive through it.

"Vancouver—I used to like it," he said. "The boys seemed to like it really well. Now, I don't want anything to do with any of it."

The grieving father told reporters that the public needed to know what had happened to his family. Children, he said, "need to know that they should listen to their parents. Something's going to happen if they don't. Don't let them wander off too far. Losing one is bad. Losing two . . . all I've got is my baby left."

In the days following the double murder, detectives concentrated on interviewing family members in an effort to reconstruct William's and Cole's activities the day they were killed. They also went door to door through the neighborhood looking for potential witnesses.

In the meantime, detectives located a young boy who had been in the park late on the afternoon of the murders. He was interviewed and, according to Acting Vancouver Police Chief Bob King, Portland police artist Jean Boylan was brought in to draw a composite sketch of a suspicious man seen in the park the day the Neer boys were killed.

"The sketch has been circulated among our police officers, and they have instructions that if this person is seen, we want to talk to him," said King, who stopped short of calling the man a suspect. "We're considering him a person of interest, someone we want to talk to about the case." King added that if his officers had no luck in finding the man, the sketch would be released to the news media.

"This is one of those cases that is so senseless," he said. "We're going to need a lot of help in solving this one. Hopefully, other people will come forward with information about others who may have been in the park at the same time. That's how these cases are made."

A short time later, police officials announced that a second person, believed to have been in the park at the time of the killings, was being studied. A witness provided detectives with a description from which a second composite sketch was prepared.

"We have reason to believe that this fellow is someone who hangs around the park quite a bit," said Captain Anderson. "Our officers are showing the sketch to people who may have been in the park Monday to see if they can help us find the man. He is only someone we want to talk to and we don't want to raise any terror in anyone."

Captain Anderson added that detectives weren't sure whether more than one killer was involved, or whether the killer was a man or a woman. He said searchers would continue until investigators were "satisfied that nothing slipped past" them.

As one day followed another, despite two police sergeants each leading a team of three detectives in their search for clues, only a few leads of any significance trickled in to the Vancouver Police Department. With little else they could do unless something substantial turned up, detectives, aided by numerous volunteers, returned to David Douglas Park and the site of the Neer murders.

"We went to backtrack where we've searched already because we may pick up on some things that may have been missed earlier," said Captain Anderson. "We especially want to look at some areas where people were seen running through the park at about the time of the crime. . . . [It's] an area that's heavily wooded and has a lot of nooks and crannies. There are a lot of leads that we have to follow up on that are routine."

One of those leads was supplied by a woman who saw a man running from David Douglas Park at the approximate time the killings were believed to have occurred. Police now had at least two persons of interest to be on the lookout for; both were men.

Investigators followed up on leads obtained from interviews with neighbors and from more than 100 telephone calls generated by the release of the composite drawings. Callers told police they had seen men resembling one or the other of the sketches driving near the park around the time of the murders and described the vehicles the men were driving. Some callers suggested neighborhoods where the men might reside. Others provided detectives with the names of companies where the men might work.

However, the investigators ran up against a brick wall at nearly every turn. The leads didn't pan out. The persons of interest had airtight alibis and witnesses who could vouch for their activities at the time of the murders. Unfortunately, by mid-September, the homicide probers were still at square one.

Investigators were relentless, however, in their perseverance in the case. They backtracked again and again. They found a reliable witness who told them he had seen the Neer boys riding their bicycles north on Andresen Road near the park at approximately 6:10 p.m. They found another witness who said he had seen the boys heading south, walking their bikes uphill along Andresen Road in the same time frame.

Despite their dogged efforts, all the investigators had been able to do was retrace the victims' activities up to about 6:10 p.m. on the day they were murdered. They were without clues as to the boys' movements from that time until the time William's body was discovered by the passerby.

At the request of the Vancouver Police Department, the FBI in Washington, D.C., worked up a psychological profile of the possible killer. The profile suggested that the killer most likely lived in the community and probably was very familiar with David Douglas Park and the surrounding area. The profile also suggested that the killer could have known the two boys and most likely was physically large enough to easily overpower them. The nature of the deaths indicated that the killer was comfortable with knives and may have used a knife in a previous assault or killing.

The senselessness of the crime, the profile said, suggested the killer could have been "acting out in response to a significant traumatic experience that happened to him in a close time frame" with the murders.

Vancouver investigators appreciated the FBI's psychological profile, but many expressed frustration that it really didn't bring them any closer to collaring a suspect. All it did was give them an insight into the mind of the type of killer they were dealing with.

Toward the end of September, when the case seemed destined for failure, investigators ferreted out yet another witness who provided them with a new lead. A passing motorist informed detectives that he saw two young boys whom he believed to be the Neer brothers in the vicinity of the park at about 6:30 p.m. on Labor Day. He recalled the boys were near a park trailhead and were talking to a man.

"Both of them had their bikes, and they were standing in the middle of the road, on the median strip, talking to this individual," Captain Anderson told the press. The witness told investigators that the man in question was in his late teens to early 20s and had dark hair. He was on foot. Unfortunately, the witness could not provide other details, such as a description of the clothing the man was wearing.

"It leads us to the possibility that, whoever this person was, he could well be the assailant," said Captain Anderson.

To everyone's dismay, citizens and police alike, no new leads surfaced, and the unknown man seen talking to the boys remained a mystery, at least for the time being.

In late October, tragedy struck again. Across the river from Vancouver in Portland, Oregon, 4-year-old Lee Joseph Iseli was reported missing by a relative.

According to the report taken by the Portland Police Bureau, Lee had gone with a 9-year-old relative to a playground at Richmond School on Sunday afternoon, October 29th. The playground, at Southeast 41st Street and Grant Avenue, was near the boy's home, located in the 3200 block of Southeast Clinton Street. According to family members, the boys played there regularly.

The older boy told detectives that at about 1:00 p.m. that afternoon, Lee was playing on a concrete-and-rock climbing knoll known as "the volcano" when he disappeared. The older boy, who was playing on other playground equipment, looked up and saw Lee talking to a man. He ran over and told Lee not to talk to strangers, and advised him to call out for him if the man did anything unusual. When he looked toward "the volcano" a few minutes later, Lee was gone. Unable to find Lee, the boy rushed home and told a family member about the disappearance.

A family member told police, "[Lee's] the kind of kid who doesn't take off, but he can get sidetracked easily."

Lee's older relative told police that the man he saw talking to Lee was in his early 30s, 5 feet, 10 inches to 6 feet tall, and thin in build. He was wearing a T-shirt and blue jeans.

Because of Lee's age, police promptly began searching throughout the boy's Southeast Portland neighborhood. Dog handlers brought in bloodhounds in the hope they could pick up the boy's scent.

There was no question that the dogs picked up Lee's scent on the school playground, but they lost it at the curb. According to the dog handlers, this strongly suggested that the boy may have been picked up by someone in a car.

Police and volunteers fanned out in the neighborhood, knocking on doors and visiting the local businesses. At one point, clerks at a nearby grocery store on Southeast 39th Avenue told police that Lee Iseli had been seen inside the store after 1:00 p.m., wandering the aisles alone. That he was seen alone in the store prompted police to consider that Lee had wandered away from the school playground after he was seen talking to the stranger. Store employees insisted they were certain of the time they saw the boy because it had been right after the beginning of the 1:00 p.m. lunch break.

"I figure if he would have left with that guy [at the school]," said a relative, "why would they go to the store? Lee wasn't seen with anybody at the store. If the guy stayed outside and gave him some money to go in and buy something, Lee wasn't the kind of kid who would have just wandered around. He would have spent it. He's never wandered off before. It's really hard to say what happened, whether he's just wandering around someplace or what.

"It might be that he saw some kids and went off and played with them. He could have wandered into somebody's garage or basement," added the relative, a hopeful tone in his voice. "It may be that he's just around, that he thinks he's in trouble and is afraid to come out."

As the day wore on and no further trace of Lee Iseli was found, relatives and police began to fear the worst.

"Four-year-olds don't run away," commented Detective David W. Simpson, a spokesman for the Portland Police Bureau. "We're getting very concerned, especially as time goes on."

As darkness approached, a bureau-wide alert was dispatched describing Lee Iseli as 4 years old, 3 feet 8 inches tall, and weighing 30 to 35 pounds. The alert also described the boy's hair as blond, with bangs down to his brown eyes. He was wearing a gray warm-up jacket with red stripes on his sleeves, a white T-shirt with writing on the front, and medium-blue pants. He may also have been carrying a sweater with him.

Unfortunately, as frantic relatives waited day and night by the telephone for any information about the youngster's whereabouts, no trace of Lee Iseli was found Sunday night. Because temperatures were only a few degrees above freezing, there was added concern about the possibility of the boy having to spend the night outdoors and suffering from exposure.

The next day, police brought in additional dogs, this time Mountain Wilderness Search Dogs, to go through the neighborhoods in another attempt to pick up the boy's scent. The searchers took the dogs through rugged areas in the parks, as well as into garages and abandoned buildings—anywhere they thought the boy could hide. By day's end, though, no traces of the boy or his scent had been found.

As fears of a kidnapping grew, police asked residents to search their garages, basements, parked boats, trailers, and cars, anywhere a small child might hide, in a last-ditch effort to find the boy. Despite everyone's noble attempts, however, there still was no sign of Lee Iseli.

As police reluctantly began to scale back their search, they began to publicly express their fears that Lee may have been abducted.

"There doesn't seem to be any other explanation," said Sergeant Terry Gray. "You can rack your brain, but you can't think of what a four-year-old boy would be doing all this time. I can't think of any other possible excuse. If he was staying overnight with a friend somewhere, I'm sure the parents would have called by now. They must know he's missing."

It was Halloween, and even though it's usually a happy holiday for children, there was little joy in Lee Iseli's neighborhood. The spirit of the night was markedly dampened as more parents than usual accompanied their children from house to house, obviously a result of their fears for their own children's safety.

Lee's Ghostbuster costume went unused, and his friends were very much aware of his absence. Many children said they missed him. Some cried openly because of the uncertainty of what had become of the boy.

One of Lee's relatives theorized that perhaps a lonely adult had abducted Lee and was taking care of him. The relative made a public plea to anyone holding the boy to release him.

"There are a lot of people out there who are lonely," said the relative. "Maybe [it's] someone who never had a child or who never got to dress up on Halloween or never got presents at Christmas. If it's someone like that, he could just drop [Lee] off at a store or street corner." Sadly, the family member's plea went unheeded.

Early the next morning in Vancouver, Washington, a pheasant hunter parked his car near the boat ramp to Vancouver Lake's south shore and unloaded his gun and small backpack. It was a few minutes shy of 8:00 a.m. when the hunter began beating the brush for his quarry in the Washington State Game Department area just off La Frambois Road. The area, open 24 hours a day, is heavily used by hunters and fishermen and is covered by wild grass, brush, and a few trees. It is an area isolated from the city and residential areas.

The Washington State Department of Wildlife stocks the area twice weekly with pheasant during hunting season, and hunting is allowed to begin after 8:00 a.m. Half an hour later, however, the hunter decided to return to his car. He had walked only a few yards on the return trip when he noticed the lily-white object in the brush just ahead of him. Curious, he walked toward it only to stop dead in his tracks after a few feet. To his horror and surprise, the hunter could see that the object was a naked little boy who was obviously dead.

The hunter ran back to his car and drove quickly to the nearest telephone. Although nearly incoherent from distress, the man managed to report his grim discovery to a dispatcher at the Clark County Sheriff's Department.

Minutes later, Clark County Sheriff Frank Kanekoa and Undersheriff Robert Songer arrived at the remote site, located at the end of a two-mile-long dead-end road, where they met the hunter.

"When I got there, there were probably twenty-five people waiting to hunt," the hunter told the lawmen. "At eight a.m., we all started walking through the fields." He explained that he and his partners split up at one point, and when he was through hunting he began walking back toward his car.

"I was coming back to the parking lot," he continued. "And there it was. I was shocked . . . that someone would . . . put a little dead boy out there. It's the worst thing I've seen in my life."

The distraught hunter led Sheriffs Kanekoa and Songer to the boy's body, which lay face up in the brush about 50 yards from the boat ramp and 50 feet from the edge of a gravel parking lot. It was obvious to the seasoned lawmen that no attempt had been made to conceal the body. There was no clothing on or near the cold corpse.

The probers noted the telltale signs of strangulation, but they found nothing at the scene that could have been used to strangle the boy. Aware of Lee Iseli's disappearance, Sheriffs Kanekoa and Songer strongly suspected that the child had now been found. The young victim matched the physical description of the Iseli boy. They called in forensic experts and notified the Portland Police Bureau of the discovery. As a result, all available Portland and Clark county homicide detectives were put on the case.

Clark County sheriff's deputies cordoned off the area. Officials declined to discuss the case with the news media until they knew more about what they were dealing with.

"We're playing this one very close to the vest," said Sheriff Kanekoa. "Obviously, you don't find a four- or five-year-old male child out in the brush every day. We're treating this case as a homicide."

Before noon, the search for Lee Iseli was officially over. Through his fingerprints, forensic experts positively identified the body of the nude boy found at Vancouver Lake as that of the missing Portland boy. Lee Iseli had been fingerprinted a few months earlier at a children's fair in Portland, and a set of those prints were used to make the identification. A Portland police chaplain was subsequently sent to the Iseli home to break the bad news and to be with the boy's family in their time of need.

An autopsy conducted later that day confirmed that Lee had died as a result of strangulation, but did not conclusively determine how long he had been dead. Authorities declined to say whether or not the boy had been sexually assaulted.

As a panicked community began to talk and rumors began to circulate, authorities initially attempted to play down any possible connection between Lee Iseli's murder and the stabbing deaths of the Neer brothers two months earlier. Detectives said the killer's method of operation was different in the Iseli case, particularly in that Lee had been strangled and the Neer brothers had been stabbed repeatedly. Arch Hamilton, the Clark County coroner, bolstered that opinion by stating that there were "absolutely no similarities at this point" in the two cases.

Detective David Simpson of the Portland Police Bureau, however, took a more cautious approach. He said this was the first case of this type in the area that he could recall. "I'd like to say it's an isolated incident, but I don't say it reassuringly," said Simpson. "We don't know enough yet about what happened. But I think we as a community need to be extremely cautious until we get more answers."

Meanwhile, Clark County investigators conducted an inch-by-inch search of the area where Lee Iseli's body was found. Anything that wasn't a part of the natural setting, items such as trash, cigarette butts, clothing, and rope, was marked on grid maps and collected as evidence. Although they remained tightlipped about what evidence, if any, was recovered, lawmen did admit that they had no suspects.

"We're up to our elbows in alligators trying to get this case to make some sense," said Undersheriff Songer. "Just that a four-year-old child was murdered doesn't make sense to begin with. What could a four-year-old do to make someone kill them?"

Meanwhile, a psychologist who specialized in sexual abuse and homicide cases provided police investigators with a profile of Lee Iseli's killer. The psychologist, Don Adamski of Portland, told probers that the killer was probably a middle-class or blue-collar working man who often fantasized about killing a child. Adamski said the killer was probably living a normal lifestyle but harboring a tremendous amount of hostility.

"The killer has been having thoughts like this for a long period of time," said Adamski. "I would assume that he has fantasized about this type of behavior.

"The other possibility," continued Adamski, "is that this could be a drug-crazed individual, but I think that that would be pretty unusual. The person probably leads a passive life and finally had to act this out."

"It's hard to say or even look at someone and say, 'This is a child killer,' " said Clark County Sheriff Frank Kanekoa. "I have a hard time handling a case where a child of any age is murdered in this fashion. I can't fathom the thinking of someone who would hurt a child who can't do anyone any harm. It's too early in the case to say. We need to gather more evidence before we come out with a profile."

Kanekoa stressed that the primary piece of evidence being sought was Lee Iseli's clothing. He said the clothes were not found at the crime scene.

In the meantime, Portland detectives questioned the subject of a composite drawing, the man who was seen talking to Lee Iseli at the Richmond School playground. The location of the man gave sleuths the first thread of hope that they were on the right track. However, the subject had been accompanied by another person who stated that they hadn't left with Lee Iseli. After additional questioning, investigators were convinced that the man was not a suspect in Lee's disappearance and murder.

Despite a telephone hotline and a $10,000 reward fund, a child killer continued to walk the community's streets while frustrated detectives quickly ran out of leads.

Barely two weeks later, on Monday, November 15th, a 6-year-old boy went with his family and friends to see *Honey, I Shrunk the Kids!* at the New Liberty Theater in downtown Camas, Washington, about 15 miles east of Vancouver. At 7:45 p.m. the boy, Tommy Staly, told his mother that he had to go to the bathroom. After sliding through a row of crowded seats, Tommy walked briskly up the aisle, passed through the double doors that led to the lobby, and entered the restroom. He passed a young, harmless-looking, dark-haired man in the foyer that separates the restroom from the lobby.

Tommy had finished his business and was alone in the restroom, preparing to wash his hands, when the dark-haired man approached him in a friendly manner. To Tommy's horror and surprise, however, the man punched him hard in the stomach. When Tommy doubled over in pain, the man hoisted him up and over his left shoulder. Thinking he'd knocked the air out of the boy, the man carried Tommy out of the bathroom and through the lobby. As he approached the front doors leading outside,

Tommy began kicking wildly and screaming as loud as he could.

"Help me!" yelled the boy. "Somebody, please help me! I don't know him!"

"Calm down, son, calm down," said the man, as he walked in a normal manner through the doors to the outside. But Tommy continued to scream.

Theater employees didn't like what they were seeing. Although the man appeared unruffled, the altercation smelled of an abduction. As a result, one of the employees quietly dialed 911 as two other employees followed the man and boy into the street.

Across the street from the theater, Les Wilson was opening the door to his pickup truck when he spotted the man carrying the boy out of the building. The man carried the still-screaming boy around the corner and approached an older, yellow Pinto station wagon. As he reached into his pocket for keys, the abductor put the boy down.

Sensing his chance to make a break for it, Tommy Staley bolted and began running back toward the theater. Crying, he met the theater employees and, recognizing safety, he embraced one of them.

By this time, Pete Mann, a friend of Tommy's family, had heard some of the commotion and began to wonder what was keeping the child so long in the bathroom. After conferring with Tommy's relative, Pete went to look for the boy. When he reached the lobby, he noticed all the turmoil and saw the theater employees walking back inside with Tommy. After telling him what had happened, Pete Mann ran outside in pursuit of Tommy's abductor.

He looked up and down the street, but the only person he saw was Les Wilson, who had witnessed the kidnapper drive away in the yellow Pinto. After giving Mann a description of the suspect and his car, Wilson told Mann that the suspect had gone north on Birch Street and had vanished. Pete Mann jumped into his own older-model car and went after him.

Mann soon found the Pinto. By some great twist of fate, the car was stalled at Northwest Sixth Avenue and Adams Street, not far from the entrance to Highway 14 that leads back to Vancouver. The car's driver was cranking it over, trying to get it started again. Mann parked his car in the parking lot of a nearby paper mill, then walked over to the yellow Pinto. He approached it cautiously and asked the driver if he needed some help.

"Looks like you're having car troubles here," said Mann, speaking to the unsuspecting abductor through the side window. "Doesn't look so good." Mann explained that he could probably fix the car, but suggested that they first get the vehicle into the paper mill's parking lot. Along the way, as they were pushing the car, Mann continued to ask "innocent" questions until he was satisfied that the Pinto's driver was the one who had abducted the boy inside the theater.

After moving the car, the driver opened the hood and stood looked at the engine with his back to Mann. That's when Mann, a burly construction worker, made his move. He wrapped his right arm around the abductor's neck in a tight choke hold and seized the suspect's left wrist with his left hand.

"This is it, you sonofabitch!" said Mann. "You've been restrained. We're going to get the cops." Mann then marched the suspect several blocks back to the theater where he pinned him against a wall while waiting for the police to arrive.

When officers from the Camas Police Department arrived, they took a statement from each of those people who were concerned about what had occurred. The only person not talking was the suspect, who sat quietly on the floor in the theater lobby. After getting enough preliminary information, the officers took the man into custody.

During questioning at the police station, officers identified the suspect as Westley Allan Dodd, 28, of Vancouver.

At first, Dodd didn't provide much information: just his name, address, and the fact that he was at the theater to watch the movie. However, responding to further questions, Dodd told the officers that he worked at a paper factory on Fruit Valley Road in Vancouver. They noted that the work address Dodd gave them was near La Frambois Road, not far from the site where little Lee Iseli's nude body was found. Moreover, his home address was less than a mile from David Douglas Park!

It was at that point that Westley Dodd became a suspect in the murders of the Neer brothers and Lee Iseli. Although he was advised of his rights, Dodd continued to talk. To everyone's astonishment, Dodd confessed to all three murders and provided information to the officers that had been withheld deliberately from the public. Dodd was promptly turned over to the Clark County Sheriff's Department.

Despite a list of 50 possible suspects — all of whom were known sex offenders — developed with the cooperation of all police agencies involved, investigators admitted that they were fast running out of clues. The Camas arrest had been a lucky break indeed, a "fluke" according to one police official, particularly since Dodd's name was not on their list of possible suspects.

After being transferred to the Clark County Jail, Dodd was interviewed by Detective David L. Trimble, a homicide investigator for the sheriff's department. In a bombshell statement, Westley Dodd explained how he had killed William and Cole Neer on Labor Day. He also told, in graphic detail, how he'd abducted, killed, and had postmortem sex with 4-year-old Lee Iseli.

Dodd explained that he'd moved to Vancouver from Seattle during the summer and had lived with relatives until he had saved enough money to rent his own place. Two days after moving into a duplex apartment near David Douglas Park, Dodd said he began trolling for victims.

"I was getting bored — I didn't have a television," said

Dodd during taped interviews with Detective Trimble and several Portland police detectives. He said he drove to David Douglas Park because he thought "it might be a place where I could find a boy and get it going."

He described how he discovered the Neer brothers along the dirt bike paths on the western edge of the park. He said he ordered the boys to go with him, but William asked why they should. Dodd told the detectives that he responded, "Because I told you to."

Dodd said that he tied the boys' hands with shoelaces, after which he ordered Cole Neer to pull down his pants. When Cole complied, Dodd said he performed oral sex on the boy in the presence of Cole's brother. When he was finished, he ordered William to do the same thing, but the boy began crying so hard that he was unable to comply. Dodd said he attempted to perform fellatio on William anyway, but was unable to do so.

When he was finished, Dodd told the children, "Okay, there's one more thing." He then raised his pant leg up and revealed a six-inch fish fillet knife. Dodd said that the boys, sensing they were in imminent danger, cried even harder and begged him, "Please don't kill us, mister!"

"I pulled the knife out from under my pant leg," Dodd told the detectives. "Billy was off to my right, about a foot off of me diagonally. Cole was off on my left. And I reached over and stabbed Billy with the knife. Then I turned to Cole and stabbed him two or three times, and while I was stabbing Cole, Billy got up and started to run down the hill back to the trail. Just—just started running up the trail towards Andresen and I ran after him. I didn't wait to see if Cole was dead or anything . . . I wanted to get Billy before he got to the road. I caught him and grabbed him by his—his right arm, stopped, spun him around. Then Billy said, 'I'm sorry.' " Dodd said he stabbed Billy again.

At that point, Billy began running again, but Dodd did not chase after him. Dodd explained that he was more concerned with returning to Cole's body to make certain that he hadn't left behind any incriminating evidence. As Dodd reached his car to head back to his apartment, he said he could hear sirens and presumed that Billy Neer had already been found.

A short time after murdering the Neer brothers, Dodd said he began thinking and planning his next attack. He said he used a map of Portland and marked off several parks where he thought he could find children playing alone. The day before he abducted Lee Iseli, Dodd said he went to several of the parks where he contemplated abducting and killing 15 to 20 children. His plans had been unsuccessful, however, and he began driving back toward his home.

He became lost along the way and happened to drive by Richmond School. Although there were children there, none were playing alone, so he left in an agitated state, frustrated and disappointed. But he returned the following day, Dodd said, and found Lee Iseli playing by himself near the volcano.

"I went up to the little boy and said, 'Hi! How you doing?' " Dodd told the detectives. "I asked him if he wanted to make some money and play some games. He was a little hesitant, but I reached out my hand and he took it." Dodd said he told Lee that his dad had sent him to pick him up, and they drove off together in Dodd's Pinto.

After driving a few blocks, Dodd said Lee began protesting that he didn't live in the direction they were heading.

"I said, 'Well, we're going to my house.' " Dodd said the child began crying a few times on the way to Vancouver, but he was able to calm him down.

"When we got there [to Dodd's apartment], I told him he had to be real quiet because my neighbor lady didn't like kids," Dodd continued. Once inside, Dodd ordered the boy to remove all his clothing. Dodd said he spent the

135

next several hours molesting Lee and taking Polaroid pictures of him.

"I asked him if he'd like to stay the night and he said no, that his brother would probably miss him. And I said, 'Nah. Your brother is probably having fun, too.' "

Dodd said he told Lee that he was sorry he didn't have any toys for him to play with. He then promised to take Lee to a nearby K-Mart store and buy him a He-Man toy and to McDonald's for dinner if he'd agree to stay. Dodd said the child eventually agreed.

Dodd said he molested the little boy throughout the night and at one point told the child he was going to kill him the next morning. When the boy became frightened and began to cry, Dodd said he tried to reassure Lee by telling him that he wouldn't kill him. Dodd then graphically described how he killed Lee Iseli at 5:30 on the morning of October 30th, before he left for work.

"So I took a piece of rope and wrapped it around his neck and I pulled it tight," said Dodd, in a chilling, frighteningly matter-of-fact tone. "I figured I'd probably been trying to choke him for two minutes or so already, and I didn't know how much longer it was going to take, so using the rope, I carried him over to the closet and tied the end of the rope up around the clothes rack in the closet and left him hanging there. Then I took a picture of it."

Because he didn't want to "hurt the boy . . . cause him any pain," Dodd said he waited until the child was dead before engaging in anal intercourse.

What did he do with the corpse when he went to work? Did he dump it at the La Frambois Road location where it was found? The detectives didn't have to press Dodd very hard for answers.

Dodd calmly explained that he placed the boy's corpse on a shelf in the closet and concealed it by placing pillows and other items in front of it "just in case the landlady decided to come in and have a look around."

When he returned home that evening, Dodd wrapped the boy's body in a plastic garbage bag and took it to the location where it was found, near Vancouver Lake. He said he then burned the child's clothing in a barrel outside his apartment, but retained the boy's underpants. Police knew that the underpants served as a "trophy" of his kill.

Armed with search warrants, homicide probers converged on Westley Dodd's duplex apartment in the 9800 block of Northeast Third Street in Vancouver. During the lengthy search, investigators found a briefcase that contained photographs in a pink 4-by-6-inch album. Many of the photos showed Dodd engaging in deviant sexual acts with Lee Iseli before and after the boy's death. One of the pictures depicted the boy hanging from a rope inside the closet.

Sleuths also seized a pair of boy's underpants, a diary, plastic garbage bags, a Polaroid camera, a roll of undeveloped but exposed 35mm film, several volumes of "Parent-Child" books, sections of Dodd's bed frame with pieces of rope attached, and numerous newspaper clippings about the murders of the Neer brothers and Lee Iseli. They also took a copy of the New Testament, still in its original box.

As a matter of routine, investigators took a number of vacuum sweepings from Dodd's apartment in their search for hair and fiber evidence. They also seized bedding, as well as the ashes from the burn barrel outside his apartment.

A short time later, Westley Dodd was charged with three counts of aggravated first-degree murder in connection with the deaths of the three boys. Prosecutor Art Curtis said he would seek the death penalty and would try the case in two separate trials. One trial would be for the death of Lee Iseli, the other for the deaths of William and Cole Neer. That way, explained Curtis, he would have two shots at getting the death penalty for Dodd.

Dodd was also charged with one count each of first-degree attempted kidnapping and first-degree attempted murder in the Camas theater case involving Tommy Staley. Despite his confession to police, Dodd pleaded "not guilty" to all of the charges. Vancouver attorney Lee Dane was appointed to represent him.

When the detectives fanned out in Dodd's neighborhood in their attempt to build a stronger, more solid case against their suspect, they found a neighbor who told them she recalled observing Dodd arrive home with a small blond boy about the time Lee Iseli disappeared.

"I thought nothing of it at the time," said the neighbor. She said the boy was no more than five or six years old and was wearing a lightweight jacket. "My feelings are asking me now if this was the little Iseli child . . . I don't even want to think about it," she said.

Dodd's landlord told detectives that Dodd was "real nice, real helpful" to her. She said she didn't know much about him and did not notice anything suspicious about his activities. "He paid his rent on time," she said. She also told the investigators that she discussed the Neer murders with Dodd right after the two brothers were killed. "He told me he hoped they caught the man who did it. He seemed concerned about it."

When the detectives began checking out Westley Dodd's background, they were told by the owner of the paper company where Dodd worked as a shipping clerk that the murder suspect was a model employee. He was very conscientious about his work and never missed a day since he started there.

"He was the last person you'd suspect," said one company official. "There was total shock" at the plant when employees were told of Dodd's arrest. "It was absolutely devastating. If you had a man who didn't miss a day of work, was willing to work weekends, was very sharp, articulate, and diligent, what would you think? The supervisors here were looking for ways to promote him."

Westley Dodd had an ominous past, detectives soon

learned, and had somehow managed to slip between the cracks in the system that was supposed to protect decent citizens from such predatory animals. Dodd, it seemed, had left a long trail of sex offenses, all involving children, and was no stranger to law enforcement in the state of Washington.

Born in Toppenish, Washington, on July 3, 1961, Dodd's family had moved to Kennewick when he was 3 years old. The rest of his life was marked by frequent family moves and the eventual divorce of his parents. Although Dodd was bright and had an avid interest in music, he held mostly low-paying jobs throughout his life.

By the time Dodd reached age 12, he began to develop a sexual attraction toward young boys. By age 16, he began seeking frequent sexual contact with children, mostly boys. Police talked to him on a few occasions, but there was never enough evidence to bring forth formal charges. At law enforcement's prodding, Dodd began voluntary counseling but quickly dropped out of a program for young sex offenders.

Dodd graduated from Columbia High School in Richland, Washington, in 1979 with a 3.0 grade point average, after which he worked as a stock boy for a local grocery store. The following year he was arrested for soliciting sex from a minor, but the case was dismissed.

Looking for a change, Dodd enlisted in the U.S. Navy during the summer of 1981. He was sent to Groton, Connecticut, where he was trained for submarine duty. After training, he was stationed at the Bangor Naval Station in Bangor, Washington, where he began spending a lot of his free time at local arcades propositioning 7- to 10-year-old boys.

In June 1982, Dodd went AWOL and attempted to solicit a sexual act from a 9-year-old boy at a Richland playground. In August of that same year, the Navy found and arrested Dodd at Camp Burton, a music camp in King County near Seattle, on charges of child molestation stemming from the June incident. He received a less than honorable discharge from the Navy.

A few months later, in December, Dodd lured a young Benton City, Washington, boy from a playground and convinced the child to undress. He was arrested and pleaded guilty the following month. He was ordered to participate in a counseling program.

Failing to meet the conditions of his court-ordered counseling, Dodd served 23 days in jail. After his release, he moved to Lewiston, Idaho, where he engaged in sexual acts with a 9-year-old boy on at least two occasions. Nearly a year later, the boy's parents reported the incidents to police and Dodd was convicted of lewd conduct with a minor. He was sentenced to 10 years in jail. Although he served time in the Nez Perce County Jail, Dodd's sentence was reduced to time served. He was released after he agreed to attend an outpatient program for sex offenders under the jurisdiction of the state of Idaho.

In 1986, Dodd moved back to Richland, Washington, where he sexually abused a 4-year-old neighbor boy over a period of five months. Again, Dodd escaped receiving any significant punishment for his deviant actions.

By the fall of 1986, Dodd was living and working as a truck driver in Seattle. In June of the following year, he attempted to lure a young boy into a vacant building. Luckily, the boy escaped, but Dodd was arrested and convicted of attempted unlawful imprisonment, a misdemeanor. He was incarcerated until October, at which time he was put on probation and ordered to undergo treatment again.

When his probation expired in the fall of 1988, Dodd quit the treatment program despite objections from officials who said he was far from being cured. Dodd was employed for the next several months at a gas station/ store, a job he had held while on probation, where he was trusted and well liked by his co-workers who, of course, knew nothing about his child molestations.

Alone and strapped for money, Dodd moved in with relatives in Vancouver in late July 1989. On September 1st, he moved into his own apartment. Within days, children began turning up murdered.

During a jailhouse interview with this writer following his arrest, Westley Dodd confessed that he would have killed the Seattle boy had the boy not escaped. He explained that this had been the first incident in which he had formed the intention to carry out a murder. Unfortunately, it had not been his last. . . .

On Monday, June 11, 1990, Dodd appeared in Clark County Superior Court for a hearing before Judge Robert Harris. In a move that took authorities by surprise, Dodd, against the vigorous objections of his attorney, announced that he wanted to change his pleas from not guilty to guilty. In low monotones, Westley Dodd confessed his crimes in court.

"On September 4, 1989, I went to David Douglas Park with the premeditated intent to cause the death of a human being," said Dodd, reading from a prepared statement. "I met Cole Neer. I raped Cole Neer, and then I killed him. I also at about the same time murdered William Neer."

He told the judge that he took a knife with him to the park with the intent of raping and murdering a child. He said he committed the murders to conceal his identity from the police. Dodd said that after killing the Neer brothers, he felt a sense of fear but soon overcame it.

"I was nervous. I was kind of afraid that I was going to get caught. And then as I watched the papers I realized that the police didn't have any clues. I started feeling a little bit more confident and realized I could do it and get away with it. The next step would be to actually kidnap a boy.

"On October 29, 1989, I kidnapped Lee Iseli from Portland and drove him to my apartment in Vancouver. I raped him, and on the morning of October 30th, I murdered Lee Iseli."

Judge Harris asked Dodd if the killing had occurred on the spur of the moment, on a whim.

"No, sir," Dodd responded. "It was premeditated."

Dodd also admitted that when he attempted to kidnap Tommy Staley from the Camas theater, it was his intention to rape and then murder the boy.

Although Dodd's admission of guilt made it unnecessary for the state to continue with a trial for a guilt or innocence determination, it was still necessary to empanel a jury to decide whether Dodd should be sentenced to death or life in prison. By pleading guilty, Dodd had relinquished the right to appeal many of the legal issues of the case, including whether the warrants used to search his apartment and car were legal and whether the confessions he made to police were valid.

The following month, after a jury of six men and six women were seated, Chief Deputy Prosecutor Roger Bennett began presenting the case. He took the jurors step by step through the case, from the heinous killings to Dodd's confessions to the defendant's lurid past. He showed them grisly photographs of the victims and a 20-minute video made by police at the scene when Lee Iseli's body was found.

But perhaps the most chilling part of the proceedings was that focusing on Westley Dodd's diary, which detailed the killings, his future plans to kill children, and a pact he made with Satan, which he described as a "Love God," to help him achieve his murderous goals. Prosecutor Bennett explained that Dodd's handwritten diary showed that he "planned to engage in a large number of long-term kidnappings and murders of young children."

Bennett said Dodd's writings showed a desire to "torture children before he killed them." The prosecutor produced schematic drawings from Dodd's diary that depicted a rack which he could use to tie up and immobilize his victims so that he could perform "experimental surgery" and dismember the children while they were still alive. His plans were to surgically remove parts of their sex organs while the children were conscious.

Dodd's diary told of numerous ways in which he could murder children. Some he planned to strangle, others he intended to suffocate. Still others would be drowned or poisoned. He referred to the planned deaths as his "experiments."

Prosecutor Bennett showed the jurors a map of David Douglas Park, drawn by Dodd, and an entry in his diary that said the park would be a "good place for rape and murder, or kidnap, rape and murder . . . a good hunting ground." Dodd also wrote in his diary that he "got more of a high out of the killing than the molesting."

"Cole and William Neer died in David Douglas Park on Labor Day as victims of 'the hunt,' " said Prosecutor Art Curtis, his voice often cracking with emotion. "At least twenty other children avoided death through fate that weekend alone. Do you wonder where those children are? Who are the lucky ones?

"Lee Iseli met a friend at the playground, a nice man who wanted to buy him a toy, wanted to give him some money," continued Curtis. "Lee Iseli did what we teach our children not to do. . . . Little did he know as he played happily at Mr. Dodd's apartment the night before his death that Mr. Dodd was sitting, writing in his diary."

Prosecutor Curtis then read a passage from the diary: "6:30 p.m. Lee is still playing. Will probably wait until morning to kill him. He suspects nothing now. That way his body will still be fairly fresh for experiments after work."

Arguing against leniency for Dodd, Curtis told jurors there was no evidence for them to consider that warranted leniency.

"Must I remind you of the crimes?" he asked. "How do you describe the enormity of the crimes for which the defendant has pled guilty—what is the appropriate word?

143

Outrageous? Appalling? Beyond belief? Horrific? It is difficult to believe a human being is capable of fantasizing about such crimes."

"Look at what Mr. Dodd likes to do in his free time," co-Prosecutor Roger Bennett told the jurors, reminding the panel that Dodd's one hobby and passion was killing. "Plan child murders. Commit child murders. Relive fantasies about child murders and write about them. With life without parole, two of those things are still available to him." Bennett then urged the jury to sentence Westley Dodd to death.

Dodd's attorney, Lee Dane, argued that Dodd should be sentenced to life without parole. Dane said Dodd would not pose a future threat to society because he killed only children, and none would be available to him if he was sentenced to life in prison.

"I'd like you to think about the effect of an execution on a community—whether it heals or hurts a community," said Dane. "The death penalty has never brought back a human life, has never elevated a community or the people who comprise it."

On Saturday, July 15, 1990, following 14 hours of grueling deliberations over three days, the jury concluded that Westley Allan Dodd must die for his crimes. They failed to find any reason for leniency.

Dodd subsequently asked that his death sentence be carried out expeditiously. Dodd said he would choose hanging over lethal injection when the time came.

In the meantime, Dodd reportedly lay in his prison cell and masturbated night and day as he wandered in and out of fantasy states, apparently reliving the gruesome murders he committed as well as those he had planned to commit.

Just after midnight on January 5, 1993, Westley Allan Dodd was executed just as he had wished, by hanging. It was the first execution by hanging in the U.S. since 1965.

# "STUCK SALT INTO HIS DYING VICTIMS' WOUNDS!"

## by Michael Sasser

Fort Lauderdale, Florida, is no different from other big American cities. It is home to some of the wealthiest people in the world and to some of the poorest. It has its share of crime. Fortunately, it also has its share of decent citizens and hardworking police officers.

Around noon on Thursday, April 19, 1990, Detective Bob Williams of the Fort Lauderdale Police Department received a possible missing-person call.

"A relative told me that a Phillip Walkins and Dorothy Haynes, his girlfriend, have been missing since late Monday night or Tuesday morning," said the officer on the phone. "Someone in the family found Ms. Haynes' rental car in an empty lot in Oakland Park. The family is worried."

"I'll check out the rental car. Let's send a uniform over to the addresses of the missing persons," Williams told the officer.

Driving north to the little suburb of Oakland Park, Detective Williams formulated in his head the usual results of a missing-person report. It usually turned out to be some type of miscommunication, or people trying not to be found. A young couple could have any number of reasons why they might not want to be found.

When Williams arrived at the location given for the car, the vehicle was gone. A quick check showed that it had been towed as an overdue rental car. After a short trip to the towing company, Williams checked the rental agreement in the glove compartment, and came up, indeed, with the name Dorothy Haynes.

While at the towing company, Detective Williams' radio toned.

"Bob," said the voice on the radio. "We've found two bodies, a man and a woman, at the home of Phillip Walkins. The place is a mess."

"I'll be right there."

"One more thing," the voice paused. "It's horrible."

Williams sped back to Fort Lauderdale, wondering what could possibly be so awful as to provoke such a response from a police officer.

At the scene, Detective Williams met with several uniformed officers and other detectives.

"What happened?" Williams asked a uniformed officer before setting foot in the apartment.

"The owner of the building flagged me down," the officer replied. "He wanted police with him when he used his passkey to get into Walkins' apartment. Some relative had called him and asked him to check on Walkins because he seemed to have disappeared."

"And you went in?"

"Yes. As soon as the door was opened, I could see that the place had been ransacked, so I told the landlord to stay at the door. I went in. The place smells. When I got to the back room, I found them lying there."

"Two people?"

"Yes, a man and a woman. Both of them were dead and had been decomposing for a while. They were tied up and there were wounds all over their bodies. It wasn't pleasant."

The area had already been roped off and the scene was crawling with officers who were talking to neighbors and going in and out of the apartment.

Detective Williams entered the crime scene. The smell hit him immediately. It was always the same, but the depth to which it disgusted him was always surprising. You'd think he'd be used to it by now, but he wasn't and probably never would be.

In the back room, Williams found the crime scene unit, a coroner's team, and several other detectives—and the bodies.

Both victims were scantily clad, decomposing, and bound hand and foot by what looked like telephone wires. Wounds all over the bodies looked like they were made by a knife. None of them looked to be mortal, though, and circular bullet entrance holes provided an idea of what would be the eventual cause of death.

There was more, though. The house was an utter wreck. In every room, things were knocked over and strewn about. Drawers were ripped out and dumped chaotically. One of the few things standing upright was a canister of salt in the bedroom. Detective Williams saw this and flinched.

Whoever had killed these people had salted their wounds along the way.

"We're about to move the bodies," said one member of the M.E. team. "Do you have any idea about the identities?"

"I'm afraid we probably do," Williams responded.

The bodies were taken to the medical examiner's office, and Detective Williams contacted the families of Dorothy Haynes and Phillip Walkins. Tearfully, the families identified the two victims as Phillip and Dorothy.

Williams spoke to Ken Davis, a relative of Phillip Walkins' and the man who had first called police about the missing couple.

"Last time I saw Dorothy was Monday night," Davis said. "And I talked to Phillip that same night on the phone. He was supposed to come and pick me up and never did."

"And you didn't hear from either of them after that?"

"No. This morning I just thought it was too strange. I asked around the neighborhood we call skid row, and nobody knew anything. So I picked up some other guys—friends—and we went looking. But there was nothing. No one answered the doors at either of their homes. Then we found the car, and I knew something was happening."

Davis had no idea who could have killed his relative—or why.

Detective Williams was sure of one thing. Because the two victims were residents of Fort Lauderdale's skid row, the people in the neighborhood were unlikely to cooperate much. And anyone who did talk might be doing so for their own advantage. Besides, the residents all knew that everyone in the district was a suspect.

The crime scene unit had come up with fingerprints in the apartment, though not a lot and most of them belonged to the two victims. There was not a lot of physical evidence available.

The coroner ruled both deaths homicides, and the cause of death was indeed a gunshot into each victim.

Between the coroner and the detectives on the scene, the police were able to confirm that the two victims were indeed tortured over several hours until finally being shot to death.

Fort Lauderdale police had a killer on the loose. And instead of having too few suspects, they had too many. The way the house had been ransacked meant that the killer had robbed the house or been looking for something. Robbery as a motive didn't eliminate anyone from suspicion.

Over the next couple of days, police combed the area. They were met with either of two responses. One was complete ignorance; the other was a complete refusal to speak to police at all.

Detective Mike Walley was assigned to work alongside

Bob Williams on the case.

On Sunday, April 22nd, Williams met relatives of Dorothy Haynes at Dorothy's apartment. Together, they entered the apartment. It was a mess. Boxes were overturned and clothes and furniture were strewn about randomly. Detective Williams was surprised. This discovery meant that the torture and killing of Haynes and Williams was not a simple robbery. Apparently, somebody had been looking for something.

Inside the apartment, Williams found a beeper that Haynes' relatives said belonged to the deceased woman. Williams checked, but the numbers stored on the beeper all belonged to concerned relatives who had been looking for the missing Haynes. It was a long shot, anyway.

Haynes' relatives said that the victim had owned a chrome .45 pistol, but Williams could not find the gun. He did find a set of keys with Haynes' house key among them, as well as keys to the home of Phillip Walkins.

Outside the apartment was a Bronco that belonged to Phillip Walkins. According to neighbors, the vehicle had been sitting there since at least April 16th.

There was little else of interest to detectives in Haynes' apartment. Williams had thought, originally, that Haynes and Walkins were the victims of a home invasion robbery. But the mess inside Haynes' apartment meant that there was probably something more diabolical beneath the surface. The crime appeared to have been more carefully orchestrated.

On Monday morning, Detectives Williams and Walley got what they thought was a break in the case. A man named Bart Oades, who lived near the area where Dorothy Haynes' rental car was found, called to say that he had seen when the car had appeared at the empty lot.

Detective Walley met with Oades at his home.

"I saw several guys getting out of the car," Oades said. "My dog started barking and I got up to see what it was. I saw three guys getting out of the car and then rub it down with a bunch of rags."

"Did you see them clearly?" Walley asked.

"Well, not really. I turned a flashlight on and they started walking away. One of them dropped something heavy—sounded like metal. Then he picked it up—I thought it was a gun—and put it in with the rags he was carrying. Then they all walked off, like it was nothing."

Oades gave a general description of the men, but he said he could not positively identify any of them. Walley thought that Oades was very lucky. If he had seen the killers that night, then they had already killed two people. Oades was lucky not to have become the third.

And Walley had wondered why so few people in the tough inner city wanted to talk to police.

According to Oades, the car had been left in the vacant lot about 1:00 a.m. The coroner's time of death was not specific, so Walley wasn't even sure if the car had been dropped off before the murders or after.

Detectives found themselves with very little to work with. They had two bodies. One, they knew, was killed with a 9mm, the other with either a .357 or .38. From the crime scene, it was obvious that both victims (who were reputed drug dealers) had been tortured for hours before death by the killers who had made tiny incisions into the victims' bodies and then salted the wounds. It seemed obvious to sleuths that the killers, in order to get information about the location of money or drugs, had cut the victims, then put salt into the wounds to increase their pain—which was their style of torture.

Detectives Walley and Williams carefully examined the information they received from the inspection of Dorothy Haynes' apartment. Because she was found in Walkins' apartment while her keys and beeper were in her own ransacked home, the detectives believed that she was quite likely kidnapped and then taken to the scene of the murder. They felt that Haynes was probably a target of an overall murder plot. No one could be sure if Haynes'

151

apartment had been searched before the two victims were killed or after.

Whatever the circumstances, the deaths seemed to result from a well-orchestrated home invasion whose plotters meant to leave no witnesses.

Continued attempts at getting information from neighborhood residents were largely in vain.

"I heard the TV playing kind of loud," said one of Walkins' neighbors. "But I didn't see them and then someone must have turned the TV off."

"Earlier in the day," said another neighbor, "I saw Phillip sitting on a car outside the building talking with one woman and a bunch of men. Don't know any of them. I didn't really pay much attention. You can't pay too much attention, you know."

Other people on the streets had information but no hard facts. According to several people, Haynes and Walkins were talking around the neighborhood about making a cocaine deal.

"They were asking around," one witness said. "Trying to set up a buyer. They wanted to move a pretty big load of coke."

Several others made the same statement. However, no one ever saw the drugs and no one seemed to be sure whether Haynes and Walkins had found a buyer or not.

Detective Williams guessed that the victims had never met with a buyer.

The word of the people on the street only strengthened Detective Williams' theory that the whole crime was deeper than it looked. In fact, he was able to put together a reasonable scenario in his head about what had led up to the killing. But he had no suspects.

Homicide still has a certain shock value in the carefully shielded, middle-class world of the suburbs. Veteran sleuths know that in the heart of the city, it has lost the power to shock. It's just one more insult to the city dweller's spirit, one more hassle to cope with and try to block out. That meant that Williams and Walley would have to work a little harder, knock on a few more doors, chase down and follow up whatever few leads they could. And there weren't many leads.

The word spread through the streets until finally on April 26th, the detectives received a call from a man who identified himself only as "Butch." Butch was calling from the state attorney's office where he had made the statement that he had information on the Haynes/Walkins murder. The detectives rushed over to meet with the man.

Butch relayed the details of Monday night, April 16th, and the following Tuesday morning. He said that he was asleep in his house when he received a call from a man named Don who was married to Butch's cousin. Don asked Butch to come and pick him up at a nearby Fort Lauderdale apartment. Butch did as he was asked.

"I knew the apartment," Butch said. "It belonged to a guy named Rich. I get there, and Don, Rich, and this guy, Tony, were standing outside. I sort of knew something was wrong because Don had blood on one of his arms."

The men asked Butch to follow them in the white car they were driving, which Butch had never seen before. Butch complied. They drove to Don's apartment.

"They had some bags with them that they wanted me to help carry into the apartment. I did, but I looked inside to see what was in them."

"What did you see?" Detective Walley asked.

Butch was very nervous, moving about the state attorney's office like a trapped animal. "I saw a bag of what looked like cocaine. And some gold jewelry and several handguns. Don asked me to take some of the stuff to my house and hold it for him until he called me or something."

"So you did?"

"Yeah, I did. I drove them back to Rich's place, and I

went home. About two days later, I looked through the stuff I was holding for them. There was a nine-millimeter handgun, a nickel-plated forty-five and a thirty-two. There was also a thick rope chain with a medallion on it inside the bag. That medallion I was pretty sure belonged to Phillip Walkins."

Butch said that he knew Walkins casually.

"Did you know at that time that something had happened to Mr. Walkins?" Walley asked.

"Not at that time. But seeing the medallion and remembering the blood on Don's arm, I kind of thought something was wrong. So, Thursday night, I brought the stuff back to Don and gave it to him."

Butch went on to describe each of the three men he had been with and also gave a phone number for Don. He knew little about Tony, except that he had a wife named Kelli, and Butch had only an approximate address for the couple.

"Do you know where any of these guys work?"

"They don't have jobs."

"What do they do?" Walley asked.

Butch was being evasive. "They rob dope dealers. Armed robbery. They rip off people making deals. When I heard about what happened to Phillip and Dorothy, I had to tell somebody what I knew."

What Butch had to say fell in line with the image that Detectives Williams and Walley had put together about the events on the night in question.

The detectives transported Butch back to the homicide offices, where he continued to be evasive. But he did manage to answer questions and deliver his statement. While at the police station, Williams was also able to run a check on the phone number that Butch had given for Don. The number belonged to Don Breed and his wife at the address Butch had given police.

In the days that followed, Don Breed became the chief suspect in the investigation. The detectives believed

Butch's explanation for how Breed made his living. To corroborate the suspicion, they compared Breed's fingerprints with those lifted from several unsolved home invasion robberies in the area.

In two cases, police came up with a match. Detectives put Breed in a photo lineup and showed it to one of the victims in one of the robberies.

"That's him," the woman said, fingering Breed in the lineup.

However, confounding the detectives, Breed's fingerprints did not show up in Phillip Walkins' house. But that didn't mean he didn't know something. Then again, Detective Williams thought, everyone seemed to know something.

On May 2nd, Detective Tim Bronson called Williams.

"I heard you guys talking about that murder that happened last month," Bronson said. "Looked like a home invasion."

"Yes," Williams said.

"I had a home invasion robbery like that in February," Bronson went on. "Unsolved. But the M.O. was similar. The perps tied the two people up and cut one of them on the face."

Bronson gave a physical description of the perps, and it matched the one given by Bart Oades. Most importantly, one of the men described looked like Don Breed.

Later that afternoon, Detectives Williams, Walley, and Bronson matched the fingerprints of Don Breed with those lifted from the home invasion robbery in February. They matched, and an eyewitness picked Breed out of a photo lineup. Unfortunately, the police still had nothing on Breed for the April 16th murder.

A warrant was issued for the arrest of Don Breed on charges related in two armed home invasions. However, police decided to set up a surveillance on Breed to see if they could come up with other suspects.

On May 4th, Don Breed was intercepted while in the

presence of a man named Richard Smith, who fit the description given by Butch of the man named Rich with whom Butch had traveled on the morning of April 17th. Smith accompanied the police willingly and agreed to be questioned and fingerprinted.

At the stationhouse, Butch positively identified Richard Smith as among the men he had been with on April 17th.

Fingerprints of Smith were taken and matched against those in the Haynes/Walkins murders and several home invasion robberies in the area. There were no matches. But Richard Smith did talk.

According to Smith, he had been at Breed's home one evening around April 16th when Tony had come over. Tony and Breed disappeared inside Breed's room, and when they emerged, Tony had a chrome .45 handgun in his pants.

"I'd never seen that forty-five before," Richard Smith said.

Police had already determined that Phillip Walkins had owned such a weapon, but they had been unable to find it during the investigation. Likewise, Butch had described seeing such a weapon in the man's bag on the morning of the 17th.

"Do you know this Tony's last name?" a detective asked.

"He goes by Tony Dupree," Smith replied.

"Do you know where he lives?"

"Yes, he lives with his wife."

Smith was released but agreed to meet later with police and show them where Tony Dupree lived.

Meanwhile, Don Breed was charged with several counts of armed robbery, and a warrant was granted to search Breed's apartment. Detective Walley and a team from the forensics division executed the search.

In the apartment, there was little of interest to the homicide case. Walley did find a .38, a Charter Arms special two-inch blue revolver. Mrs. Breed said it belonged to her husband, but she carried it in her purse while moving about town.

Walley took the weapon and had it tested against the information they had acquired about the murder weapon.

"This isn't it," the ballistics expert told Walley.

Walley wasn't surprised. He and Williams had two suspects, but there wasn't a shred of evidence against either of them in the Walkins/Haynes murders. The sleuths did, however, have Don Breed on robbery charges.

In this case, the detectives had determined, every clue was colored a different shade of gray. There was no black and white. Their suspects were guilty in varying degrees. But they still didn't know who, in fact, was guilty of the brutal double murder. Could it be Tony Dupree, whose name did not show up on the police computer?

Richard Smith did show detectives where Tony Dupree and his wife, the former Kelli Carson, lived and which vehicle was theirs.

One woman who lived near Bart Oades came forward to say that she had seen three men walking past her house away from a white car on the early morning of April 17th. Detectives verified that the car the woman saw was the same one Oades had seen, which was the vehicle rented to Dorothy Haynes.

However, when a photo lineup of suspects was presented to the woman, she was unable to positively identify anyone. Likewise, Oades had not been able to pick anybody out of a lineup.

Detectives Williams and Walley hadn't absolutely eliminated any of their suspects from suspicion. But now, they moved to concentrate on the mysterious Tony Dupree.

A check of local pawnshops revealed nothing. None of the possible suspects had a recent record of pawning any jewelry or firearms.

Detective Williams became curious about the exact identity of Tony Dupree. He had received information that Dupree was married in Fort Lauderdale in May 1990.

Williams contacted the Broward County marriage license bureau.

Apparently, Kelli Carson had indeed been married in 1990. The name of her husband was not Tony Dupree, however, but Antonio Van Dyke Dorsett.

Williams ran a check on Tony Dorsett. No record came up, but Dorsett had been ticketed by Davie, Florida, police for driving without a license, an offense for which Dorsett was not arrested. It was not a strong lead by any means. But since Williams knew that Dorsett didn't have a license, it provided the detective with the opening he needed to pick Dorsett up.

Williams proceeded to Kelli Carson's workplace, where he happened to see Antonio Van Dyke Dorsett driving a bronze Nissan. Knowing that he had no license, Williams pulled Dorsett over. Dorsett was calm and cooperative as he was taken into custody and transported to the Fort Lauderdale Police Department. At the police station, Dorsett agreed to answer questions.

When told that Don Breed had been arrested and charged with at least two home invasion robberies, Antonio Dorsett claimed to have known Breed for only a few months.

"Do you know Phillip Walkins and Dorothy Haynes?" Williams asked.

"I knew Phillip. Don't know no one named Haynes," Dorsett replied.

"Where do you know Phillip from?"

"Just the streets."

"Did you ever have any reason to be in Phillip Walkins' apartment?"

"No. Never."

Dorsett agreed to be photographed and fingerprinted, as was procedure for the arrest for the license violation. But with nothing to hold Dorsett on, police had to let him go when he posted $25 cash bond for the infraction.

But detectives had gotten what they wanted—

fingerprints. The lab did the work on Dorsett's fingerprints. They were able to positively identify Dorsett's prints as several of the unidentified prints in the cases in which Don Breed was already charged. So that strongly implicated Dorsett in the home invasion robberies.

Then a check was done in the Walkins/Haynes murders. Antonio Dorsett's fingerprints matched a print on the phone in Walkins' apartment. The print on the phone was not where a normal print would be if someone had merely been using the phone. The print was upside down, near the point where the phone cord had been pulled out, apparently before it was used to tie up both victims.

Finally, Detectives Williams and Walley had the big break they needed.

On May 16th, a warrant was issued for the arrest of Antonio Van Dyke Dorsett on two counts of armed robbery. There wasn't time to prepare a case yet on the homicides. But at least a dangerous man could be taken off the streets.

At seven o'clock that evening, Detectives Williams and Walley arrested Tony Dorsett at his residence. Dorsett went with police willingly and was returned to the Fort Lauderdale Police Department. Williams and Walley questioned Dorsett again after telling him that he would be charged with the murders of Phillip Walkins and Dorothy Haynes.

Again, Dorsett denied knowing anything about the murders. He said he knew Walkins but had never been inside Walkins' home and had never had reason to handle Walkins' phone.

Walley gave Dorsett several openings to explain his role in the crime, if indeed Dorsett hadn't committed the crime alone. But Dorsett simply denied knowing anything about it. Nevertheless, Dorsett was charged with the grisly torture murders of Phillip Walkins and Dorothy Haynes.

In the days that followed, police continued to locate any evidence to link other people to the crime. Walley and

Williams had a hard time believing that one man had kidnapped Haynes, transported her to Walkins' apartment, tied and tortured the two, then shot each with a different weapon. The weapon issue concerned detectives most. Why would Dorsett use two different weapons on his victims?

That question would never be answered. Dorsett continued to profess his innocence, and no guns were ever recovered.

Finally, in court, Antonio Van Dyke Dorsett was convicted of two counts of first-degree murder along with two counts of robbery with a deadly weapon, two counts of armed robbery, and two counts of armed kidnapping. He was sentenced to two consecutive life sentences.

Questions still abound about what exactly happened on the night of April 16, 1990. Because Tony Dorsett chose not to testify, he carries the burden of his guilt alone. Judging from the details of the crime, Detectives Williams and Walley know that it is a heavy burden. And judging from the horrible torture inflicted on Dorothy Haynes and Phillip Walkins, the detectives know that Dorsett will one day face a judgment from an authority even greater than the law.

EDITOR'S NOTE:
*Ken Davis, Bart Oades, Butch, Don Breed, Richard Smith, and Kelli Carson are not the real names of the persons so named in the foregoing story. Fictitious names have been used because there is no reason for public interest in the identities of these persons.*

# "TORTURE KILLING OF THE WEALTHY STOCKBROKER"

## by Joseph McNamara

**WHITESTONE, N.Y.**
**JUNE 13, 1980**

In the Whitestone Section of Queens, just off Powell's Cove which borders the East River and across that waterway from the mighty stone towers of Manhattan, there is an enclave of some 70 acres which offers large sumptuous homes for some 450 families. If these are not mansions, they will fill the bill in the eyes of all but the most discriminating. Some homes cost as much as $1 million and are owned by many of New York City's most influential citizens—judges, politicians, Wall Street tycoons and other assorted luminaries. The area is known as Malba.

In this northernmost section of Queens, with commanding views of the river and of Long Island Sound, burglaries have become a nuisance to the wealthy owners, the city police and the special security force that has been hired to patrol the area. But violence does not rear up to terrorize the inhabitants. All this, however, was changed on a sun-drenched day in February, 1980, when a Wall Street stockbroker was brutally murdered in his home there.

The victim was George F. Robb, 74 years old, who had

his own seat on the New York Stock Exchange. A senior partner in the firm of Robb, Peck, McCooey & Co. — the second largest specialist firm in the Wall Street community — Robb had been ill and rather inactive for two years and was considered semi-retired.

He was attacked with such ferocity that Captain Roy Richter of the Queens Homicide Squad reported: "Robb received a horrible beating. He was stabbed repeatedly."

Robb was found dead in his $300,000 12-room Cape Cod home by his wife and their married daughter who lived nearby. The two women had gone on a shopping trip to Manhattan about 11 a.m. on Friday, February 1, 1980, leaving the elderly millionaire alone in the house. Upon returning at 5 p.m. they found Robb lying on a blood-soaked rug in the foyer.

The victim's wife almost passed out upon making the gruesome discovery and it was left to the daughter to summon police officers by the 911 emergency number. A doctor was immediately called to treat Mrs. Robb.

Uniformed radio patrolmen responded to the scene, quickly followed by homicide men of the Queens office, headed by Captain Richter. He noted that the front and the back doors to the green and white house were open and that the house had been ransacked. In fact, it was in shambles. A trail of blood led from one room to another, attesting to the drawn-out nature of the beating.

The old man had been jabbed dozens of times in the arms, face, back and chest, police theorized, in an effort to get him to reveal where he stashed his valuables. Kitchen knives — taken from drawers for this purpose — were found in different parts of the house, some of them with their blades bent or broken. So fierce was the attack that blood was even found on some ceilings.

Tragically, there was not much of value kept in the lavish home on its one-and-a-half acre setting. But if the ailing victim, dragged from room to room while being beaten and knifed, told his assailants that, they apparently did not believe him.

It was presumed by homicide men under Captain Richter that at least two killers were involved, perhaps more, because of the injuries inflicted and the damage done. Seasoned detectives found it difficult to believe that one man could have caused so much mayhem.

Richter was led on a tour of the home by Robb's wife to determine if anything had been stolen. From the outset, the captain believed the slaying was robbery motivated. Meanwhile, he had sent for forensic units to begin fingerprinting the entire house. And Detective Sean Grennan was brought in to handle the case.

The detectives, based on an inventory by the family, discovered that the most valuable item stolen from the place was an antique ring ripped from the finger of the victim with such force, his finger was broken.

The ring contained a large amethyst, surrounded by a grapelike cluster of smaller amethysts. It had been owned by Robb's father and the slain man had worn it since his dad's death. The ring was considered priceless since there were only two like it ever made.

Robb's wristwatch had been snatched from his wrist so forcibly it was ripped from its case. It had stopped at 12:13 p.m. Why the thieves left it behind was puzzling to police, who reasoned the killers figured they had damaged it too badly to be worth much.

A police artist, working with members of the Robb family, produced a sketch of the missing ring. It was later distributed to jewelers and to gold dealers by the detectives, who also questioned known fences trying to get a lead on the bauble.

Meanwhile, the forensic people had turned up several fingerprints in the house—prints that did not match those of any member of the Robb family. These were run through the computers and records by the forensic men seeking a matchup in the police files. It was a long, laborious process.

In seeking to reconstruct the crime, detectives noted that there was a narrow common driveway behind the

Robb house used by six homes in the exclusive enclave. Cars that are driven into the lane are concealed from the street. It was possible that the killers had parked a car there. Only a white picket fence and some shrubbery would deny anyone access to the rear of the house.

In the meantime, detectives had been questioning the Robb's neighbors and they found one who had seen a young man running from the death scene in the direction of a nearby bus stop. The time was around 1:10 p.m., the detectives were informed. According to this neighbor, the young man was black, about 20 years old. This neighbor could not provide any additional information, but it was a good start. It shot holes in the theory that a car might have been parked behind the house for the killers to escape in, and it left open the possibility that the killers may have come by bus, or, at least, have left that way.

Detective Grennan and his partner, Michael Giovanniello, began the next phase of the operation—talking to bus drivers in hopes of locating the one who might have picked up the young man seen running from the house.

Also, a special police number was set up for the use of anyone with any information about the shocking murder, with the usual promise of anonymity given such callers. And the residents of the area did indeed find the crime shocking. One resident of the affluent community told reporters:

"Burglaries, yes, we get 'em. But this is the first murder that I can recall having been committed in Malba."

Moreover, there was an immediate rush on new locks, added locks, reenforced security and such. Many locksmiths in adjoining areas reported the heaviest business they had in years. One electrician said he was kept busy moving doorbells to the outside of outer doorways instead of inside, so doors could be permanently locked.

Among the items strewn about near the body of the slain man was a claw hammer. And this, the medical examiner of Queens reported, was the object that crushed Robb's skull and inflicted the fatal wound. Also, the post mortem revealed, Robb had been stabbed at least 12 times by his killers. Since his wristwatch had stopped at 12:13 p.m. and one of his suspected killers was seen running from the house at 1:10, it suggested to the investigators that Robb had been tortured for about an hour in an effort to make him divulge the hiding place of his valuables.

However, as police had learned, Robb kept his valuables in a safer place than his unlocked home. The doors to the house were left unlocked since people moved freely in and out, the authorities were told. Also, the family cat used the rear portal and this was usually kept ajar in the daytime, it was learned.

The killers had apparently entered through the unlocked rear door and surprised Robb watching TV from an easy chair, as he convalesced from a recent operation. The television set was still turned on when police arrived after discovery of the murder.

By now, Robb's wife had completed her inventory of the home she had shared with her gentle husband for many years, the happiest of their 52-year marriage. She found that a gold watch and chain had been stolen by the killers. Detectives Grennan and Giovanniello added this valuable to the ring as they hit the jewelers circuit. But it was tough work . . . and long.

Robb, who is survived not only by his wife and the daughter who found him dead, but by 2 sons, 13 grandchildren, and 3 great-grandchildren, was laid to rest on February 6 following a Requiem Mass in St. Fidelis Catholic Church in College Point. The final tribute provided investigators with an opportunity to talk to other members of the dead man's family.

They told the probers of the kindness of the man, of his love for horses—he was a breeder and owner of some note. The relatives spoke of how he was always ready with advice for neighbors, with a warm knee for great-grandchildren and a deep-bred conviction that man acquires things through his own invention and industry. At one point in the investigation, probers wondered if this philosophy had contributed to his death—a reluctance to tell his killers where his valuables were kept. But the detectives had since decided that Robb simply told the truth—that there were no valuables kept in the house and that the slayers really did not believe him.

A clear picture of a self-sufficient man who had made it on his own came through to the investigators, but it shed no new light on the killing itself. And, in a way, the detectives really didn't expect it.

"Hey, you do things by the book," one prober noted in reference to the long odds. "Sometimes you get lucky. But most times you just keep piling up details until you get that one break in the case."

The investigators realized they could use that one break. Grennan and Giovanniello had been doing things "by the book." They were busy quizzing all neighbors to the Robbs, as well as those who lived in the vicinity of a bus stop, the nearest stop from Robb's home in the direction the young man was seen running from the death scene. It was a half mile from the house.

They located one witness who had seen a young man splashed with blood get aboard a Q44 bus just after 1:10 p.m. on the day of the murder. Consistent and determined questioning of others eventually increased the number of witnesses to four.

The youth, according to these accounts, was between 17 and 20 years of age. He was about 5-foot 9-inches tall and weighed about 150 pounds. All had agreed that the young man was wearing a brown nylon ski outfit that had white or yellow stripes lining the chest and both arms.

"There was blood splashed across the jacket of his ski outfit," one witness told authorities. "And it was on the pants, too. A lot of blood."

This witness said that the gore was possibly on the man's blue sneakers, which appeared to be a pair of Pumas.

To say that this witness was startled was a vast understatement. The shock of the blood was obvious in the wide eyes of the witness, for the young man felt constrained to tell the witness, unasked, that he had cut himself while skiing. The witness did not buy that—and promptly called the police, which led directly to this one witness.

The most distinguishing feature of the suspect, Grennan learned, was a round scar, about the size of a half dollar, on his right cheek. The man also had a small scar by his left eye. The description was filled out to a short black Afro hairstyle, brown eyes and medium complexion.

It was at this point that the questioning of bus drivers paid off for Detectives Grennan and Giovanniello. They located a driver of a bus on the Q44 line, a driver who said he had picked up a man who fit the description of the guy seen running from the murder scene.

"Was there anyone with this man?" the driver was asked.

"No, he was alone."

"Are you sure?" the detective pressed.

"He got on alone. I'm sure there was no one with him," the driver replied. The other witnesses agreed they saw no one else.

Grennan and his partner now began to change their thinking about the number of killers involved. They began to lean towards the lone slayer theory. They had no proof that more than one man had been involved in the murder; only the belief that the frenzied violence perpetrated on the elderly Robb had to have been the product of more than one twisted mind and body. It was quite possible, now even probable, that a single killer—bent on robbery—angered at finding little of value to take at the rich man's spacious home—had resorted to such fury.

Further interrogation of the bus driver and the witnesses on the Q44 bus revealed that the bloodied young stranger had left the bus at 163rd Street and Jamaica Avenue. Questioning of residents in that area, however, failed to yield any further clues as to the young quarry. No resident could be found who had seen the ski-suited youth leave the bus.

Nevertheless, investigators felt they had uncovered a tangible line of pursuit. The witnesses, including the bus driver, were put in touch with a police artist, who, after conferring with them, came up with a composite drawing of the suspect.

In the meantime, Detectives Grennan and Giovanniello ran the suspect's description through the police computers in hopes of getting a clue to his identity. But nothing turned up on the computer that fit the suspect very well. The probers kept digging, however.

By now, business associates of the brutally slain man were offering a reward of $10,000 for information leading to the arrest and conviction of his killer. The special police telephone number that had been set up for anyone with information about the vicious bludgeon slaying, was emphasized by the authorities. The phone number was circulated through newspapers and local television and radio outlets.

In early March, investigators began circulating the composite sketch of the suspect seen boarding the Q44 bus. Once again, newspapers and radio and television stations were asked to cooperate. And did. At the same time, the sketches were made available for the bulletin boards of every precinct house throughout New York City, with special emphasis on the borough of Queens.

"That circular scar might be a help," one investigator noted. "Every witness we found mentioned it in describing the suspect . . . it must have made an impression on each of them. Maybe it will impress someone else now."

The investigation kept perking along through the month of April, although the probers were becoming a bit discouraged. An exhaustive search of the fingerprint files failed to produce any link to the several prints found in the home of broker Robb. This probably meant that the suspected murderer did not have a record of prior arrest

168

in New York City.

Throughout the weeks, the search for the killer continued. Detective Grennan made it his business to interview just about every burglary suspect collared in the Queens area. On several occasions he was heartened. One young fellow bagged in a supermarket robbery in Jamaica, fit the description of the Robb killing suspect incredibly well. Grennan leaped into his auto and sped to the precinct house to interview the man. This suspected burglar denied any knowledge, however, of the slaying in Malba's green and white mansion.

"Where were you on the afternoon of February 1?" the suspect was asked.

"Holy hell, I dunno. That's a couple months ago," he answered.

"When is the last time you were in Malba?" the sleuth shot out.

"Where's Malba?"

The investigators felt they might have a "live one" here. But further questioning dashed their hopes. The accused burglar said he had been picked up for questioning by police in early February about a liquor store heist in mid-January.

The probers dug into the case and found, that indeed, their hopeful suspect had been picked up by detectives of the Jamaica squad on February 1 and spent the afternoon being grilled about this case—a crime that could not be pinned on him. And he was released.

"Talk about alibis!" one detective noted in disgust. The youthful collar was turned over to the burglary squad, who were making a better case of the supermarket job.

Still Grennan pursued his quest among the burglary suspects in Queens. At the same time, other detectives combed the pawn-shop beat, hoping to turn up a clue to the stolen amethyst ring or to Robb's missing gold watch and chain. They were getting nowhere fast on this.

It was on June 3 that Detective Grennan got good news on the case. Just the night before, a 17-year-old youth had been arrested during what the authorities characterized as an attempt to burglarize a Howard Johnson's Motor Lodge in Jamaica. The lodge was just eight blocks from the home of the suspect, Ronald Donaldson, who lived on 132nd Street, South Ozone Park.

During the questioning of the suspect at the Jamaica station, one alert detective noted a circular scar on the teenager's cheek. The scar bothered him. He knew that somewhere, somehow he had seen this peculiar scar before. But for some four hours, he could not place it. And then he remembered — it was on the precinct house bulletin board. It was in reference to a circular on the suspected slayer of George Robb.

Bright and early the next morning, Grennan was notified about the possible connection with the Robb murder. The detective came to the Jamaica precinct and questioned the burglary suspect. At the same time, Grennan got copies of the suspect's fingerprints to compare them with those lifted from articles at the scene of Robb's murder.

Afterward, Grennan went to Queens Borough District Attorney John Santucci and asked that the entire investigation be turned over to a grand jury for possible indictment for murder.

Although Robb's ring, watch and chain had never been found, Grennan felt that he had a strong case for murder against Ronald Donaldson, and detectives working on the case with him felt the same. This feeling was buttressed when word came down to them from the fingerprint laboratory. But the probers wanted to get grand jury action in the case. There was no pressing need to charge Donaldson. He was already jailed in the Johnson Motor Lodge job.

So DA Santucci presented the matter to a Queens grand jury. On June 9, the panel returned the indictment, charging the South Ozone Park man with second degree murder, first degree robbery and second degree burglary in connection with the heinous slaying of George Robb.

Donaldson pleaded innocent to the charges when arraigned in Queens Supreme Court. He was held without bail and remanded to Rikers Island prison to await trial. But that was not the end of Donaldson's woes. Four days later, on June 13, the grand jury indicted him in another murder, that of an 84-year-old blind woman, Myrtle Dehart of South Ozone Park.

Dehart had been slain in her home on March 23, about seven weeks after Robb was killed. Like the millionaire stockbroker, the woman had been bludgeoned and viciously stabbed. Investigators also reported they had found a thermometer shoved down the elderly woman's throat. The viciousness of the two crimes had intrigued investigators.

Grennan, whose eight-man task force had pressed the Robb case, and Lieutenant Joseph Pirrello said that neighbors of Dehart had identified a picture of Donaldson as the person seen in the vicinity of the victim's home shortly before the slaying. He also awaits trial for that murder.

Investigators working the cases noted with irony how similar the methods of the slayings—how disparate the victims: the aging millionaire in his mansion and the blind woman in her modest home, likened only in their frailty and their abject helplessness.

Ronald Donald was convicted and sentenced to 6-18 years for manslaughter, 8-24 years for burglary one, and 5-15 years for burglary two. He is serving his sentences concurrently at the Sullivan Correctional Facility.

# "48 HOURS OF RAPE AND TORTURE!"

by Barbara Geehr

ORLANDO, FLA.
APRIL 11, 1986

Levi had just raped her again, and she felt like throwing up. Mark, naked and sitting on the side of the other bed with gun in hand, still had the weapon pointed dead at her. He'd held it like that all during the rape to make sure she did everything Levi demanded for his sexual gratification.

Levi stumbled out of bed and headed for the bathroom. Mark put the gun on the night table between the two beds, stretched out and pulled up the covers. She wanted to kill them both for what they had done to her, but she dared not reach for the gun. Mark was wide awake and watching her every move.

It was mid-morning of Tuesday, November 12, 1985, and 21-year-old Karen Weber was in a top-floor room of a four-story motel in Daytona Beach, Florida, with two men she knew only as Levi and Mark. They had abducted her shortly after 10 o'clock on the preceding Sunday night after saying they would drive her home from a Fern Park night spot in their van. The van, which she had since learned they'd stolen, was parked at the foot of three flights of stairs outside the motel room.

As she lay on the bed mentally calculating the number of hours of rape, torture and physical abuse she'd survived, Karen wondered for the hundredth time how and when the nightmare would end.

Wearily, she got up and put on her fancy western shirt — which wasn't looking quite so fancy any more — and her boots. Levi was still in the bathroom, a towel now wrapped around his middle. Mark still lay in the bed, naked. "Damn you all!" she flared at Mark. "I'm going down to the van to get the aspirin."

Before Mark could react, she opened the door and walked out. She made her way down the steps and to the van, cautiously. She did not dare to run, believing Mark by this time would have jumped out of bed, grabbed the gun from the night table and called Levi from the bathroom. They were probably pulling on their pants at this very moment to come after her, she thought.

Sliding open the side door of the van, Karen spotted, at a car parked nearby, a curly-headed man with glasses. He was wearing shorts and a yellow sport shirt.

"Hey, dude!" she called in a loud whisper. "Get the police. Tell them I've been kidnapped and am being raped continuously by a couple of weirdos. They've got a gun. I'm sure they're watching me out the window right now. If I try to run, I'll be dead."

"What room are you in?" the stranger asked.

"I don't know the number. Just watch what room I go to when I leave here."

She rummaged through the backpack in the van, found the bottle of aspirin and then started back up the stairs. Midway, she stopped to glance at the window of the room where she'd left Levi and Mark. The drapes were drawn, and she could not tell whether either of her abductors was peering out at her.

Hoping they might not yet have gotten their act together, she mustered up her last shred of courage. "The hell with it!" she said. "I'll chance it."

173

Abruptly, Karen swung around, ran back down the steps and to the motel office. There, she managed to tell the desk clerk to call the police. "I've been raped and raped and raped," she cried, her voice quivering. Then she broke down.

Daytona Beach Police Department Detective Debbie Bramlitt arrived at the scene on the heels of responding officers. The first officer to reach the motel advised Bramlitt he'd found the terrified victim hiding in the closet of the motel manager's office but had not found either of the suspects in the room where the rapes occurred. "They must have fled on foot because their van is still parked at the foot of the stairs," he said. "It's the 1980 red-and-white Chevy with the Brevard County plates." He gave the tag number.

"Fan out and search the immediate area," Bramlitt directed. "I'll go and talk to the victim."

The detective found Karen Weber in the motel manager's office, trying without success to drink the cup of coffee set on the desk beside her. Trembling hands made it impossible for the victim to pick up the cup without spilling its contents.

Bramlitt, introducing herself, noted that not only were Weber's hands shaking, but so, too, was her entire body. The detective also observed that the woman's eyes were wide with fear and that her face had a torn lip and bite marks. She tried to dispel some of the terror. "You're safe now," Bramlitt said. "Your attackers fled but left the van. Officers are searching the area; we'll have the van towed away. I'll drive you to the Halifax Hospital for rape examination and treatment of your abrasions, but I need descriptions of your two assailants before we do that. Are you okay enough to tell me what they look like?"

"Yeah. I'm still kind of shaky; but other than that, I'm beginning to feel okay," Karen responded.

She first described the man she knew as Levi as in his late 30s, about 5 feet, 10 inches tall and weighing about

140 pounds. He had blond hair, blue eyes, a mustache and beard. And, oh yeah, he had the tattoo C.B. on his upper left arm," she added. "He was the one in charge. Mark, the other guy, did everything Levi told him to do."

"Explain that," Detective Bramlitt said.

"Well, if Levi told Mark to go to the store to buy me a bathing suit, Mark went. If Levi told Mark to keep the gun on me while Levi raped me, Mark did that. Somewhere along the line, they mentioned they were half-brothers. Levi seemed quite a bit older, so it looked like a case of a younger brother hero-worshipping an older one."

"Okay," Bramlitt said. "What about Mark? What did he look like?"

"He was younger, as I said, but taller by two or three inches. He also was of medium build with blond hair and blue eyes, but he didn't have either a beard or a mustache. He did have a couple of tattoos, though—a lady's face on his right arm and something that looked like the Harley Davidson motorcycle emblem on his left arm."

"Good enough for now," the detective said. "Let's get you to the hospital."

Before pulling away in the police car, Bramlitt radioed descriptions of the suspects and of the stolen van to headquarters. "Put a BOLO out for the men," she instructed. "Get the van towed to the police compound and run a check on the tag number and the stolen-vehicle reports."

At the Halifax Hospital, Karen Weber underwent a rape examination and received treatment for her various abrasions and bruises. She then agreed to go with Detective Bramlitt to Daytona Beach police headquarters to answer questions. There, in a small interview room and with a cup of coffee which she could now handle, she recounted the bizarre events which began on the Sunday night of November 10th at the Tempest Lounge in Fern Park, a small area north of Orlando, known mainly for its jai-alai tournaments and its night spots featuring topless and nude dancing.

Karen worked as a dancer at the Tempest Lounge, performing in total nudity for customers willing to pay from one-to-five dollars a dance. "I'd only been working there about three weeks and was on during the day hours," she began. "Sunday was the first time I got assigned to the six-to-ten o'clock night shift. I was pretty happy about that because the next day was my birthday, and I was counting on making enough that night to treat myself to some new clothes."

She stopped talking as quickly as she had begun; and Bramlitt sensed, from past experience with victims of rape, that the woman was feeling ashamed and embarrassed about recounting her traumatic sexual experience. "Why don't you just try telling me in your own words what happened once you got to work on Sunday evening?" she suggested.

Karen took a deep breath and then plunged headlong into her story. "Sunday was a lousy day to start with," she said. "The night before, I'd had several beers at a bar next to the Royal Motel, which is where I live, and I spent the whole day in my room, nursing a hangover. I still felt buzzy when I arrived at work, and I was a half-hour to forty-five minutes late. They slapped me with a five-dollar fine for that. As though that wasn't bad enough," Weber went on, "midway through the evening, the lounge hostess called me over the mike that I was to report to the disc jockey's booth at once.

"When I got there, she told me one of the other dancers reported smelling marijuana in the bathroom right after I had walked out of there. The hostess said they were going to have to search my locker and purse. That was okay because I knew they wouldn't find any pot in either place."

"When and how did you become involved with Levi and Mark?" Detective Bramlitt asked sympathetically.

"It was just after those two incidents. I was on the

176

stage, dancing in just my tee-strap, and they were drinking beer at one of the tables. They never took their eyes off me, and I couldn't help looking back at them because I thought the one I later knew as Levi—the one with the beard and mustache and long hair—looked like the guy in ZZ Top. But it was the other one, Mark, who came up to the stage and handed me a dollar."

"What happened after that?"

"When I finished with the stage dancing, I went to my locker and put on my fringed western shirt and fancy boots. Another dancer at the lounge was also there, putting on a shirt. She'd been dancing for Mark earlier in the evening and told me to introduce myself to these two guys because they had a lot of money. When we got our shirts and boots on, we went over to their table."

Karen said she introduced herself, that the other dancer again began dancing for Mark and that Levi asked her to dance topless. "I did one dance like that and then Levi told me I could put my shirt on. I danced four more dances for him with my shirt on."

"Did he pay you?"

"Yeah. Five dollars a dance."

"What happened then?" the detective asked.

Karen answered it was then time for her to go back to the stage to perform and that, as she left the table, Levi handed her another five-dollar bill. By the time she finished dancing on the stage in only her tee-strap, it was 10 o'clock and time to quit, she said. "I saw that the table where Levi and Mark had been sitting was empty and that the other dancer, already dressed, was heading out the door. I needed a ride home because I'd only made fifty-three dollars and didn't want to spend money for a taxi, the next day being my birthday and all."

After hurrying to the dressing room, pulling on her black leather pants and grabbing her white dress, her boots and her overnight bag from her locker, Karen said, she ran out and caught the other dancer in the parking lot. But the woman couldn't "drive me because she had to pick up her boyfriend. She told me Levi and Mark were still in the parking lot and to go ask them. She walked over to their van with me. The guys said dropping me off was no problem, so I got into the van. They were both pretty drunk, but I wasn't expecting any trouble."

"What was the seating arrangement in the van?" Bramlitt asked.

"Mark was doing the driving, and Levi was in the seat on the passenger side. There were a couple of bucket seats behind the front seat, and I climbed into the one behind Levi. I told them I lived at the Royal Motel and that it was only a couple of miles up the street. When Mark pulled out of the parking lot, I thought that was where he was going to take me."

It took only a few moments for Karen Weber to realize otherwise. According to her statements, the van was barely out of the parking lot before Levi stumbled to the back, pulled her out of her seat and onto the floor behind Mark. Before she realized what he was up to, he had a gun pressed against her face.

Karen then told what happened after that. "Levi said, 'Do you know what this is?' I was too frightened to answer, so he said, 'This is a gun that's going to kill you if you don't be a good girl and do what we say.' Then he told me to take off my pants. I did, and that's when he began sexually molesting me."

"How long did he keep that up?" Detective Bramlitt asked.

"All the way to a motel in Altamonte Springs."

"Did you try to fight him off?"

"I kept trying to push him away so I could look out the window and see where I was. Every time I did, he yanked me back down by my hair and slapped me. I couldn't do much because the gun was right there on the floor beside him."

The drive from the Tempest Lounge to the Altamonte

Springs motel was a relatively short one. Arriving there, Weber said, Levi—with gun now in hand—pulled her out of the van and dragged her into a room on the ground floor. "The room must have already been paid for, because Mark had the key to open the door."

"Had you put your clothes back on?" Bramlitt asked.

"No. Levi wouldn't let me. I didn't have anything on but my fringed shirt and my tee-strap. I was carrying my boots."

In the room, Weber said, Levi threw her on the bed, walked across the room and turned on the TV. "There was already a lot of beer in the room and both men were pretty drunk. Levi told me to get up and dance. He put some bills—three one-hundred dollar ones and a fifty—inside one of my boots and told me I was his for the night. Then he told me to take off my shirt and dance again. I did. Then he told me to take off my tee-strap and dance some more.

"After one dance in the nude, he told me to go take a shower and cut off my pubic hair. When I got out of the shower, he handed me a scissors. He stood beside me and watched while I cut off the hair. We were at the wash basin in the bathroom; there was a big mirror on the wall over the basin. He stood me in front of it and nearly pulled the hair out of my head while telling me to look at myself in the mirror."

"What happened after that?" the detective asked.

"Levi held my hands behind my back and pushed me out of the bathroom. He said he had to go out for a short time and to go have sex with Mark. He put it in a lot cruder way than that, but there was no mistaking what he meant.

Weber said she tried to stall for time by asking for a drink of water. "Levi was drinking a bottle of beer. He just laughed and poured the beer all over me."

"Where was the gun during this time?" Bramlitt asked.

"Mark had it. He was keeping it pointed at me to make

sure I did everything Levi told me to do. When Levi shoved me over to the bed to have sex with Mark, Mark laid the gun on the bed. He saw I had some bills wrapped around my finger. It was the fifty-three dollars I earned that night. He took the money off my finger and put it in his wallet."

"Why would you have the money wrapped around your finger?"

"When you dance in the nude and someone pays you, you don't have any place to put the money so you wrap it around your finger and secure it with a small rubber band."

Answering Bramlitt's question as to what happened next, Weber said the two men decided to take her rings. They got a couple of them off my fingers but couldn't get the last one. They were going to cut my finger off to get it. Before they could do that, I managed to pull the ring off myself and give it to them."

Following Levi's leaving of the room, according to Weber's further statements, Mark pulled her down on the bed and forced her to have oral, vaginal and anal sex. "I thought it would never end, and it probably wouldn't have if Levi hadn't come back to the room," the woman said. "Mark got up, and then I had to go through the same kind of sex business all over again with Levi."

When the assaults were over, the victim continued, Levi got up and told her to put on her white dress but to leave her boots and tee-strap off because they were going to Daytona Beach to get $1,500 which someone owed him.

"I told him I couldn't go to Daytona because I had to pick my daughter up from a babysitter's," she explained to the detective. "But that wasn't true—about my little girl being at a babysitter's, I mean. I do have a child, but she lives with her father in another state. Anyway, the lie didn't work. Levi told me I was going to Daytona, or else. He had the gun; and after I got into my white dress, he made me get into the back of the van with him. Mark got

180

into the front and did the driving." On the way to Daytona, Weber said, Levi again sexually abused her. "I tried to fight him off, but he ripped my white dress down the front, held the gun on me, and asked if I was going to be a good girl. I had to do all the disgusting things he told me to, or I would have been dead. When he finally finished with me, he wanted to see blood, so he bit my lips until they bled."

"What happened when you got to Daytona?" Bramlitt asked.

"We didn't get there—not that night, anyway. When we'd gone about halfway, Levi told Mark to turn around and go back to the Altamonte Springs motel. I didn't have anything on when we got there and had to cover myself up with my torn white dress while Levi was forcing me back into the room. There, the nightmare got even more terrifying."

According to Weber's statements, Levi made her line up cocaine on the bible in the motel room, snorted it, and again demanded that she do a couple of dances in the nude. Following that, he tore one of the bed sheets into strips, threw her on the bed, tied her hands behind her back and bound her feet together. Then, as he ran a knife up and down her chest, he forced her to fulfill more of his wild sexual fantasies.

"When I asked for a drink of water, he again poured beer all over me," the victim said. "And he kept me tied up all the rest of the night."

Weber said she fared a little better on Monday morning and recounted how Levi sent Mark to a shopping mall to buy her a dress, how Mark came back not only with the dress but also with a new watch for Levi and a bottle of aspirin. They gave me all but one of my rings back, because they said only the one they were keeping was worth anything," she added.

"Then they ordered me to get dressed because we were going to Daytona. When I put on my western shirt and boots, I discovered the three hundred and fifty dollars Levi had put into my boots the night before was gone."

"What do you think happened to it?" Detective Bramlitt asked Weber.

"I suspect Mark took the bills—the same as he took the fifty-three dollars I earned Sunday night—and put it in his wallet."

According to Weber, the drive to Daytona was relatively quiet, with both men nursing hangovers with aspirin they'd put in their backpack upon leaving Altamonte Springs. Arriving at a Daytona Beach motel, Levi held her at gunpoint in the van while Mark went to the office and got a top-floor room. On his return, Mark drove the van to the side of the building and parked it at the foot of the stairs leading up to the room.

Once all three of them got inside the room, Levi decided he wanted to go to the beach and sent Mark out to buy Karen a bathing suit. "Levi kept the gun in clear view all the time Mark was gone. I told him I wanted to look at the ocean, so he told me to go out and stand on the balcony. Out there, I walked a short distance around the back of the building and saw a guy in maroon shorts lounging by the pool below. I mouthed the words, 'Help me, help me,' but he didn't understand. By then, Levi came out and stood next to me. He told me I had to come back to the room."

Continuing with her story, Karen said Mark returned with the bathing suit, that she changed into it and that the three then went down to the beach. They stopped for hot dogs as they made their way through the sand to the boardwalk area.

"You never had an opportunity to escape during all this time?" Detective Bramlitt asked.

"I was never alone at any time. Either Levi or Mark was always at my side; and whichever one it was, he always had the gun."

Karen went on with her account of the happenings.

"Levi decided to rent a dune buggy for a drive along the beach. We had to walk a block off the beach to a service station to get one. I sat on a bench outside the office while Mark went inside to make the arrangements. Levi, with the gun in his pocket, was standing a short distance away. Some guy getting gas at the station came up to me and asked if anything was wrong. Before I could alert him to what was going on, Levi was right there, telling the guy not to bother me."

"What about when the three of you were driving on the beach in the dune buggy?" Bramlitt asked. "Didn't you see any officers in patrol cars you could have signalled for help?"

Karen explained that police cars passed them on two occasions, but she'd been afraid to make any kind of move because of the gun. "Besides," she said, "both Levi and Mark seemed to know I was looking for an opportunity to escape, and they were staying closer to me than ever. After we returned the dune buggy, they took me to a place a block away for lunch. Before we even went inside, Levi warned me to be quiet and not to say anything to anybody."

Weber said they spent nearly two hours inside the restaurant, during which time she tried to get the attention of a man and woman who were shooting darts. "Levi knew what I was doing, and he told me to get up and tell everybody what was going on if I wanted to. I thought he was testing me, playing games, but I pushed my chair back a bit. Mark immediately told me to sit still and shut up or I was going to be a dead lady."

The rest of the afternoon was spent on the beach, following which the three returned to the motel room and dressed for an evening on the town. Karen said the night started with dinner at a seafood restaurant where she ate only a shrimp cocktail and was not allowed to get up from her chair.

Following that, they went to a saloon, which she immediately knew was a bikers' bar, because there were about 200 Harleys and a lot of people dressed in leather outside. "But it was inside where I got really scared," she said. "A couple of bikers beat the daylights out of some guy and threw him into the street. A couple of others were throwing stools across the bar. I was afraid I was going to get gang-raped before we got out of there."

When they left and got into the van, Karen continued, Levi told Mark to head back to Fern Park. "I was in the back of the van with Levi, and I noticed for the first time that there was a shotgun there. Levi also still had the handgun. He was very drunk, very tired and talked quietly. He told me he was from Colorado, was married, had two sons and a dog named Coty."

The drive was uneventful, Karen said, until Mark reached an area about a mile and a half from the Royal Motel. "Then Levi suddenly told Mark to turn around and drive back to the Daytona Beach motel. There, Levi made me sleep in the van with him; Mark went up and slept in the room. When it got daylight, Levi took me up there with him. I got raped again. It was ten o'clock this morning before I finally found a way to escape."

Detective Bramlitt commented on the complexity of the case, due to the crimes taking place in two different counties—Seminole and Volusia. "I can put out warrants for the arrest of Levi and Mark on the Daytona Beach crimes. The warrants will have to be made out for John Doe number one and John Doe number two, since you knew these men only as Levi and Mark. You'll have to report the Fern Park and Altamonte Springs assaults to the Seminole County Sheriff's Department in Sanford. Warrants on the crimes allegedly committed there will have to come from that office."

Weber said she knew Sergeant John Thorpe at the Seminole County Sheriff's Department and would talk with him in the morning. Bramlitt then arranged for the victim to be transported to the Royal Motel in Fern Park.

The following morning, Wednesday, detectives set about obtaining warrants, charging each of the two men with two counts of sexual battery between November 9th and November 12th at or near Daytona Beach, without the consent of the victim and using or threatening to use in the process a deadly weapon: to wit, a gun. They also charged the men with physically striking the victim several times and holding her against her will in a van they both occupied.

An incoming report on the 1980 Chevy van with the Brevard County tag number said the van had been stolen in Brevard County on October 25th. Processing of the vehicle had turned up a number of latent prints and some photos. Bramlitt, believing the van was of no further value in the investigation, arranged to have Brevard County deputies pick the vehicle up for return to its rightful owner.

On that same morning, Sergeant John Thorpe of the Seminole County Sheriff's Department was not surprised at receiving a phone call from Karen Weber. "Can you come to the office and make a statement?" he asked.

Weber reminded him that she had no transportation, so Thorpe told her to stay at her motel and he would drive there to pick her up.

During the trip from Sanford to Fern Park, Thorpe mentally reviewed the happenstance under which he'd met Karen Weber. It took place in mid-October, at which time the woman was living in Sanford with a man named Henry. On the night of the incident, she was supposed to play her guitar with a local band at a barn-type night spot; and according to her story, she walked to the city park at 9:00 p.m. to practice.

Strumming away on a park bench, she suddenly felt someone behind her. She turned around and saw "the guy in the red bandanna," who, she said, had been following her for the past five weeks. She told Thorpe she'd seen this man at least five times a day during that time. "He

185

was always walking past my house," she had explained. "He never said anything, just stood and stared."

Frightened at seeing her mysterious follower in the park, she ran home. There, Henry, upset that she hadn't kept her band engagement and so would not be bringing money home, wouldn't let her into the house. She didn't know where to go so she just began walking aimlessly. A car with two men in it pulled alongside, and one of them said something she didn't catch. Then she saw that the other man was the guy in the red bandanna. In stark terror, she ran to a store across the street and telephoned the sheriff's office.

Sergeant Thorpe responded to her call; and upon seeing how near to hysteria she really was, arranged through an Orange County deputy to have her taken to a crisis center in Orlando. After a few days there, she telephoned Thorpe to tell him she had a job at the Tempest Lounge and one of the customers had helped her get a room at the Royal Motel on credit.

Thorpe reached the motel, picked up Karen and drove her back to his office. Once there, he had her sign a cover sheet for the statements she was about to make. "Your signature indicates your statements will be truthful and accurate," he explained.

Following that, Karen recounted in detail the 48 hours of rape, torture and fear she had earlier described to Detective Debbie Bramlitt.

At the close of the interview, Thorpe had a deputy drive the victim to her motel while he went about the business of obtaining arrest warrants on charges of kidnapping, five counts of sexual battery with a deadly weapon and robbery with a firearm or deadly weapon.

Shortly after Weber's return to the Royal Motel, Volusia County Detective Bramlitt got to her with photos recovered from the Chevy van. The victim identified the subjects in the photos as the men she knew as Levi and Mark. Bramlitt then went to the Seminole County Sheriff's Department where she gave copies of the photos to Sergeant Thorpe.

Despite nationwide alerts and the release of composite sketches of the two John Does through the news media, nothing in the investigation moved forward. Then on November 26th, in a seemingly unrelated incident, a Winter Park female police officer, checking tag numbers for a stolen 1978 black van, spotted the vehicle outside a local motel. As she radioed for backup, two men came out of the ground-floor room and headed toward the van. Seeing the police car, they jumped into the van and sped away.

The female officer followed in what turned out to be a 15-mile, high-speed chase. Despite her flashing lights, the driver of the van did not bring the vehicle to a halt until he reached Altamonte Springs and a convergence of other officers in police cars. The men refused to give their names or other identifying information. They were arrested as John Does and booked into the Seminole County Correctional Facility on a charge of grand theft auto.

Events moved swiftly after that. Officers at the correctional facilities, believing the two auto-theft suspects fit the descriptions of the two men being sought in the Karen Weber case, contacted Sergeant Thorpe. Thorpe, with photos of the men (identified by Weber as her kidnappers) in hand, proceeded to the facility. There, he found a perfect match of the arrested men and the photographs.

He quickly drove to Fern Park, picked up Karen Weber and took her to the correctional facility. There, the woman identified the two John Does as the Levi and Mark of her real-life nightmare.

A comparison of Levi and Mark's fingerprints taken at the jail with those lifted from the stolen 1980 Chevy van led to the identification of Levi as Robert Charles Buroker, 38, and of Mark as Stormy Dee Faddis, 23. Buroker, as he told Weber, lived in Colorado; his half-brother Faddis had escaped in late September from the

Cocoa Correctional Facility where he was serving a 10-year sentence on a burglary conviction.

Further investigation revealed charges outstanding against Buroker and Faddis in three Orange County rape cases strikingly similar to the Weber case. All three assaults had taken place during a two-week period shortly before the Karen Weber abduction.

Buroker and Faddis went to trial in Seminole County on April 7, 1986, facing charges of kidnapping, armed robbery and five counts of sexual battery. Before jury selection, Circuit Judge Emory Cross ruled that prosecuting attorneys could present testimony about the three Orange County cases during the trial.

On April 11th, a six-person jury convicted the two half-brothers of kidnapping, armed robbery and four of the five counts of sexual battery.

Seminole County Assistant State Attorney Dan Marblestone recommended life imprisonment for both Buroker and Faddis on each of three of the sexual battery counts; on each of the remaining charges (one sexual battery, kidnapping and armed robbery), Marblestone recommended 100 years for Buroker and 70 years for Faddis.

EDITOR'S NOTE:
*Karen Weber and Henry, and the Tempest Lounge and Royal Motel are not the real names of the persons and places so named in the foregoing story. Fictitious names have been used because there is no reason for public interest in the identities of these persons and places.*

# "BEHEADED AND CASTRATED ALIVE!"

## by Christofer Pierson

At 3:30 p.m. on the warm spring afternoon of Thursday, May 18, 1978, a Rutgers University bus driver pulled into the stop near St. Peters Medical Center in New Brunswick, New Jersey. Boarding the bus was a paunchy, middle-aged man with greasy brown hair that fell in a jumble over his horn-rimmed glasses. Behind his dirty lenses, the man's gray eyes focused into an intense, if somewhat vacant stare. The passenger nervously asked to be taken to the Rutgers Mental Health Clinic in Piscataway and took his seat directly behind the driver.

As the driver pulled his bus back onto the street, he glanced into his rear-view mirror. His eyes were met by the deadened stare of the strange man behind him. The driver casually glanced at other passengers on the bus and returned his attention to the road. Within seconds, the driver sensed the icy gaze of the passenger behind him, apparently probing him from the mirror. The driver looked up. The passenger was now staring straight at him.

The driver shook off a cold shiver running down his neck. He looked back at the road, trying to put the strange man out of his mind. Too soon for the driver's comfort, the reflection of the passenger's eyes in the rear-view mirror etched into the driver's brain. He looked up again. The unblinking passenger's eyes were riveted to his own in the mirror.

After what seemed like an eternity of enduring the passenger's gaze, the driver pulled the bus into the stop in front of the mental health clinic. The strange man stood up and quietly left the bus. The driver watched the man step onto the curb and then slammed the door shut behind him. The driver wiped the sweat from the back of his neck with his hand and pulled his bus back into the street, relieved that the strange passenger had gotten off. What was *that* guy's problem? the driver wondered to himself.

About an hour later, at 4:00 p.m., the New Brunswick police received a call from Dr. Kris Fischer, a psychiatrist at the Rutgers Mental Health Clinic. Dr. Fischer told the dispatcher that a patient at the clinic had just told him a strange story about a dead body in a van he had left parked in front of the county jail.

New Brunswick police received a similar call at 11:30 that morning.

"I'm in trouble," the nervous man on the other end of the line had stammered into the phone. "I think—I think I hurt somebody last night."

The dispatcher calmed down the caller and elicited the information that the man had left a car parked in front of the old jailhouse. There was something in the car, the man said—it was a dead body.

The dispatcher asked the caller if he would be willing to meet police in front of the jail. The man agreed and quickly hung up.

Moments later, officers were standing on the sidewalk outside the jail, alternating their attention between the vehicles parked on the street and passersby on the pavement. There were several cars of all types parked in front of and on the sides of the Victorian-age jail, a squat, forbidding-looking brick building just outside the modern county administration complex, which houses the Middlesex County Prosecutor's Office and its bureau of detectives.

The officers sized up each vehicle from the exterior. It was impossible to fathom which was the one the nervous man had spoken of. The minutes ticked by with no sign of the caller surfacing. The officers took a slow walk around the block, eyeing all the vehicles parked on the streets.

It occurred to the officers as they took a third or fourth stroll around the block that the caller might have altered or withheld a part of his story. Perhaps the caller had actually left a different kind of vehicle—a van or a pickup, or perhaps not any vehicle at all—and had only said he'd left a car there to throw cops off his scent in case he changed his mind about showing up. The caller, if he wasn't just a crank, might have been fighting two contradictory impulses: one to confess, and one to get away with murder.

As the minutes passed by, and then an hour, with no sign of the nervous caller coming to claim his car, the police knew that the second of the two impulses had probably gotten the best of the would-be confessor. The cops looked at each other, shrugged their shoulders, and returned to headquarters, frustrated by their wild goose chase.

At 1:30 that afternoon, the nervous man called again. This time he told the dispatcher that the body was in a "blue van" parked near the county jail. The police returned to the street immediately, but there were no blue vans parked anywhere near the jail. Frustrated again, the cops returned to headquarters.

Police did not know it then, but there really was a body in one of the vehicles parked near the jail.

The night before the police received the calls about the body in the van, Joey Pichirallo, a 31-year-old restaurant worker and amateur flower arranger from Bricktown, New Jersey, went with a relative and her boyfriend to the

191

restaurant where Joey worked to have a few drinks on his night off. They were planning a little excursion that night to Asbury Park. Nationally famous as the home of Bruce Springsteen, Asbury Park has long enjoyed a reputation among central New Jerseyites as something of a hot spot. Joey and his companions were in the mood to party, and they knew that Asbury Park was the place to go for it.

On one of the city's main drags, there's a restaurant/ bar that most passersby probably wouldn't give any attention to. From the outside, it looks like a typical neighborhood hole in the wall. The exterior seediness, however, masks a luxuriously decadent interior. Through the front door, the bar beckons patrons of different sexual inclinations in three different directions. To the right, a comfortable room attracts heterosexual singles. Down the plush hallway and to the left, a large dance floor is crowded primarily with gay men most nights of the week. At the far end of the gay men's portion of the bar, a staircase leads to a lesbian club on the second floor.

This was the bar Joey Pichirallo and his companions had come to on the night of Wednesday, May 17, 1978. The trio met up with other friends and partied well into the night. At 3:30 a.m., a boisterous crowd of friends was gathered on the sidewalk outside the bar, deciding what to do next.

Joey excused himself from the group and slipped down the street away from the bar. A couple in the group turned away from the discussion and watched Joey disappear into the night. Did Joey meet someone? his friends wondered as he vanished from view. The fleeting glimpse would be the last time anyone in the group would see Joey Pichirallo before he met his grisly fate.

Joey had, in fact, met someone that night. That person would be seated in a room at the Rutgers Mental Health Clinic the following afternoon, telling doctors a strange story about a dead body in his van.

Shortly after 5:00 on the afternoon of May 18th,

Detective-Sergeant John F. Cannon and Detective Ron Valdata of the New Brunswick Police Department received a call from headquarters to investigate the red van parked in the vicinity of the old jail. The police had finally received an accurate description of the van and its location: a red Ford with New Jersey license plates 763-IRN parked on Kirkpatrick Street in the Kennedy Square area.

The detectives stepped up to the vehicle and peered into its dark interior. The window curtains were drawn, and what little light filtering through them was not enough to reveal the van's secrets. Detective Cannon walked over to the front of the vehicle and noticed a parking ticket stuck under the windshield wiper. Apparently, it had been issued that day at 1:49 p.m., only moments after the second call to police headquarters reporting the body in the van.

Not wanting to break into the van for fear of damaging evidence in the process, the detectives decided to drive to the mental health center in Piscataway and meet the van's owner. They hoped he would provide them with the keys.

At the center, the detectives met Dr. Rachel Kline, the psychiatrist who had examined the van's alleged owner when he first showed up at the clinic. She directed the sleuths to a paunchy, middle-aged man in her office. The man with the intense stare identified himself as John Pinte of Old Bridge, New Jersey.

Detective Sergeant Cannon introduced himself and Detective Valdata to Pinte and asked, "What seems to be the problem?"

"I have many problems," Pinte said matter-of-factly. "I think I hurt someone last night. There's a dead body in my van."

"Is it a man or a woman?" Cannon asked.

"I don't know," Pinte replied. "I don't even know how it got there."

"We found the van," Canon said. "It had a ticket on the

windshield. You want us to check it out for you?"

Pinte said that he would. He reached into his pocket, pulled out a set of keys, and handed them over to the detective.

Moments later on the street in front of the jail, Detective-Sergeant Cannon and Detective Valdata approached the red van. Cannon slid the key into the lock on one of the side doors, turned the key, and pulled the door open.

Sunlight flooded the cavernous interior of the van, exposing a pile of heavily blood-soaked newspapers and plastic bags in the center of the floor behind the driver's seat. Protruding from under the pile was the muscular form of a bare male leg. The bloodless pallor of the bare leg indicated to the sleuths that the body beneath the papers was quite dead.

Detective Cannon took a step back and exhaled the breath he had been holding. He relocked the van and returned to his own car to radio headquarters for homicide detectives and an identification expert. The New Brunswick police immediately notified the Middlesex County Prosecutor's Office.

Detective-Sergeant James Marko of the New Brunswick PD was between shifts at headquarters when the call came over the radio reporting Detectives Cannon and Valdata's discovery. Marko and Detective Charles Stankovitz radioed Cannon, who directed them to go with Detective Valdata to the mental health clinic and bring John Pinte into headquarters for questioning.

While the suspect was being picked up, Detective-Sergeant Robert Velloso, the "ID man," arrived at the crime scene. The area in front of the jail was suddenly buzzing with activity as officers and crime scene technicians made a barrier around the scene's periphery. Cannon drew a diagram of the area while Velloso snapped color and black-and-white photographs of the body in the van as it was found. When the preliminary work was done, the two investigators carefully removed the blood-soaked coverings from the body.

It was instantly clear where all the blood had come from. Apparently, the body had been viciously mutilated. The victim, a young white male with shoulder-length dark hair, lay in a slightly twisted position on his back. He was naked but for a blue windbreaker that was open and barely covering his upper body. The victim's almost completely severed head was connected to his shoulders only by a thin thread of flesh. All that was left of the nose and upper lip were bright red wounds where they had been torn away with some kind of serrated blade. A gash, 12 inches long and 2 or more inches wide, ran up the victim's abdomen, exposing muscle and tissue. The victim's intestines had been removed and placed—along with the severed nose and lip—in a plastic bag between his legs. The scrotum was also slashed open. The body was otherwise marked with multiple puncture wounds and large, dark blue bruises.

Detective-Sergeant Cannon observed on the dashboard a bloodstained serrated steak knife, which appeared to have been the weapon that caused at least some of the damage to the victim's body. The abrasions on the victim's legs resembled those that occur when a person is struck or run over by a moving vehicle, Cannon noted.

At 6:45 p.m., Detective Anthony Tauriello of the Middlesex County Prosecutor's Office arrived at the scene and was briefed by New Brunswick's Detective Cannon. (Homicide investigations in New Jersey are shared by detectives not only from the local police force, but from the county sheriff's and the county prosecutor's offices as well.) While Detective Velloso photographed the exposed body, Cannon called for the corpse to be removed to Perth Amboy General Hospital for autopsy. He then called for the van to be taken to New Brunswick Police Headquarters for a detailed investigation of the vehicle's interior. Once the scene was cleared of the evidence, at approximately 8:30 p.m., Detectives Cannon and Tauriello left for headquarters.

Detectives Marko, Stankovitz, and Valdata, in the meantime, had gone to the clinic and spoken with Dr. Fischer, Dr. Kline, and another psychiatrist. The doctors told the sleuths that they hadn't believed John Pinte's story at first and had asked him to undergo sodium amathol treatment. Like the related compound sodium pentothal, sodium amathol acts as a "truth serum." Pinte had told the physicians the exact same story after receiving the treatment. The doctors said they had no reason to doubt him then, and that was when they decided to notify the police.

Detective Stankovitz advised John Pinte of his rights and had him sign a "rights card" with the Miranda warnings printed on it. The detectives then transported the suspect to headquarters. Detective Cannon, now back from the crime scene, again advised Pinte of his rights. The suspect was led into an interrogation room by Detectives Marko and Tauriello.

While John Pinte chain-smoked the better part of two packs of filterless cigarettes, he told Detectives Tauriello and Marko what he claimed to remember about the previous night, Wednesday, May 17th, and the early hours of Thursday, May 18th.

John Pinte recalled being at an Alcoholics Anonymous meeting in Bradley Beach early that Wednesday evening. He said he was one of the guest speakers and didn't leave the meeting until sometime after 10:30. A fog had descended upon the Jersey shore by then, and as Pinte was driving his red van home, he got lost. After a while, Pinte said, he came upon a tavern and decided to stop and have some drinks. He couldn't say where he was exactly, but he thought he might have been at a bar that he frequented in Long Branch or, at least, one similar to it.

Though vague about which bar he was in — or even which town the bar was in — Pinte was somewhat better able to describe the establishment's interior. He recalled being waited on by a female bartender, and he remembered seeing pinball machines and a pool table inside. He was not sure how long he had stayed, but he knew he had eight drinks before he bought a six-pack to take with him on the road. Pinte said the bar was still relatively busy, and he assumed it was well before closing time when he returned to his locked van in the tavern's crowded parking lot.

It was at this point in the story that the suspect became vague, not only in his memory, but in his relation of what he said he could remember. The night had apparently become a blur to Pinte, and he could only recall a few extraordinary details.

Pinte said he thought it was when he returned to his van that he first saw the mutilated body in the back. He couldn't stand to look at the dismembered corpse, he said. He had to cover it with papers. He was frightened, he said — frightened of the dead body.

In one of the more incredible portions of his story, John Pinte said that while he was driving in the fog and fretting over the body in his van, a police cruiser pulled him over. Three officers from the cruiser approached Pinte's van. All they wanted, Pinte said, was to tell him he was driving without lights and to ask him to switch them on. Pinte did so and, leaving the officers behind, he continued to drive his red van with the dead body in the back through the foggy night.

The suspect related that he thought he was driving on Route 35, but he wasn't certain. He remembered passing through a rural area and suddenly coming upon a place where there were a lot of people. He passed a sign with the words "Asbury Park" on it, but he wasn't sure if he was actually in Asbury Park. He didn't know what time it was, either, only that it was "very late."

Pinte said he finally found his way home at about 7:30 in the morning. His wife was angry with him for being out so late, he said. He lay down only for about an hour and then got up. He said he told his wife he had to go to work.

In fact, Pinte told the two sleuths, he wanted to find some place to get rid of the body. He left his house at about 9:30 and drove to his office in Edison—"to pick up parts," he said enigmatically. He then drove to Bedminster and almost stopped twice to dump the body there along Route 22. But he decided that he couldn't just dump the body. He resolved instead to turn his van over to the police.

So Pinte drove to New Brunswick and left the van near the jail. He said he tried to call police several times and couldn't get anyone to help him, so he decided to walk to St. Peters Medical Center to see if he could get psychiatric help there. A receptionist in the hospital's emergency room directed him to the Rutgers Mental Health Clinic.

"I know something's wrong with me," Pinte told the detectives. "I wish someone would help me find out what it is."

When Detective-Sergeant Marko left the room momentarily to get coffee for the suspect, Pinte told Detective Tauriello that there was a pair of bloody gray trousers in the closet in his apartment. Before Tauriello could pursue the point, Marko returned, and Pinte resumed speaking about his mental health.

The suspect told the sleuths that he had been institutionalized "at least twice before." On one occasion, Pinte said he had stabbed a woman 16 times, but he couldn't recall actually wielding the knife in the attack. In that incident, he told the sleuths, he had been drinking heavily in a Jersey City bar when suddenly "people were chasing me.

"I didn't think I did it until I read about the evidence later," Pinte said of the earlier incident. "I had to have done this. It couldn't have been done by anyone else."

Police would find out from a background check on the

198

suspect that, in September 1974, John Pinte had indeed followed a woman into the ladies' room at a Jersey City bar and had stabbed her 17 times. The victim, whom Pinte did not know, had survived, and after a trial in June 1975, Pinte was given a two-to-three-year sentence in the New Jersey State Prison for atrocious assault and battery. (It was probably from documents produced at that trial that Pinte had "read about the evidence" and "convinced" himself of his guilt.) He was released on parole after only two years.

Pinte told Marko and Tauriello that his violent past included an earlier attempt to strangle a boy, whom he also chose at random, on a street in Jersey City. He claimed he had been drinking heavily prior to that attack as well. Pinte told Marko and Tauriello that he had stopped himself and turned himself in to police. No charges were filed against him, and he voluntarily checked himself into Meadowview Hospital in Secaucus for observation. *"They* didn't find out what was wrong with me, either," the suspect said.

It was getting late, and Pinte said he didn't think he should say any more. He was taken to a cell in the old jail outside of which he had left his red van earlier that same day.

While the suspect was being interviewed, New Brunswick and Middlesex County detectives continued to probe the evidence at hand.

Detective-Sergeant Cannon had obtained John Pinte's signature on a set of search warrants for his impounded vehicle, his house, his person, and others of his vehicles. Detective Velloso had also taken samples of the suspect's hair and fingernails and had photographed him. Cannon and Velloso then proceeded to the garage where the red van was waiting for a thorough going-over.

Behind the red van's front seat, the detectives found a brown paper bag that held a wallet and several pieces of identification papers and credit cards. The paper and plastic had all been ripped to shreds. Cannon pieced together the shredded driver's license and made out the bearer's name and address: Joey Pichirallo of Bricktown, New Jersey.

The victim's identity would be confirmed by a positive comparison of prints Detective Velloso took from the body with those made of Joey Pichirallo in Bricktown after he had been the victim of a burglary some years before.

In the paper bag that held the victim's wallet and identification papers, the detectives also found a receipt from a local grocery store chain. The receipt had on it the number 570 or 579 — the last digit was partially obscured — and the sleuths reasoned it referred to the particular store in the chain from which the purchases were made. Another number on the receipt was presumed to refer to a particular cashier or cash register at the store.

Also found in the van on the first night of the investigation was a pair of men's undershorts that were stained on the front with blood. They appeared to be too large to have belonged to the victim, but could very well have been John Pinte's. A partial pack of filterless cigarettes different from those Pinte smoked was also found between the driver's and passenger's seats. It was later discovered to be the preferred brand of the victim.

The most significant piece of evidence found in the van were those the detectives had found earlier in the day: the serrated steak knife, a box of plastic garbage bags, and a pair of bloodstained plastic gloves. All these items appeared to be brand new. They were presumed to have been purchased at the grocery store whose receipt was found in the brown paper bag amid Joey Pichirallo's shredded identification papers.

It was not known at the end of the first day of the investigation — though it would soon become painfully clear — that John Pinte was unwilling or unable to help detectives reconstruct the events leading up to Joey

Pichirallo's death and mutilation. Pinte never changed his official story. He continued to maintain that he merely found an already dead and mutilated body in his van. It was up to the sleuths to retrace Pinte's steps and determine where and when the murder had occurred. It was up to the law to prove John Pinte murdered Joey Pichirallo.

Toward that end, the detectives would have to locate the bar where Pinte claimed he spent the evening of May 17th—and possible witnesses at the bar—to confirm or refute his story. They would have to find the supermarket where the items used to mutilate Joey Pichirallo's body were bought and verify whether or not Pinte, in fact, had purchased the items. The interior of the van, the serrated knife, the plastic gloves and other items found at the scene would have to be raked thoroughly for fingerprints. Joey Pichirallo's relatives would have to be questioned for possible information that might prove helpful in establishing a time frame and possibly a motive for the murder.

The mystery did not clear on the morning of Friday, May 19th, when Dr. Marvin Shuster, New Brunswick's Detective-Sergeant Velloso, and Detective Casimir Smerecki of the prosecutor's office met at the Perth Amboy General Hospital Morgue for the autopsy on Joey Pichirallo's body. Although some previously undetected details came to light, the autopsy mostly confirmed what the first detectives on the scene had suspected about the nature of Joey's death.

Joey Pichirallo had apparently been stabbed numerous times, with most of the stab wounds centered around his chest. One knife thrust had penetrated the victim's left lung, but it was unlikely that it was the sole cause of death. The knife had not cut any major arteries there, and bleeding would have been slow, depending on the body's exertions.

The victim had also suffered numerous broken ribs and a ruptured spleen, injuries thought to have been caused by his having been run over by a vehicle. Also noted on the right side of the victim's skull was a bruise where he seemed to have been struck with some kind of blunt instrument.

Dr. Shuster examined the areas of mutilation on the body and discovered that one of the victim's testicles was missing. It appeared to have been manually removed rather than to have escaped through the gash in the victim's scrotum. The missing organ was not in the plastic bag in which the victim's intestines, nose, and upper lip had been stuffed, and it was never found by investigators.

It was impossible to determine the order of the injuries to Joey Pichirallo's body. Because blood doesn't circulate after death, superficial injuries to corpses do not leave bruises. Thus, pathologists can usually determine whether an injury was sustained before or after death by the presence or absence of bruises under the skin. In Joey Pichirallo's case, there were bruises, but Dr. Shuster was cautious about the significance of this finding.

Joey Pichirallo had been completely drained of blood. The drainage had probably occurred while the killer was attempting to decapitate the body. The body's almost complete absence of lividity marks, which result after death when uncirculated blood gravitates into patches on the underside of a body, suggested that the victim's blood had drained quickly after he died—and possibly even as he was dying.

Dr. Shuster was, therefore, unable to determine whether the victim had died as a result of being stabbed, run over by a vehicle, or mutilated alive. The only thing he could say for certain about the order of the injuries was that they had occurred in a very short time frame, one right after the other.

At 2:30 on the afternoon of May 19th, John Pinte was arraigned before Superior Court Judge John Bachman at the Middlesex County Courthouse on one charge of murder. Judge Bachman set bail at $150,000, and Pinte was remanded to the county jail in lieu of that amount.

Meanwhile, detectives were feverishly trying to reconstruct the events leading up to Joey Pichirallo's death.

Detective Jack Taormino of the New Brunswick PD was assigned to retrace Pinte's footsteps from the moment he arrived in New Brunswick to leave the van at the county jail until his arrest. Taormino located witnesses at the hospital and mental health clinic, as well as the Rutgers University bus driver who had transported Pinte to the clinic. All these people remembered the disturbed man from their encounters with him the previous day.

Meanwhile, Detective-Sergeant Cannon interviewed the couple who had last seen Joey Pichirallo alive. They had never seen or heard of John Pinte, and, as it turned out, neither had any of Joey's relatives or other acquaintances. No one could offer any reason why Pinte might have wanted to kill Joey, whom he clearly hadn't met until May 18th. Cannon also went to a bar in Bradley Beach that Pinte had mentioned in his interrogation with Detectives Tauriello and Marko. None of the bartenders recognized either Pinte or Joey Pichirallo from photographs.

Also on the 19th, Cannon and Lieutenant Charles F. Aumick of New Brunswick went to Pinte's apartment in Old Bridge and spoke with the suspect's relatives. One relative told Cannon that Pinte had called him in the middle of the night to say he was "in big trouble and may have hit or hurt someone." Lieutenant Aumick conducted a search of Pinte's apartment and turned up some items of interest: the trousers Pinte claimed to have worn the night before, some wet articles of men's clothing, and several serrated steak knives similar to the one found in the van. A search of Pinte's other two vehicles, as expected, failed to produce any worthwhile evidence.

The Pinte investigation slowed to a near standstill over the summer of 1978 as detectives struggled to find any threads that would lead them to the full story behind Joey Pichirallo's murder. While sleuths managed to track down the grocery store where the items found in Pinte's van had been purchased, no one at the store remembered dealing with Pinte.

Detectives John Mandeville and Harold Bott of the prosecutor's office spent a good part of the summer trying to locate a bar — *any* bar — along the route Pinte had described where witnesses might have seen Pinte and Joey Pichirallo together. The detectives' footwork, while it provided them with an education on the wilder side of New Jersey nightlife that they hadn't bargained for, ultimately proved fruitless. None of the dozens of potential witnesses Detectives Mandeville and Bott questioned remembered seeing the suspect and the victim together on May 18th.

The first real break in the case came in September when the FBI sent back results on their test of some of the items the New Jersey investigators had submitted for analysis. The FBI technicians concluded that bloody fingerprints found on the inside and outside of one of the rubber gloves found in Pinte's van were, in fact, John Pinte's. The detectives were puzzled over the appearance of a single bloody fingerprint on the *inside* of the tight-fitting glove, but the FBI was unable to answer their question about how it got there.

The positive match on the prints was the next best thing to the "smoking gun" that Prosecutor Richard S. Rebeck and Assistant Prosecutor Thomas Kapsak, who would prosecute the case, were hoping for. It would be very difficult for Pinte's attorney to argue against the bloody fingerprints as proof positive that Pinte had actually participated in Joey Pichirallo's death.

However, while they were compelling pieces of evidence, the fingerprints remained, after all, circumstantial. Assistant Prosecutor Kapsak would require some substantiating evidence to ensure a conviction. A plausible version of events on the night of May 17th and 18th would help, but investigators continued through the fall to be frustrated in their attempts to reconstruct the murder.

And John Pinte was still not talking—at least, not to prosecutors.

On December 25, 1987, Ronnie Monaco composed a letter to Prosecutor Rebeck's office from his cell in the Middlesex County prison. "I'm writhing in regards to the case of John Pinto [sic]," Monaco wrote. "I'm sure your office is interested in conversations I've had with John Pinto. I've become very friendly with him." Monaco went on to write that Pinte (whom he persisted in calling Pinto) had told him he "killed a queer in a graveyard . . . and then cut him up with an ax and hacksaw after Pinto left a AA meeting. . . .

"If you think I'm b-----g," Monaco's letter continued, "why don't you talk to me and find out?"

Monaco's missive was received in the prosecutor's office on December 27th after the Christmas holiday. The prosecutors read the letter, as Monaco had predicted, with considerable interest. But their interest was mitigated by caution.

Assistant Prosecutor Kapsak was well aware that jailhouse informants are not the most reliable witnesses. Juries tend to be suspicious of any con who tattles on his peers, if only because a tattling con is still a con. Furthermore, snitching involves a very high degree of selfishness. No prisoner informs on another without expecting some deferential treatment from the authorities in return.

But the risk involved in informing on other cons is extremely high: It's usually punishable by death, according to the brutal, unwritten code of prison society. A prisoner would have to be crazy to dabble in snitching just to get a cell with a better view. Snitches have to know what they're doing.

The problem with expert snitches, from a prosecutor's standpoint, is that they are masters of a dangerous game. They might be holding aces, but they could just as easily be bluffing. Prosecutor Kapsak knew that Ronnie Monaco was an expert snitch. Monaco had achieved some fame beyond New Jersey judicial circles for serving as a jail-house informant in a well-publicized case a few years before. Kapsak decided to communicate to Monaco that he had reservations about the letter of December 25th.

Monaco was undeterred, however, and sent another letter to the prosecutor's office a few days later. Kapsak remained cautious and returned with another expression of his reservations about the veracity of Monaco's information.

To Kapsak's surprise, Monaco sent a third letter a few days later, this time with an astonishing piece of news. Monaco, who was undoubtedly aware that the prosecutor needed solid evidence before he'd believe the informant, had gotten John Pinte to draw him a map of the murder scene. If a handwriting expert could prove that the map was by the suspect's hand, Kapsak would have a damning piece of evidence against Pinte. Now the prosecutor was ready to talk with Monaco.

When Monaco was finished with his story, the transcription came to 32 pages. Although Kapsak remained skeptical about some of the information Monaco supplied, much of Monaco's story explained the evidence in a way that only someone who had witnessed the murder would be able to.

Monaco was unclear about when and where John Pinte and Joey Pichirallo had first met. At one point, he said the pair had met early in the night of May 17th at the restaurant where Joey worked and where he was dining with his relative on his night off. Later, Monaco said Joey met Pinte in Asbury Park inside the bar from which Joey disappeared, and at another point he said they met outside the bar after Joey left the group he had been with. In any case, Monaco was more credible about events after Joey walked away from his friends outside the bar in Asbury Park.

Pinte told Monaco that Joey had been arguing with his relative about whether or not they should end or continue

206

the evening. The consensus among Joey's friends was that enough was enough for the night; it was time to go home. Joey didn't like the idea, and when he left his friends, Pinte said, Pinte took Joey into his van, concealing him from view.

The two men sat parked on a street near the bar and watched the group Joey had been with as they searched for their missing companion. Pinte told Monaco that Joey was enjoying the attention his friends afforded him in his absence. When the crowd finally gave up on Joey and dispersed, Pinte said, he and Joey had sex in the parked van.

Monaco related that things began to go sour between Pinte and Joey after the sex. The pair began to argue as they drove off in search of a six-pack of beer. The argument only got louder as Pinte drove his red van, with six-pack in tow, toward the Monmouth Memorial Cemetery at the intersection of New Jersey Highways 33 and 34. At that point, Pinte told Monaco, he got sick of Joey's remonstrations. Pinte grabbed a mallet he kept between the driver's and passenger's seat and slammed it into Joey's head.

While Joey was reeling from the blow, Pinte drove into the entrance of the graveyard. He reached over and opened Joey's door and pushed the wounded man out of the van. As Joey lay on the ground struggling to recover, Pinte opened one of the beers and watched his victim writhing in agony. Slowly and unsteadily, Joey stood up and stared into the bright headlights of the van. Pinte revved the van's engine. He put the car in gear and drove straight for Joey, knocking him back to the ground and running him over. Pinte bragged to Monaco that Joey was pinned under the van's wheels, and Pinte had to put the van in reverse to free the vehicle from its victim.

With Joey writhing on the ground in the van's headlights, Pinte grabbed the serrated knife he had been keeping handy and sprang out of the van.

"I'm gonna fix you, you queer bitch!" Pinte yelled at Joey.

"What are you doing this to me for, John?" Joey allegedly said. "Why don't you leave me alone?"

Pinte told Monaco that he dragged Joey to the side of the van and flourished the knife.

"I'm gonna fix you," Pinte said. "You don't want me, you ain't gettin' nobody!" Pinte bragged that he then sliced open Joey's scrotum.

Monaco did not give a coherent account of events after the half-castration, but he unwittingly answered a question that had still been puzzling Assistant Prosecutor Kapsak and the detectives who had been working the case. Pinte told Monaco that, at one point in his mutilation of the body, he paused to have a beer. Pinte said that he took off his rubber gloves during his beer break, which explains how a bloody fingerprint came to appear on the outside of one finger of the glove. It also suggests how the fingerprint came to appear on the inside. Since Pinte's hand must have been bloody in order to leave the first print on the outside of the glove, it must have been bloody when he put the glove back on.

Assistant Prosecutor Kapsak, Detective Casimir Smerecki, and Detective-Sergeant Velloso investigated the cemetery on January 9, 1979, but by then, there was no evidence worth collecting. In order to verify Ronnie Monaco's account, the investigators gave him a polygraph test, which he passed with distinction. Monaco was moved to a new cell while he, Kapsak, and Pinte waited for the murder trial to begin on January 29, 1979.

John Pinte was represented by Thomas Spinello of the Public Defender's Office in Newark. Spinello's objective was to discredit Ronnie Monaco as a witness. He argued before the jury that because Monaco was a longtime informant, he knew well how prosecutors build their cases. Spinello asserted that Monaco had constructed a clever lie about John Pinte, because Monaco knew just what As-

208

sistant Prosecutor Kapsak wanted to hear. Spinello called Superintendent Clinton Pagano of the New Jersey State Police to testify to that effect.

After Monaco had been an informant for Superintendent Pagano during an earlier case, the informant and the superintendent had a falling out. Monaco turned on the state police and accused them of reneging on the deal they had allegedly made in exchange for his undercover work for them. Pagano testified at Pinte's trial that Monaco's information had to be scrutinized carefully. Some of the information was good, but some of it was not good at all. Pagano testified that he had once called Monaco "a pathological liar."

Assistant Prosecutor Kapsak immediately objected to Defense Attorney Spinello's tactic. Pagano, Kapsak said, was a police superintendent, not a psychiatrist. Superintendent Pagano's definition of a "pathological liar" was not one that was legally meaningful. What *was* legally meaningful in Superintendent Pagano's testimony, Kapsak argued, was that concerning Pagano's own field of expertise, namely, the treatment of an informant's information. Pagano had advocated "scrutinizing" Monaco's information, and that, Kapsak said, was exactly what the prosecutor's office had done.

Kapsak called to the stand a psychiatrist who testified that John Pinte exhibited the signs of a classic "sadistic homosexual." The sadistic murder and Pinte's earlier attacks against strangers—against the young boy and the woman in Jersey City—were all consistent with the psychological profile of a repressed homosexual who harbors great resentment against women and who enjoys humiliating his victims sexually.

Pinte's repeated conversations with Ronnie Monaco, the psychiatrist testified, showed another classic trait of the homosexual sadist: Sadists aren't satisfied merely committing a violent act; they have to brag about it. Pinte did not want to tell police what he had done for fear of winding up in prison for life, the doctor asserted, but he had to tell someone. Pinte knew Monaco from another prison and trusted him — as it turned out, not wisely. He trusted Monaco enough, at any rate, to use him as a sounding board for his perverse re-creations of the murder.

Assistant Prosecutor Kapsak also called to the stand a handwriting analyst, who testified that the map Monaco had provided was consistent with John Pinte's handwriting. He asked them to consider why Pinte would have kept a steak knife, a mallet, a hacksaw, plastic garbage bags, and rubber gloves in his van if he had not planned to use them in the manner in which he finally did. To nail his case down, Kapsak stressed that the key pieces of evidence he wanted the jury to consider were the pair of bloody fingerprints matching Pinte's found on the inside and outside of the glove.

On February 21, 1979, the jury found John Pinte guilty of murder in the first degree in the death and mutilation of Joey Pichirallo. Judge Robert Longhi sentenced Pinte then and there to life in prison.

John Pinte is serving his sentence at the Trenton State Prison. He will be eligible for parole in 1993.

EDITOR'S NOTE:
*Dr. Kris Fischer, Rachel Kline and Ronnie Monaco are not the real names of the persons so named in the foregoing story. Fictitious names have been used because there is no reason for public interest in the identities of these persons.*

# "HE WON'T TALK? TORTURE HIM!"
## by Bud Ampolsk

Monday, September 26, 1988, dawned as one of the saddest days in the memory of New York's Catholic worshipers. It was on that day that 500 of them crammed into every available inch of space at the Holy Trinity Church in the Whitestone section of Queens. They were there to listen to their spiritual leader, John Cardinal O'Connor, pay a glowing final tribute to a simple man whose life had been a living monument to the precepts of his faith.

They were there because they had come to realize that even the interior of one of their most hallowed cathedrals was no longer a sanctuary from the madness and violence which held their city in a lethal grip.

They were there because the life of 77-year-old John Winters, a volunteer usher at St. Patrick's Cathedral, had been instantly snuffed out before the famed church's high altar by a deranged, street person wielding a prayer stand who had entered the sacred building's confines to vent his rage at mankind in one final burst of bloodlust.

Both Winters and his assailant, 32-year-old Jorge DelGado, died in the terrible moments following the invasion. Winters succumbed to the blows rained down around his head and shoulders by a maniac's incredible strength. DelGado was killed by police bullets as he turned to assault the officers who had moved in to restore the peace.

In the ensuing days, the faithful heard the Archbishop

of New York say, "Mr. Winters was a man who loved this cathedral and literally gave his life to this cathedral.

"This mighty cathedral, so powerful-looking, is really vulnerable, delicate and fragile. This is true of each one of us, true to life. So often we feel so powerful and invulnerable, but each one of us is so delicate, so fragile, so easily shattered. What happened here last night (the deadly assault of Winters) is a reminder that each one of us must be prepared to face Almighty God at any time."

Now, on this pleasant early fall morning, they heard Cardinal O'Connor tell them, "It is important to remember that he (Winters) died defending what he loved."

As the mourners followed the simple coffin containing the mortal remains of the gentle 77-year-old who had given his life in "the defense of the faith," they had no way of knowing that even at this moment the message of human frailty and the gallantry of a fallen victim, would not be applicable to Winters alone.

They had no way of knowing that even as Cardinal O'Connor was returning to his Manhattan offices from the Trinity Church rites for Winters, he would receive yet another tragic shock. This would come to him when word was flashed that one of his own priests had been murdered in the Bronx.

This time the victim was the Reverend Lazer Sheldija, leader of the SS. Peter & Paul Albanian Center in the Eastchester section of the Bronx.

Upon receipt of the terrible news, the Archbishop immediately ordered his chauffeur to change course. Within minutes, his limousine was drawing up before the ramshackle Sheldija home on Eastchester Road. There he was greeted by grim-faced crime-site homicide detectives going about the ugly business of securing the scene, making preliminary forensic tests and searching for any possible scrap of meaningful evidence.

From the officers, Cardinal O'Connor heard of the consummate brutality, so reminiscent of what had happened to Winters, that had claimed the fallen priest.

According to what was then known of the case, Sheldija, a 60-year-old Albanian refugee, had last been seen alive on Thursday, September 22nd as he paid a 6:30 p.m. visit to a nearby barbershop.

Because the elderly priest lived alone, his absence had not been noticed until Sunday, September 25th, when parishioners of Holy Rosary Church, some seven blocks from his home, convened to celebrate Mass. They were surprised by the failure of their priest to make an appearance.

On Sunday afternoon, a group of church members had gone to the Sheldija home to investigate his absence. But, receiving no response to their bell-ringing and seeing no signs of a forced entry or violence, the parishioners decided that they had become unduly worried over the priest's not being on hand for regular services.

It was not until Monday morning, September 26th, when Sheldija had still failed to surface, that the concern of his congregation turned to alarm.

A decision was made to seek the aid of police.

Even before arriving officers spotted Sheldija, their experience warned them that they were about to discover a harrowing sight that would cause them to swallow hard against the bile burning their throats. This came with the sickly sweet stench that accompanies the advanced decomposition of a human body.

Indeed, the beloved priest was dead, and had been for several days. Preliminary estimates of representatives from the Bronx Medical Examiner's office would place the approximate time of death at sometime between Thursday and Friday evenings, September 22nd and 23rd.

Had Sheldija died of natural causes, the discovery of his unattended corpse would have been macabre enough. But the Albanian exile had not died naturally. All signs indicated that he had been sadistically assaulted, beaten about the head and shoulders, and strangled. A wound in his forehead had possibly come from a lethal bullet which had finally ended his agonies.

Fully dressed in a black suit and a clerical collar, Sheldija's corpse was sprawled across a reclining-type chair in the living room of his house. An electrical cord was tightly wrapped around his neck and throat.

According to a police spokesman, Detective Joseph McConville, Sheldija had apparently been shot in the forehead. His body also had other lacerations around his head, attesting to the possibility that he had been beaten and otherwise tortured over a period of time by his killer or killers.

Although taking an inventory of possible missing valuables was proving a lengthy and complicated process, probers learned that an Oldsmobile sedan from the late 1970s, which had been owned by the priest, was missing.

(During the evening following the discovery of Sheldija's cadaver, officers searching city streets came upon the missing vehicle. It had been parked in front of a building at Astoria Avenue. According to another police spokesman, Sergeant Maurice Howard, the recovered automobile was towed to headquarters of the 114th Precinct, where it was impounded for further inspection.)

Meanwhile, there was a growing police feeling, triggered by interviews with friends, colleagues and acquaintances of the slain clergyman that his murder might have been the result of a misconception concerning the prelate's financial holdings.

For example, there had been the theft several years before of his coin collection. A fellow priest of nearby Holy Rosary Church estimated that the collection had been valued at $100,000.

Also supporting the robbery theory was the condition of two upstairs bedrooms of the Sheldija house. They had been ransacked. Papers were strewn across the floor. The personal property of the slain priest lay scattered about.

That Sheldija might have known his killer or killers, or at least allowed them to enter his home, was seen by the fact that there were no signs of forced entry to be found on the premises.

Said Robert Colangelo, Chief of New York City detectives, "At this point robbery looks like our best guess."

Giving further weight to the robbery theory was the dream which Sheldija had had during his lifetime. Considered the pastor of some 50,000 Albanian immigrants now living in the Metropolitan New York area, the priest had set his heart on building a church they could think of as their own. Contributions from a number of Albanian civic groups for the purpose of buying a weed-filled lot adjacent to Sheldija's home had amounted to from $300,000 to $500,000, according to informed estimates. Despite the collections, however, some said the funds had not been ample enough to allow construction to begin on the dreamed-of church. Some even reported that there had been the threat of foreclosure on the property.

There was neighborhood gossip concerning a split among the sponsoring fund-raising civic organizations. But none of those reporting the possible dissension would elaborate on the details.

What was learned was that when Sheldija had fallen in arrears on city taxes on the still undeveloped lot, the New York Archdiocese had finally stepped in to pay the delinquent fees.

Although Sheldija had been in financial straits, at one point having had the water and electricity turned off in his home during the last year—neighborhood legend had it that he kept vast sums of money around the house.

Whether affluent or impoverished, however, the prelate had constantly maintained the respect of the Albanian community.

Typical comment was that of the Reverend Toner, who said of his martyred colleague, "He was like a parish priest. He was a dedicated guy. He must have been lonely, yet he served those people. He took care of all the weddings, baptisms and funerals—all that—and he was with the people. He always had a few of them with him. I always admired him. He was ordained in Rome in 1950, but was never able to get back into his country because of

215

communism."

Others expanded on the ill-fated odyssey which had brought Sheldija from his native land to the Bronx.

His goal of becoming a priest with his own flock had taken him from Albania to Rome, Brazil, and finally the Bronx.

Sheldija had been one of eight brothers who had grown up while serving in the anti-Nazi underground of his native land during the oppressive World War II occupation. He had told friends that the post-World War II years had seen him escaping from the Albanian Communist regime in 1953.

Said the administrator of Our Lady of Good Counsel Church in the Bronx, "He fled from Albania to Yugoslavia and then to Rome, where he was ordained. He went to Brazil, where he served as a missionary for ten years."

Sheldija, who spoke a number of languages, finally arrived in the Bronx in 1973. He became a priest at Our Lady of Refuge Church, near the Bronx Campus of Fordham University.

"We often had lunch together," said the administrator. "He loved his country and his people. He was on a mission to help his people."

There had been some controversy swirling around Sheldija's head. This was said to have revolved around a youth center he had opened at the site of his proposed church.

Residents of the largely close-knit Eastchester area reported that the youth center had been popular among local teenagers who had gone there to shoot pool and play video games. But some adult neighbors had contended the center attracted rowdyism, as well.

The youth center was said to have been destroyed by an arson fire set in 1987.

Whatever the issues involved between Sheldija and the community, they had never eroded the personal affection Eastchester residents had felt for him. Said one resident of Italian origin, "He always had a smile on his face.

"The man was kind of quiet, but every once in a while he'd talk to parents and give them advice on their problems.

"He was very big on making sure that kids went to school."

Although he spent the greater part of his time away from the church alone in his house reading, Sheldija had displayed a great thirst for knowledge.

One woman neighbor recalled that she had been giving the priest lessons in Korean so that he might add to the seven languages he already spoke fluently. She commented, "He always wanted to learn things."

In talking about the recent events which had claimed his attention, Cardinal O'Connor called the murder of Sheldija the climax of "one of the worst weeks of my life—a shattering experience."

The grimness had started with the death (from cancer) of Monseigneur Raul del Valle, one of the archbishop's closest friends. Only hours after the Monseigneur's death, Cardinal O'Connor had been called upon to conduct the funeral mass for a young AIDS victim who had been baptized by the cardinal on Christmas Eve.

Then there had been the violence inside St. Patrick's, which had claimed two lives. This had been followed by a strong police suggestion that Cardinal O'Connor don a bulletproof vest and be accompanied by guards as he went about his church business. (He had turned the advice down.)

This final blow had been the learning of Sheldija's murder. Said Cardinal O'Connor, "I've never heard of so many traumas in so short a time."

An aide said of the prince of the church, "He's feeling shell-shocked."

As a cadre of homicide detectives sorted out the emerging details of Sheldija's church and private lives, major questions remained unanswered.

One concerned what role, if any, had been played in his murder by his reported dabbling in real estate. Several friends acknowledged that the prelate had once owned a 90-unit apartment house said to be located on 261st Street and Broadway in the West Bronx. However, one close associate reported that the building had been sold several years ago.

Those who had known him best refused to believe he had any substantial hidden assets. They maintained that any would-be burglar or robber could not have picked a more destitute target.

On the forensic side, the medical examiner's report, which was issued on Tuesday, September 27th, dashed any hope that a bullet to the head had cut short Sheldija's death agonies.

The autopsy showed that the priest had died of strangulation and head injuries caused by a blunt instrument. The victim's skull had been fractured and he had suffered massive brain hemorrhaging, according to the findings.

Detective Chief Colangelo was sticking to his original estimate of the crime. "My judgment is that it is robbery, but we are not ruling out other possibilities."

The "other possibilities" included the theory that somebody might have sought vengeance for some real or fancied hurt done by Sheldija.

Could it have been political motivation?

One longtime friend talked of Sheldija's strongly-held political views. The friend said of the dead man, "He was a great man, a religious man, and anti-communist. And he was dedicated to his community. He was pro-Albanian."

Could there be some ill will over the amount of money lost by those who had contributed to the priest's dream of an Albanian home of Catholic worship? It was estimated that over the past decade, some 400 to 500 families in the Albanian-American community had contributed from $350,000 to $400,000, but all of that sum, plus an additional $15,000 raised in Detroit, had gone to purchase the parcel of land on which his private home stood.

It was said that the land had been paid off only within

Winston Hemsley,
famed choreographer,
was slain in his
Las Vegas home.

Robert Mayfield,
Hemsley's killer.

A headless body found by the side of a Texas road
turned out to be 26-year-old Jeanette Sue Fain.

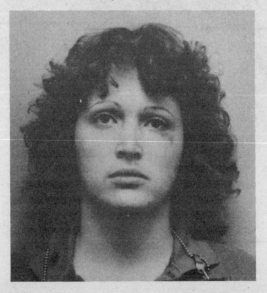

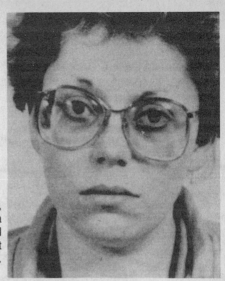

Waltraud Wagner, ringleader of a gang of lethal nurses who killed at least 15 patients.

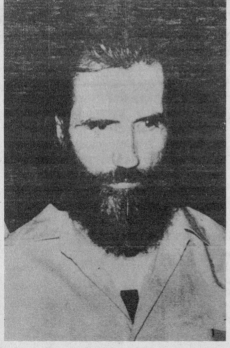

Gary Heidnik, who kept women chained and tortured in his basement and their body parts in his refrigerator.

Lawrence White was tortured to death by his crack-dealing buddies.

Tracy Turner may have helped a second victim escape but did not save Lawrence White.

Child killer
Westley Allan Dodd.

Two of Dodd's victims,
tragically, were the
Neer brothers—Cole, 11,
and William, 10.

4-year-old Lee Iseli,
Dodd's third victim.

John Pinte called the police and told them there was a dead body in his van, but claimed he didn't know how it got there. A jury found otherwise.

Antonio Dorsett poured salt into his victims' wounds to increase their pain.

30-year-old Dassa Jackson was a beautiful woman before her husband dumped her—alive— into a vat of acid.

Cecil Jackson.

Her bloodstained bible was
found near the body of
Donna "Dee Dee" Friesenhahn, 16.

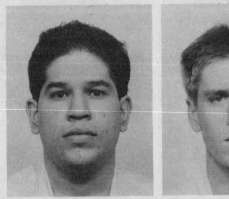

Friesenhahn's killers, Rolando Rodarte
and Ty Wesley Gunnerman.

Lance Wood and
Michael Archuleta
blamed each other
for the torture slaying
of college student
Gordon Church.

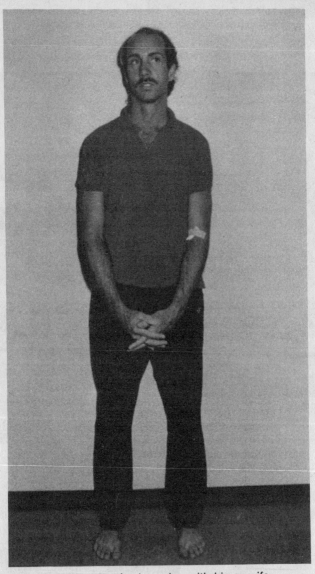

David Harrison's obsession with his ex-wife, Anne Jenkins, ended in her death.

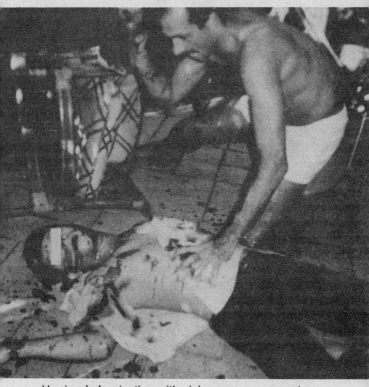

Harrison's fascination with violence was apparent
from this staged photo in which he pretended
to stab a friend.

Harrison owned a number of books on bomb-making
and on getting revenge.

the last year. Now the Albanian community was attempting to raise an additional $2 million for the proposed building itself. Said one man who knew the background intimately, "When it came time to build the church and the time to give the money, a lot of the parishioners backed off."

Could it have been the hatred of former tenants of the priest? It was said that Sheldija had carried out eviction proceedings against commercial tenants of a brick structure situated on "church land" to make way for the proposed construction program.

In September 1987, on the 21st, 24th and 25th, there had been separate fires on the disputed property. According to Fire Department spokesman John Mulligan, these three conflagrations resulted from arson.

Could it have been the victim's own personality? Said a priest who had been an intimate confidant of the dead man, "He was a very opinionated man. He never equivocated on any issue. And he was a rabid anti-communist."

As more information became available to them, investigators felt that Sheldija had known and had reason to trust his killers.

Now the reported police theory was that either Sheldija had opened his door to his slayer, or he had accompanied him to his home. It was said that the prelate had been attacked while in the middle of eating his dinner.

It was now revealed that several empty beer cans, as well as coins from the clergyman's American collection, had been discovered among the debris on the living room floor.

One police source held that Sheldija might have been tortured by his assailant in an attempt to force him to reveal the hiding place of items of value being sought by the killer.

One thing on which there could be no argument was the sadistic cruelty with which the Albanian patriot had been slain. Commenting on the crime, New York Police Commissioner Ben Ward, who had been attending a ceremony at Police Headquarters in Manhattan, stated, "I don't think it means it's going to get worse. I just think it is a bitter commentary on our times."

On Friday, September 30th, the rites, which had been delayed to allow Sheldija's relatives who reside in Albania to be informed of his death, were held at Holy Rosary Church in Eastchester.

Cardinal O'Connor led a packed assemblage of 800 mourners in paying their last respects to the slain cleric. The cardinal said of Sheldija, "He laid down his life for Albanian people here."

The Archbishop told the assemblage, "Every death is a reminder that we do not begin to understand life itself."

Turning to the recent St. Patrick's Cathedral bloodshed and regarding it together with the Sheldija tragedy, Cardinal O'Connor stated, "We pray that the death of Father Lazer will be the last of the tragedies that have been visited on the archdiocese."

By an ironic quirk, the interment of Sheldija's remains in a grave at St. Raymond's Cemetery in the Bronx came within hours of the burial of Jorge DelGado, the drifter who had caused panic and consternation in St. Patrick's Cathedral when he battered usher John Winters to death, slashed at a police officer, and went to his own doom in a hail of answering police fire. DelGado's coffin, with only 30 mourners in attendance, was lowered in a narrow grave in the same cemetery only a few yards from Sheldija's final resting place.

While the final rites were being performed, a police task force was still hard at work attempting to come to grips with the mystery of the Albanian cleric's slaying.

Thus far, there had been no real progress to report, according to Deputy Chief Dennis Ryan. Ryan, who had attended Sheldija's rites, said that detectives were still canvassing the Woodside, Queens area where the priest's aging Oldsmobile had been discovered. The detectives were also continuing their interviews with Sheldija's friends and acquaintances.

Commented Ryan, "A priest is a symbol of authority in the community. The death of a member of the clergy is certainly a serious matter. Especially in circumstances like this."

On Tuesday, October 4th, there was a seemingly important development. It came when police spokesman Maurice Howard announced that a 38-year-old suspect had been arrested at his apartment in the Norwood Section of the Bronx and had been charged with second-degree murder in the cleric's killing.

However, the spokesman noted that no details would be forthcoming as to what had led to the arrest. The only information divulged was that the suspect in custody was an Albanian. A registered alien, he had arrived in the United States in 1983. Most recently, he had been working as a kitchen helper in a Manhattan restaurant.

The chef in the eatery where the suspect had been employed reported that the man started his job there two weeks before the slaying. Commented the chef, "He worked midnight to eight. We close at four and after that he was here alone, cleaning up.

"He was supposed to work last night and tonight, but he didn't show up."

If there was jubilation among the arresting officers concerning their apparent breaking of the difficult case, it was to be short-lived.

To the consternation of police brass and detectives, on Wednesday, October 5th, Bronx District Attorney Paul Gentile declined to prosecute and the suspect was released. Gentile contended that his office did not have sufficient evidence against the kitchen helper to go to court.

For his part, Deputy Chief Ryan took strong issue with the D.A.'s actions in releasing the man in question. Stated Ryan, "We checked with our legal department. They said we had probable cause to charge him." The deputy chief added that detectives would continue trying to construct their murder case against the suspect.

Meanwhile, the released suspect's wife who lived with

him and their two children in the Bronx apartment was quoted as saying, "We go all the time to Father Sheldija's church. My husband is not guilty. He is clear."

The woman also added that her husband "likes the priest. He never fought with him."

She made a point of saying that her husband had cooperated with the cops, and had answered all their questions. "We are not upset with the police," she said. "We understand they were doing their job."

A family friend who refused to be identified said, "We're from a communist country, so we're used to a lot worse than this. But we want it to stop now."

Unofficially, the difference of opinion between detectives and Gentile's office appeared to revolve around fingerprints said to be identifiable as those of the suspect and which were alleged to have been found in Sheldija's home. Some sources argued that the kitchen helper had been a frequent visitor at the priest's home, and that accounted for the prints.

But police sources claimed that some of the man's prints had been discovered in areas of the house where they shouldn't have been a part of the house where the alleged suspect had denied having been in.

Ryan revealed that the man, after having been taken into custody on the prior night, had been questioned at the Eastchester Road station and had "voluntarily made statements."

The D.A.'s office remained steadfast about its position in the matter. Said Ed McCarthy, Gentile's spokesman, "There wasn't any evidence there." And there was a statement by the district attorney himself. "We will not go into court until we have a legally sufficient case."

It was learned that after police had decided to charge the man with second-degree murder, representatives of the prosecutor were brought into a conference. The D.A.'s personnel had decided there was insufficient evidence to bring the man before a judge. Thus the man had been released at 10:30 p.m. on October 4th.

One confusing point that remained was why the police department had allowed its Public Information Office to announce the arrest after the suspect had been released.

The case was to remain in limbo for three days. Then, on Friday, October 7th, a second man was taken into custody and charged with Sheldija's slaying.

According to police spokesman Howard, the suspect, whom police identified as 24-year-old Eurik Shabani of Cambreleng Avenue, the Bronx, an Albanian native, had been taken into custody at 10:30 p.m. in Ardsley, New York, and had been taken to the 49th Precinct stationhouse in the Bronx for questioning.

In making the announcement, Howard said that Shabani would be arraigned on Saturday. He said that the Bronx D.A. had agreed to prosecute Shabani.

Filling in some of the details of Shabani's questioning and arrest, Bronx Deputy Chief Ryan, who had been in charge of the investigation, alleged that Shabani had made statements "implicating himself in the murder."

Ryan said that the motive for the murder had been robbery, despite the fact that Sheldija had lived in a shabby, ill-furnished house without running water, and had a checking account balance of less than $100.

Added a detective who had been closely associated with the intensive probe, "The word on the street was that Sheldija had a lot of money."

Investigators were still expressing continuing interest in the first suspect who had been arrested and released. They alleged that the man and Shabani were friends.

However, the original suspect was said to be among the missing. One police theory had it that the man might have fled the country to avoid further complications with the New York City Police Department.

Their fears were said to have been triggered by their inability to locate the man at the apartment where he resided or at any of his usual haunts.

The heightened desire to bring the man in had been caused in part by statements allegedly made by Shabani which the police said implicated the first suspect.

One theory had it that the man being sought was indeed somewhere in the Metropolitan area, lacking the funds necessary for an extended trip. Said one investigator, "He simply does not have the money to leave the country."

Saying that the man had probably gone into hiding in local environs, the source reported that detectives had checked airlines, immigration and shipping officials, as well as Albanian authorities in their ongoing search.

"If he'd gone back to Albania, we'd know it by now," the detective commented.

On Monday evening, October 10th, detectives of the 49th squad in the Bronx received a major surprise when the wanted man voluntarily walked into the stationhouse.

Lieutenant John Rudden of the 49th Precinct detective squad would add that the man had been questioned for a short time in the presence of an assistant district attorney. The man had been released and had left the Eastchester stationhouse at about 7:00 p.m.

Declining to comment specifically on the Sheldija case, D.A. Gentile would merely say, "We will not take a case to court unless we have sufficient evidence to prosecute the case. As in every other case, we will review the evidence, and if it's sufficient to prosecute we will and if it is insufficient, we will not."

As of this writing, Eurik Shabani remains the lone charged suspect in the slaying of the Rev. Lazer Sheldija. He is awaiting further court action on the second-degree murder charges lodged against him.

It should be remembered that under the United States Constitution, Shabani has the right to be presumed innocent of this charge, until and unless proved otherwise under due process of law.

# "GHOUL KILLERS TOOK TURNS STABBING HER 120 TIMES!"

by Bruce Gibney

**SAN DIEGO, CALIFORNIA**
**FEBRUARY, 1983**

Homicide Sergeant R.E. MacLennan was halfway through an interview on April 25, 1983, when he told the interviewer: "I have been in this business a long time and I have seen a lot of things that I can't understand, but this Anna Weerts case just left me with my jaw hanging. I don't understand how so many kids could know about that murder and not tell us. You consider the way the poor woman was murdered and what those killers did. I mean, it makes you wonder about these kids, what their values are and what they are going to be like when they grow up."

A lot of people were wondering about the new generation. Said a former high school teacher, "A lot of these kids are time bombs. When they'll explode is anybody's guess. Good luck to whoever's around them when they finally do."

Eighty-six-year-old Anna Weerts was from an older, much gentler era. "Anna was the nicest person I knew," a neighbor remarked once. "She took on everybody else's problems but never shared any of her own."

The oldest of the five Weerts children, Anna, grew up in an 11-room house on Park Boulevard in the Normal Heights section of San Diego, California. The house was built by her father, Frank, a carpenter who also built three other stately homes in the neighborhood. The big family house was the only one Anna ever lived in and the only place where she felt comfortable. When relatives suggested she might be happier in a smaller place or a convalescent home where she could be looked after, Anna nixed the idea.

"She said it was the house her father built and she wasn't going to move," a relative recalled. "We argued, but there was no changing her mind once it was made up."

In her youth, Anna was an accomplished seamstress who designed hats and dresses and even worked with furs. She enjoyed sewing and crocheting gifts for her sisters, grandchildren, and great grandchildren. Gardening was also a passion, and her pride and joy was the huge flower and vegetable gardens she cultivated in her spacious backyard. Neighbors marvelled at the joy she took in watching things grow.

"She loved every plant, every blade of grass," one neighbor recalled. "She couldn't bear to kill the weeds in her garden."

Anna remained active until the past few years when the ravages of old age began to take their toll. She first gave up sewing, then her beloved gardening, and by mid-1982, she was pretty much confined to the house she loved so much.

Vic Barry lived in a residential hotel just a couple of doors down from the Weerts home. He was sound asleep early Thursday morning on April 8, 1982, when an explosion made him sit up in bed. He rushed to his window and saw flames shooting out of the front window of the Weerts home. He grabbed the telephone and notified the fire department.

When firemen arrived minutes later the house was engulfed in flames. Two firemen climbed through a front window that had exploded from the heat and began a frantic search for the elderly occupant. They found Anna curled up on a burning couch, her frail body partially covered by ashes and plaster that had fallen from the ceiling. They made no attempt to revive her; she was already dead.

The blaze that destroyed the home of Frank Weerts and took the life of his oldest daughter had begun in the living room, then spread to the upstairs. The fire, however, had not been an accident. Newspapers and other incendiary materials had been piled around the couch and underneath the woman, then deliberately set. When this determination was made, firefighters retreated from the living room and contacted police.

Sergeant R.E. MacLennan was on his way to work when he learned of the fire over the radio. He switched directions and headed for Park Boulevard. He was joined shortly by Homicide Detectives Barbara Harrison, David Ayers and Larry Lindstrom.

Detectives quickly determined that entry into the home was made through a rear door after they discovered a light bulb had been unscrewed in a fixture above the threshold and a window pane cut out of the door.

A motive for the break-in appeared to be robbery. A neighbor told Detective Harrison that Anna had been repeatedly robbed.

"I think she's been hit nineteen times in the ten years that I have known her," he said. "She was really an easy mark. All the kids in the neighborhood knew about Anna, and even some of the senior citizens. They all took advantage of her."

Anna would not allow a security system to be installed in the house. She was also reluctant to tell her family about each of the break-ins.

"I think she felt that if her family knew about all the break-ins they would make her leave the house," another Park Boulevard resident explained.

It was common knowledge that Anna kept thousands in cash, jewelry, rare coins and other valuables in the house. Relatives begged the elderly woman to put her money into a checking account but Anna rejected the idea. Even after her house was hit regularly by thieves she still felt better about having her cash in the house rather than in a bank.

Investigators learned one break-in occurred just two days

before the fire.

"Anna said she caught this teenage kid stealing some things from her bedroom," a relative said. "She chased him away with a broom but not before he stole some jewelry and money."

Anna had described the crafty intruder as a young man in his teens or early 20s, of medium height and weight with blond hair worn shoulder length.

It was logical, sleuths theorized, that the intruder might have come back to steal more from the elderly woman. Either that or he had told some cronies, who then decided to try their luck. But why burn down the house?

The answer was apparently to hide the fact that Anna had been beaten, then stabbed to death. According to the pathologist's report, Anna had been hit on the head with a hammer-like object, then stabbed approximately 120 times in the chest, neck and face with a long-bladed knife. The pathologist said he counted as many as 20 stab wounds in the victim's tongue. There was no explanation for the excessive number of knife wounds, except that perhaps the killer or killers were caught up in a frenzy or were acting out some sort of death cult ritual.

The senseless killing hit a responsive chord in the city of nearly one million. In a *San Diego Tribune* editorial an elderly woman was quoted as saying that she could sympathize with Anna. "There are people living in terror, common people, people who built this city. I won't ask for pity, just that people be conscious, that they help us."

Another woman told a reporter that "some people think Anna was crazy for staying in the house after it was robbed so often. But I could understand it, my house has been robbed and what am I supposed to do? I could move in with the kids, or go to an old folks home. I would be safe. But what about my pictures, my life? What would remain? What would I do if there were no weeds to cut?"

Phone tips, due in part to the barrage of news stories, lit up the police switchboard. They came from all parts of the city, from people who were outraged by the vicious killing and thought they could help. Investigators checked out 100 such tips, but it was not until April 13th that they hit paydirt.

The call came from a resident in North Park, an older blue collar community east of Park Boulevard. "All the kids in the neighborhood can talk about is that murder," the tipster said. "They seem to know who did it."

Detectives jotted down the teenagers' names. A few discreet inquiries put them in touch with a 17-year-old high school student. He said on the Saturday following the murder he had attended a Black Sabbath rock concert at the Sports Arena. At the concert he noticed that two buddies who didn't work and were usually scrounging for money were flashing rolls of money around.

"They were bragging about killing that old lady," the teenager said. "I thought they were shining me on."

The two buddies with the bank rolls were 16 year-old Denis Marsh and 17-year-old Jeffrey Inglett.

"I don't like what happened to that old lady," the informant said. "They were bragging about it. They said they took turns stabbing her."

Marsh was a bean pole of a kid, with a thatch of dark hair that fell to his shoulders. He lived in an apartment complex on Adams Avenue two miles east of Anna Weerts' home. Neighbors said that the parents both worked and Denis and a bunch of his friends were always hanging out at the apartments after school. "They were always around here underfoot," a neighbor said. "Because the parents worked the kids went any which way they wanted to."

Denis had a record—three run-ins with authorities because of curfew violations, trespassing and battery—but he didn't have a reputation as a bad kid.

"Denis just sort of went along with whatever was happening," a school chum said.

Jeff Inglett was another case. A big, bull moose of a kid, with long dark hair and ham-sized fists, Inglett had been in trouble since his early teens. Records showed that between January, 1979, and April, 1982, Inglett was arrested by police a dozen times for a variety of offenses, including petty theft, burglary, possession and sale of marijuana, discharging and brandishing weapons, and trespassing.

A neighbor said it seemed like there was always a police car pulled up in front of the youth's modest middle-class home on 28th street. Exactly what turned Inglett into a bad apple remained a mystery. According to one neighbor, "Jeff was spoiled. He always had the best bike or the best skateboard, the best of everything." Apparently the best of everything wasn't good enough because in 1979 he was arrested as a runaway and spent time in Southwood Mental Health Center in Chula Vista. The hospital, which specializes in therapy for emotionally disturbed teenagers, had had little effect because, upon Inglett's release, he ran away from home again.

The teens were not exactly candidates for the youth achievement award, but their records did not indicate they were the type of fiendish psychopaths who could have committed as ghoulish a crime as the Anna Weerts murder. Still, investigators had no reason to doubt the information provided by the tipster, particularly after a second teenager contacted police a few days later and gave essentially the same story.

"They were joking about it," the teenager said. "How can you joke about doing something like that?"

Investigators attempted to find an answer to the question. In the next few days they talked to neighbors, school officials, juvenile officers and friends of the two teenage suspects. They learned the two were part of a group of kids who hung out at an apartment on Suncrest Drive, a two block street just a mile from the Weerts' home. The apartment was rented to Douglas Fletcher, a 21-year-old machinist who neighbors described as an average working stiff, who liked to work on his car on weekends and occasionally played his stereo too loud. Teenagers at Garfield High School said the apartment was a good place to party and get high on coke and crystal meth.

Marsh and Inglett were frequent guests at the Fletcher

230

apartment. So were Trudy James, 15, and Debbie Gilliam, 16. Trudy was a tall, strickingly pretty brunette who did well in school despite the fact she liked to cut classes to be with her friends. Debbie was described as an impressionable teenager who sometimes hung out with the wrong crowd.

The common thread that ran through their lives was that all four teenagers had attended Garfield School in North Park. The school housed 450 teenagers who transferred there with parental consent because they could not succeed at other city schools. The problems varied from poor health, slow achievement or a need to work during the day to chronic truancy, social or physical immaturity and anti-social behavior. Many had been high school dropouts.

School district literature described Garfield as a "guidance-oriented high school offering an alternative educational plan which is student-success centered."

The rumor on campus had it that Jeff and Denis had been the ones who killed "that old lady" and set her house on fire. The rumor was fueled by the fact that a couple of students swore they overheard Denis and Jeff joking about the crime. One informant who talked to police only after they contacted him first said the rumor had been going around school for a couple of days.

"The old lady was supposed to be rich," the kid said. "They got enough to buy a motorcycle."

One reason kids did not call police was for fear of repercussions from Inglett. "The guy was always picking fights," one youth said. "But he goes psycho if you hit him."

For ten days investigators kept tabs on the youths. Surveillance teams were put on their homes and the places they frequented. Word that the cops were nosing around and asking questions apparently got back to Inglett, because on April 20th the informant who attended the Black Sabbath concert with Inglett and Marsh contacted police.

"Jeff said if I told anyone about the Weerts thing he would find me and kill me," the informant said.

The following morning police learned that Inglett and Marsh were planning to leave San Diego and take an ex-

231

tended vacation through the northwest and Canada. Ironically, that same day the investigators were scheduled to meet at the D.A.'s Office to draw up search warrants. The warrants would have to wait.

"We have to move on this before those two take off," Sgt. MacLennan said.

The others agreed. If Inglett and Marsh split, they might never be caught.

A plan was devised. Detective Harrison would assist a deputy district attorney with the warrants, while the others headed for Normal Heights. They no sooner reached the neighborhood when they received a radio message from a surveillance team that Inglett and Marsh were on a motorcycle headed east on Adams Avenue.

Ayers and Lindstrom took off after the cycle. They turned onto Adams Avenue, weaved through the slower traffic and were just a hundred feet behind when the cycle took a left and zigzagged onto Collier Street. The detectives took a street that ran parallel, found themselves going the wrong way on a one way street, made a quick U-turn, zigzagged along several narrow streets and screeched to a stop in front of Denis Marsh's apartment. Parked next to the front entrance was the spiffy new motorcycle.

Inside, Inglett, Marsh and a pal were drinking a few beers and listening to Black Sabbath records. The party was over when Ayers and Lindstrom walked in and placed the merrymakers under arrest. The teens were taken to the central police station where they declined to make any statements concerning the murder of Anna Weerts and the burning of her house.

Police had better luck with Trudy James and Debbie Gilliam. The two showed up at Marsh's apartment looking for their friends. Instead, they found detectives busy sifting through evidence. Since the names of the two had surfaced during the investigation, they were arrested and taken in for questioning.

Their statements when added to those of other witnesses created the following scenario: Hours before the Anna

Weerts slaying, the two girls and their teenage boyfriends were sitting around Fletcher's apartment on Suncrest Drive getting high on alcohol and their favorite drug, crystal methamphetamine. By midnight, the group had consumed the last of the booze and dope and were discussing where to get more when Inglett burst into the apartment.

Inglett was probably the last person the group wanted to see. Earlier in the day he had severely beaten Debbie, his on-again-off-again girlfriend.

"He hit me and wrapped his legs around my stomach," she related later. She was taken to the hospital for x-rays after spitting up blood.

Inglett's mood hadn't improved any and he grabbed one of the partygoers by the front of his shirt and started punching him. The fight — actually Inglett did the punching while his friend passively absorbed the blows — continued out onto the lawn, where the commotion caused neighbors to call the police. The fight had broken up by the time a cruiser pulled in front of the Suncrest Drive apartment but police arrested Fletcher for public intoxication and took him to county jail.

"We went down to bail him out," Debbie said. "Jeff and Denis stayed at the apartment."

It was almost four in the morning by the time the teenagers got Fletcher out of the slam. When they returned to the apartment they found Inglett and Marsh in the living room.

The two had been very busy boys. Two days earlier Marsh had boasted about breaking into Anna Weerts' house and stealing jewelry and a few fistfuls of greenbacks. Marsh had grabbed about $800 before Anna discovered him and drove him out of the house. But Marsh knew there was more — a lot more. Marsh and Inglett got on Marsh's motorcycle and drove back to the Weerts home, carrying with them two knives they had purchased earlier at a hardware store.

The two said they parked the bike two houses away in the alley and went to Anna's back door. Marsh crept up onto the back porch and unscrewed a light bulb above the door, pitching the rear entryway into darkness. Inglett then cut a

233

hole in the glass pane in the rear door, reached inside and unlocked it.

They took a few steps through the kitchen when they were confronted by Anna Weerts. Inglett then gripped the handle of a hammer and brought it down on top of Anna's head.

"I asked him why he did that and he said, 'Well, she saw me,' and he didn't want to have her around to identify him," Debbie said.

Inglett said he brought the body into the living room and lay it on newspapers they had spread out over the couch. Inglett then started stabbing the woman with a hunting knife. After stabbing her several times — maybe 50, he wasn't really sure how many — he handed the knife over to his buddy. "I'm sure he did something with the knife," Inglett said. "But I'm not sure if he stabbed or poked her or whatever."

Inglett then put newspapers around the couch and lit them with a lighter provided by his friend. Back at the house, Inglett and Marsh went into the bedroom and showed the impressionable girls the booty taken in the robbery.

"I just went, 'Wow'," Trudy recalled. "There were a lot of bills, some of the bills even had blood on them."

In all, the two had collected about $5,000 in cash, rare coins, jewelry and other valuables. With so much money the teenagers went on a spending spree. Inglett purchased beer, cocaine and a motorcycle; Marsh bought clothing, cocaine and marijuana, while Debbie took a gift of $200 from Inglett to buy some new clothes and a pocket book.

The good times came to an end on April 21st when Trudy and Debbie were held in juvenile hall on suspicion of murder, robbery and burglary. Charges against Trudy were dropped, while Debbie was allowed to plead guilty to one count of receiving stolen property. Both agreed to testify against their former friends.

In July, Marsh and Inglett appeared at a hearing in juvenile court to see if they would be tried as juveniles or adults. Judge Robert J. O'Neil described the crime as "one of such

234

outrageous proportion that I can find no mitigating factors" and declared the two unfit for juvenile proceedings. In August, they were arraigned on charges of murder, burglary and arson. Bail was set at $250,000 each.

Then in October Jeffrey Inglett surprised everyone and entered a plea of guilty. Before the judge accepted his plea Inglett was ordered to make a full admission to his participation in the murder. The boastful murderer, however, became bashful before the courtroom full of reporters and the proceedings were moved to Judge Thomas Duffy's private chambers. There Inglett admitted cutting the throat of Anna Weerts, stabbing her in the chest, and moving her to the living room couch with the help of Denis Marsh and stabbing her more than 50 times.

Inglett was at a loss to explain his decision to kill Anna Weerts.

"I don't know why," he said. "We just went to get money, and I don't know why it ended the way it did. I was so high on drugs, I don't know why I was stabbing her so much."

Outside the courtroom, Defense Attorney Michael McGlinn said Inglett's decision to plead guilty was "from our perspective, the best thing for him. Nothing was getting better. Jeffrey has never denied his involvement. The question was, what was going to happen to him? We wanted to get this young man started on his sentencing, to start rehabilitating himself."

He will have a long time behind bars to work on self improvement. In February, 1983, he was sentenced to 26 years to life in the state prison. The chunky teenager received the bad news stoically before he was escorted back to his cell at the county jail.

Partner in crime, Denis Marsh, went on trial in April, 1983. Although he admitted committing a solo robbery of the Weerts' house on April 6, 1982, and participating in the robbery with Inglett two days later, he denied taking part in the murder. In a non-jury trial, Judge J. Perry Langsford, however, found Marsh guilty of murder, robbery, arson, burglary and conspiracy to commit burglary. The youth,

235

however, was found innocent of committing arson with intent to do great bodily harm because Weerts was apparently dead before the fire was set.

Marsh also faces a term of 25 years to life in state prison. Both men will be eligible for parole after serving 23 years behind bars.

EDITOR'S NOTE:
*Vic Barry, Debbie Gilliam, Douglas Fletcher and Trudy James are not the real names of the persons so named in the foregoing story. Fictitious names have been used because there is no reason for public interest in the identities of these persons.*

# "HE DROPPED HER IN A VAT OF ACID!"

## by Philip Westwood

For Fred and Betty Elmore, February 25, 1991, started out just like any other day. They began it at their home, an apartment no different from any of hundreds of other apartments in the row of multistory buildings littering the skyline of London's Forest Gate district. The Elmores had made their home as nice as their senior citizens' pension checks permitted. Both were in their late 60s, and both wanted nothing more than to be allowed to live out their final days in peace. That was why they had invested in the sturdy, solid wood front door with its collection of dead bolts and locks. There's a lot of crime in Forest Gate.

The elderly couple considered themselves lucky. They had never been the victims of a crime and had never had any contact, even remotely, with the commission of a criminal act.

At least, they hadn't until February 25, 1991.

That day, being a Monday, meant that Fred and Betty would take their weekly trip down to the local shops.

"Get your coat on, dear," Fred advised his wife as the living-room clock struck 11:00. "It looks a bit cold out there." The couple always left the apartment at 11:00 on a Monday morning.

Because of the Elmores' advanced years, the local coun-

237

cil that owned the building had given them an apartment on the first floor. For Fred and Betty, it was just a short walk along the corridor to the building's main entrance before they stepped out into the weak, morning sunshine.

"You were right, Fred," said Betty, as the chilly air hit her face. "It *is* cold out here."

"Come on," said Fred. "We'll take the shortcut."

The shortcut to which Fred referred entailed the couple making their way round to the rear of the block and along an alleyway past the lockup garages provided for residents who owned cars. A great deal of the crime in the Forest Gate district concerns theft of—and from—cars.

Betty didn't really like the shortcut. In places, the alleyway was narrow and lined with tall shrubs and bushes. Betty thought it was an ideal place for a mugger looking for easy pickings. She would never have used the alleyway on her own. But she didn't mind too much when Fred was with her, and at least it meant that the walk to the shops would take only half as long as it would going by the more conventional route.

But that morning, the couple never reached the shops. They never reached that part of the alleyway that Betty feared was inhabited by lurking muggers. In fact, they never even got past the row of lockup garages.

Only moments into the excursion, Fred stopped suddenly and was inclining his head like a bird listening for an underground worm. "What was that?" he said.

"What was what?" inquired Betty.

"That!" Fred answered, after a short pause.

Betty cocked her head and listened. She thought she heard something, too, a strange, muffled sort of metallic sound. It seemed to be coming from one of the garages.

"What is it, Fred?" Betty wanted to know.

Fred couldn't answer her with any certainty, but he thought it might be some animal that had become inadvertently trapped in one of the garages. "It probably crept

238

in there for a sleep after the owner had left it open," he mused. "Then the owner came back and locked it without noticing the animal. The poor creature must be half scared to death. We'll have to let it out."

But first, they had to locate the exact garage from which the sounds were emanating. That wasn't difficult. What was difficult was getting the garage open. Not only was it locked, but the owner had gone in for some extra security in the form of a padlock.

"Well, that's it. There's not much we can do," concluded Fred, as he tugged at the unyielding padlock.

"But we can't just leave the poor creature in there," protested Betty. She put her face against the garage door and started to make cooing noises in an attempt to soothe the unseen animal.

Fred was starting to point out that there was not much he could do against the robust padlock, when Betty, her face still pressed against the garage door, suddenly ordered tersely, "Be quiet!"

Fred was somewhat taken aback. Betty didn't usually speak to him like that. He started to remonstrate with her, but he didn't get very far.

"Be quiet!" Betty snapped once more. "I thought I heard something else."

"Heard what?" Fred asked.

"That creature in there," Betty replied. "I think it spoke. I think it said, 'Help me!' "

"Don't be ridiculous!" retorted Fred. "You're letting your imagination run away with you."

But Betty insisted that she had heard something, and she made her husband put his ear against the garage door.

Fred listened. From inside the garage he heard a series of scuffling noises — long, slow, drawn-out scuffling noises, as though something was being dragged across the floor in an effort of terrific proportions.

And then Fred heard the voice.

"Help me," someone seemed to be saying from inside the garage.

Fred stepped back from the door and shot his nervous eyes at Betty's.

"We've got to do something" said Fred, his heart starting to thump at the prospect of what they had stumbled upon.

"But what?" Betty asked. "We don't know who owns the garage, and by the time we get to a phone and call the authorities, it might be too late."

Fred thought for a moment. "I know!" he suddenly announced. "Herbie Johnson! If anyone can get that door open, Herbie can. And I know he's at home. That's his van parked over there. I'll go and get Herbie."

Moments later, Fred was back with a large, 250-pound man carrying a formidable-looking toolbox.

"I'll soon have this off," said Herbie Johnson as he pulled from his box the biggest pair of bolt cutters that Fred had ever seen. Herbie did not exaggerate. One mighty flexing of his huge muscles against the handles of the bolt cutters and the padlock snapped as if it had been nothing more than a withered twig.

With the padlock out of the way, Herbie bent down and studied the lock of the garage door. It was a small, round keyhole set into the middle of the chromium-plated handle.

"That looks pretty straightforward," Herbie announced after a few seconds of study.

Herbie took a piece of bent wire from his toolbox, inserted it into the keyhole, and jiggled it about. A few seconds later, Herbie pulled the wire from the hole and gave the handle a twist. It turned.

"Got it!" Herbie proclaimed. "Right, let's see what we've got in here."

Herbie gave an almost imperceptible tug on the handle and the door swung up and over in one smooth movement. A shaft of sunlight streamed in lighting up the garage's formerly dark interior.

Betty, Fred, and Herbie looked into the garage and all gasped at once. Betty clutched her chest. Fred clutched his stomach. Herbie just stood there with his mouth open.

Shuffling toward the trio from out of the garage's gloom came a ghastly, female form dressed in the tattered remnants of a once-pretty dress. Long strands of flesh dangled from the woman's arms and legs. From her lower left arm and hand, the flesh was gone altogether, leaving the skeletal bones clearly visible. Her head hung weakly as she made her way on legs more bone than flesh toward the open door. Except for a few strands of hair, the woman was bald. Her scalp appeared to be covered with thousands of bubbles that fizzed and popped underneath a thin, grayish-white vapor rising from her head.

Herbie couldn't comprehend what he was seeing. "Good God!" he uttered.

At the sound of Herbie's voice, the woman stopped and raised her head, exposing the most horrible face that any of the three witnesses had seen and ever hoped to see.

The first thing that struck Herbie Johnson was the size of the woman's teeth. They seemed to be enormous. Then he realized why. *She had no lips.*

There was just a jagged edge where her bottom lip should have been, but all of the flesh from her top lip right back to her nose was gone. Her nose, too, had suffered some damage. It was only partially intact. The tip and the nostrils were missing.

But the worst thing Herbie would recall was the woman's eyes. The pupils were gone. The eyes were totally white, like two saucers of solidified milk.

"Help me," the woman tried to say.

It was too much for Herbie Johnson. Pausing only to shout to Fred and Betty that he was going to call for an ambulance, he ran.

"Call the police, as well!" called Fred, still clutching his stomach.

Herbie had scarcely returned from his task when blaring sirens and screeching tires announced the arrival of an ambulance and a police patrol car. The vehicles drew to a halt a few yards from where Betty Elmore courageously cradled the stricken woman in her arms. Two paramedics, closely followed by two uniformed police officers, moved swiftly toward the little group.

One police officer took Fred and Herbie to one side. He received a brief account of the activities of the previous 20 minutes, writing it all down in his notebook.

His partner, meanwhile, helped the two paramedics gently remove the woman from Betty's arms and start to render what assistance they could. The officer was having difficulty coming to terms with the sight that greeted him.

It was a couple of minutes before he managed to ask the medics what could have caused such horrendous injuries.

"Acid," one replied. "She's been burned with acid."

"Will she be all right?" the officer asked hopefully. But he knew the answer was negative as soon as he spoke the question. Even if the woman survived, the damage done by the acid was simply too great. Plastic surgery can work miracles, but it has its limits. And the woman was way beyond those limits.

"We've got to get her to the hospital fast," said the paramedic. "It doesn't look good."

"I'll ride along with you," said the officer.

As the paramedics carefully placed the woman on a stretcher and loaded her into their ambulance, the two policemen conferred.

The one who had assisted the paramedics told the other that the woman had been burned with acid. His partner was not surprised. After talking to Fred and Herbie, the

242

officer had taken a look inside the garage in which the victim had been imprisoned. In one corner of the garage, he told his partner, stood a large vat that was almost full of hydrochloric acid. "She must have fallen into it," the officer concluded. "Unless, of course, someone pushed her into it."

So, while one officer rode in the ambulance with the victim, his partner stayed behind to radio in for detectives and a forensics team.

In the ambulance, the victim was fading fast. "I don't think we're going to make it," said one of the paramedics.

The victim seemed to hear what the paramedic said. She turned her head toward him and her mouth moved. A sound came from the back of her throat.

"Did you catch what she said?" asked the police officer.

"It sounded like 'husband,'" the medic replied.

"Yes," said the policeman. "That's what it sounded like to me."

The woman made it all right to the hospital, but she didn't make it any further. Despite the valiant efforts of a team of doctors, the victim died two hours after she was admitted.

Back at the scene of the woman's ordeal, detectives had been working fast. The woman had been identified as 30-year-old Dassa Jackson, a resident of the same apartment block that was home to Fred and Betty Elmore. She had lived with her 37-year-old husband, Cecil, though he was not at home when detectives called to break the news of his wife's death. Neighbors told the officers that Cecil was at work. So it was at his workplace where Cecil Jackson learned that his wife was dead. He seemed genuinely surprised and grief-stricken.

"Have you any idea how your wife came to be locked in the garage?" Jackson was asked. He replied that he hadn't though he agreed that it was his garage and that he held the only keys to the lock and padlock. Asked if he had those keys on his person, Jackson replied that he did not. He had taken his car out of the garage in order to drive himself to work, and then he had locked and padlocked the garage and taken the keys back to his apartment. "I left the keys with my wife during the daytime," Jackson explained. "There were things that we kept in the garage that Dassa might need."

Jackson explained that the garage stored such items as cleaning fluids and detergents, which Jackson, through his work with a chemicals company, was able to buy in bulk quantities. Detergent isn't cheap when you have to buy it in little bottles from the supermarket, he told the officers. Purchasing it wholesale in five-gallon containers brought the cost down considerably.

"There wasn't room in the apartment for such large containers," he went on, "and, anyhow, Dassa didn't like having stuff like that around the apartment. She thought it was dangerous."

Not unnaturally, the detectives were curious as to why Jackson kept a large vat of hydrochloric acid in the garage. Again, the grieving husband expressed a surprise that seemed genuine. He didn't know anything about a vat of acid, he claimed. He had no idea how it could have gotten there.

But further questioning of Cecil Jackson began to throw some light on a possible motive for Dassa's murder. It also brought to the surface the name of the possible killer: Vince Drury.

Drury, Jackson said, had been a good friend to both him and his wife. Unfortunately, he had been a better friend to Dassa than he had to Cecil, a fact that Cecil only discovered when he arrived home early one day and found his wife and his friend in bed together. What followed was the heated exchange that such a discovery would inevitably bring about, and Cecil had literally thrown Drury out of the apartment.

Cecil Jackson told the detectives that he and Dassa then had a long talk about things. Dassa admitted that she had been a fool. She said she had become infatuated with Drury, and the couple began an affair that lasted several months. Dassa knew it was wrong, but she couldn't help herself. Eventually, she told her husband through tears, she had wanted to end the affair, but Drury wouldn't let her go. He threatened to tell Cecil everything if Dassa didn't agree to go on seeing him and doing what he wanted. Jackson said his wife was glad that he had found out because Drury no longer had a hold over her.

But, Jackson continued, Drury still wouldn't let Dassa go. Drury would call her up when Cecil was out at work, pleading with her to go away with him. But she refused. He started calling round at the apartment, but Dassa wouldn't open the door. Finally, he started to make melo-dramatic threats, intimating that if he couldn't have her, no one would. At first, Dassa was frightened, but Cecil said he persuaded her that it was nothing to worry about and that Drury wouldn't really do anything.

"How wrong I was," he sobbed to the detectives. "But I never imagined that Drury would go that far."

Neither did the detectives who questioned Vince Drury. Dassa's former lover was a quiet, rather timid man who looked as though he couldn't possibly pose any physical harm to anyone. He strenuously denied Cecil's allegations that he had virtually blackmailed Dassa into continuing their affair. He also denied that he had made unwanted visits to Dassa's home. "It's Jackson that you ought to be talking to about Dassa's death," Drury advised the detectives. "It's him that she was afraid of, not me. The man's an animal."

The detectives were inclined to agree. Statistics show that when an ordinary housewife meets a sudden, unexpected death, chances are her husband has had a hand in it. Usually, a husband will do the job himself, either in a momentary fit of anger or in a carefully calculated plot designed to make the killing look like an accident or the work of some mysterious third party.

A spur-of-the-moment killing presents no problem for experienced sleuths. The murderous husband is so shocked by the results of his violent outburst that he makes little or no attempt to conceal the truth. Similarly, the planned killing also presents few problems for detectives. The husband may think that he has been clever and has thought of every angle. But he is a novice in the killing game. And pitched against him are experienced homicide investigators, backed up by every scientific aid that this sophisticated technological age can muster. Right from the outset, it is no contest.

Cecil Jackson thought he was being clever when he feigned surprise and grief upon hearing of his wife's death and then casually introduced into his interview with police officers the subject of Vince Drury's affair with Dassa. But routine police work quickly established not only that Drury was not involved in Dassa's death but that Cecil Jackson had a motive for wanting his wife dead. Besides learning about his criminal record, which spoke for itself, sleuths discovered the matter of the insurance policy that Cecil Jackson had recently taken out on his wife.

Cecil Jackson, sleuths learned, had a criminal record for violence. Some years earlier — before he was married to Dassa — a girlfriend had told him that she wanted to end their relationship. Jackson's reaction had been to imprison her in her apartment and to try to get her to change her mind by beating her up. But quite understandably, she didn't change her mind. And all that Jackson got for his trouble was two years in jail.

Under the terms of the insurance policy on Dassa's life, Cecil stood to collect almost $100,000 to help soothe his grief at not having her around anymore. But, sleuths found out, the policy had been taken out only a week before Dassa's death. And even the most elementary student of murder knows that it is both wise and respectful to wait a little longer than seven days before cashing in on a policy. Such indecent impatience is bound to prompt suspicion.

Even though the investigators could prove that Cecil had both the motive and the opportunity to kill his wife, it took several hours of interrogation before Cecil Jackson decided to talk. And even then, he claimed that Dassa's death was an accident.

Jackson claimed there had been an argument between himself and Dassa on the night of February 24th. One thing led to another and Dassa hit him. So, he said, he hit her back. Then he grabbed her round the throat. He meant only to frighten her, nothing more than that. His hands were only on her throat for a few seconds. But in just that time, Dassa's body went limp. He thought he had killed her. He didn't know what to do. He took her down to the garage and locked her in. Why he did that, he didn't know. He couldn't explain it. He was not acting rationally. His mind was in turmoil.

The next morning, before he went to work, Cecil looked in the garage. Dassa was still lying on the floor where he had left her, so he locked the garage up again. He never thought about the acid, he said, and he certainly didn't put her into it. He wasn't that callous, he said.

Jackson told the detectives that he was ready to admit to a charge of manslaughter on the grounds of diminished responsibility — accidentally killing Dassa during an argument while he was angry and not in control of himself. Conviction on such a charge often carries for its perpetrator just a few years of jail time or even a period of probation. But the homicide investigators were unmoved. They told Jackson he would be charged with murder.

So it was that, in February 1992, Cecil Jackson stood

trial at the Old Bailey on a charge of murdering his wife Dassa. He insisted on pleading guilty to manslaughter, even though his defense counsel advised that his cause was hopeless. And his present attorneys weren't alone in that opinion. All four sets of counsel whom Jackson hired — and subsequently fired — felt the same way.

Finally, Jackson announced to the stunned court, he would conduct his own defense. The judge, Mr. Justice Hidden, advised Jackson against such a course of action, but Jackson was adamant. He said he could do a better job than any trained lawyer.

Prosecutor John Bevan, Q.C., detailed to the court the appalling injuries and agonizing death that Dassa had suffered. He also spoke of her great courage. Blinded, crippled, and with her flesh hanging in shreds, Dassa still had sufficient strength of character to identify her killer. "Husband," she had told the paramedic and the police officer who traveled with her in the ambulance.

Prosecutor Bevan also dismissed Jackson's claim that the killing had been an accident. It was a planned and premeditated murder, Bevan said. This was demonstrated by the fact that Jackson had spent weeks, and possibly months, gathering acid, ounce by ounce, until he had 50 gallons — more than enough to dispose of Dassa's body. Police believed that he intended to strangle her and then dissolve her body in the acid. That Dassa was still alive, although unconscious, when Jackson dumped her into the vat was a mistake on his part. The prosecutor asserted that Jackson's surprise when he learned of Dassa's death was genuine. But it was not that she was dead that surprised him. It was the way in which she died — and the fact that her body had been discovered — that came as such a shock to him.

To the legal process, Bevan continued, the method of the murder did not matter. What counted was whether death was intended. And in the minds of the jury, there was no doubt that Cecil Jackson intended that Dassa should die.

On Thursday, February 20, 1992, Cecil Jackson was convicted of murder. He showed no emotion as the verdict was announced.

"You are a dangerous man with an enormous capacity for evil," Judge Hidden told Jackson before sentencing him to life imprisonment. The judge added that Jackson must serve at least 18 years before parole can be considered.

Life at the apartment block in Forest Gate goes on much as it did before. Each Monday morning, promptly at 11 o'clock, Fred and Betty Elmore set off for their trip to the local shops. Only now they no longer use the shortcut through the alleyway that runs past the garages at the rear of the block. Betty says that she doesn't like the thought that muggers might be lurking in the bushes. And Fred agrees. That alleyway is a mugger's paradise.

EDITOR'S NOTE:
*Fred and Betty Elmore, Herbie Johnson, and Vince Drury are not the real names of the persons so named in the foregoing story. Fictitious names have been used because there is no reason for public interest in the identities of these persons.*

# "BIBLE-CLUTCHING GANG-RAPED TEEN!"

## by Bill G. Cox

Young people knew the undeveloped lot on the northeast side of San Antonio, Texas, as a "lover's lane." Teenagers who often parked and partied there called it "The Circle." Plans for a residential development never quite got off the ground, but a paved road runs through the otherwise vacant field.

The Circle wasn't exactly a scenic spot to engage in drive-in romance, but its isolation served the purpose.

Besides offering a place for carefree sex, it was a handy spot for drinking beer or doing drugs. The piles of litter and discarded junk attested to its being an ideal spot to dump trash, as well. The kids didn't mind the environmental clutter and hardly noticed it when they went there to make out.

At about 3:45 on the afternoon of Thursday, October 26, 1988, a San Antonio resident was driving to the site to dump some trash when he saw a strange form by the side of the road. When he got out to look closer, a horrible, bloody mess met his gaze. He jumped back in his truck and sped to the closest phone to report his sickening discovery.

Patrolman Brian Custard received the call from the San Antonio Police Department radio dispatcher. The "body found" location was given as near the intersection of

250

Jester Court and Royal Lane. Custard wasn't far from the area and he radioed his arrival within minutes.

When Custard saw the body on the ground, he was sickened as he had never been before. Months later, he would still remember the terrible, gory sight. The body was dressed in women's clothes, but the face had been beaten to such a pulp that it looked neither male nor female. The uniformed officer radioed for homicide detectives and a crime scene team.

Among the first investigators to arrive was Homicide Sergeant Billy Ewell. He could hardly believe his eyes when he viewed the pitiful human remains lying face up in the tall grass. The body, about 25 feet from the street curb, appeared to have been dragged there, Ewell noted.

Ewell knew that the body's facial features would not be much help in making an identification. As if that weren't bad enough, the jaw bone had been broken, and several teeth were scattered on the victim's chest and over the ground. As it turned out, however, identification was quickly made by other means.

Despite the victim's face being bludgeoned beyond recognition, her sex was not a mystery. The obviously female victim was wearing a white T-shirt, a denim miniskirt hiked above her waist, white socks, and white sneakers. She was not wearing panties. Looking inside a purse that was lying near the body, the detectives found a wallet containing a Texas Department of Public Safety identification card bearing the name of Donna Friesenhahn and giving her age as 16 years old. The card bore an address in the nearby town of Cibolo, which is between San Antonio and New Braunfels.

Other contents of the purse were strewn over the area. Sleuths found two Bibles near the corpse, one with the girl's name embossed on its white, bloodstained cover. A search of the immediate vicinity failed to turn up a weapon that could have battered the victim so savagely.

The investigators surmised that cuts on the body could

have been inflicted by broken bottles they found scattered around the area. Bloody glass fragments that appeared to be from the smashed beer and wine-cooler bottles were found on the ground and on the victim's body.

The searching detectives and criminalists who photographed and processed the site for evidence, however, were unable to find anything in the area that might have been used to bludgeon the victim.

"Somebody stomping her face could have done that, too," one investigator suggested.

A radio unit sent to the Cibolo address to notify the victim's relatives found a large mobile home at the address, but no one was at home. Later, the medical examiner's office located a relative with whom the teenage girl lived and requested that he come to the morgue to identify the body.

Questioning the relative and another family member who lived nearby, detectives learned that Donna, whose nickname was "Dee Dee," was a pretty teenager with a very trusting nature. She made friends easily. Donna's mother was deceased, and her life had been somewhat unstable in recent months, especially after she dropped out of high school in the spring of 1987, the relatives said.

At one point Donna decided that she wanted to move to Houston, where another relative lived, and go to school there. But her high school transcript took two months to reach the school, which prevented her enrollment, the detectives learned. Since school already was under way by then, Donna returned to San Antonio, but she had not gone back to school.

When an autopsy was conducted by a pathologist in the medical examiner's office, the full horror of the savage assault on the girl became apparent. She had been sexually assaulted, probably more than once, but it was the extent of her injuries that sickened the veteran investigators.

The autopsy report revealed that the young girl had been beaten so badly, nearly every bone in her face was crushed. The report stated that the victim's injuries included crushed upper and lower jaw bones, eight teeth knocked out or damaged, multiple skull fractures, and numerous lacerations on her face, head, and body. The pathologist said, "The majority of the injuries were to the head. Small fragments of bone were actually in the brain [from the severe force of the blows]. The jaw bones and the nose were all crushed to the extent that, if you pushed on the face, the bones gave way."

The pathologist said a large wooden splinter had been removed from a gaping wound in the victim's forehead, which seemed to indicate that the bludgeoning weapon had been a wooden club. No such weapon had yet been found.

Submitted with the report where numerous color photos, taken during the autopsy, that made investigators wince when they viewed them. Detectives said the victim's injuries were evidence of one of the most brutal murders in the entire violent history of crime in the city where the Alamo stands.

When they first discovered the slain girl, detectives speculated that she had been a victim of a serial rapist who had been terrorizing the city's North Side. The violence the attacker exhibited in the rapes led sleuths to fear that he would eventually kill a victim. Now, the sleuths believed, the serial rapist had gone over the edge and had turned into a cold-blooded, sadistic killer.

But in spite of several detectives having been assigned to the serial rapes, no arrest had been made.

While working on this theory, detectives started backtracking Donna Friesenhahn's last known itinerary. But relentless digging failed to bring a good lead to the identity of her killer.

The whole investigative picture changed within a short time when the North Side serial rapist was nabbed and charged in several sexual assaults. But the investigators could find nothing that linked him to the brutal murder of the teenage girl found in The Circle.

Three long, frustrating months passed since the sex-killing of Donna Friesenhahn when, out of the blue, an informant phoned the Bexar County Sheriff's Department from Houston, 100 miles to the east.

"I've got a good lead for you on the murder of a girl last October," the tipster said. The caller said that he knew of a youth who had been told about the girl's slaying by someone else. The caller gave the name of the youth who told him about the rape-murder, but he said he didn't know the name of the original source.

The tip was relayed to San Antonio detectives. Over the next few days, the detectives quizzed several youths whose names they learned from the person named by the Houston tipster.

The first witness whom the sleuths grilled said that everything he knew about the murder had come from an acquaintance of his. According to the witness, this acquaintance had actually been led to the body of the slain girl on the morning after her killing.

After tracking down the second possible witness, the investigators heard a bizarre story. The youth admitted he had viewed the girl's body after being taken to the site by a 16-year-old friend of his, whom he had known in high school.

"I couldn't even tell it was a girl when I looked," the nervous youth said. "She was beat so bad, man, it made me sick to my stomach."

Noticing his reaction to the shocking sight, the witness said, his friend who had brought him to the scene suggested they "go buy a Coke. Maybe it'll make you feel better."

The witness said that his friend, who was limping at the time, mentioned that he'd injured his foot kicking the girl as she lay bruised and bleeding.

"He just said they, like, kicked her and stuff," said the witness. The friend with a limp gave the witness a plastic trash sack full of bloodstained clothing and a pair of bloody sneakers and asked him to get rid of it. The witness put the bag beside his family's garbage for regular sanitation pickup, he recalled.

The witness named his friend as 16-year-old Ty Wesley Gonnerman, whose home address, the sleuths noted, was only one block from the field where the victim's body had been found.

When quizzed a short time later, the teenager provided no details of the murder. As a prosecutor would later describe it, "He didn't deny it, or he didn't admit it. He just didn't talk period."

After hearing the story of the witnesses and talking to Ty Gonnerman, detectives charged the youth with murder under the juvenile code, since he was only 16. Under Texas law, anyone to be charged as an adult offender must be 17.

The suspect's name was not disclosed to the press at that time, but police did say that other suspects were being sought. Detective-Sergeant Ewell told reporters, "A combination of information that was received—plus circumstantial evidence gathered at the scene—helped us put the case together."

From the witnesses with whom Gonnerman had talked about the slaying, investigators learned that the suspect had met Donna Friesenhahn at a teenage club the evening before her body was discovered in the field.

Detectives went to the club, a teenage hangout that specialized in video games and served only soft drinks. They were told by club employees who knew Donna that she had left there in the company of Gonnerman and two other young men they had been playing pool with.

The other two youths were identified as Rolando Rodarte and Bob Adkins, both approximately 19 years old. Witnesses said that Rodarte had tossed a $100 bill on a table and told the club manager to call a limousine for the departing group of teenagers.

The three men had been playing pool with Donna about two hours before they all left in the pale blue limousine that responded to the call.

After Gonnerman's arrest, Rolando Rodarte came to the police station voluntarily to talk with detectives. He said he had been with Donna Friesenhahn and Ty Gonnerman earlier at the club, but he denied any knowledge of what happened to the girl after he left them that evening.

Rodarte mentioned another man who was with Gonnerman that night, whose name he thought was Frank or something like that. He gave the name of a street on which he thought Frank lived.

But detectives who walked door-to-door on the street failed to come up with anyone named "Frank."

Meanwhile, detectives obtained the name of the limousine company that had dispatched the limo to the teenage club that night and tracked down the driver. He was of little help. The driver related that during the ride, he had heard noise in the backseat that prompted him to slide open the partition between driver and passengers and ask if there was a problem. He'd closed the partition after one youth answered no.

He remembered that one male passenger had instructed him to go to an address at about 2:00 a.m. There, after a few minutes, they picked up another man. The driver didn't hear his name, but he said that the address was on a different street from the one on which Rodarte had thought the mysterious "Frank" lived.

Later, the limo chauffeur had been instructed to go to the site known as The Circle. The girl and two of the males had been dropped off there, the driver recalled.

While the murder probe continued, Rolando Rodarte, who was a member of a youth gang known as "The Clan," was arrested for the burglary of two business establishments. He was convicted of the charges and sentenced to 10 years in prison.

Meanwhile, the state wanted to have Ty Gonnerman certified as an adult so that he could be tried in state district court rather than in juvenile court. A district judge signed papers ordering the suspect to undergo psychiatric testing as a preliminary move toward trying him as an adult.

An assistant district attorney who headed the juvenile prosecution unit said, "We have to see if he is sophisticated and mature enough to be treated as an adult."

At a hearing following the mental examination, Gonnerman was certified as an adult. He was indicted for the murder by a Bexar County grand jury.

With the young suspect bound over for trial, police and the district attorney's office continued the murder investigation. They felt certain, based on the story that Gonnerman had told his friends, that others were involved in the murder, primarily Rodarte.

Gonnerman's trial was delayed by the temporary loss of the so-called "rape kit," which contained samples of blood, hair, semen and other evidence from the victim and the crime scene. Actually, the state learned to its relief, that the kit had not been lost—only temporarily misplaced when the DNA laboratory in the medical examiner's office was reorganized and new personnel took over.

With the evidence now in hand and Gonnerman's trial about to start, the D.A.'s office had Rodarte transported back to San Antonio from prison on April 19, 1991, as a possible trial witness and also to take blood and bite samples from him.

Assistant District Attorney Mary Ellen Smythe, who would prosecute the case, also wanted to make renewed efforts to locate the man known only as "Frank," whom Rodarte and the limousine driver had mentioned in the early phases of the probe. She believed he might be a vital witness.

They ran a check on Rodarte's visitors to the jail, hoping to find someone who recognized the name Frank. One of the visitors did and was able to give them the general area where "Frank" lived. It wasn't the street mentioned by Rodarte or the chauffeur.

"I think Rodarte sent us down a bunny trail," one detective said to his partner. "And the chauffeur just didn't remember what street where he picked up the guy."

Homicide Detective John Campa and District Attorney Investigator John Lobello launched a house-to-house search of the street named by Rodarte's jail visitor, talking to residents they found at home and leaving their cards in the door when no one was at home. As a result, someone who knew "Frank" got word to him that he was being sought by the police. Apparently the heat generated by the detectives' street pounding prompted "Frank" to come in voluntarily.

Frank Marino, as he gave his name, had a shocking story to tell. His account linked Rolando Rodarte to the rape and murder of Donna Friesenhahn. He said he had witnessed the girl being beaten and raped in the limousine's backseat and said that Gonnerman and Rodarte dragged her from the limousine at The Circle, after which the limousine had driven away.

The dental imprints taken from Rodarte and compared with bite marks on the victim's body were inconclusive. But DNA testing of both the semen samples from the victim's body and of Rodarte's blood positively linked him to the rape-murder.

Meanwhile, on August 27, 1991, Ty Gonnerman, now 18 years old, at long last went on trial for the murder in San Antonio's 226th State District Court. In her opening statement to the jury, Assistant D.A. Smythe said Donna Friesenhahn "was begging for her life as she was being beaten about the face."

In his opening remarks, the defense attorney said that

Gonnerman never took part in the rape or beating death of the victim, contending that the real killer was Rolando Rodarte, as yet not charged or indicted in the case.

Jurors winced when a color video of the teenage victim at the crime scene was shown. Detective David Anderson, an evidence specialist, told the jury, "I didn't have a picture, but I couldn't have recognized her."

The friend of Gonnerman who had been led to view the victim in the field the morning after her death told the jury that Gonnerman claimed he "just went along with Rodarte" in the vicious beating of the teenager.

Another youth testified that Gonnerman gave his friend a sack of bloody clothing and sneakers to get rid of "because they were bloody from kicking the girl . . . [and] because he didn't want to be caught with them." The witness added that Gonnerman told him the girl was beaten until her body stopped moving.

The most riveting testimony came from Frank Marino, who was on a 10-year probation for a drug offense. The witness said he became involved in the party when the limo stopped at his house so that Rodarte could buy some cocaine and Rodarte invited him along for the ride.

At one point during the drive, Rodarte tried to force himself on the girl and she bit his lip. That was when the savage beating started, Marino said. He said that Gonnerman punched Donna in the face three times as Rodarte raped her. Marino said he didn't interfere for fear of being attacked himself.

The witness said that the sobbing girl tried to leap from the speeding limo at some point along Interstate 10, but she was pulled back. He recalled that the driver lowered the privacy panel and asked if there was a problem. Rodarte said no, and the driver closed it. Then the beating and rape continued. The witness testified that both Rodarte and Bob Adkins raped Donna.

During the assault, the victim reached into her purse and pulled out a white Bible, Marino said. She clutched the book to her chest and prayed to God for help as she was being raped and beaten. Marino quoted the girl as crying, "Stop it! God, please help me!" as Gonnerman held her down for another man to rape her.

"She was just fighting for her life," Marino told the jury. "She did have some strength . . . but after they kept on hitting her, she stopped saying anything. I thought she was unconscious."

Just before Gonnerman, Marino, and the victim were dropped off at The Circle, Marino said, Donna was sobbing and shaking and had her arms crossed upon her chest, still clutching the Bible. The last words he heard her say were, " 'God bless you all,' like she knew her life was coming to an end," Marino said.

Marino finished his harrowing story, telling jurors that he offered the limo driver $20 and some cocaine to take him home.

"I wanted to get the hell out of there," Marino said. Adkins had also left the party sometime after the rape, the witness said.

The star witness for the defense was the blond-haired Ty Gonnerman himself, who claimed he never attacked Donna and even tried to help her after Rodarte had raped and beaten her senseless. He said Rodarte used a four-inch thick post to pound the girl to death.

The youth said he watched, frozen with fear, as Rodarte and Adkins raped the victim repeatedly in the limousine. He said Rodarte urged him to rape Donna but he refused.

When they got out of the limo at The Circle, Rodarte took the victim into a field and raped her once more, Gonnerman testified. Continuing, Gonnerman said, "He got up and walked over to me. That's when he said he couldn't let her live."

As the jury listened, horrified, Gonnerman said that Rodarte "picked up a bottle. He hit her with it in her head. She was crying and asking why he was doing that.

He had steel-toed boots on. He'd kick. He'd stomp. Anything. Like a place kick, sometimes; other times, he'd step down with it."

The attack lasted 10 minutes and the victim was lying face up, sobbing, he said. Rodarte then took a broken beer bottle and sliced her face and neck with it. "She was crying and screaming out," Gonnerman said, "like 'Help me! Please God, help me! Why are you doing this? I don't even know your name!' "

After trying to choke the badly beaten and cut-up victim with her sweater, Roland then rummaged through her purse. "I walked over to her," the defendant said, "I tried to help her get up. She was holding her neck. I knew she was bleeding."

Gonnerman said he put his arm under the victim to support her, and the two began walking away. But Gonnerman testified, "Rodarte said, 'Where are you going?' I said, 'Don't worry, I'll take care of her.' He said, 'Put her down.' She was still crying, 'God help me! Why did this happen to me!' "

Gonnerman said he lowered the badly injured victim to the ground, and Rodarte exclaimed, " 'Look, either you're with me, or you're with her.' I thought he was going to beat me up. I thought he was going to kill me. I said, 'O.K., O.K., I'm with you.' "

Then, trying to appease Rodarte, Gonnerman kicked the victim in the leg, scuffing his foot on the ground, the only blow he said he struck. His foot was sore the next day, he recalled.

Then came the shockingly graphic conclusion of Gonnerman's testimony:

"I started walking toward the curb. I saw him pick up what looked like a heavy post. He had to hold it with two hands."

Gonnerman demonstrated how Rodarte held the post — like a post-hole digger — and brought it down three times on the victim's head.

"I thought he might have knocked her out. I kind of had a feeling that she might be dead. I just felt sick."

In final arguments before the jury of five women and seven men, Prosecutor Mary Ellen Smythe clutched the white Bible that was stained with the murder victim's blood and dramatically declared, "Donna Friesenhahn cannot be here to tell you what happened. I have to be her voice."

Although Gonnerman testified that he had not delivered the fatal blows to the victim, another prosecutor on the team explained that it was not necessary for Gonnerman to have done so to be convicted of murder. A provision of a Texas law provides that actions such as urging, soliciting, aiding or attempting to aid a murder constitute murder itself.

Said the assistant prosecutor, "All during this trial the defense has put Rolando Rodarte on trial. We can only try one person at a time. Another day, Rodarte will have his day in court. Both Rodarte and Gonnerman are guilty of murder."

The jury took only 85 minutes to decide that Ty Gonnerman was guilty of murder.

The same jury took 90 minutes when deciding the convicted killer's punishment. They returned with a verdict of life imprisonment. Prosecutor Smythe, wiping away tears, said the trial had drained her emotionally and that she had nightmares of Donna Friesenhahn "running in a field and someone grabbing her legs and her falling."

Shortly after Gonnerman's trial, an indictment charging capital murder, which could carry the death penalty, was returned against Rolando Rodarte. His trial began on June 1, 1992. Key witness Frank Marino repeated his blood-curdling testimony about what he observed in the limousine backseat on the murder night.

But the most damning evidence came when forensic experts testified about the DNA test results. The experts told the jury that DNA structure of the semen found in

262

the victim's vagina matched the genetic structure of Rodarte's blood. The witnesses testified that the semen samples did not belong to convicted killer Gonnerman.

The experts explained that DNA, or deoxyribonucleic acid, is contained in human cells and bears a chemical genetic code that, similar to fingerprints, is unique to each individual.

Although Gonnerman was listed as a possible witness in the trial, he was not called because of feared reprisal in the prison where he was serving his life term. Gonnerman's attorney told the jury that Rodarte could have made contact with prison gangs while serving his burglary conviction.

"If Gonnerman testified and it is true that Rodarte has buddies in prison, it could cost him his life," the lawyer said.

A female witness took the stand to testify that she had heard Rodarte brag about the sexual assault and fatal beating of the victim.

When prosecutors finished their case, the defense did not call any witnesses, contending the state had failed to prove the charge against Rodarte. In final arguments, the defense attacked the credibility of Marino, a convicted drug dealer, and other witnesses.

After deliberating, the jury found Rolando Rodarte guilty of capital murder, which is punishable by either life in prison or death by chemical injection.

During the punishment phase of the trial, the state presented eight law officers who testified about the defendant's violent nature.

Bexar County jail guards described Rodarte as the violent leader of a jail gang who terrorized other inmates and attacked the jail guards. The witnesses said they had once seen Rodarte and his buddies severely beat an inmate over a dispute about a telephone.

A weeping relative of the defendant pleaded with the jury to spare his life.

"Please don't kill him!" she cried as she wept on the witness stand.

The jury spent over five hours deliberating the fate of the convicted killer. When they returned to the courtroom, they decreed that Rodarte should be imprisoned for life instead of put to death. Later, a jury member told newsmen that two jurors philosophically opposed the death penalty and could not be persuaded to change their minds. Texas law requires that in the case of a jury deadlocked in the punishment phase of a capital murder trial, a life sentence is automatically required.

Bob Adkins, who, witnesses testified, also raped Donna Friesenhahn twice in the limousine, left the state, clear of any charges in the case. It was a decision that left the prosecutors highly frustrated. The district attorney's office was helpless because state law provided that Adkins could not be convicted on the testimony of accomplice witnesses.

Also, forensic experts testified that DNA samples taken from the victim's body pointed only to Rodarte.

Rolando Rodarte and Ty Gonnerman are serving their life sentences in the Texas Department of Corrections.

EDITOR'S NOTE:
*Frank Marino and Bob Adkins are not the real names of the persons so named in the foregoing story. Fictitious names have been used because there is no reason for public interest in the identities of these persons.*

# "TWISTED TORTURE TOOLS OF THE RUSH-SEEKING SICKOS"

## by Jerry Spangler

It was a brisk evening but not bitterly cold, as you might expect on a November night in a mountain town. The relative mildness prompted the local young folk to take to their cars in observance of the town's traditional courting ritual. The teens would drive back and forth from one end of Main Street to the other, pausing now and then at the curb to flirt with a pretty girl or handsome boy on the sidewalk.

In Cedar City, a small college town in southern Utah, there's not much else to do. And since most of the kids already know each other, it is usually a predictable ritual. But on Monday, November 21, 1988, the rite took an unusual twist when Nancy Johnson approached a friend's car as it idled on the street.

"You okay, Gordon?" Nancy asked her friend through the car's window. Gordon Ray Church, a 28-year-old theater arts major at nearby Southern Utah State College, seemed subdued as he sat between two men, one of whom was driving Gordon's white Ford Thunderbird. Nancy thought it odd that Gordon wasn't driving his own car.

"Wanna go somewhere and talk?" the driver of the car

cheerfully shot back. Nancy didn't recognize the man, but since there was nothing else to do and two new faces were the most interesting objects to appear in Cedar City in weeks, Nancy and a friend followed the three men to a nearby parking lot. After about 30 minutes of playful conversation, the two women turned down an offer to go further than conversation.

It was just another night on Main Street for Nancy Johnson. But to Gordon Ray Church, it was destined to become a horrible night of torture, terror, and death. Before the sun would rise, Church would become a victim of one of the worst torture killings ever recorded in Utah. He would be raped, the skin peeled off his back with pliers, his arm and his jaw broken, his neck slashed, and a lug wrench pushed so far up his rectum it would puncture his liver. Incredibly, Gordon's attackers also used jumper cables to link his genitals to a car battery, and followed that by clubbing their victim about the head so viciously that portions of his skull would be found 40 feet away from the site where the killing occurred.

Moreover, all this occurred with no particular motive.

Homicides are probably no more rare in southern Utah than they are anywhere else in rural America. But torture murders of this magnitude are unusual regardless of where they occur. Gordon Church's death was one in which the public justifiably demanded the full resources of local law enforcement be brought to bear. And before this investigation would be completed, the case would involve the state's best forensic experts, a national blood-spatter expert, and cooperative efforts by at least eight different law enforcement agencies.

"It was a perfectly investigated case," Millard County Prosecutor Warren Peterson would later say. "There were no mistakes."

In this particular case, investigators were not trying to piece together a classic whodunit. Rather, they used a complicated array of hair, blood, and fiber evidence to unravel a tale of "which one did it more." And, as a result, one man now sits on Utah's death row, while another will spend the rest of his life in prison as an accomplice.

It was Wednesday, November 23, 1988—two days after Nancy Johnson last saw Gordon Church on Cedar City's Main Street—when John Graff, a parole office for the Utah Department of Corrections, received a phone call. Lance Conway Wood, a 21-year-old parolee, was nervously blurting out that he had witnessed a homicide and wanted to take deputies to the body. He said the killer was Michael Anthony Archuleta, a roommate and fellow parolee. Wood told Officer Graff he now feared for his own life and wanted protection from Archuleta.

After picking up Wood at a Cedar City store, Graff quickly assembled the Iron County prosecutor and investigators for the Iron County Sheriff's Department to listen to Lance Wood's story. It was a convincing story, enough so that Graff immediately dispatched officers to arrest Michael Archuleta on a technical parole violation until the facts of Wood's story could be verified. Under Utah law, officers could hold Archuleta for 72 hours without filing charges.

Stuffed between two deputies in the back of a patrol car, Lance Wood directed officers to a lonely stretch of road about 40 miles north of Cedar City immediately adjacent to Interstate 15. Having crossed the boundary into Millard County, they were joined by Millard County investigators.

Evidence of a homicide was all around: blood spatters, pools of blood, pieces of hair, flesh, and bone. And, noted Millard County Sheriff's Captain Robert Dekker, "We saw a stack of cedar boughs in a grave-like fashion. And protruding from that, I could see some legs with gray stockings. The body was lying face up with a red gag in its mouth, naked from the waist down, and wrapped in tire snow chains. The neck had been slashed in an X-fashion."

Officers immediately cordoned off the entire crime

scene area, photographing everything and anything in the vicinity whether it appeared relevant or not. Everything was just as Lance Wood had initially described it.

Michael Archuleta did it, case closed. Right? Wrong.

As detectives would soon discover, it was anything but an open-and-shut case. Upon his arrest on a parole violation, Archuleta immediately countered with a story of his own, which said that he had been a simple bystander; it was actually Wood who had committed the murder.

Only a careful recording of the crime scene, in particular blood, fiber, and hair evidence, would unravel who was really telling the truth. Not wanting to take any chances, both men were repeatedly given Miranda warnings. Lawmen also confiscated the clothing of both men.

A careful canvass of the crime scene revealed considerable evidence. Deputy James Masner found several bone fragments and hair samples in a blood-stained area near where the body had been concealed, as well as large amounts of blood in different areas. Pieces of a broken car jack were recovered, as were an empty condom package, jumper cables, and bungie cord. There was blood on the jumper cables and bungie cord. Gordon Church's wallet and watch were missing from the body.

Meanwhile, some 150 miles to the north, in the Salt Lake suburb of West Valley, the victim's abandoned vehicle was recovered. "I observed on the rear bumper what appeared to me to be blood spatter," reported West Valley Patrolman Thomas McClachlan. Hair samples were also taken from the bumper.

Deputy Masner was immediately dispatched to West Valley City, where he searched the vehicle and dusted it for prints. Michael Archuleta's fingerprints were discovered on a small lamp in the trunk of the victim's car, and Lance Wood's fingerprints were located near the car's trunk area.

In addition, hair was found on a bumper jack that had been in the trunk, but no fingerprints were on the jack. According to state criminologist Robert Brinkman, the hair from the bumper matched the victim's hair.

Church's body was removed from its shallow grave and taken to the State Medical Examiner's Office in Salt Lake City, where forensic pathologist Sharon I. Schnittker conducted the autopsy. She reported the victim had abrasions and lacerations all over his body, none of which were lethal. Rather he probably died of severe blows to the head, most likely administered by a ratchet and jack leg found at the crime scene.

"I thought there were a minimum of eight to nine blows to the head," Schnittker said. "Injuries to Church's skull were so severe, it would be like your head being run over by a large car or truck. That's the kind of magnitude of force we are talking about."

Schnittker added that Church "died fairly quickly from the head injuries," but he suffered two stab wounds to the liver that also would have proved fatal. Those were likely inflicted by a tire iron found in the trunk of the victim's car. In addition, his neck had been cut, but not deeply. There were also injuries to the victim's genitals, and he had multiple abrasions to his legs, hips, thighs, and knees. His left arm and lower left jaw had been broken—strong bones that likely were not broken by a simple punch or kick. Schnittker suggested the victim had suffered a tremendous amount of pain before he died.

The victim, who had been wearing a purple sweater over a shirt, had four lesions on his penis, and his liver and diaphragm had been punctured by a long instrument, probably the tire iron recovered from the victim's car. She estimated those injuries occurred one to 30 minutes prior to death. The victim died three to five minutes after the first blow to his head, based on swelling of the brain and limited fluid in the lungs, she said.

Gordon Church was unquestionably the victim of a homicide. But at whose hand? Detectives began the arduous task of retracing the exact activities of both Lance Wood and Michael Archuleta, trying to confirm or refute the contradictory statements of both. Both men were obviously not telling the truth. Perhaps neither one was.

Lance Wood, 20, was a hyperactive high school dropout who suffered as much from a learning disability as he did from his association with the "wrong crowd." Shortly after he turned 18 years old, he stole a motorcycle and wrecked it. He was paroled from a Cedar City prison one month before the Church killing.

According to Lance Wood's statement to Deputy Charles Stewart, Wood was mortally afraid of Michael Archuleta and had repeatedly warned parole officers that Archuleta was involved in gang activities. Wood said he was so frightened of Archuleta that he feared if he moved out of the apartment they shared, Archuleta would hunt him down.

Wood described in detail the events leading up to the Church homicide. He related how he and Archuleta had cruised Main Street in Gordon Church's car, and how the three men eventually drove to a wooded area just outside of town. Investigators would later visit the scene and recover a kitchen knife blade and an appliance cord.

At the remote spot, Wood said, the three men started talking about sex, and Church admitted he was gay. It was then, Wood said, that Archuleta impulsively pulled out a knife and slashed Gordon Church's throat. Church said something like "ouch," after which Wood grabbed Archuleta's arm and allowed Church to flee. Wood didn't flee himself because, he said, "I didn't have no place to go." Wood said Archuleta tackled Church, breaking the victim's arm in the process. He then placed Church in the car's trunk and began driving on Interstate 15 toward Salt Lake City. About 40 miles north of Cedar City, at the Dog Valley exit, Archuleta pulled onto the frontage road, sodomized Church on the hood of the car, and then killed him by clubbing his head with a car jack.

At first Wood said he stayed in the car the whole time, but later recanted that, saying, "I got out of the car when Mike told me to get out of the car. I didn't have no involvement in the crime. I thought admitting being outside with him would involve me in the crime." According to Wood, he was nothing more than a helpless bystander unable to intervene on Gordon Church's behalf.

Michael Archuleta's account, however, was substantially different from Wood's. Archuleta told interrogators that he and Wood had been drinking heavily when they linked up with Gordon Church on Cedar City's Main Street. And when Lance Wood drank, he turned crazy, Archuleta claimed. Making matters worse, Wood was having problems with his girlfriend.

"I feel that this happened because of Lance wanting blood. He didn't care whose blood it was. He wanted revenge because his girlfriend went to Arizona to see another guy," Archuleta said.

Archuleta's story to Deputy Stewart was essentially the same as Wood's, except with the roles reversed. After cruising a while, Archuleta said, the three men drove to a wooded area just outside of town where they parked on a dirt road. When talk turned to sex, Church admitted he was homosexual. That's when *Wood* pulled out a knife and tackled Church as he tried to run, Archuleta asserted.

"We chained Gordon up, tied him up, and put him in the trunk. I don't know why we did that," he said. Archuleta thought they were going to turn Church loose alongside the road somewhere and take his car. "I thought maybe Wood was thinking the same thing I was, that we were going to leave him up there."

As Wood kept driving, "I knew Gordon wasn't going to leave the canyon alive," Archuleta said. "I was up to my neck already. It was one event after another."

After driving about 40 miles north toward Salt Lake City, they pulled off the freeway. At that location, Wood slashed the victim's throat and tried to shock him by attaching jumper cables to his genitals, Archuleta said.

"It was just as Lance was in front of me, he sliced Gordon's neck. At first I said to him, 'What are you doing?' The dude tried to take off, but Lance chased him down and cut his throat. When hitting him on the head with the

271

jack handle didn't kill him, Lance hooked the jumper cables to the victim's genitals to shock him to death. I hooked the cables to the car battery. I don't know why. I was just scared," Archuleta said. It was Wood who had raped the victim with a lug wrench, he said.

Despite the torture, claimed the suspect, the victim never pleaded for his life. "I guess he more or less knew what was going to happen. I didn't tell him we were going to kill him or anything. All I remember is Lance saying we were in trouble."

After the victim fell to the ground, "I heard a smack, something hitting something else. He [Wood] had his foot on Gordon's face and was swinging the jack like a golf club or like a mallet when you play croquet."

Archuleta said the memory of the scene haunted him. "I was seeing Gordon. He was right there. I could see Gordon saying, 'Why are you doing this to me?' I could see Gordon laying on the ground. I could see the shallow grave Gordon was in. I could see myself standing right next to Gordon looking at him. I still see him. It will never go away," Archuleta shuddered.

When Deputy Stewart prodded the suspect for a motive, Michael Archuleta responded, "I don't know why he was killed. He just kept saying he wouldn't rat on us. There was no motive at all. A little alcohol and you go off the deep end. We just got scared, you know. We didn't know what to do. We didn't start out planning on killing the dude."

That may have been true. Nothing in either Lance Wood's background or Michael Archuleta's background indicated a propensity toward homicide. An investigation into the 27-year-old Archuleta's background revealed he had been abused as a child and still carried the scars of burns on his arms and buttocks. He had been suspended from several different public schools and received treatment at a mental health center.

Archuleta was first sent to prison at age 18 for stealing a firearm and was paroled a year later, in 1982. He was again sent to prison in 1987 for distribution of a controlled substance and was paroled on October 11, 1988 — about a month before the murder. Neither suspect had the criminal profile that would indicate a depraved killer.

The painstaking process of determining who — if either — was telling the truth began on the streets of Cedar City. Officers there located two witnesses who remembered seeing Gordon Church sitting between the two men in the front seat of his own car. One also remembered seeing a knife strapped to the belt of one of the men, later identified as Archuleta.

An employee of a local truck stop also identified Archuleta as the man who had purchased gasoline for a white Ford Thunderbird sometime after 11:00 p.m. on November 21st. She didn't notice whether he was driving alone.

The owner of another service station about 200 miles north of Cedar City told officers that Archuleta and Wood had purchased gasoline at about 5:45 a.m. on November 22nd. He remembered Archuleta because he mistook him for someone else. The pair looked like they "had worked all night. They were dirty and their clothes [were] wrinkled and soiled," the witness recalled.

According to one witness, Archuleta showed up at his home about 1:00 p.m. on November 22nd — the afternoon after Gordon Church had last been seen. When he left the next morning, he left behind a wristwatch. Police identified the watch as belonging to Church.

Detectives then questioned a friend of Archuleta's who told them that Archuleta and Wood had arrived at her West Valley City apartment on the morning of November 22nd, "smelling of sweat, alcohol, and blood." Archuleta's pants were bloodstained, and as the men entered her apartment, the witness said, "My cat and dog almost attacked his [Archuleta's] legs. His pants were rolled up, and they had a lot of blood on them.

"The animals went a little wild. I had to get them off of Mike. The dog jumped up on his leg and was smelling

273

him, and the cat was, too. I had to lock them in another room."

According to the witness, Archuleta told her they had been rabbit hunting, "and rabbits bleed a lot." When their car broke down, they said, they hitchhiked to Salt Lake City. The witness told officers she then drove them to the apartment of a relative. "He kept saying he wanted to get out of his bloody clothing. It seemed urgent to him to get out of his clothes."

A clerk at a local thrift store identified Michael Archuleta as a man who had entered her store about 9:30 a.m. and purchased some pants. He was carrying a portable radio at the time, she recalled. (The radio was later recovered and identified as belonging to the victim.)

Four blocks away from the thrift store, detectives located Archuleta's discarded blue jeans in a drainage ditch in Salt Lake County. Also recovered were personal papers, a telephone calling card, and pieces of a photograph belonging to Gordon Church, said Captain Robert Dekker of the Millard County Sheriff's Office.

Stare forensic experts examined Archuleta's pants and shirt and determined the blood was that of Gordon Church. They were unable to type blood samples taken from Archuleta's boots and leather jacket, according to tests conducted by Pilar Shortsleeve of the State Crime Lab.

Forensic expert Martha Kerr, also with the State Crime Lab, testified that human blood found on Lance Wood's pants and shoes was also consistent with that of the victim. Hair strands belonging to the victim were found entangled in the laces of Lance Wood's shoes, indicating that Wood probably kicked the victim in the head. Kerr also identified blood found on the wristwatch, as well as on the car jack and battery jumper cables, as that of the victim.

Experts noted there was more blood on Archuleta's pants than on Wood's, even though Archuleta's pants had been submerged for a day in the drainage ditch. The amount of blood indicated that Archuleta was nearer to the victim when the fatal blows were administered.

Investigators had considerable evidence to work with, including large amounts of blood. Robert M. Bell, a blood spatter expert for the Sacramento County, California, Sheriff's Department, was brought in to assist with the investigation. He concluded that the blood on Wood's pants and jacket indicated he was standing within three feet of the victim at the time the victim received multiple blows. "The wearer of this jacket had to be in close proximity to this assault," Bell said. He went on to explain that powerful, violent blows produce smaller drops of flying blood. Those drops, one millimeter or less in diameter, fly a maximum of three feet. Wood's clothes had drops that small on them in the pattern predicted by Bell. Furthermore, a splash of blood drops, like shotgun pellets, spreads out over distance. Some groups of blood spots on Wood's clothes were close together and therefore flew only a short distance.

"In this case, the blood patterns were caused by bludgeoning. The blood spatters and velocity are indicative of the power generated in this attack," Bell said. "Blood conforms to all the forms of physics," allowing investigators to reconstruct a lot about the killing. "There was such a profusion of blood on the back of the car, it was relatively easy to determine the way this attack took place."

Church was struck at least once while he was standing, once while his head was at bumper level, and once while he lay on the ground. There was brain matter on his clothing, indicating the force of the blows. Bell concluded that Archuleta was the one who had inflicted the blows, with Wood standing two or three feet away.

While fiber and blood evidence formed the core of their case, detectives went back to the time-proven practice of canvassing potential witnesses and tracking down potential evidence that would shed light on the perpetrators' state of mind at the time of the killing. After repeatedly questioning friends of the two suspects, one girlfriend finally admitted that Archuleta had called her from the Millard County Jail and told her, "Don't worry. They won't find any fingerprints." When she asked why the killing had been so sloppy, Archuleta said it was because they hadn't had time to plan it. "If it had been planned, it would have been neater."

Archuleta also told her that it was Wood who had done the killing. They had met Gordon Church after being denied entrance to a Cedar City bar, and they paid him to take them around in his car. "When talk turned to homosexuality, that's the point when Wood pulled a knife on him [the victim]," the witness said.

Investigators also questioned a man who had shared a jail cell with Archuleta during the time just after his arrest on the parole violation. "He told me that it was the ultimate rush. He said the evil had completely taken over him, and once they started, he couldn't stop. He said drugs could not compare to the high they got from killing."

Sergeant Charles Stewart again questioned Archuleta, probing inconsistencies in his story and confronting Archuleta with lies. Finally, Archuleta admitted he'd punched the victim once in the face, but it was not a hard punch. "I hit him with my hand. I just tagged him one time." Evidence from pathologists suggested otherwise, however,

Archuleta also admitted lying about having sex with the victim. "I'm lying about that. I did do it. But he was asking for it." Archuleta claimed that Church even asked his assailant to wear a condom.

According to Lance Wood's account, Wood was sitting in the car when Archuleta picked Gordon Church up, set him on the hood of the car, and said, "I'm going to get him in the butt!" Church said, "You had better use a condom" and gave him one. (An empty condom package was recovered from the crime scene.)

Special Prosecutor Carvel Harward would later argue, "Archuleta admitted putting his penis in the victim's rectum at a time when the victim was already a hostage and injured, and it is a fair inference that it was without his consent. The jumper cables that inflicted injury upon his penis was a separate act from the act of sodomy or object rape. The object rape is based upon the penetration of Church's body cavity with the tire iron. Evidence showed the wrench end was inserted into the rectum for a distance of forty-seven centimeters [about 18½ inches]."

Two things became increasingly clear to investigators and prosecutors: Michael Archuleta was the dominant individual in the relationship, and Lance Wood could have gotten out of the criminal episode at several different points but chose not to. For that reason, both men were charged with capital homicide, aggravated assault, aggravated kidnapping, aggravated sexual assault, possession of a stolen vehicle, sodomy, object rape, and forcible sexual abuse.

"Both Wood and Archuleta were there," Prosecutor Harward said. "Both engaged in the execution in an especially heinous, atrocious, cruel, and exceptionally depraved manner." But it was Archuleta who drove Church's car from Cedar Canyon to Dog Valley, who bought the gasoline for the car, who had taken Church's watch, and who controlled the relationship with Wood. It was Archuleta who suffered from a "convenient loss of memory" when confronted with contradictory evidence. And it was Archuleta whose fingerprints were found on objects removed from the victim's trunk and whose pants were stained with more of the victim's blood than was on those of his partner in crime.

But the investigation had also revealed that Lance Wood had filled the car with gasoline while Gordon Church was still in the trunk, and that Wood's shoelaces had strands of Church's hair in them, indicating Wood had kicked the victim in the head. "He has lied when he claimed that he was a mere observer," the prosecutor said of Lance Wood. "The evidence proves he is a liar as well as a killer."

It was Wood's hand print on the rear of the car, the prosecutor said. And not only could Wood have gotten away when they stopped to gas up the car, but Wood had in his possession the pliers used to peel the skin off Gordon Church's back and legs.

"They did it because, once [Church was] injured, they couldn't let him go," Prosecutor Harward said. "In assessing the risk, they elected to take his life . . . [forcing] the victim into the trunk of the car, they knew that Gordon wouldn't live to see the sun rise on November twenty-second."

What troubled investigators most was that everything that was done to Gordon Church was not necessarily done to kill him. Gordon could have survived the cut on his neck and the broken arm. He could have been taken to the hospital and let go. Did they do that? No. "They continued to terrorize him. When they left that canyon, they knew Gordon Church wouldn't see the sunrise," Prosecutor Harward said.

"The number and nature of the wounds, the separate instrumentalities used, and draping the corpse with tire chains [all] evidenced mutual participation by Wood and Archuleta—except that Archuleta is alone responsible for the act of sodomy," Harward said. "Because of the time span, the geographical territory involved, and the relationship of the parties, it is clear that they both participated directly and actively."

Harward also argued that application of the jumper cables to the victim's genitals and insertion of the tire iron into Church's rectum showed sexual intent. This was an important point in that homicides committed during a sex crime can carry the death sentence in Utah.

And given the evidence, prosecutors wanted nothing less than a death sentence for both men. Both defendants were tried separately, each using the defense that it was the other who had committed the crime. Michael Archuleta was convicted of first-degree murder, and was sentenced to death. Lance Wood was also convicted of

278

first-degree murder, but was spared the death sentence when the jury could not unanimously agree on a death sentence. He was sentenced to serve the rest of his life in prison.

Said one prosecutor, "Justice was done. It's not a happy occasion for anyone. But the jury did a tough job. They followed the evidence. They did what the statute called for and that's their verdict. It was the proper verdict under the evidence."

A relative of the victim agreed, telling reporters, "I think the Millard County Sheriff's Department and the Millard County Attorney's Office have done an outstanding job in reference to professionalism, integrity, and pursuit of justice. I would like to thank them for their efforts.

"I am still heartbroken that Gordon is gone and that he had to suffer so much at the hands of these criminals. We miss him, and society will not be able to benefit from the good he had to contribute."

Both defendants are currently serving time in the Utah State Prison. Michael Archuleta's death sentence will be automatically appealed to the Utah Supreme Court.

EDITOR'S NOTE:
*Nancy Johnson is not the real name of the person so named in the foregoing story. A fictitious name has been used because there is no reason for public interest in the identity of this person.*

# "RABBI SUFFOCATED WITH HIS SKULLCAP!"

by Joseph Pedreiro

**BROOKLYN, N.Y.**
**MARCH 4, 1985**

December 19, 1974, began as a quiet morning on Montgomery Street in the Crown Heights section of Brooklyn. A relative of Rabbi Nathan Friedler awoke early, as was her custom, and prepared breakfast for him. The rabbi lived in a ground floor apartment in the same building as his relative.

Rabbi Friedler was a retired principal of Hebrew Studies at the Solomon Kluger Yeshiva on the Lower East Side. Despite having reached the advanced age of 98, he remained in excellent physical condition. A devout and well-read man, he was unusually alert for his age. He had retained all his faculties and was proud of the fact that he did not even need glasses to read. Born in Poland, Rabbi Friedler spoke English as well as he spoke Yiddish. His neighbors said of him that he had more strength and more brains in his head than many men 50 years younger.

However, Rabbi Friedler had recently been experiencing difficulty walking and had only occasionally left the house to walk the two blocks to the Congregation

Rayim Ahuvim synagogue. He had lived on Montgomery Street for over 10 years, and he often told his neighbors and friends that he would never go into a nursing home.

This was Rabbi Friedler's firm opinion, despite the obvious changes in the neighborhood, an area which was once safe and was now becoming somewhat dangerous. A relative of the rabbi's had been mugged in their building several weeks earlier, and similar incidents had been occurring to their friends and neighbors with increasing frequency.

But Rabbi Friedler wanted to stay in the neighborhood where he had lived for so many years. As one of his friends remarked, "Nathan wants to stay here with us and die in his own bed."

That morning, the Rabbi's relative made Rabbi Friedler his usual light breakfast. She knocked on his door at 8:00 a.m. promptly, having given the rabbi sufficient time to complete his daily morning prayers. He did not answer the door. She knocked repeatedly, becoming more concerned. She then called his name, but still, there was no answer.

Alarmed, the woman ran upstairs to her apartment and got her key to her relative's door. Having opened the door, she ran to the old man's bedroom, afraid that he might have fallen during the night and had been unable to get up off the floor.

The sight that met her eyes when she entered the bedroom shocked her into immobility. Rabbi Friedler lay upon the bed with his arms and legs tied to the bedposts with his phylacteries (small leather boxes containing scriptural passages, with leather straps attached to the corners. The rabbi's frail body lay broken and bruised, with one eye blackened and swollen shut. His mouth gaped open, and the edge of his skullcap protruded from between his lips.

Even from where she stood near the door, the relative could see that the rabbi's chest was still and that there was no sign of life in those contorted features. An inexpressible horror arose within her. Vivid memories of the years of Nazi terror in Poland flashed before her eyes. She had thought that dreadful chapter in their lives was closed, that such atrocities could never happen again, that they had escaped from all of it.

The relative fell to her knees, screaming helplessly. How could such a thing happen here, in the country to which they had fled for the freedom to practice their religion in peace?

Neighbors came running, roused by the cries of the overwrought woman. They pulled her away from the awful sight, hardly believing their own eyes. One of the neighbors ran to his apartment to call the police while the women gathered around the grieving relative in a vain attempt to comfort her.

One woman shook her head and said to the others, "This is the greatest, greatest sin in the whole world. To kill a man using the tools of his religion like that—the brutality, the disaster . . ."

Police officers arrived promptly on the scene. Word of the horrible crime had spread rapidly throughout the Jewish community of Crown Heights, and the detectives assigned to the case were alert to the sensitive issue of anti-Semitism. However, the detectives refrained from any comment upon the nature of the crime, knowing full well that the religious symbolism might have little or nothing to do with the true motives of the criminals, and might even have been used deliberately to conceal the intentions and identities of the killers.

Upon inspection of the crime scene, detectives were able to come up with several clues right away. First of all, it was clear that entry was made through the bathroom window. The apartment was on the ground floor, but the windows were high off the ground. Although the bathroom window was closed when the detectives began their search of the apartment, there were footprints right underneath the window, and scuff marks on the wall where the murderers had climbed up.

The detectives, working with the forensic section, combed the apartment for clues. After several hours of painstaking work, they made an important discovery. The found several latent fingerprints on the glass of the bedroom window. However, there was no way to know how recent those prints were. Fingerprints on glass, unless the glass is wiped, will stay there forever.

Nevertheless, the placement of these prints was telltale. Although there were fingerprints left by the deceased man and his family on windows throughout the apartment, the placement of the prints on the bathroom window indicated to sleuths that these prints were left by a person opening the window from the outside, not the inside. This important piece of evidence led the detectives to strongly suspect that these were the fingerprints of the actual killers.

In addition, probers found evidence that the killers had left the apartment through the kitchen window. A blanket had been placed over the sill for a quick exit.

The detectives gently questioned Rabbi Friedler's relative about the contents of the apartment. The rooms appeared to have been ransacked and, according to the relative, there was a stereo or Gerard turntable missing. She wasn't sure if cash had been stolen, because she wasn't certain exactly how much money the rabbi had kept in the apartment.

It seemed evident to the detectives that burglary was the primary motive. The investigators were not sure if the burglary was an inside job, done by a person familiar with the layout of the house, or if it was an outside job done by random robbers. It seemed plausible that the burglars might not have originally intended to kill the old man, but were surprised by him during the act of burglary.

In the experience of the detectives, most burglars did not enter an apartment without a weapon of some type, such as a gun or knife. No weapon was found in the apartment, and there was no evidence upon examination of the body that any weapon other than fists were used to subdue the old man. So it seemed likely that the burglars' intent was to rob rather than to kill.

It also seemed likely that the old man surprised the intruders and was then beaten, tied down and gagged in order to prevent his raising an alarm. Probers reasoned that the phylacteries were probably the only readily available instruments for binding him to the bed, and the yarmulke (skullcap) was handy as a quick gag. Although the medical examiner's report ultimately identified the cause of death to be asphyxiation by the skullcap, it did not appear certain that the yarmulke was intended as anything more than a gag. In fact, it was possible the killers had no idea what the religious significance of these articles was at the time they were used in the horrible deed.

However, the detectives could not overlook the equally likely possibility that the killers were aware of the religious significance of these articles and used them with callous disregard to brutalize and bind the aged Jew. It was clear that the crime would receive great publicity and that many would interpret the act as vicious anti-Semitism. Sleuths knew it was vitally important that these killers be apprehended, brought to justice and their true motives ascertained before this heinous crime could spur any acts of retaliation or other repercussions in the community.

The 71st Precinct gave the Nathan Friedler murder the highest priority. Roughly 30 to 40 detectives were assigned to the case. These investigators were instructed to fan out over the surrounding area and perform an extensive canvass.

All the residents of the apartment building where the victim lived were questioned in depth. Even though the mode of entry did not suggest an inside job, the superintendent of the building was questioned closely for any information related to the Friedler case which they

284

might be willing to barter with the police.

On December 21st, two days after the killing, the detectives got their first possible description of the killers. One of the people interviewed said he had attended a party held in a downstairs vacant apartment in his building in Crown Heights. He began speaking with four young black males. The informant gave sleuths the name of one of the men and described him as "6 foot 4 inches, 190 pounds, with brown skin, yellow teeth, and a large part on the right side of his head."

According to this witness, the man described stated to the group, "We did a job on an old man last night. He wouldn't have gotten hurt if he'd cooperated with us and told us where the money was." The informant told probers that he questioned the man at that point, asking him, "How did you do it?" And another one of the men in the group answered, "Mind your own business." The informant stated that he believed the unknown male had just been released from prison.

This informant was taken to the district attorney's office to repeat his story. He then stated that he was told the old man was tied down.

The district attorney's office assigned investigators to check out the description given by the informant. They questioned all the other people who were present at the party, but everyone gave them different and conflicting statements. They reviewed local prison records to identify prisoners who had been released recently, but were overwhelmed by the numbers, since this was Christmas time and there had been seven or eight hundred prisoners released around that time. Then the investigators checked to see if there were any crimes of a similar nature committed recently. But this facet of the investigation turned out to be a dead end, too.

Another informant came forth to corroborate the first informant's story about the four black men at a party. However, both of the informants had been arrested for other crimes, and it soon became evident to detectives that they were friends who were trying to sell this story to the police in an effort to better their own situation. Enough information had been published in the newspapers about the Friedler case for the men to put together a superficially convincing story. But it was nothing more than that, sleuths concluded.

Now the detectives concentrated on the fingerprints found on the bathroom window. They barraged the latent section with requests for comparisons with prints from known burglars operating in the Crown Heights area. There were two distinct sets of fingerprints, suggesting that more than one person had been involved in the killing.

The technician in the latent section was kept busy comparing prints day and night. Since one fingerprint technician is usually assigned to compare all the prints for a single case, the man assigned to the Friedler case found himself extremely busy with all the prints submitted for analysis. Although the latent section does have a modern computer to do print analysis in addition to the fingerprint technicians who do manual analysis, the computer has its limitations.

Fingerprints are classified on latent prints found at the scene of the crime, at least seven points are needed. If only one print—say, a thumb or an index finger—is found at the crime scene, there are not enough points to make a comparison from the computer. If a criminal leaves a full set of prints from both hands, they can be fed into the computer and classified, and the criminal is then usually identified right away. But it is rare that a criminal leaves two hands of prints. Usually, detectives are able to find only one or two fingers. And that is simply not enough to use the computer.

So one technician was handed the enormous task of sorting through and comparing each set of prints submitted for analysis. It takes an expert technician a good three or four hours to do one set of prints. In most cases, detectives will submit perhaps 20 sets of prints to the latent section for comparison with prints found at the scene of a crime. The results on the entire set are generally completed and available within two months.

In the Nathan Friedler case, detectives submitted over 500 sets of prints for comparison. Working day and night, the technician provided results in record time on all the prints submitted. They were all negative, however. None of the prints of any of the suspects matched the prints found on Rabbi Friedler's apartment.

Weeks passed as the detectives poured every bit of energy into finding the killer or killers of the aged rabbi. Every lead that turned up was investigated thoroughly, no matter how flimsy the story. But the detectives could only come up empty-handed. As the weeks turned into months, the police department despaired of ever identifying and bringing to justice the men who had perpetrated this awful crime.

Time passed, and the trail grew colder. The Crown Heights section deteriorated further, and the community served by the 71st Precinct changed. An area which had been a quiet, safe, rather elegant and predominantly Jewish residential area now became a poor and very transient neighborhood. Many of the new people were West Indians who were illegal aliens. These new residents moved quickly and frequently, often changing identities and names in order to avoid deportation. Buildings would burn down mysteriously and people would vanish. The job of the detectives assigned to the 71st Precinct became more difficult by the day.

By the time several years had passed, the detectives originally assigned to the Nathan Friedler case had all been transferred to different departments or had retired. The case, however, was never closed. There is no statute of limitations on homicide. A homicide case that is not solved or cleared is never closed.

As new detectives were assigned to the 71st Precinct, all the unsolved cases were passed on to them from the detectives whose positions they were replacing. On occasion, the new detectives received information on homicides that had occurred several years earlier but had never been solved. At that point, the investigator's main problem would become one of locating the witnesses and individuals involved.

In 1980, Detective Raymond A. Apo was assigned to the Homicide Squad of the 71st Precinct. Detective Apo was instructed to take over all the cases that a previous detective had been assigned, including the Nathan Friedler killing, a case which was by now a dim memory to most of the personnel involved.

Detective Apo reviewed the file accumulated over the years. He looked in vain for some loose end, some clue that had bene overlooked or insufficiently investigated. But try though he might, he could offer no new insight into the solution of a crime that appeared to be almost perfect.

And so, Detective Apo set the Friedler case back on the shelf, hoping that some day some new information might surface which would shed light on the mystery of who killed Nathan Friedler and why.

And Detective Apo was certainly kept busy enough not to dwell on a homicide case which was now over six years old. There were only six detectives handling all the homicides that came into that precinct, and they were doing an average of 50 to 70 cases a year. As the new cases kept coming in, the old, unsolved cases kept piling up. The detectives were able to solve 60 to 75 percent of their cases yearly, leaving perhaps 25 percent that were not cleared. Of those 25 percent, in at least four or five instances the detectives identified a prime suspect, but they were unable to put together sufficient proof to bring the case to trial.

In Brooklyn, every homicide is reviewed by the Brooklyn District Attorney's Office, and it is up to the district attorney's office to determine if sufficient proof exists to bring a suspect to trial. Although a police officer need only show probable cause to arrest a suspect, the critical question becomes one of whether or not that probable cause is enough to make a guilty verdict likely or even possible from the standpoint of a jury. The harsh reality of the situation is that New York City is overwhelmed with criminal cases and it is simply not in the best interests of the city to spend $100,000 to bring a case to trial when there is insufficient proof to make a quality verdict possible.

So the unsolved homicides, including those in which sufficient proof was lacking, continued to pile in the files of the 71st Precinct, as well as elsewhere throughout the city of New York.

In 1981, in response to the tremendous volume of work and the large number of robberies, the New York City Police Department instituted a Central Robbery Division. Certain Precincts, in particular those heavy with robberies, were selected for the formation of Robbery Identification Program (RIP) Units. The 71st Precinct contributed a number of detectives to form a RIP unit, and the detectives assigned to the unit shared the office with the 71st Precinct.

While these changes were occurring around him, Detective Raymond Apo was immersed in the many other homicides assigned to him. He gradually pushed the Nathan Friedler case to the back of his mind.

Then suddenly, one day—April 30, 1983—several years after Detective Apo had begun working in the 71st Precinct, he got a surprising visit from two detectives who were accompanying a woman.

Earlier that day at about 1:30 p.m., an unknown woman had telephoned the 60th Precinct in Coney Island. She spoke to Detectives Danny Rizzo and Mark Mischel, and said, "I've got information on the killing of an old Jew."

The two detectives tried to talk the woman into coming down to the precinct house, but she said she did not want to do that, and hung up. Later that day, the woman called again. She told Rizzo and Mischel that she thought her information, even though it was given over the phone, would be enough to arrest the killers. She was extremely reluctant to appear in person at the precinct house.

The detectives patiently explained to the woman that more proof than a telephone conversation would be necessary to arrest a suspect on a homicide charge. Once the suspect was arrested, it was unlikely he would make a spontaneous confession, and a stronger case had to be put together before the police would be able to act on any information which she might give them.

The woman refused to identify herself on the phone, either by name or by address. Detective Mischel had once worked in the 71st Precinct, and he remembered the case the woman was describing. He and Detective Rizzo tried to talk the witness into meeting them at some location outside the precinct house. After calling a total of four times, she finally agreed to meet with them outside the precinct in a car.

When she walked up to the car, Rizzo and Mischel saw a slender black woman with a ravaged face and an anxious air about her. Detectives Mischel and Rizzo explained to her that it would require more than just an accusation to convict someone of murder. After much persuasion, she agreed to come in to the 60th Precinct to give a statement. She seemed hesitant regarding the name of the alleged murderer, but after much reassurance, they managed to elicit from her the name Andrew Harris as the person involved. The detectives glanced at each other; they were acquainted with Harris' past record and knew him personally. One of them took a photograph of him from their files and added several others and then asked her to pick out the one of Harris. The woman looked through them, picked out the correct one and said, "This is Andrew Harris."

At this point, armed with the statement and a photograph of the suspect, Detectives Rizzo and Mischel explained to the woman that, since the killing had taken place in the 71st Precinct, the case was technically out of their jurisdiction and would have to be pursued further from there. The witness agreed to go to the 71st only when Rizzo and Mischel promised to personally escort her there.

In the meantime, Detective Apo had arrived for work at the 71st Precinct at 4:00 p.m. as scheduled. Detectives Rizzo and Mischel brought the woman into the precinct house, and asked for the name of the detective working on the Nathan Friedler case. Detective Apo stepped forward, took the woman into the interrogation room and began questioning her.

The woman's demeanor was calm. At Apo's request, she identified herself as Sandra Johnson and gave an address in the Coney Island area.

As Sandra Johnson spoke with Detective Apo, a somewhat confused and contradictory story emerged. The woman said that, nine years earlier, she had been staying with her sister, who had been going out at that time with a man named Andrew Harris. One day, Andrew Harris burst into the apartment very excited and acting very scared. He blurted out that he'd just killed "an old Jew" in Crown Heights.

Apo asked Sandra Johnson what her sister's name was. She responded that her sister had been missing for the past two years. Apo again requested her sister's name, so that he could check to see if a missing person report was on file for her. At this point, the woman became evasive. She told him she thought her sister must be dead, because "she would never do anything like this."

Detective Apo spoke with the woman for approximately an hour. Afterwards, he called the district attorney's office to find out if they would take a statement from her at that time. Even though Apo did not believe everything the woman had told him, he felt it would be useful to get her story down on tape before the district attorney.

291

At the D.A.'s office, repeated the same story she had told Detective Apo, stating that she had overheard this conversation between Andrew Harris and her sister. The sister appeared to be a phantom whom the woman insisted could not be found.

Detective Apo mulled over the woman's statement in his mind. Somehow, the whole story about the sister didn't seem to jibe with the rest of her statement. He thought about it for a while and then decided to speak with Sandra Johnson some more.

He confronted her with his deductions. "What is the relationship between you and Andrew Harris?" he asked.

The woman was evasive, refusing to answer the question directly.

The woman then said she wanted to go home after giving her statement, since it was now almost 8:00 p.m. Detective Apo told her he would keep in touch with her regarding developments in the investigation. She agreed to speak with him in the future regarding any further details which she might be able to offer.

Apo offered her a ride home in the precinct car. He did so because he wanted to check her address against the one she had given at the 71st Precinct, as well as be able to contact her at a later date. She accepted the offer, and, together with Detectives Mike Poliseno and Mischel, Apo drove the woman back to Coney Island.

Early the next morning, Detective Apo submitted a request to the latent section to compare Andrew Harris' prints with the fingerprints found on the glass in Nathan Friedler's apartment. Several hours later, he got his answer. The results were negative.

Stymied once again, Apo had to ask himself if this witness was really telling the truth or if this was all some pathetic story fabricated by an unstable woman trying to avenge herself on an old boyfriend. Somehow, his intuition told him that Sandra Johnson was telling the truth.

Apo made an appointment to meet with Miss Johnson

again. His goal was to gain the woman's confidence so that he could get her to tell him the simple truth without any embellishing lies.

In their next conversation, Sandra Johnson revealed to Detective Apo that there had been another person involved in the killing with Andrew Harris. She said she didn't know this person's actual name, but that his nickname was either "T" or "D". She wasn't sure of the exact pronunciation. She described this man as a person who was 5'10" or 5'11", very skinny, and very dark-skinned — she described him as "the blackest person I have ever seen."

Apo and Poliseno went back to the 71st Precinct and checked through the nickname file. They came up with five persons with those nicknames. Apo requested photographs of these five men, and discovered that none of them even remotely matched the description given by Sandra Johnson. In addition, Apo submitted requests for fingerprint comparisons between these men and the latent prints from the victim's apartment. All were negative.

Detective Apo sighed and made another appointment to speak with Sandra Johnson. He still thought she had something she was holding back, and the key to finding that was to communicate with her constantly.

For the next month and a half, Apo and Poliseno were persistent. They spoke with the witness frequently, stressing to her the points that were necessary to put the case together. Apo listened patiently as she went over her story again and again. Most of all, he reassured her repeatedly that no harm would come to her if she told the whole truth.

Finally, one day Detective Apo decided it was time to take a different tack. He told the woman, "Look, why are you lying to me?" He went on to say that he knew there was more to the story than she was telling him. He confronted her with the inconsistencies and contradictions in her statements. "You talk about your sister, and, frankly, I don't believe you even have a sister," he said.

He pointed out that she refused to allow him to corroborate any part of her story. She wouldn't let him talk to her mother. She wouldn't give him her mother's name, telephone number, or address. In fact, he wondered if he should believe anything she had told him.

Finally, Sandra Johnson broke down. She admitted that she was the woman going with Andrew Harris back then, but, she claimed, she had not lived with him since 1975 or 1976. Sobbing, she confessed that Harris had been beating her in the street every time he saw her. She had had him arrested on two separate occasions for assault and kidnapping.

At this point, Detective Apo felt he had something to work with. He went over her story again and corroborated that she had no sister. Furthermore, she had not simply overheard the conversation in which Andrew Harris confessed to the killing. Now, it was no longer hearsay. Harris had spoken to her directly.

As her story now went, Andrew Harris was living with her at one of his relatives' apartments at the time of the killing. To the best of Sandra's recollection, on the evening of December 19, 1974, she was watching television in the relative's apartment and heard a news story about a Jewish man who had been found in his ransacked apartment, the victim of a homicide. Sandra had last seen Andrew Harris the day before at approximately five or six o'clock in the evening, and she did not see him again until the following night.

The fact that Harris did not come home the night of the 19th was unusual, she said, because he had never been gone for two days at a time. He would often go out at night, not tell her where he was going, and return to the apartment around four or five o'clock in the morning. She had been worried in the past about what kind of trouble he was in, particularly since, at that time, Harris was using drugs. But he had never been gone two days without coming home.

Sandra Johnson had never been involved in drug use. At that time, she recalled, she was 16 or 17 years old. When Harris left on the 18th, all he told her was that he was "going to do a sting in Crown Heights." He left with a man by the name of Jimmy.

Detective Apo asked if this "Jimmy" was the same "T" Sandra had been describing earlier. She admitted that she had fabricated the nickname. The reason she gave was that this other man had never done anything to her and she saw no need to involve him. The only person she wanted arrested was Andrew Harris. Apo pressed her for the man's last name, and she finally identified him as Jimmy Jackson.

She went on to say that when Harris came home on the 20th of December, he was agitated and "scared out of his mind." He came into the apartment and told Sandra, "I've got to talk to you." He took her into the bedroom and said, "We just did a sting in Crown Heights with an old Jew and we stuck a yarmulke in his mouth."

Sandra remembered the news program from the day before, and cried out, "Oh, my God, he's dead! You killed him." She wasn't sure from Harris' reaction to her statement whether or not he had been aware that the old man had died. Nothing else was said, and Harris warned her to keep her mouth shut.

Later that night, Jimmy Jackson came over to the apartment, and all three of them went into the bedroom. Harris told Jackson, "I told her." And Jackson responded, "I hope you're going to keep your mouth shut, Sandy." The two men spoke for a few minutes, and they mentioned a third person. Harris asked Jackson if this person would keep his mouth shut and Jackson answered, "He's OK. He won't say a word."

Sandra recalled that Harris and Jackson said they hadn't meant to kill the old man. They punched him around a little bit, but they didn't want to really hurt him. They stuffed the yarmulke in his throat to muffle his cries. Sandra said that she tried to act as though she didn't want to know about it.

This was the last time anything was ever said about the killing. Sandra never brought it up again, and neither of the two men ever referred to it.

So Detective Apo now had some solid information to investigate. He began by looking for Jimmy Jackson. A computer check yielded a list of 120 James Jacksons on file. The only way for Apo to pick out the right man was to use Sandra Johnson's description of "T," which she admitted was actually an accurate description of James Jackson. Unfortunately, Sandra's description was of James Jackson as he had appeared almost 10 years earlier. His appearance could have changed considerably.

Detective Apo pulled the computer file and prepared to check every James Jackson manually against her description. In addition, he checked descriptions of all the people who had ever been arrested with Harris to see if any matched Jackson's description but was using a different name. None did.

According to procedure, Apo checked in with his supervisor, Sergeant Timothy Dowd, who was the sergeant in charge of homicides. He told Dowd that he had a case and described the information and leads he had picked up. Apo then went over to BCI and checked a computer printout of all the James Jacksons in the area.

On May 31, 1983, while Detective Apo was wading through piles of paper at the BCI, Sergeant Dowd was working in the office which the 71st Precinct shared with the Robbery Identification Program (RIP) Unit. It so happened that day that the sergeant of the RIP Unit was not available, and Sergeant Dowd took over his duties.

That afternoon, one of the officers of the 71st Precinct, Officer Eddie Wilton, was on patrol with his partner in Crown Heights when suddenly they heard a woman screaming for help. They drove in their unmarked car around the corner and found a young Jewish woman crying out that her purse had been wrested from her grasp by a young black man. She pointed out the direction in which he had escaped and told the officers that they arrived no more than five seconds after the man had fled. The two officers gave chase and pursued the man into an abandoned building, where they cornered him and arrested him.

The officers brought the suspect to the 71st Precinct, where he identified himself as Michael Williams. They put him in a lineup to see if the victim of the pursesnatching could identify him as her attacker. Sergeant Dowd, acting as supervisor of the RIP unit that day, had to oversee the lineup. The young woman made a positive identification. The officers ran an identity check on Michael Williams and discovered that the name was an alias. The man had used four or five different names on different arrests, but his actual name was James Jackson.

When Sergeant Dowd heard the true identity of the robbery suspect, he immediately recalled Detective Apo's case.

Dowd contacted Apo and got Sandra Johnson's description of James Jackson. The description matched the James Jackson being held for the purse-snatching. Elated at this sudden stroke of good luck, Detective Apo returned to the 71st Precinct as quickly as possible. He got the robbery suspect fingerprinted for comparison with the ten-year-old latent prints from the Friedler apartment.

He then went through the man's file of previous arrests and found prints documented on an earlier occasion. He submitted the prints to the latent section technician, Guillermo Jaramillo, and hoped his luck would hold. Unfortunately, Jaramillo was not available to look at the prints that day, so Apo went home that evening without knowing the outcome of his request.

When he got into work the following morning, a message was waiting for him. The word from Jaramillo was that the prints were positive. Apo couldn't believe his ears.

We've finally put a case together, he thought. He felt that between Sandra Johnson's testimony and the matching prints, there was sufficient evidence to bring James Jackson to trial for homicide.

He still had to convince the district attorney of the reliability of his witness. Even though Apo had gathered enough evidence to arrest Jackson, the district attorney's office had to authorize the arrest first.

Apo went to the district attorney's office and spoke with one of the homicide supervisors. The supervisor felt that Sandra Johnson's testimony was critical to the case, but he was not certain that she was telling the truth. He decided to submit her to a polygraph test. Even thought the results of the polygraph would not be admissible as evidence in court, the district attorney's office would have a better sense of whether or not the woman was lying. After all, she admitted she wanted to have Andrew Harris locked up. Perhaps she had cooked up the whole story out of revenge for his shabby treatment of her.

From a more technical standpoint, the district attorney also wanted to know if Sandra Johnson was lying about Harris' confession being told to her directly. If in truth she had only overhead a conversation between others, her testimony would be hearsay and carry much less weight than if the statement was made directly to her.

Detective Apo contacted Sandra Johnson and raised the possibility of a polygraph. At first she refused, saying that those sorts of things frightened her. He persisted, reassuring her that the results of the lie detector test could not be used against her in any way. Finally she gave in, and the polygraph was scheduled.

During the lie detector test, Apo found his ability to communicate with the woman tested to the utmost. She had a very high-strung personality, and simply getting her to sit still for five minutes without her anxiety interfering with the sensitive measurements of the test was a major task. In addition, Sandra kept throwing the test results off by holding back irrelevant details. These registered as lies on the test and kept skewing the readings, making the polygraph technician's job difficult.

At one point, Apo took Sandra Johnson aside and instructed her to calm down. "Look," he explained, "these questions are routine. We aren't really interested in whether or not you ever smoked marijuana in your life. When we ask you that, just tell us if you did or not. Don't try to hide anything. We're not going to lock you up for it."

Finally, Sandra seemed to realize that she had to be completely honest in her responses to the questions, and that half-truths would register as lies and invalidate her entire testimony. She relaxed and told her whole story again. And the lie detector supported her testimony as truthful.

The district Attorney's office decided to act on her testimony. With Sandra Johnson as a witness and prints matching Jackson's in the apartment, the story was consistent and corroborated.

In addition, the district attorney's office considered the possibility that Jackson might subsequently attempt to defend himself by stating that his prints were legally in the victim's apartment. One plausible defense could be that Jackson did repair or maintenance work in the apartment at some point prior to the killing. As it turned out, the superintendent had stated at the time of the homicide that he had hired local youths to do odd jobs for him in the building. Jackson could claim to have been working for the super.

The district Attorney's office began a long and tedious search for the man who had been the superintendent in Nathan Friedler's building ten years ago. They managed to track him down in Puerto Rico via relatives, and arranged for him to be a standby witness. However, the key piece of evidence in the case remained Sandra Johnson's testimony. The fingerprints alone would be insufficient to convict Jackson for homicide. Without a witness, it would be a simple defense for Jackson to plead guilty to a fictitious burglary committed several weeks prior to the killing, and deny any involvement in the homicide. But with Sandra Johnson's testimony, a conviction seemed not only possible, but likely.

The stage appeared to be set for Jackson's arrest and trial. But where was Jimmy Jackson? After being taken into custody on the robbery charge, Jackson was transferred to a prison facility. Detective Apo checked all the city facilities where Jackson would have been sent, since he committed the robbery in the city. But Jackson was nowhere to be found.

Apo grew increasingly frustrated as he maneuvered through the delicate and complex bureaucracy of the prison system in an attempt to locate Jackson. Finally, he discovered that when Jackson was arrested for the robbery by Officer Wilton, he had also violated parole, which was a state offense. Jackson had been paroled after serving four years for a rape and robbery in a Brooklyn apartment. Since he had violated his parole, Jackson had to do the time he owed in a state institution. Apo continued his search for Jackson for some time, coming up with several leads, but none of them panned out for him. After fruitlessly spending much time looking for Jackson in the upstate region, Apo managed to locate him in a state facility in Long Island City.

The district attorney's office pressed Detective Apo to get Sandra Johnson to commit herself to testifying. Apo realized that the many months he had spent gaining the woman's confidence were about to be put to the test. He decided to take a gentle but firm approach, stating that she would never see Andrew Harris come to justice if she did not openly testify in court. She responded that she feared for her life since Harris' family lived in her neighborhood and would be likely to seek revenge.

Apo assured her that, if she felt her life was in danger or if she was harassed by any member of Harris' family, she would be moved to a different location for her protection. But Sandra refused to accept this, saying, "I've lived in Coney Island all my life, and this is where I want to stay."

At this point, the district attorney's office informed Apo that they wanted Sandra Johnson to go before a grand jury and testify before they proceeded further with the case. This was somewhat unusual, as the district attorney's office generally shied away from an "open indictment," where the person was not in custody at the time of the indictment. The more common procedure was to first arrest the suspect, charge him, and then go to the grand jury. The problem with going to the grand jury without the suspect in custody was that the suspect could flee to another state and the indictment would sit in the D.A.'s office for years without their being able to act on it.

But the district attorney wanted to be certain that Sandra Johnson was a reliable witness who was willing to testify and capable of convincing a jury that she was telling the truth.

Apo spoke at length with Sandra Johnson. He pointed out that she would never feel secure with Harris out free on the streets. He appealed to her sense of justice, reminding her of the frail old rabbi, brutally beaten to death. He asked her if she could let someone she knew to be a killer go without punishment so he could be free to kill again.

Sandra Johnson was frightened. She thought about the elderly man. She thought about her fear of getting up on the witness stand. She imagined all the dreadful possibilities if Harris was not convicted and was set free. He would probably hurt others, but she would be his first victim.

Finally, Sandra Johnson decided she would testify. It took a great deal of thought and more courage than she even knew she possessed for her to reach that decision, particularly in view of her nervous personality and profound anxiety.

Detective Apo wasn't certain how Sandra would handle testifying before the grand jury. The district attorney's office was represented by John Fairbanks a man who was fortunately capable of reassuring Sandra and calming her anxiety. He talked to her, and she testified. When they came out of the courtroom, Fairbanks told Apo she did a beautiful job. The grand jury came back with an indictment.

Now Apo had an arrest warrant for both Jimmy Jackson and Andrew Harris. He didn't have to worry about arresting Jackson, since Jackson was already in jail. The person he wanted now was Andrew Harris.

The detective returned to Harris' neighborhood. For the better part of a week, he attempted to locate Harris. He had his photograph, and Sandra had told him all the places that Harris liked to hang out in. But the detective kept missing him narrowly. At one point, Sandra Johnson would call Apo and say, "I just saw him in the street." Apo would jump into his car and drive down immediately. But every time he got there, Harris would be gone. He missed Harris sitting in front of his relative's house, missed him sitting on the stoop of his new girlfriend's house, missed him going into a bar, and so on.

Finally, Detective Apo decided to use a more direct approach. He went to Harris' relative's house, knocked on the door, and told her that he wanted to talk to Harris on an unrelated matter, something about a recent crime committed in the 60th Precinct which he thought Harris might have some information on. Apo did not give his name and address at the 71st Precinct, figuring that Harris might become suspicious and think, "I haven't been in the 71st Precinct in almost ten years—

why are they looking for me now?" Apo did not want Harris to guess at the real reason he was searching for him. He left the name of a Detective Joe Scarpatti who had previously worked in the 71st Precinct but was now assigned to the 60th Precinct.

Detectives Mischel and Rizzo, being personally acquainted with Harris, also spoke to his relatives, telling them that they had to speak with him regarding an assault he had allegedly been involved in.

Several days later, on July 6, 1983, while Detective Apo was in court on another case, he received a message that Andrew Harris had come in to see Detective Scarpatti and that he was being held in the 60th Precinct for Apo.

Apo went to the 60th Precinct immediately, took Harris into custody, and returned to the 71st Precinct. He took the man into an interview room, sat him down and said, "You must be wondering what you've been arrested for."

Harris, who had a hostile and belligerent air about him, demanded to know why he was being held. Apo informed him that he was being charged with homicide. He asked Harris if, by any chance, he remembered an apartment in the Crown Heights area and an old man with a yarmulke stuffed in his mouth.

Apo went on to inform Andrew Harris that he had been indicted by a grand jury and that he had a warrant for his arrest. The detective read him his Miranda rights.

Harris' reaction was not one of shock or even surprise. On the contrary, the suspect coldly responded. "I didn't do anything like that. I don't know what you're talking about. I never have committed any crime in Crown Heights." Harris was currently free on $500 bail on an unrelated assault charge.

Apo hinted that it was one of Harris' associates who had turned him in, hoping that Harris would respond by accusing Jackson or the unknown third perpetrator of committing the actual killing. But Harris did not take

303

the bait. Apo then informed Harris that the police were aware that Jimmy Jackson was one of Harris' close friends. Harris admitted to knowing Jackson, but said that he had never committed any crime with him. When Apo suggested that Jackson had implicated him in the crime, Harris responded calmly, "I don't know what he's talking about and I don't know what you're talking about."

The detective told Harris that Jackson had been arrested two weeks earlier. At the time, Apo didn't know if Harris was aware that Jackson had been arrested on a robbery charge. Harris did not respond. The detective implied that Jackson was interested in striking a deal with the police in order to get off on the robbery charge, and that the proposed deal involved implicating Harris as the killer of the aged Jew. Harris remained unmoved, however.

The questioning continued for over four hours. Apo showed Harris a photograph of James Jackson, and Harris admitted that he was an acquaintance, but no amount of questioning or suggestion would budge Harris from his story. Harris, a veteran of over 20 arrests, was an old hand at remaining cool and composed under interrogation.

Finally, Detective Apo shrugged his shoulders and began to draw up the arrest papers on Andrew Harris. Apo hadn't really expected Harris to break down and give a confession during the interview, considering his long criminal record and his personality as described in detail by Sandra Johnson. But it was always worth a try.

The detective took Andrew Harris over to Brooklyn Central Booking and lodged him. In cases involving open arrest warrants, the suspects do not go to Criminal Court rather, they go directly before a judge for arraignment and are then sent over to the Supreme Court. Once a person has been indicted, the case is no longer a Criminal Court matter, and the suspect goes right over to the Supreme Court.

The trial was set to take place on November 3, 1984. Andrew Harris and James Jackson were named as co-defendants in a joint trial. Assistant District Attorney Stewart Orden put together an airtight case for the prosecution. The charges were murder during the commission of a felony, manslaughter in the first degree, and burglary in the first degree.

The brutal aspect of the crime and the helplessness of the frail, elderly victim were placed before the jury. It was revealed during the trial that Jackson and Harris were both over six feet tall, while Nathan Friedler was a mere five feet two inches and weighed no more than 120 pounds.

Rabbi Friedler's relative, elderly and frail herself by this time, was unable to testify in the proceedings because of her ill health and the emotional impact of reliving the awful memory of that day when she found the rabbi dead.

Much of the prosecution's case centered upon the testimony of Sandra Johnson and the fingerprints which corroborated her statement placing Harris in the rabbi's apartment. Ms. Johnson was extremely anxious prior to her courtroom appearance but gave her testimony in a calm and convincing manner. It was her heartrending story that, without a doubt, had the greatest impact upon the jurors hearing the case.

Assistant District Attorney Orden explained that Sandra Johnson had waited so long to come forward because "it took that long for her social conscience to override her fear and for her hatred of Andrew Harris to grow to such a degree that she was prompted to turn him in."

The trial lasted four days. The jury deliberated for a mere four hours before returning to the courtroom. On November 5, 1984, the foreman stood up and pronounced the verdict: guilty as charged.

Judge Sybil Kooper set sentencing for November 27th. Interviewed by reporters prior to sentencing, James Jackson complained that he did not get a fair trial and had been given a Jewish attorney, George Sheinberg, over his objections. Despite these statements, Jackson admitted that he had no complaints about Sheinberg's work.

Before Judge Kooper sentenced James Jackson, Assistant District Attorney Orden commented on what he called Jackson's history of robbing elderly Jews. As he called for the maximum term, Orden said, "Vermin like him should never see the light of day."

Calling the crime "a despicable and heinous act," the judge sentenced James Jackson to a term of 25 years-to-life for the slaying of Nathan Friedler. Two days later, Andrew Harris received the same sentence.

At the sentencing, Andrew Harris told Judge Kooper, "It's a shame the old man died, but it was never proven I committed the crime." The judge responded that the jury had thought otherwise.

Judge Kooper commented about Harris, "I can't believe this man was arrested twenty-one times. His arrest record is absolutely appalling."

Jackson's sentence was added to the five-to-ten year term for which he had already been convicted for robbery. Harris' sentence would be consecutive to a two-to-six year term for which he had previously been convicted for selling drugs.

When asked to comment on the sentences given, one of the victim's relatives responded, "At times like this I'm sorry there isn't an electric chair."

District Attorney Elizabeth Holtzman commented, "Justice has finally been done after ten long years," Holtzman added, "The fact that a witness came forward made the difference in this case and shows how important it is for people who know about a crime to report it to the police."

Detective Apo refused to take any special credit for the solving of the case. "This case just fell into my lap," he said in an interview.

Apo's supervisor, Lieutenant Anthony Santora,

summed the case up. "That's the way a detective thinks. If this woman hadn't come forward, this case would still be in a box in the back of the record room. She opened the door. Ray walked through the door and did a real good job."

Santora added, "I think the biggest problem that Ray had with this case was the informant. He had to gain her confidence, and it took him four months to do that.

"He stayed with a difficult witness for four long months and didn't quit until the case was solved. That's what being a good detective is all about."

EDITOR'S NOTE:
*Sandra Johnson is not the real name of the person so named in the foregoing story. A fictitious name has been used because there is no reason for public interest in the identity of this person.*

# "BOUND SEX SLAVE HAD HER THROAT SLIT!"

## by Patricia Lieb

Sheriff's Deputy Carlos Douglas was on routine patrol in the early-morning hours of April 9, 1987, making the rounds at businesses in Spring Hill, Florida. The community was one of the fastest growing areas in Hernando County, about 60 miles north of St. Petersburg.

Douglas, a handsome, young deputy with a friendly manner and a ready smile, slowed the cruiser as he neared one of many convenience stores in the area. The area had been plagued recently by a rash of abductions of store clerks working the night shift. Some had even wound up murdered.

Douglas kept an eye on several different convenience stores in Spring Hill. He would pass the Presto store on U.S. Highway 19 and Forest Lake Boulevard at about the same time every night he was on duty. At about 2:55 a.m., the beautiful, young store clerk on duty would always come to the window and wave to assure Douglas that everything was fine.

On the morning of April 9, 1987, Douglas pulled into the parking lot and glared at the store. Instantly, his gut feeling told him something was wrong. The store looked empty. The girl's truck was parked near the store, but he could not see her. The deputy knew that the conscientious store clerk would never go away and leave the store unat-

308

tended. He pulled his cruiser closer to the store and manipulated the vehicle's spotlight so it shined inside. When the clerk did not come into view, Douglas parked his cruiser and went into the store. Perhaps the girl was in the washroom, he reasoned, or maybe she was stocking beer in the cooler.

With his hand on the gun that rested on his hip, Deputy Douglas walked cautiously through the store. As he peered around the aisles, he called out the young woman's name. "Lee Ann, you there? Lee Ann?" But 23-year-old Lee Ann Larmon did not answer.

As Deputy Douglas walked about the store calling out for Lee Ann, he became more anxious, hoping any second to see the pretty woman with light brown hair and the smiling face, laughing and chatting about country-western singers, or quietly engrossed in her studies.

Douglas walked behind the cash register and looked around. Lee Ann's multicolored purse and jacket were lying there. Pinned to the purse strap was a button proclaiming Lee Ann's enthusiasm for country-western star Conway Twitty. Lee Ann would never leave the store willingly without her purse, Deputy Douglas thought to himself.

Douglas walked from behind the cash register to the counter where a microwave oven sat. A hot hamburger on the counter was still steaming and a container of relish was sitting beside it. It appeared as if someone had just left the store. Could that person have kidnapped Lee Ann? Douglas wondered. Fear, already worrying the officer, now made his heart pound. He knew something had to be done quickly. Lee Ann Larmon had surely been kidnapped.

Deputy Douglas hurried from the store and got on his radio with the police dispatcher. "The girl that works the night shift here is missing," he explained. "She knows what time I make my rounds. I think she's been kidnapped. It's very suspicious."

Spring Hill is an unincorporated area with no police department of its own. The area, which is made up of thickly populated sections of new homes and shopping centers, lies in the county's southwest corner and covers most of the area to the southwest of Brooksville, which is located in the center of the county. Except for a couple of small communities in between, Spring Hill is separated from the Gulf of Mexico by the Weeki Wachee and the Chassahowitzka swamps. Except for Brooksville, all law enforcement in the entire county is handled by the Hernando County Sheriff's Office (HCSO), the Florida Highway Patrol, and the Florida Department of Fresh Water Fish and Wildlife.

Upon receiving Douglas' call, sheriff's deputies were dispatched to comb the county. *We've got to find her,* Douglas thought while he waited for backup officers to arrive at the store. He knew Lee Ann could not have been gone long.

Officers went to Lee Ann Larmon's home and awakened her relatives. She had not come home, they said, and they had no idea where she might have gone. They said that a friend of Lee Ann's had mentioned that a former boyfriend of Lee Ann's might have returned to town. He could have picked her up at the store and they could have gone out someplace to talk. Perhaps they were getting back together. Perhaps she left with him in his vehicle. That would explain why Lee Ann's truck was still at the store's parking lot. But if she had left with him willingly, why would she have left her purse?

Lee Ann's relatives told officers that they knew nothing about Lee Ann leaving work with anyone. They had heard nothing from her since she had left the house to go to work. At that time, everything had seemed normal. Lee Ann had dressed as usual in a pair of jeans and shirt. She had slipped her multicolored purse over her shoulder, got into her truck, and hurried off to work at the convenience store. She had said nothing about going away somewhere else. Lee Ann would not have left the store to go anywhere, relatives assured the officers. She took her job seriously and was working her way through Pasco-Hernando Junior College.

"Lee Ann Larmon did not leave on her own accord," deputies concluded, "She was kidnapped."

Sheriff's Lieutenants Jerry Calhoun and Royce Decker were awakened at their homes by telephone calls. "You've got to do an air search," they were both told. Both men quickly got dressed and hurried through the fog to the sheriff's office airplane hangar, located at the Brooksville Regional Airport, about five miles south of Brooksville.

Through the wee-morning hours, both officers sat impatient in the helicopter, wishing the thick fog that covered the west end of the county would lift. If they tried to take the chopper up in such a white cloud, they would not be able to see their hands in front of their faces. They had no choice but to wait and pray that the fog would lift soon.

Deputies in patrol cars circled through Spring Hill parking lots where young people had partied in the night hours. In Spring Hill and other areas in Florida, parking lots are popular hangouts for teenagers who stay out late at night and have nothing else to do. Often, young people will meet in parking lots, and from there, they will go to secluded sinkholes that have filled with water and become lakes, or to houses where they can drink beer and smoke marijuana, without the threat of cops or parents popping in on them.

Sheriff's detectives and deputies looked in every direction, checking out every road that might possibly lead to Lee Ann Larmon's whereabouts or to her abductor. There was one other possibility, detectives acknowledged—the newspapers, which were delivered in the early-morning hours, had been delivered to the store as usual. Maybe the carrier who brought them had seen something.

Sleuths contacted and questioned the newspaper carrier.

311

Yes, he said, he had been at the store at 2:00 a.m. that morning. Lee Ann had been on duty. When he left the store, she was fine, he said.

Another person deputies felt they should contact was the store manager. He told officers that Lee Ann was a nice girl. He said he knew she was working the night shift at the store so she could go to school during the day. But he was unaware of anything that might have happened that night.

HCSO Detective Jim Blade also knew Lee Ann Larmon. Blade went into the store occasionally and drank coffee while Lee Ann was on duty. He knew no one who would want to hurt her.

Meanwhile, the helicopter's propeller whirred with an impatient whining hum. And as Sheriff's Lieutenants Calhoun and Decker waited for the fog to lift, they too became more and more anxious. Radio communications with the sheriff's office convinced the lieutenants in the helicopter that Lee Ann Larmon had been kidnapped from the Presto store. Officers were swarming western Hernando County in search of Lee Ann. And as day started to break, Calhoun felt he could wait no longer. Although there was still too much fog to go up safely, Calhoun decided he would have to risk it.

The chopper was soon hovering over areas near the Presto convenience store where Lee Ann had last been seen. It then veered to other areas where new construction was going up, to housing developments and shopping centers.

The chopper then headed slowly up the east side of U.S. 19, a well-traveled highway that runs down Florida's west coast, from the northernmost part of the state south to Naples. At night, U.S. 19 in Hernando County north of Spring Hill is dark and eerie. The country is scantly populated, with deep woods marked by signs that warn of bears. Sinkholes and dusty lime-rock roads lie to the east, and wildlife preserves and swamps to the west.

312

If Lee Ann had been kidnapped, which officers believed was the case, her abductor might have left her someplace along the highway. She could be trying to get back from some isolated place at that very minute. Lieutenant Decker climbed out of the helicopter and positioned himself on its runner, in order to get a better look at the ground below. Through the thick mist, both officers kept their eyes looking downward, combing the ground over which the chopper hovered slowly. Reaching the northern part of the county, Calhoun turned the chopper, swooped across the highway, and started back south on the west side of U.S. Highway 19. There the swampy area was mostly wooded with scrub-oaks, dressed with Spanish moss, and thick, prickly palmetto bushes.

At about 10:00 a.m., while flying over the long swampy area adjacent to the gulf, deputies in the helicopter spotted a pickup truck that appeared to be stuck in the swamp. With Decker still sitting on the helicopter runner, Calhoun made a sweep, passing over the blue Ford truck. Two men were trying to get the vehicle out of a mud hole. A woman stood near a car behind the truck. She looked up at the helicopter and waved.

Calhoun got on the radio and reported the incident. The sheriff's dispatcher sent a patrol car to the scene. Without help, the people involved could be stranded in the swamp indefinitely.

While patrol deputies were still searching throughout the county for Lee Ann Larmon, deputies were dispatched to the swamp where the people were stranded. The middle-aged woman identified herself as a relative of the truck passenger. The owner of the truck was an acquaintance who had been to her house before, but she did not know him too well. The two men had come to her home earlier that morning to ask for help, she said. They needed equipment to free the truck. The dirt road through this part of the swamp was often used by people to illegally dump garbage.

A deputy walked in front of the car to the pickup truck. "Y'all have a problem here?" he asked.

"Yeah," both men agreed. The truck was stuck in the mud and had been for sometime.

"What were y'all doing out here this time of morning?"

"We've been mud-bogging," they both replied.

"Mud-bogging," or driving a truck through a swamp for sport, was a popular form of recreation around the Florida wetlands.

With Lieutenant Decker still on the helicopter runner, Lieutenant Calhoun made another sweep over the truck. He saw that help for the people below had arrived. Still, Calhoun put the helicopter in hovering mode and stared down at the swampy area around the stuck truck.

Suddenly, Calhoun's eyes widened. Below, about 400 yards from the stranded truck, a female form was lying in a cluster of palmetto bushes. "Take a look down there," Calhoun said, but Decker's eyes were already focused on the nude girl. Portions of her body were bound with wire, and she was curled up in a fetal position. Looking closely, the men could see the girl was wearing nothing but socks.

Without hesitation, Lieutenant Calhoun got on the radio. "Don't let those two men out of sight," he ordered. "Keep them there. They might be involved in what has happened out here." Calhoun felt that even if the men were not involved, with a girl lying in the bushes only about 400 feet away, they might have seen something.

While other police cars were dispatched to the swamp, deputies kept the woman and the men talking.

*My God*, officers thought when they went to the palmetto bushes where the girl lay. *Who could have done such a thing?* The men at the truck, when asked moments later, shook their heads. They didn't know anything, they said. They were out mud-bogging. They had seen nothing.

The men identified themselves. The one with long, straggly light brown hair, peach-fuzz moustache and goatee said he was Phillip Frantz of Spring Hill. The

314

other, with shorter, wavy black hair, black piercing eyes, and a thick black goatee, identified himself as Todd Mendyk of Shady Hills, an area south of Spring Hill in adjoining Pasco County. Both men were 20 years old. Neither one had much to say to police.

While officers from the sheriff's office started gathering evidence, Jeff Cario, an assistant in the state's attorney's office, and Jane Phifer, an investigator for the state's attorney's office, were sent to view the crime scene and watch officials gather evidence.

As they walked alongside the yellow crime-scene tape that stretched across a large area of ground around the stuck truck, Phifer, who had been to many crime scenes previously, felt a cold chill come over her.

Investigator Phifer could not make any sense of what had happened. The beautiful girl lay nude except for a pair of socks. She was bound with electrical wire and gagged. Phifer thought about her own daughters. The sadness that had been coming over the investigator deepened. The beautiful girl had been discarded in this illegal dump, as if she was no more than garbage. On the victim's face, Phifer could see the torture the girl had suffered.

Detective Jim Blade, who had known the victim, was called to the scene. He identified the dead girl as Lee Ann Larmon. He followed the ambulance to Lykes Memorial Hospital morgue in Brooksville where the body was turned over to Dr. John Sass, pathologist and assistant medical examiner for the state's 5th Judicial Circuit.

The Presto store manager was called to the morgue to identify the body. He, too, identified the dead girl as Lee Ann Larmon, the store's night clerk.

In the swamp where the body had been found, Detective Ralph Decker (no relation to Lieutenant Royce Decker), of the HCSO, found articles of clothing. These were later identified as having belonged to Lee Ann Larmon and had been thrown into the swamp. The clothing

315

was sent to the FBI lab in Washington, D.C., to be analyzed.

A knife was found in the mud underneath a truck wheel; it, too, was sent to the FBI. They subsequently determined that it had been the knife used to cut the electrical wire which had bound Lee Ann's neck, wrists, and ankles.

Other FBI agents became involved in the case. Raymond Rawalt, an expert mineralogist, compared soil samples taken from the bottom of the stranded motorists' shoes with samples taken from the area where Lee Ann's body had been dragged and tied to a tree and from the palmetto bush where she was later ditched. The FBI found that the soil samples at the scenes matched the soil samples taken from the bottoms of Todd Mendyk's shoes.

FBI Agent Michael Malone determined that hair which had been vacuumed from Todd Mendyk's truck had been taken from Lee Ann's head by some act of force.

As Sheriff Thomas Mylander, detectives, and deputies dug into the incident, Phillip Frantz and Todd Mendyk were ordered to be held for the murder and kidnapping of Lee Ann Larmon. The men were then indicted by the grand jury.

Frantz and Mendyk were held in jail until the case went to court in October 1987. Phillip Frantz agreed to exchange a guilty plea for a life sentence, which would put him in jail for 25 years without parole, rather than be subjected to the electric chair. In order to get this deal, Frantz had to agree to testify against Todd Mendyk, who, detectives said, was the "mastermind" of the crime.

But there would be no plea bargaining for Mendyk "unless he wants to plea for high voltage," Assistant State Prosecutor Tom Hogan said to reporters outside the courtroom on the day of Frantz's pleas.

Hogan kept his word. No plea agreement was offered to Mendyk. Due to enormous publicity about the case, the trial was moved from Brooksville to Tavares, in Lake

316

County, about 60 miles northeast of Brooksville. There, an impartial jury was selected.

On Monday, October 12, 1987, a chained Todd Mendyk was escorted to a black vinyl court chair where his shackled feet were locked to the defendant's table. He made some type of a facial gesture to Prosecutor Tom Hogan. Hogan walked toward him and asked Mendyk what he had said. "I thought you were talking to me," Hogan said, visibly annoyed.

Mendyk replied, "I'll get out, and I'll be back to get you. Your court clerk can put that on her record."

During the proceeding, Mendyk sat with a pen in his hand, drawing what appeared to be a dagger. And during the trial, he would point the "dagger" at the judge, at witnesses, at jurors, and at cops and reporters in the courtroom.

But a hush came over the courtroom when Prosecutor Hogan made his opening statement. "April ninth was the last day of Lee Ann Larmon's life. She was twenty-three, working the night shift at a convenience store and going to junior college."

Hogan described the kidnapping, telling how Lee Ann had walked around the counter to get relish for Mendyk, how he had then grabbed her around the neck, how he had forced her into his truck and held her on the floor while Phillip Frantz drove away. Hogan told how Lee Ann had begged for her life, and how Mendyk told her to shut up.

The most damning evidence against Mendyk was delivered by Detective Ralph Decker. Decker had worked on the kidnapping and murder case from the beginning. On October 16th, he was called to the witness stand to testify against Mendyk.

Decker used a toy truck placed over a poster-size drawing he had made to show the route the truck belonging to Mendyk had taken on the night of the kidnapping and murder.

317

Mendyk's public defender, Alan Franter, objected to that type of testimony, arguing that the drawing and the toy truck was not to scale. However, Judge L.R. Huffstetler Jr. agreed with Hogan that the demonstration would help the jury in knowing where the incident had occurred. The judge allowed the testimony.

Decker testified that Mendyk told him that he and Frantz had been riding around looking for a "target" when they went to the Presto store. The two men hung around the parking lot for a while, waiting for a customer to leave the store. The time was approximately 2:40 a.m. This was not the first time Mendyk had been in the store; he knew what the clerk looked like, Decker said.

According to Decker, once inside the store, Mendyk ordered a hamburger. Then he grabbed Lee Ann around the neck, hit her to "make her know he meant business" and, holding her upright, he forced her to the truck.

While in the truck, Larmon was asking, "Where are you taking me? What are you doing?" Mendyk told Lee Ann to be good and everything would be alright.

Frantz drove the truck into Pasco County while Mendyk tied Lee Ann's wrists together with stereo speaker wire. Mendyk continued to fondle Lee Ann in the truck while she begged and pleaded.

They went to a place familiar to Mendyk in Shady Hills, where Mendyk had hoped to rape Lee Ann. Finding the gate into the property locked, they went to an area in the swamp that was familiar to Frantz.

After reaching the swamp, Frantz parked the truck near the illegal garbage dump. With the headlights shining, Mendyk made Lee Ann bend over a sawhorse he had taken from his truck bed and tied her wrists and ankles to it. While she was tied helplessly to the sawhorse, Mendyk sexually molested her with a stick and forced her to perform fellatio. Mendyk then dragged her to two scrub oak trees and using electrical wires, he tied Lee Ann's wrists to the limb of one tree and her feet to the other. Her body

318

formed a quarter-moon against the dark night.

With Lee Ann tied to the trees, still alive, Mendyk and Frantz decided to find a shovel and bring it back to bury Lee Ann, in case they decided to kill her.

At this point, the two men had not decided whether to kill Lee Ann. The idea of keeping her there, tied to the trees, and making Lee Ann their sex slave appealed to them.

Mendyk started to drive the truck out of the swamp, and on the way out, the wheels bogged down in the mud. Mendyk left Frantz to work on the truck, and went back to the trees where Lee Ann was mercilessly tied with electrical wires. Mendyk talked to Lee Ann, telling her he was unsure about what to do with her. Should he kill her or should he make her his sex slave?

Lee Ann kept saying, "Trust me. I won't tell anyone. Please don't kill me. I'm too young to die." But, Mendyk told Lieutenant Decker, the idea of her begging him not to kill her excited him. Mendyk left Lee Ann again and went back to the truck where Frantz was still trying to get the vehicle out of the mud.

"She's still there," Mendyk said to Frantz. And then in a little while Mendyk went back to check on Lee Ann again.

"Trust me, trust me, I don't want to die. I'm too young to die," was Lee Ann's final plea.

After telling this story to Lieutenant Decker, Mendyk said, "Anyone will say anything to get out of dying." That was when he put a bandanna around the victim's neck, and using his knife as a tool, he tightened it slowly. Lee Ann was shaking, so Mendyk wrapped her neck with wire, cut her down from the tree and took her to the palmetto bushes where he stabbed her in the throat.

Killing the helpless girl gave him an "incredible high," Mendyk told Decker.

One day, while Mendyk was in the county jail awaiting trial, Detective Kim Curlew asked Mendyk how he felt about killing the young girl. Mendyk responded that he wasn't sorry. He told Curlew that he would do it again if he had it to do over, Curlew testified.

When co-defendant Phillip Frantz testified, he corroborated Decker's testimony. Frantz, who had pled guilty to first-degree murder and to being a principal to kidnapping and a principal to sexual battery, said he did not help kill Lee Ann and did not sexually batter her, although he admitted that he stood by and did nothing to stop Todd Mendyk from committing the crimes.

According to Frantz, he and Mendyk had been looking for a girl before they stopped at the Presto store on the morning of April 9th. Frantz said that on April 8th, the day before the murder, he was in his room playing his bass guitar when Mendyk showed up uninvited.

At about 10:30 that evening, the two decided to go out. Frantz said he drove Mendyk's truck because he didn't trust Mendyk's driving when he was drinking.

They picked up a six-pack of beer, then went out looking for the house of a female friend in Brooksville. When they could not find her, they went to Spring Hill in the hopes of finding a party someplace. They drove by a couple of 7-11 stores where kids usually hung out in parking lots, but they couldn't find a party. By this time, their beer was gone.

The two men then drove to a friend's house and partied there for about half an hour. When they were ready to leave, their truck wouldn't start, so they stole a battery out of a car and put it in Mendyk's truck. When they left, they went to the Presto store to get something to eat.

"As we were getting out of the truck, Todd said, 'Let's grab this babe,' and jokingly I said, 'Yeah, right.'"

Inside the store, they went to the cooler and looked at sandwiches. "Todd got a hamburger and put it in the microwave. I was talking about wishing we had money to get beer." Frantz said that about that time, a man came into the store and looked him directly in the eyes.

"Todd asked the girl for onions, and she said she didn't have any. Then he asked for relish. When she got the relish for Todd, Todd stepped behind her and grabbed her around the neck. She asked what he was doing and he walked her out the door. He told her to get in the truck and she did," Frantz added that Mendyk told him to drive to Shady Hills.

Public Defender Alan Fanter asked Frantz if he knew what was happening at the time. Frantz replied, "I had a good idea. We were kidnapping the girl. We were going to do something. She wanted to know if we were gonna kill her. Todd said, 'No. Just be a good girl.' "

After going down a road near Mendyk's house off Shady Hills Road and finding a no-trespassing sign and a locked gate, the men drove to the swamp where Lee Ann Larmon was later sexually battered and murdered. Frantz claimed he stood about six feet away while Mendyk tied the victim to the sawhorse with black guitar strings, sexually battered her with objects, then tied her to the trees.

When they were ready to leave the swamp, Mendyk insisted on driving. When the truck got stuck and Mendyk went back to kill Lee Ann, Frantz said he did not try to stop him.

After the killing, Mendyk appeared to be the "normal Todd," Frantz testified. Frantz said he never went back to look at the body. But together, he and Mendyk threw the victim's clothes in the swamp, locked the truck, and started walking to find help in getting the truck out of the mud.

Evidence showed only one set of footprints going to the trees where Lee Ann had been tied. They belonged to shoes worn by Frantz, while tracks made by shoes worn by Mendyk had left several sets of prints between the stuck truck and the trees. Evidence also showed prints belonging only to Mendyk's shoes going to the palmettos where the body was found. This evidence showed that Phillip Frantz was telling the truth about what had happened in the swamp.

Upon delivering his closing statement to the jury, Prosecutor Hogan walked rapidly across the courtroom. With an angry look on his face, he pointed to Todd Mendyk, who sat comfortably in the vinyl chair, his feet still shackled to the legal table. "This is the last face Lee Ann Larmon ever saw," he said with a raised voice. "This is the face Lee Ann Larmon saw while she begged for her life. While she pleaded that she was too young to die!

"Three hours of terror for Lee Ann Larmon. Why?" Hogan asked. Then he answered his own question. "So Todd Mendyk could practice his domination. His lust."

In less than an hour, the jury of three women and nine men returned to the courtroom with their verdict. While Judge Huffstetler read the verdict over to himself, the courtroom was full of anticipation. Huffstetler handed the written verdict to the court clerk to read aloud. While she read the verdict, four bailiffs moved closer to where Mendyk sat shackled. Mendyk laughed lightly and whispered something to his public defender. The bailiffs never took their stare off Mendyk while they heard the verdict.

Mendyk was found guilty as charged of first-degree murder, two counts of sexual battery, and the kidnapping of Lee Ann Larmon.

The same jury recommended unanimously that Mendyk be sentenced to death in Florida's electric chair.

Todd Mendyk was sentenced by Judge Huffstetler to die in the electric chair for Lee Ann Larmon's murder. The judge called it "heinous, atrocious, cruel, cold, calculated, and premeditated."

Mendyk has been on death row at the Florida State Prison in Starke since his 1987 sentencing. The case went to the Florida Supreme Court in June 1989, at which time, the death sentence was unanimously upheld.

# "HE RAPED HER, BASHED HER, AND BURIED A COMPASS IN HER ARM!"

## by Bill G. Cox

A few minutes past 3:00 on the cold afternoon of Monday, January 7, 1991, the supervisor of the Pilot Community Center in a rough-and-tumble neighborhood of Oklahoma City returned from a doctor's appointment and received the worst shock of her life.

For the hour that she'd been gone, the supervisor left the center in the able hands of Elaine Marie Scott, a pretty, 21-year-old education major at the University of Oklahoma in nearby Norman. Although it was winter break, and many of her friends had left campus, the dedicated junior from Tulsa chose to spend her vacation working with the youngsters who were the lights of her life. Elaine was planning to become a special education teacher, and her part-time job at the community center, working with kids who were troubled and deprived but full of promise, gave Elaine the perfect opportunity to practice her skills. Her family and friends occasionally worried aloud about Elaine's safety, but Elaine would downplay their anxiety with a smile and a shrug, saying the neighborhood's risks were minimal compared to the boons she got being with the kids.

Ordinarily, the center's gymnasium would have been booming with the sounds of children at play. But on this afternoon, the only sound in the deserted building came from the supervisor's shoes as she walked the empty corridor to the two-room main office where she expected to find Elaine.

When she stepped into the office and peered around the door, the supervisor gasped as her eyes fell on a horrible sight.

The nude body of Elaine Scott lay sprawled face down on the floor in a widening pool of blood in the door between the inner and outer office. It seemed that blood was everywhere. The supervisor whirled, ran from the building to her car, and drove two blocks to an automobile parts store that was open. From there she called 911 to report her grisly discovery.

The uniformed patrolman who had received the call from the emergency dispatcher took one look at the bloody office scene, and after determining that the woman was dead from what appeared to be head wounds, radioed for homicide detectives. The first homicide investigators at the scene included Detectives Vance Allen and Eric Mullinex.

As they studied the office and the form on the floor, the detectives saw that Elaine Scott had been savagely assaulted and apparently bludgeoned to death. A large gash was visible on the side of her head, presumably the result of a tremendous blow. The ferocity of the attack was evident from the blood and what looked like brain tissue that had splashed on the walls up to seven-feet high.

The investigators noted that the victim's blood trailed across the ceramic floor, to a bathroom. Traces inside the bathroom indicated that the killer had probably tried to wash up — and perhaps even tried to clean his blood-stained shoes and clothing. There was a definite pattern to the bloody prints on the bathroom floor. They looked like the soles of athletic shoes.

Near the body was an overturned wooden coat tree and a metal golf club, both of which, the officers surmised, had been used to beat the coed to death. Later, the sleuths would learn that the golf club had been in the center office for some time, apparently left by someone who had forgotten it. From all appearances, it looked like the killer had grabbed at anything for a weapon in a frenzy to beat the pretty recreation staff member to death.

The victim was still wearing short, white socks, but otherwise she was nude. The investigators found her clothing — including a shirt, jeans, and panties — piled beneath a bulletin board in the inner office, where she had probably been forced to disrobe.

In addition to the furious bludgeoning, the coed had also been stabbed with a drawing compass that was still embedded in one arm. Blood had run from five puncture wounds, apparently inflicted by the compass, in the victim's neck. The amount of blood that had flowed from the wounds indicated that Elaine was still alive when the killer tortured her with the compass thrusts.

Not until an autopsy was done would the investigators be positive whether the pretty victim had been sexually assaulted, but the fact that she was nude made it probable that a sex motive had triggered the violent attack. A preliminary search of the office failed to turn up Elaine's purse, which indicated that robbery was probably also a factor.

Also reported missing was the victim's red Ford Taurus, which had been parked outside the recreation center. The sleuths presumed that the killer left in the victim's car after finding the keys in the coed's purse.

While technical investigator Sergeant Don Wilson took still photographs and videotaped the body and the scene, detectives began interviewing several young men who were among the crowd that had gathered, with the arrival of police, across the street from the center.

The investigators asked the young onlookers if they had seen anyone around the center that afternoon. One witness said he had seen a young man drive away in the red Ford owned by the victim. The witness described the driver as a black man who was wearing a black jacket and a red stocking cap. The suspect was thought to be in his mid 30s or younger. He had black hair worn in a short cut, and was under 6 feet tall and weighed 150 to 160 pounds.

A bulletin for the Ford Taurus and the unknown driver was broadcast to all local and area law enforcement units with a warning to use caution when approaching the vehicle.

At least part of the description—a black male wearing a black leather jacket and stocking or ski-type cap—fit the general description of a serial rapist who had attacked at least 11 Oklahoma City women in the past three years.

But Elaine Scott's killer had not followed the M.O. of the elusive rapist who had struck only during hours of darkness, usually in the early-morning hours after midnight. So far, his victims had been young black women—sometimes mothers with small children—in their homes.

The rapist had threatened the women if they did not submit but had not beaten or harmed them other than sexually, the detectives recalled.

But the detectives had a growing fear that the physical violence of the rapist might increase to the point of murder at any time, not an uncommon occurrence with sexual offenders.

The detective most familiar with the rapist's past forays, Captain Ted Carlton, head of the sex crimes division, said he could not rule out a connection between the coed's murder and the serial rapes at this point, but there was no link other than the meager description of the driver of Elaine Scott's missing car. In the Scott murder, Carlton pointed out, the driver had not been wearing a mask as had the serial rapist in all of his known attacks.

Barely an hour after the discovery of Elaine Scott's battered body, a police unit found her automobile about a mile north of the recreation center. It had been abandoned near the intersection of Northwest 15th and McKinley in a quiet residential area.

The vehicle was photographed and processed for fingerprints and other possible evidence, but nothing was found initially that would lead to the driver's identity. The vehicle was towed to police headquarters for further examination.

Meanwhile, the questioning of the spectators at the murder scene turned up one witness who said he knew someone who might have seen something that would help the police.

"There's a guy named Brian who said he had been at the center, and there was these two guys who were giving Elaine a hard time," the youth said. "He lives in a pink house over at Sixth and Douglas."

The witness did not know "Brian's" full name, but when detectives drove to the mentioned area, they quickly spotted the pink house. Inside, they introduced themselves to a teenager who gave his name as Alfred Brian Mitchell.

When asked if he had been at the center and seen anything that afternoon, the youth confirmed the story related earlier about "two guys giving Elaine a hard time." He had left because he was afraid and didn't want to get involved, he said.

If for no other reason than to eliminate Mitchell as a possible suspect, since he admitted to having been at the center that afternoon, the detectives asked Mitchell if he owned any tennis shoes. The teenager said he did. He went to get them and when he gave them to the officers, they noticed the shoes were damp, as if they had been recently washed. To make matters worse for the young man, the tread pattern on the soles appeared to be similar to the tracks left in the victim's blood.

The youth gave detectives permission to take the shoes for further examination. Before leaving, they asked him to come to the police station the next morning to make a written statement about what he had seen at the center.

When they returned to their office, the sleuths ran a background check on Alfred Brian Mitchell. What they found in his records made him loom as a primary suspect in the murder of the coed.

Only 17 days before the murder, Mitchell had been released from the state juvenile detention facility on his 18th birthday. When only 16 years old, he had been confined as a juvenile delinquent for the rape of a 12-year-old schoolgirl in 1988. The sexual assault had occurred after Mitchell kidnapped the young girl as she walked along the street to catch a school bus. He had taken her to a vacant building and raped her, the reports showed.

Under the state law, a juvenile delinquent is released from the reform school on his or her 18th birthday, unless for specified reasons the authorities of the institution decide to hold them for a longer time. If a petition is filed, an offender may be kept behind bars until the age of 19.

The detectives learned in reviewing Mitchell's files that in addition to the rape conviction, Mitchell's record also included a juvenile conviction for unauthorized use of a motor vehicle. Not only that, during his confinement, the psychiatrists and psychologists at the state facility had diagnosed the teenager as a sociopath, describing him as being "dangerous and volatile."

When Mitchell's tennis shoes were scrutinized by police laboratory experts, they found specks of blood on the shoes and the shoelaces, in spite of their having been washed. The soles appeared to match perfectly with the pattern seen in the bloody tracks found near the body.

The autopsy on Elaine Scott's body disclosed the full extent of the savage and humiliating attack that Elaine had undergone before being finally bludgeoned to death with the coat rack and the metal golf club.

The medical examiner's report to the investigators stated that the victim had suffered a crushed skull from the fierce blows to her head. The killer had bludgeoned her with such force that slivers of wood were embedded in her skull. Tests showed that the slivers matched wood splinters found near the body that had come from the coat rack.

The autopsy also disclosed that Elaine Scott had been raped and sodomized. During the autopsy, unidentified black, wool fibers were found under the victim's right thumbnail. It was believed the fibers were from the killer's clothing—snared under the thumbnail as the coed struggled with her attacker.

Alfred Mitchell came to police headquarters voluntarily on the morning after the murder, as detectives had asked him to do, so that a statement about what he had seen at the center could be taken. But as the questioning began, the youth became a strong suspect instead of a witness.

He was quizzed by Detective-Sergeants John Maddox, Willard Paige, and Eric Mullinex. Mitchell continued to deny any involvement in the rape and murder. He initially tried to focus on the two men who "gave Elaine a hard time," but as the interview progressed, the suspect changed his story numerous times.

At one point, Mitchell placed the blame on a gang member who he said bludgeoned the young woman to death with a golf club and wooden coat rack after he raped her. Mitchell claimed that he himself looked on, fearing for his own life, then fled from the center.

Outside of the suspect's presence, one detective told his colleagues that Mitchell was giving accurate details of what happened in the center office, but he was dumping the blame on someone else.

The investigators realized from listening to Mitchell's sordid story that he could not have known these explicit details without having been there since none of the information had been publicized. In telling the condemning details of the crime, the suspect had backed himself into a corner.

After the lengthy questioning session with Mitchell, the detectives went to his home again and talked with a relative, who recalled that the youth had been wearing black sweatpants on the day of the slaying. The sleuths took possession of the pants and a black jacket that had been part of Mitchell's apparel on Monday afternoon when Elaine Scott was slain.

In interviewing co-workers and friends of the victim,

detectives found another witness who added to the growing amount of evidence — physical and circumstantial — against Alfred Mitchell.

A fellow employee at the recreational center told detectives that he and Elaine had become good friends through their work together at the center. He said they frequently went to lunch or ran errands together in Elaine's car. The employee recalled that Elaine had confided to him that she feared Alfred Mitchell, who had been coming to the center recently. The coed said that Mitchell made suggestive remarks to her.

"She said he was saying some stuff that really frightened her," the center worker told sleuths. "She asked me once to walk out in the hall with her because Mitchell was talking to her while I was playing basketball in the gym."

The detectives also received information from two other witnesses. Two youths said that they had been walking in the vicinity of Northwest 15th and McKinley on the Monday afternoon of the slaying and encountered Alfred Mitchell walking toward them. He was coming from the area where a red Ford Taurus, later identified as Elaine's, was parked, they recalled. They had not seen him actually inside the car, they said.

As a result of the intensive police investigation, Alfred Brian Mitchell, 18, was charged three days after the coed's death with first-degree murder, robbery with a dangerous weapon, and larceny of a motor vehicle. At this point, no charges were filed in the sexual attack, pending the results of laboratory DNA tests comparing body fluids from the victim with those obtained from the suspect.

Undergoing tests by Oklahoma City police chemists and subsequently the FBI laboratory in Washington, D.C., were the victim's bloodstained blue jeans, shirt, and panties. Also undergoing tests were the clothing reportedly worn by the suspect on the day of the murder, his white tennis shoes, the black fibers from underneath Elaine's thumbnail, and the golf club and coat rack thought to be the bludgeon weapons.

Meanwhile, District Attorney Robert H. Macy and other officials criticized the Oklahoma Department of Human Services (DHS), which has jurisdiction over juvenile offenders, for releasing Mitchell on his 18th birthday instead of holding him longer for additional rehabilitation—especially in view of the psychological report that he was a sociopath who was "dangerous and volatile."

Said the outraged D.A., "In this business, you see a lot of bad crimes, but this had to rank as one of the worst. Here was a girl who dedicated herself to helping underprivileged kids, and she is bludgeoned to death. This should never occur in a civilized society. Mitchell should not have been released from custody for another year. Had he been handled properly, this would not have happened."

In response, a spokesman for the DHS said that offenders who reach the age of 18 must have successfully finished a behavioral modification program before they are released. But another DHS official said it is difficult to predict the future behavior of young offenders.

An examining trial for the accused killer was conducted on March 13, 1991. Oklahoma City police chemist Joyce Gilchrist testified that blood found on the victim's clothing matched that of Mitchell's blood type. According to prosecutors, Mitchell suffered a cut on his finger during the attack and left traces of his blood on the victim's panties, shirt, and jeans. The blood on the suspect's tennis shoes matched that of Elaine Scott, the chemist added.

According to the police chemist's testimony, semen samples taken from the victim's body matched Mitchell's blood type and genetic markers. Semen was also found on the girl's underwear, the witness said.

Detective Maddox testified that when interviewed, Mitchell eventually admitting that he struck Elaine Scott three or four times with "a wooden thing" and stepped in her blood and tried to wipe and clean his shoes.

Based on the testimony, the judge ordered Mitchell to

stand trial for first-degree murder, robbery, and car theft. Charges of rape and forcible anal sodomy would be added after chemical tests were completed.

Mitchell smiled at the hearing's conclusion, saying only "They got to prove it."

Still smiling, the bespectacled Mitchell went on trial in June 1992, in state district court in Oklahoma City's modern downtown Courts Building. In opening testimony, the state displayed to the jury 20 enlarged color photographs or the body and the crime scene, along with the video that scanned the scene and showed the bloody footprints.

Police chemist Gilchrist repeated the testimony about blood samples on the victim's clothing matching the blood type of Mitchell. She said that semen samples taken from the body were consistent with samples from the defendant, and bloodstains on a pair of Mitchell's black sweatpants matched the blood type of Elaine Scott, the witness added. The chemist also told the jury that black fibers found beneath the victim's right thumbnail matched those in a black wool jacket found at Mitchell's home the day after the slaying.

FBI Agent Gary Kanaskie displayed to the jury enlarged diagrams of shoe print impressions taken from the bloody prints on the ceramic tile floor inside the Pilot Center and around the body. He compared the sole, arch, and heel areas of a white sneaker belonging to Mitchell to the impressions in the blood, saying they "absolutely and positively" matched.

Also testifying was the youth who had seen Mitchell walking away from Elaine's car on the afternoon of the murder, and the co-workers who had been told by the victim that she feared Mitchell because of suggestive remarks he made to her during visits to the recreational center.

When testimony ended and the prosecution made its summation arguments, Assistant District Attorney Don Deason asked the jury to convict Mitchell of the savage murder, saying, "He wanted her, stalked her, humiliated her, and then got excited by what he saw. She fought him. Fibers from his jacket were embedded in her thumbnail. Then he robbed her, took her purse, but most importantly, he took her life."

Deliberating for less than three hours on June 24, 1992, the jury found Alfred Mitchell guilty of first-degree murder, rape, forcible anal sodomy, and theft of a vehicle. The same jury would decide whether the killer would be given the death penalty, life in prison, or life without parole.

When testimony began in the punishment phase, the victim's family were allowed, under a new Oklahoma law, to tell of the emotional pain they suffered as a result of Elaine's death. The law, allowing victim impact statements in court before a defendant is sentenced, was authored by Oklahoma state Senator Brook Douglass, whose parents had been murdered by robbers in their rural home in the 1970s. Douglass and his sister, both children at the time, barely escaped with their lives after witnessing the killings of their minister father and mother.

Another witness was the teenage girl who was raped by Mitchell when she was 12 years old.

Arguing for the jury to give the convicted killer the maximum penalty—death—Assistant District Attorney Steve Deutsch referred to Mitchell as "a man filled with rage who charted his own destiny the day Elaine was killed.

"He never showed any remorse—not one thread," said the prosecutor. "He sat here grinning at times. What kind of man would beat a helpless woman so savagely that brain tissue and blood splattered seven-feet high?"

Commenting on the stab wounds with the drawing compass, the assistant D.A. told the jury, "We know she was alive when she was stabbed. She bled profusely."

The defense attorney fought hard for a life sentence instead of a death sentence for his client, describing him as "a tormented young man who sought but never received affection and approval. . . . The bad part of him snapped the day he approached Elaine Scott."

But Prosecutor Deason described the defendant as a "predator," reminding the jury of the testimony by the 12-year-old rape victim two years before the murder of Elaine Scott.

On June 25, 1992, the jury returned a verdict of death against Mitchell, who showed no emotion as the verdict was read in the courtroom. Outside the courtroom, the defendant smiled his usual broad smile at reporters.

Besides giving him death, the jury also assessed a penalty of 100 years in prison for the rape, 20 years for forcible anal sodomy, and 30 years for the robbery conviction, just in case the murder sentence was overturned somewhere along the long process of appeal to higher courts.

A boyfriend of the victim told reporters after hearing the verdict, "I was disgusted that he could walk out of here smiling like it was all just a big joke. . . . There are lots of scars from this."

On July 10, 1992, state District Judge Dan Owens pronounced the death sentence on Alfred Brian Mitchell. When the judge asked him if he had any questions about the sentencing, Mitchell shrugged his shoulders and smiled.

The judge told Mitchell that they would meet again after all appeals are filed in the death penalty case. He added, "I hope someday somebody will take that smile off your face when you realize what you have done."

As this is written, Mitchell is confined on Oklahoma's death row awaiting the outcome of the appeal on his sentence.

# "RAVAGED, THEN BURNED ALIVE!"

## by Tammy O'Reilly

Nestled in the Pocono Mountains of Pennsylvania lies the city of Scranton, a relatively safe place with a population of 112,000 and a fairly low crime rate. People who live there feel secure in leaving their doors unlocked, and at ease walking the streets at night. Children from around the neighborhoods are allowed to play outside unsupervised because residents know that bad things seldom happen in Scranton. Or at least they didn't, until that Sunday, May 14, 1989.

It dawned warm and sunny, a perfect day. Many people gave a sigh of relief at the lovely weather. Most of them were planning family gatherings and hoped to hold them outdoors. This Sunday wasn't just an ordinary Sunday; this Sunday was Mother's Day.

Thirty-nine-year-old Joyce Brent spent most of the day as it should be spent, with her mother. Joyce worked the nightshift, and as the day wore on and evening approached, she forced herself to start getting ready for work. Shortly after 11:00 p.m., she said goodbye to her family and left the house, having every intention of reaching her job on time. Sadly, she was mistaken.

The dirt road Joyce traveled was narrow and heavily wooded. As she approached the bottom, she could see

335

flames and thick smoke. Slowing her car as she neared the fire, the 39-year-old woman thought she could see the outline of a face. Confused, she looked harder and saw that indeed it was a face, a small face on a small body.

Horrified and stunned at the realization that this fire was fueled by a person, a human child, Joyce Brent turned her car around and raced back to her family home to summon help.

Accompanied by a relative, Joyce returned to the site of the blaze and together they extinguished the flames. It was very evident that there was nothing else they could do. The two shocked individuals simply waited at the scene until police arrived.

The sight that greeted Pennsylvania State Police was a nauseating one. The tiny, charred body still smoked and the stench was strong enough to turn even the strongest stomach. But these men, like all lawmen, had a job to do and they wasted no time. Lieutenant George Kamage, who would head this investigation, ordered the scene secured and an intensive search of the area was begun. Soil samples were taken from near the body and surrounding areas, as were samples of the victim's clothing. These would be sent to the crime lab for analysis. About four feet from the body, Trooper Michael Morrissey found a tire track in the mud. After a closer examination, he noticed that embedded in the middle of it was a footprint.

Trooper John Fox, Dunmore State Police Barracks Records and Identification specialist, was called over. He proceeded to make a cast of the footprint.

Though the body was badly burned, police were fairly certain who it was. Only an hour earlier, they had received a call from a man who wanted to report a missing child.

Pretty, nine-year-old Renee Waddle had a nine o'clock curfew, so when she failed to return home by it, her family immediately began to worry. Had she been an adult, they might not have been so concerned, but Renee was only a child, and darkness was falling. By 10:30 p.m., after phone calls to friends and a search of the neighborhood disclosed nothing, the distraught family called the police.

And now a body had been found, a child's body. And there was evidence that this was the missing second grader. The height was about the same, 4 feet 6 inches, and samples of the victim's clothing closely matched the description provided by her family. Coroner William Sweeny also told investigators that the body appeared to be that of a female in her pre-teens. However, police refused to confirm the victim's identity until after the autopsy.

But people who worked at the bubbly, dark-haired girl's school didn't need confirmation. They knew. They watched sadly and silently as police converged there Monday morning seeking Renee's dental records.

If you were to ask any law enforcement officer what the worst part of their job is, there is no doubt they would tell you it is having to inform someone that a loved one is dead. But a job equally, if not more, distasteful, would have to be taking someone to identify a loved one. That was the position Pennsylvania troopers, accompanied by a relative of Renee Waddle, found themselves in on Monday afternoon. The family member, visibly upset and shaken, was able to make a positive ID, despite the condition of the body.

Dr. Halbert Filinger, a forensic pathologist who specializes in arson deaths, was called in from Philadelphia to assist in the autopsy scheduled to be done late Monday afternoon.

While this procedure was under way, sleuths swept into the little girl's neighborhood, knocking on doors and stopping passing motorists. They intensified their search in the area where the victim's body had been found, and sent out the word that anyone with information contact the Dunmore State Police Barracks.

337

Shortly before 6:00 p.m., lawmen announced that the burning body found on the isolated road was definitely that of nine-year-old Renee Jean Waddle.

Feelings ran strong in the community. Residents were both shocked and outraged at the brutal murder of one of their children, a young girl described as extremely friendly and trusting, never too busy to wave a big hello. But along with the shock and outrage, most people felt an underlying tinge of fear.

No one had forgotten the murder of a college coed only a year and a half earlier. The similarities between that crime and this one were uncanny, and there were few people who missed them. At that time, police discovered the badly beaten body of a 19-year-old girl, also in flames, on a Scranton street. Evidence showed that the young woman had been raped and that she had died from violent blows to the head. It was a barbaric crime in all respects, and one that remains unsolved to this day.

Renee's grade school principal was brought to tears by the news of her death, as were many of the victim's friends. Plans were made to bring in counselors to help the young students deal with their tragic loss and conflicting emotions.

Holding a press conference Tuesday morning, Lackawanna County Coroner William Sweeny stated that the second grader had died from a traumatic head injury. He also announced it was his opinion that the child was already dead when her body was set on fire. That there were numerous other injuries to the victim was not denied, but he refused to comment on them. He took the same stand when asked if she had been sexually assaulted.

With the victim positively identified and the manner of her death known, the Scranton area was thrown into one of the most exhaustive police investigations ever. With 30 troopers working the case full-time and another 50 pitching in often, roadblocks were set up on the main highway near where the victim was found and in the residential

338

areas where the little girl lived and played. Officers' feet ached from pounding the pavement, questioning the slain child's neighbors over and over again in the hope they would remember something previously not told. Despite all their efforts, police still didn't come up with anything concrete and they were frustrated. They knew better than anyone that if a case wasn't resolved within 48 hours the chances of solving it declined drastically; so far, they had come up with little. But they refused to give up, and within 24 hours, their luck would change.

It was on Wednesday, three days after the murder of the sweet little grade schooler, when a woman came in to see the investigators. She brought with her a small plastic earring and explained that it had been found in a man's auto repair shop on Monday, by a family member.

After confronting the man with it—he made the comment that it looked like a child's earring and claimed one of the neighborhood kids must have lost it—the man's relative began a search for the missing earring's owner.

On Tuesday, newspapers printed a map of the area where Renee Waddle's body had been found. It was an area that the relative knew the man frequented. Combining this fact, the fruitless effort to locate the owner of the earring and what she described as strange behavior on the man's part that Mother's Day, the relative became suspicious.

Though careful not to show it to her, lawmen were very interested in the woman's story. Although it had never been revealed to the public, there was evidence that Renee Waddle had been wearing earrings.

While performing the autopsy, doctors had noticed that Renee's right earlobe was torn, a wound consistent with an earring being yanked from a pierced ear. But people in law enforcement know better than to get their hopes up. For all they knew, the man from the garage could very well be telling the truth and this earring could have no connection whatsoever to the case. Nevertheless, they took the purple, clam-shaped piece of jewelry and thanked the woman for coming in with it. What relevancy it might have the police didn't know at the time, but they were soon to learn a very interesting fact.

On Saturday, May 13th, only one day before she would die, Renee Waddle had gone shopping with a family member. While at the store, she purchased a strip of earrings, 12 in all, for 99 cents. On the afternoon she disappeared, she had gone through the earrings, trying on several different pairs, before finally choosing to wear a set of purple ones, shaped like clam shells. Renee had seemed pleased with her choice, as she showed them to a family member, asking her if she thought they were pretty. She then asked the same question of a girlfriend she played with later in the day and the girlfriend's mother.

When police retrieved a similar strip of earrings from the store, they noted that the only ones missing from the strip Renee had were a pair of purple, clam-shaped ones. This was a set of earrings matching the single one found in the man's garage.

Pennsylvania state troopers now had a suspect to focus on in the case, 44-year-old Frank Osellanie, an auto mechanic who owned his own business. Described as a big man with an explosive temper, Osellanie was not unknown to the police, having been picked up before on various charges. When it came to murder, however, the auto repairman claimed he was innocent. He stated to police that he had worked late at his garage that night, returned a vehicle to its owner at 10:30 p.m., and then gone home. But police weren't buying his story because, like the pieces of a puzzle falling into place, evidence that seemed to have little meaning before Osellanie came under suspicion, now took on crucial importance.

Frank Osellanie's garage was located only a few blocks from the Waddle residence. In their door-to-door canvass of the neighborhoods, police had come across a woman who had seen Renee around 6:30 p.m. on that fateful

Mother's Day, walking north in an alley. On first learning of this, the importance of it had been lost to officers, but now it was to become a critical piece of evidence. If Renee had kept walking north along that alleyway, she would have come upon Osellanie's garage in only two short blocks.

Another puzzle piece fell nicely into place when a witness came forward to tell of seeing the victim right outside the auto mechanic's garage that same evening sometime after 7:00 p.m. The garage doors had been up, and the lights on, the witness further stated, indicating someone had been inside at that time.

Things were fitting together neatly now, but it still wasn't enough, and the Pennsylvania State Police knew it. They had a positive identification on the earring, and the witnesses who saw the victim outside Osellanie's garage at a vital time. It was all good evidence, but still not enough to secure a murder conviction. They needed more, and, unbeknownst to them, they were about to get it.

The tire track found near the nine-year-old's body was a mystery. It hadn't come from any vehicle the 44-year-old mechanic owned. It was then that police began to wonder about all the different autos Frank Osellanie had access to that weekend. It was a tedious process, but with no other avenue to explore, police began locating and checking every vehicle left at the garage that Sunday. Their efforts paid off when they discovered a commercial van that was taken to the garage on Saturday and returned by Frank Osellanie on Sunday night. According to the owner, however, the mechanic had returned the vehicle but hadn't fixed it. He also claimed that after the suspect brought the van back, the suspect had told the owner he should give it a good cleaning.

Looking over the van, state troopers noted that the tires looked right. Taking this into account along with the owner's statements, lawmen were prompted to impound it. They did this, much to the displeasure of the owner,

341

who had no other means of transportation.

The irate owner then phoned Osellanie to voice his objections to the mechanic for possibly using his van in a criminal act. In the process, the man tipped off Osellanie to the fact that the police were zeroing in on him.

State Trooper John Fox, who had the unenviable task of comparing numerous tires with the track left at the crime scene, finally hit pay dirt with the commercial van's left front tire—a perfect match.

Investigators were now faced with a hard decision. They needed, and wanted, more time to wrap up their case, but they were also aware that their suspect knew they were on to him. It was a problem they dwelled upon until May 21st, when it suddenly resolved itself.

On that date, in an action that would surprise everyone, police armed with search warrants arrested the 44-year-old auto mechanic on a charge of sexual assault unrelated to the murder, and also announced that he was a suspect in the death of Renee Waddle. Served with a search warrant for his home and garage, the arrested man was also made to give blood and hair samples.

While the intensive searches were being conducted, Frank Osellanie was taken into custody and held in lieu of $200,000 bail.

The officers' good fortune crumbled shortly thereafter, however, when the sexual assault charge against Osellanie was dropped because the statute of limitations had run out. At that time, lawmen had no other choice but to arrest their suspect for the Waddle murder, and State Trooper Walter P. Carlson did just that.

The once successful mechanic was charged with first, second and third-degree murder, voluntary and involuntary manslaughter, kidnapping, rape, and involuntary deviate sexual intercourse.

This was the first time residents heard that the pretty, dark-haired girl had been raped. They were to learn a lot more at the defendant's trial, which opened on May 31,

1990, before Judge Carlson M. O'Malley.

District Attorney Michael Barrasse, in his opening statement, promised the jury a vast amount of physical, direct, and circumstantial evidence that would prove beyond a reasonable doubt that Frank Osellanie was Renee Waddle's vicious killer. He also announced that he would be seeking the death penalty in the event the 12 jurors returned a first-degree murder conviction.

The defense maintained that Osellanie wasn't guilty of any crime, and the reason he now sat in that defendant's chair was a direct result of a relative's malice.

But Pennsylvania State Police had done their job well. Along with the victim's earring, the two witnesses who placed the slain girl near the defendant's garage on that fateful Mother's Day, and the tire track, they introduced 160 other pieces of evidence. Included in that was a solvent by the name of Drydene, taken during the search of Frank Osellanie's garage. Drydene is a solvent commonly used by mechanics for degreasing car engines. It just happened to have the same chemical makeup as what was used to set little Renee Waddle on fire.

George Surma, a state police forensic scientist, took the stand. He told of soil samples taken from the youngster's sneakers that matched, in all respects, soil taken from behind Frank Osellanie's garage.

Another witness testifying for the prosecution claimed to have seen Osellanie leaving his auto repair garage in the commercial van between 10:00 and 10:15 p.m. on the night the body was discovered.

Undoubtedly the saddest, and most shocking evidence the state brought out was the medical examiner's findings. Not only had the nine-year-old second-grader sustained traumatic head injuries, but she had also been badly beaten about the body. Discovering that she had been raped was horrible enough, but the rape had been uncommonly vicious and brutal, causing massive internal injuries that medical examiners, at one time, thought might

343

have caused her death. But perhaps worst of all, and contrary to earlier statements, there was now evidence that Renee Waddle hadn't been dead when set on fire, but had still been breathing when her body was doused with accelerants and ignited. It was this last finding that caused D.A. Michael Barrasse to seek the death penalty, charging that the young child had been tortured horribly and had suffered terribly before her death.

The defense brought out that a DNA analysis had been done, but had come back inconclusive. In a bizarre twist, the defense actually used investigators' meticulous efforts in the search of Osellanie's home and garage against them. Speaking candidly, the defense attorney told of state troopers going so far as to remove the lint filter from a clothes dryer and the floor drains from his client's garage in search of evidence. And yet, despite such a painstaking search, police had netted only the Drydene, a solvent readily available to anyone.

The jury also learned from a witness that Frank Osellanie had admitted that on that Mother's Day afternoon he had been in the area where Renee's body was later found (a fact the prosecution never discovered). The jury was asked if that seemed like the actions of a guilty man.

The case went to the jury on Thursday, June 14, 1990, exactly one year and one month after little nine-year-old Renee Jean Waddle was found dead.

The jury deliberated a total of 13 hours before returning with a verdict finding Osellanie guilty of second and third-degree murder, voluntary and involuntary manslaughter, kidnapping, rape and involuntary deviate sexual intercourse.

Frank Osellanie, who showed no emotion when the verdict was read, will be spending the rest of his life in a Pennsylvania State Prison.

EDITOR'S NOTE:
*Joyce Brent is not the real name of the person so named*

*in the foregoing story. A fictitious name has been used because there is no reason for public interest in the identity of this person.*

# "HANGED HER, THEN YANKED OUT HER TEETH!"
## by Barry Bowe

A few minutes before 3:00 a.m. on Sunday, December 13, 1971, a bearded man walked up to the back of an apartment building in Folcroft, Pennsylvania, a tiny borough five miles outside of Philadelphia, and knocked on the door. Small puffs of breath were coming out of the man's mouth as he waited for an answer to his knock. Two adjacent buildings, which stood end to end and contained store fronts and apartments, made up the 1500 block of Chester Pike. A narrow driveway split between the two buildings and led to a two-story, ramshackle garage another 50 feet behind the buildings.

Inside one of the apartments, 20-year-old Roscoe "Eddie" Edwards was trying to sleep. His wife stirred next to him, upset that somebody had the nerve to knock on the door in the middle of the night. Edwards rolled out of bed, peered out onto the landing, and saw his friend who rented the garage out back standing outside. Edwards opened the door.

"I want to show you something," said the friend.

"Man, can't it wait 'til tomorrow?" Edwards asked.

"No, you got to come now," his friend said. "Out back in the garage, c'mon back."

"Okay, be out in a few minutes," Edwards said.

Edwards got dressed and went outside. His friend had made it sound as if it were a matter of life and death, but Edwards didn't have the slightest clue about what could be so urgent. When Edwards reached the garage, he pushed the door and it squeaked open. Edwards stepped into the eerie darkness, but his friend was nowhere in sight.

"Up here," his friend said. Edwards looked up. His friend was standing at the edge of the loft, above him, holding a flickering candle. "C'mon up."

Edwards started up the stairway in the dark, his eyes adjusting to the gloomy light as he climbed. When he reached the top, Edwards stopped in his tracks.

A naked woman was hanging from a rope. One end of the rope was noosed around her neck and the other was tied to the rafters above. It was too dark for Edwards to see the woman's face until his friend moved closer to the dangling body. In the glimmering candlelight, Edwards saw long blonde hair. Then he recognized the woman's face. It was his buddy's girlfriend. She looked ghastly pale. Her head was drooping to one side at a weird angle and her tongue was sticking out. Slobber was oozing out of her mouth and glistening in the spooky light.

The scene shocked Roscoe Edwards, but not his friend, who was staring at the body, smiling.

"Eddie, look what I done here," his friend said. "I killed her. I hung her. Now she won't bother me anymore."

"I'm getting the hell out of here," Edwards said.

"I want you out of here," his friend yelled. "Get the hell out of here!"

Edwards went back to his apartment, trembling with fear. For all he knew, his friend was going to burst in at any second and string him up next. His friend was running on meth. He had seen it in his eyes. His friend was dangerous when he was like that, a madman.

When a Philadelphia family returned from a week's cruise to the Caribbean the following Saturday, letters overflowed their mailbox. Unopened Christmas cards addressed to Liz Lande leaned against the front door of the two-story home in the 7600 block of tree-lined Overbrook Avenue in West Philadelphia.

"I knew immediately Liz hadn't been there," Liz's father would later recall. Inside the tastefully furnished home, Liz's pictures adorned almost every wall, but there were no signs of Liz when her father inspected the premises.

"Nothing was missing except a pair of dungarees, which we assumed she was wearing, a pair of platform shoes, and an overcoat," Liz's father would later remember. "No luggage was missing of any type. No hand grips. Nothing."

When Liz's cat Venus wandered into the kitchen, mewing weakly from hunger, Liz's father was certain that no one had been in the home during the past week.

Elizabeth "Liz" Lande was petite, only five feet tall, with green eyes, a peachy complexion, gleaming white teeth, and 110 well-proportioned pounds on her tiny frame. Her blonde hair was her trademark: long and silky, it cascaded over her shoulders.

Liz had won a few beauty contests as a teenager and had tried to parlay her physical attributes into an acting career. But a successful semester of night school the previous spring had changed her plans, and she had enrolled at Philadelphia Community College as a full-time student that September. Now, her family feared she was missing.

When Liz's father reported her missing, the desk sergeant at Philadelphia's 19th Precinct at 61st Street and Haverford Avenue was sympathetic but unmoved. In the crime-ridden city, missing persons were nuisances. From a legal standpoint, Liz Lande was 21, and under Philadelphia Police Department standards in 1971, adults did not qualify to be missing persons.

At that time, Elmer Andress was the chief of police in Collingdale, a small borough between Overlook Park and Folcroft. Chief Andress offered a notebook, bulging with reports, to explain police attitudes toward missing persons.

"They take off if they have a fight with their mothers or their boyfriends," the chief said, "or if they do bad in school. We get the call and a day or so later they show up at a friend's house. There's just too many runaways to keep track of them all."

But Liz's father sounded too persuasive to be dismissed as a crank. Inside, city detectives asked him about the last time he saw Liz.

"We decided to take a trip," Liz's father began. "I didn't really feel right about it, but Liz wanted us to go so much that we decided she'd be all right by herself. So we left, knowing friends would be staying with her if she needed them.

"We left for a week's cruise out of New York," the father said, adding that they departed around noon on Friday, December 11th. "Liz walked down the pavement toward the car because she had a beauty parlor appointment at that same time. And we said goodbye. We all walked out together. We reminded her to study for her final exams, which were beginning the following Monday. She told us not to worry; she was looking forward to her finals."

Liz's father told the detectives that Liz had neither a credit card nor a bank account and only $25 in her pocket when the family left on their trip. Liz's father had already checked with the dean at P.C.C. Liz apparently never showed up for any of her final exams. Liz's father also mentioned Liz's telephone compulsion.

"Liz would call so many times with trivial, unimportant things," he said, "it was more than an attachment. It was unnatural for a twenty-one-year-old. But since our return, not one phone call."

But what worried her father the most was Liz's ex-boyfriend. The man said that Liz had been dating a member of the Warlocks, a local motorcycle gang rumored to be involved in drugs and assorted criminal activities. When Liz tried to break off the relationship the previous summer, the boyfriend and a bunch of his buddies circled the block almost every day on their motorcycles, trying to intimidate Liz into changing her mind.

"One night," Liz's father recalled, "just to let her know they meant business, I guess, they put a bullet through our back-room window. It went through the ceiling and lodged in the rafters. We called the police, but Lizzie wouldn't let us press charges."

The detectives had heard enough to begin an investigation. They started by interviewing friends of Liz Lande's and knocking on doors in Overbrook Park. Two of Liz's neighborhood pals told the detectives that they had kept Liz company on the first night home alone. They ate a pizza and were watching the "creature feature" on channel 10. Venus was sitting in Liz's lap on the sofa when, just before midnight, the phone rang.

Liz answered the phone while her two friends eavesdropped. They couldn't swear for sure who was on the other end of the conversation, but they both thought it was probably her old boyfriend, the biker. Liz agreed to some sort of meeting, but after hanging up, she was evasive with her friends, saying only that she was going out. Her friends then left in a huff, and they hadn't seen her since.

The detectives talked to a neighbor across the street who had observed something that might prove helpful. On the night Liz was last seen, the neighbor remembered seeing a gold Toronado pull up to the curb outside the Lande home.

It was just before 2:00 a.m., and Liz came out a few minutes later, got in the car, and the car drove off. The neighbor said it was dark; he could only describe the driver as a young white male.

Smelling a rat, Detective Raleigh Witcher visited Liz's

ex-boyfriend's home in Darby. With the ex-boyfriend's family members present, Detective Witcher told Bobby Nauss that he wasn't a suspect in Liz Lande's disappearance and wasn't in custody, but Witcher advised him of his rights in case he should say something incriminating.

Robert T. Nauss Jr. was 20 years old, ruddy-complexioned, and a 1970 graduate of Monsignor Bonner, an all-male Catholic high school in Upper Darby. He had long, wild dark hair, a beard like a wolfman, and a mustache. Tattoos marked both arms and made him look like someone not to mess with, despite his being only 5-foot-8 and 128 pounds.

In the interview with Detective Witcher, Nauss admitted that he knew Liz and had dated her. But, he told the detective, he heard that Liz had a boyfriend who was a "nut," and since then, he had steered clear of Liz. He added that he hadn't heard from her in quite a while and had no clue where she might be. When the detective fished for the gold Toronado, Bobby Nauss told him that he owned a blue '56 Harley motorcycle, but no car.

Detective Witcher went back to the police station and reviewed what he had so far: a mysterious telephone caller, an unidentifiable driver of a gold Toronado, and a cooperative suspect who swore to his innocence. The consensus around the station was that Liz Lande had run away and, like millions of other young people in that era, was probably headed for California to become a hippy. Witcher agreed and closed the investigation.

But Liz's family members refused to accept that theory. They turned to the FBI, but a special agent immediately begged off the case. From where he sat, the special agent saw no proof of Liz's being kidnapped or forcibly taken across state lines, no proof that any federal laws had been broken. He referred Liz's father back to an inspector at the Philadelphia PD headquarters, known as the Round-house, at Eighth and Race Streets. After hearing the father's story, the inspector reopened the case and assigned it to the West Philadelphia Detective Bureau at

351

55th and Pine Streets.

The following March 15th, Detective Phil Formicola hauled in Liz Lande's ex-boyfriend for another interview. With a buddy present, Bobby Nauss was told that he wasn't being arrested. Then the detective advised Nauss of his rights and questioned him. When Nauss walked away from the interview, Formicola had learned nothing new.

In July, Detective Tom Salerno got no further with Nauss on a third interview. At that point, the Philly PD closed the case for the second time.

"I knew I'd have to track her down myself," said Liz's father, who printed posters with Liz's picture and offered a $2,000 reward. Already fearing the worst, he haunted every seamy bar and strip joint in Philadelphia and across the river on the other side of the Ben Franklin Bridge, along Camden's Admiral Wilson Boulevard, a notorious region for prostitution and pornography.

"I figured the kind of people who may have killed her would be hanging out in places like these," he would later recall. "Everybody said they could help and figured me for an easy mark. It was always the same. I'd flash her photo and ask if anybody knew anything about her. The bartender would swear he'd seen her in there, and a couple minutes later, they'd call me over to a side table, insist they knew where her body was, then put a price tag on the whole thing. At first, I paid everybody. Then I realized how pointless it was. They didn't know any more than I did."

Next, Liz's father hired a private detective.

"I didn't have the money," he explained, "but I hired him anyway. I think he asked for a hundred dollars a day plus expenses. He said he was certain he could find Liz.

"Around that time I decided to work through the Warlocks. I figured they knew who killed Liz, and for a two-thousand-dollar reward, somebody was bound to turn him in. But they don't operate that way. I don't know what it is, but you can't turn them. I don't think they would have cooperated with me for two million dollars.

"I went to their clubhouse out in Southwest Philly one day with the private detective," the concerned father continued. "All I wanted to do was talk to them and leave some reward posters with them. We were parked across the street, just sitting there, trying to work up enough nerve to go in.

"Pretty soon, they came over and surrounded the car. The next thing I knew, this tough-guy detective takes off like a jet down Woodland Avenue, scared to death. That was the last time I used a private eye."

Later, Liz's father went back to the clubhouse alone and confronted Bobby Nauss.

"I'll never forget how he laughed at me when I asked him to help me find Liz," the father recalled. But Liz's father refused to give up. He followed lead after lead, but got nowhere. In addition to his own lack of progress, the police had given up on the case twice, the FBI wouldn't touch it, and a private detective proved worthless. In reality, the probability of anyone ever getting to the bottom of Liz Lande's disappearance appeared to be extremely remote.

The years passed—1972, 1973, 1974—with no new developments. By 1975, Liz Lande was all but forgotten by the law enforcement community when, suddenly, more young girls in the county started to disappear.

Two young girls, age 15 and 16, vanished from an Upper Darby Street on Holy Thursday night in March. Philadelphia marine police and fireboat crewmen pulled the girls' bullet-riddled bodies out of the Schuylkill River on Easter Monday. A 19-year-old girl disappeared in May and her body floated to the surface of the Tinicum Marsh in October. A 20-year-old disappeared in August and rabbit hunters found her skeletal remains in the same swamp in January 1976.

Investigators of these four murders by detectives from the Delaware County Criminal Investigation Division

(CID) revealed certain similarities: three of the four victims were from the Stonehurst Hills section of Upper Darby, all four girls knew each other, all four girls frequented the MacDade Mall in Ridley Township, and all four girls associated with members of the Warlocks Motorcycle Club. It was this last coincidence that caused the CID to re-examine the Liz Lande disappearance.

The unsolved murders rated constant press coverage in the city and the county newspapers for the better part of a year and the issue became a political football. When Frank Hazel took over as the county's new district attorney in 1976, solving the unsolved murders ranked at the top of his list of priorities.

"When the [last victim] turned up dead with a bullet through her head," said Detective Paul Schneider of the Upper Darby PD, "[the Warlocks] turned up the heat on themselves. The press made it a federal case and, for the first time, a concentrated force was established to try to stem the tide of biker violence, the rapes, the murders."

Frank Hazel created the Major Crimes Task Force, a hand-picked corps of elite operatives spearheaded by John Riley, the first-deputy D.A. In addition to Detective Schneider, Hazel also selected a pair of state troopers, George Ellis and Bill Davis, to man the topnotch staff, which Hazel charged with only two objectives: stemming the wave of biker crimes and cracking the unsolved murders.

"In the beginning," recalled Trooper Ellis, "we looked at Nauss on four or five of the unsolved cases—one of which was the Lande girl. The connection was too obvious to overlook: He was the girl's boyfriend. Later, we definitely ruled him out in two of the killings."

Despite the concentrated efforts and intensive probing by the elite corps, months passed without a single new lead being developed. Then, in the fall, the stale investigation got its first breath of fresh air in years.

On October 31st, Tanya Weston pressed charges against four Warlocks, swearing they had forced her at knife-point to perform sexual acts with them. The strike force dug in.

"The girl they raped from Media was a prostitute," Trooper Ellis would say later, "and she was one hard bitch, on the fringe of the bikers. But she was really pissed off because they kidnapped her and really worked her over.

"We put two of the perpetrators into the Witness Protection Program," Ellis said, "and we made the rape case, which took us into the drug case. At this point, we knew Nauss killed the Lande girl but lacked evidence. But we knew the Warlocks were in the drug business. We knew if we worked long enough and hard enough through the drugs, focusing on Nauss the whole time, taking it one step at a time, infiltrating further and further into the Warlocks, we had a chance to break the case."

State troopers went undercover, growing their hair long, not shaving, dressing like bikers, and buying drugs.

"In time, we got enough on the drug case for a probable cause to search [Nauss'] house in Aston. [Nauss was married by then and living at a new location.] That's when Liz's father dropped the evidence to Bill Davis that opened up the murder case."

With the information the strike force had gathered by infiltrating the motorcycle gang, they arrested Bobby Nauss and 48 other Warlocks in May 1977 on charges of drug manufacturing, distributing, and conspiracy. More importantly, Trooper Bill Davis had unearthed two vital pieces of information in the murder investigation.

"We now had Roscoe Edwards' name and the address of the apartment he rented on Chester Pike in Folcroft," Trooper Ellis said.

The state troopers ran the rental information and located Edwards' landlord. The landlord remembered a tenant named Roscoe Edwards, but the landlord also remembered that Edwards had mysteriously disappeared one day, without giving notice. The landlord dug out his records, which showed that Edwards had vanished in the middle of December 1971, five and a half years earlier, without leaving a forwarding address.

The troopers asked to see the rental application. On the seven-year-old document, they found out that Edwards had listed his mother's address for reference purposes. The troopers sped to the address listed on the old rental application, a house in Philadelphia. Outside, a vehicle with Florida tags was parked at the curb. Inside, at that very moment, Roscoe Edwards was visiting his mother.

"We brought [Edwards] in and found out he was wanted on an outstanding bench warrant for an old shooting charge," Trooper Ellis recalled. In the process of questioning Edwards, the troopers advised him that they were considering arresting him as an accessory to the murder of Liz Lande. Feeling the heat, Roscoe Edwards spilled the details of the gory murder, then told the troopers that he had returned to his apartment afterwards. Around 6:00 a.m., Bobby Nauss knocked on Edwards' door again.

"Come on out to the garage," Nauss had said calmly. "You got to help me with the body. I can't do it myself."

"You're nuts," Edwards replied, trying to keep his voice down so he wouldn't wake up his wife. "I don't want anything to do with it. Just get out of here, man, and leave me the hell alone."

"Look, Eddie, you're more or less implicated already," Nauss said. "You know what I mean?"

"No, I got no idea what you're talking about," Edwards replied.

"You call the fuzz?" Nauss asked.

"Come on, man, you know I wouldn't dime you to the heat."

Bobby Nauss told Edwards that that was exactly why he was implicated. Since he had neglected to call the police, he was an accessory. Now Edwards had no choice. He had to help Nauss dispose of the body.

"No way," Edwards said. "I'm not going to help you."

"Look, Eddie, you know the kind of people I hang

356

around with, the kind of people I know," Nauss said. "Things could happen." Nauss talked about cars crashing and catching fire, burning with the driver trapped inside at the wheel, or houses catching fire in the middle of the night and burning while the people slept peacefully inside, or "something might happen to your wife one day while she's at the store."

Edwards told the troopers that when he went back out to the garage, the body was lying on the floor, near the door. It was wrapped in a sheet, the head was covered, and parts of the legs and feet were sticking out at one end. Edwards bent down and grabbed the feet while Nauss took hold of the head. Together, they threw Liz Lande's corpse into the trunk of Edward's white '65 Pontiac Bonneville convertible.

A few seconds later, they learned why morticians called cadavers "stiffs." In death, Liz refused to cooperate with Nauss. Apparently, rigor mortis had frozen her legs and her knees were sticking straight up. When Nauss tried to close the trunk, Liz's knees resisted. Finally, on the eighth or ninth try, Nauss sealed Liz into the only coffin that would ever hold her.

An hour later, Roscoe Edwards and Bobby Nauss were steering a course into the New Jersey pine barrens, 1.3-million acres of wilderness. Edwards was driving along a two-lane side road heading deeper into the timberland when he spied a dirt road. He turned onto the path and braked to a stop between clumps of pine trees.

Quickly, the two men dug into the sandy soil and tossed Liz's body into a shallow grave. Then Edwards walked around to the front of the car while Nauss finished the burial. He needed space to breathe, away from the corpse. Edwards was leaning against the car when the notion hit him that, just maybe, Nauss was going to try to "do" him next. Edwards knew the Warlocks believed that the only good witness was a dead witness. Suddenly, Edwards was terrified, so scared that he knew he and his wife had to pack their bags and move to Florida, almost immediately.

The new evidence thrilled the two state troopers, but they knew there was no time for celebration. With Edwards' statement, they had only circumstantial testimony, which Bobby Nauss would surely swear was a lie. It boiled down to one man's word against another's. The lawmen knew they needed more evidence, more witnesses and, most of all, the body. The troopers interrogated Roscoe Edwards again and milked more information.

Edwards now told the troopers about stopping at an auto repair shop on the way to the Jersey pine barrens. Edwards went inside with Nauss, looking for Ace Wiggins. Trooper Ellis would later describe Wiggins as someone on the fringe of the bikers who was involved in altering the manufacturers' numbers on stolen cars, in chopping and fencing stolen parts, and probably in the drug trade, as well.

The troopers located Ace Wiggins at once and informed him that they were considering pressing charges against him as an accessory to the murder of Liz Lande.

"I don't think he had much choice," Trooper Ellis would later say, commenting on Wiggins' willingness to cooperate. "If he didn't testify, he knew he was in the soup with Nauss."

Ace Wiggins told the investigators that Bobby Nauss had told him he had murdered Liz Lande, and Nauss wanted Ace to go to the Jersey pine barrens to help dispose of the body. Ace didn't like the idea and told his friend that he had too much work to do.

At that point, Nauss handed him a crumpled paper bag. Inside were the jeans, blouse, overcoat, bra, and panties that Liz had worn the night before. Wiggins tossed the clothes into a 55-gallon drum, poured lacquer into the barrel, and torched the evidence.

On July 2nd, Trooper Davis drove to the Folcroft garage to photograph the loft. Two-by-four beams ran horizontally overhead. Davis measured seven feet, nine and three-quarters inches from the tops of the beams to the floor. Taking Liz Lande's height and Roscoe Edwards' descriptions of the murder scene into consideration—the length of rope and the victim's feet dangling a foot and a half to two feet above the floorboards—Edwards' story added up. Meanwhile, Trooper Ellis was speeding to the Jersey pine barrens with Edwards to search for Liz Lande's body.

"We spent a lot of time digging," Ellis would recall, "almost a week. We used bulldozers. We leveled two acres and tried everything to find the body. We even borrowed a special dog from the New York State Police, a dog specifically trained to sniff out dead meat. The dog found a lot of dead meat, but not what we wanted. I suspect Nauss went back, dug up the body, and moved it."

Without the corpus delicti, District Attorney Frank Hazel faced a difficult decision. As a rule, prosecutors shied away from alleged murder cases without bodies. So far, the evidence was circumstantial, and the distinct possibility existed that the witnesses against Bobby Nauss might be influenced into recanting their testimonies. Everyone involved in the investigation believed that Bobby Nauss had murdered Liz Lande, but the case might never go to trial without Liz's body. For now, the decision would have to wait. It was time for Nauss' drug trial to begin, and with the precarious nature of the homicide investigation, the D.A. wanted to make sure that he put Bobby Nauss behind bars on something.

"I guess I was sort of like his runner, his flunkie," a self-confessed drug dealer swore at the drug trial. "[Bobby Nauss] would give [methamphetamine] to me up front, and I would pay him after I sold it."

On August 4th, a federal jury convicted Bobby Nauss of attempting to distribute methamphetamine, a conviction that would prove monumental a decade later. The rape case began in September.

Tanya Weston, the alleged rape victim, told the jury that three Warlocks had abducted her and demanded to have sex with her. When she refused, they pulled out

359

knives and threatened to slash her throat. Fearing for her life, she crawled into the backseat and stripped.

Weston swore that Bobby Nauss forced wine laced with barbiturates down her throat and forced her to perform sex acts with him. First, the defendant made her perform oral sex, Weston testified. Afterward, he performed oral sex on her. Next, he punched her stomach and legs repeatedly. The jury gasped upon hearing the details, but the worst was yet to come. Weston told the court that Bobby Nauss inserted the neck of a liquor bottle inside her vagina, then stuffed ice cubes up her rectum.

Next, the three Warlocks drove her to a strange apartment. A fourth biker joined the group inside and they "trained" her, a motorcycle-gang euphemism for gang rape. If at any time she displeased the defendant, he ordered his friends to whip her with a belt. After that came the anal-genital sex. Then, the bikers allowed her to sleep on the couch while they took turns standing guard over her. Later that night, the bikers woke Weston again for another "train."

Tanya Weston said she escaped the next morning and rushed to the hospital. While someone called the police, a hospital physician treated her for extensive bruises and documented the sexual abuse.

"She was a nymphomaniac who voluntarily engaged in sex acts with my friends," Bobby Nauss testified. He said one of his buddies was alone with the woman in a bedroom when the buddy yelled, "Come see this freak!" Nauss entered the bedroom and saw his friend beating the woman with the belt. At that point, Nauss claimed the woman voluntarily performed oral sex on him.

"I remarked to him that she was terrible," Nauss testified, "and my friend hit her with the belt. And she was still bad, and I stopped. I never even finished with her."

On September 21st, the jury sided with the victim and convicted Bobby Nauss of rape, kidnapping, involuntary deviate sexual intercourse, simple assault, and indecent assault. By that time, the D.A. had decided to proceed with the homicide charges, even without the body of Liz Lande.

Nauss' murder trial began two months later in front of Judge William A. Toal and a jury of eight men and four women. Assistant D.A. James DelBello prosecuted for the Commonwealth; Edward Savastio provided the defense.

DelBello introduced Liz's family members, who provided the victim's background and character. He called Roscoe Edwards, who described seeing the victim's dangling body in the candlelit loft and told of her burial. Next came Ace Wiggins.

"[Bobby Nauss] told me he killed Liz Lande," Wiggins testified, then described how he himself had burned the victim's clothing. "All that was left was a pile of ashes," Wiggins said.

The prosecutor called a girlfriend of one of the bikers, who described a conversation she had with Bobby Nauss three months after the murder.

"Where's your girlfriend?" the witness remembered asking Nauss on that occasion.

"What was the defendant's reply?" Prosecutor DelBello asked.

"He said he killed her," the witness replied. Nauss had also said, "I couldn't stand it any longer. She was making me mad. I started choking her and went too far."

Finally, the prosecution called Richie DiPaolo. "DiPaolo and Nauss were good friends, Warlocks, and they had this deal they pulled a lot," Trooper Ellis would later say. "Nauss would drive some unsuspecting girl out behind the airport with DiPaolo hidden in the trunk. Kids used to go behind the airport in those days to park. Later, after Nauss started having sex with the girl, DiPaolo would let himself out of the trunk and join in. . . .

"It shows the contempt they had for women and the contempt Nauss had for the Lande girl."

From the witness stand, Richie DiPaolo recalled a conversation that had taken place six months after Liz

Lande's disappearance.

"[Bobby] said, 'Richie, I killed her. I strangled her. I pulled all her teeth out and cut off her hands and feet," DiPaolo recalled on the stand.

DiPaolo's testimony shocked the packed courtroom, adding savage tones to an already gruesome story.

Despite the absence of a corpse, the defense never denied that Liz Lande was dead. Instead, the defense attorney tried to paint a picture of the victim as being an emotionally troubled person. Defense Attorney Savastio called witnesses who labeled Liz Lande a nymphomaniac and a masochist. Other witnesses called Liz suicidal, manipulative, schizophrenic, and paranoid.

"She was high," Bobby Nauss testified, describing the night of his girlfriend's death. After having sex with him, the defendant said Liz "consumed uppers and downers. She was slobbering, hunched over from doing drugs. We argued about it, but she said doing drugs made her feel better. She said, 'I can't understand why nobody likes me. Nobody loves me. I just feel worthless.' "

Nauss swore he then left Liz alone in the loft while he and Roscoe Edwards went out to hunt for a 1970 red Cadillac convertible they had planned to steal as part of their car-theft ring. When Nauss and Edwards returned, Nauss went back up to the loft.

"I got to the top," Nauss testified. "I stood there and froze for a minute. Liz was hanging. A crate was underneath her. Liz hung herself."

The assistant D.A. called two rebuttal witnesses. One was Roscoe Edwards, who denied any complicity in a hot-car ring with Bobby Nauss. The other witness was a clinical psychologist.

"[Liz Lande] was too immature to attempt a true suicidal gesture," the psychologist stated. He said Liz was the type of person who might fake a suicide attempt to attract attention to herself but, in his opinion, she definitely lacked the courage and commitment "to carry the attempt to a conclusion."

On December 9th, six years after the gruesome murder of Liz Lande, the jury convicted Bobby Nauss of first-degree murder and sentenced him to life imprisonment. But society had not heard the last from the man who epitomized the bikers' anthem: "Born to Be Wild."

"Absolutely," Edward Savastio announced, when a reporter asked him if he intended to appeal his client's conviction. "And we'll win," the defense attorney said. "We already have ten or twelve points [of law in our favor]."

So Bobby Nauss entered prison feeling confident that his murder conviction would be overturned, spending his first year and half of confinement in the Delaware County Prison under the watchful eye of Warden Tom Rapone, a former schoolmate. Then, in August 1979, the state transferred Nauss to Graterford State Correctional Institute, a maximum-security prison 25 miles northwest of Philadelphia. Bobby wore number AM2456 and was assigned to cellblock B. He took a job in the prison woodshop where he met 41-year-old Hans Vorhauer. Vorhauer was serving 13 to 27 years for a $39,000 robbery at a MacDade Mall jewelry store, plus an additional 10 to 20 years for larceny, conspiracy, and armed robbery.

While his appeal slowly made its way through the appellate courts, Nauss reported to the woodshop at nine o'clock every morning for the next three years. He honed his carpentry skills. The prison allowed inmates to make furniture in the shop and sell it to private citizens on the outside, with the proceeds going to the inmates' welfare fund. Soon, Nauss was making and selling furniture. He was also maintaining his outside contacts with his biker friends, smuggling drugs into prison, and selling them to the cons. But one day in 1982, the State Supreme Court upheld the lower court's verdict. Bobby Nauss had run out of appeals and this unexpected development called for a new strategy.

"[Bobby Nauss] came to my desk with another inmate,"

the prison woodshop instructor would say later, referring to the morning of November 17, 1983. The instructor said Bobby and Hans Vorhauer approached him at 7:00 a.m. "They told me they were going back to the block and I issued them a pass," the instructor recalled.

But Nauss and Vorhauer had lied to the instructor.

"A head-count of inmate population did not come out as correct," remembered Captain Creighton Caison, a Graterford guard on duty that day. Caison ordered a bunk check. When both Nauss and Vorhauer missed that check, Caison called the warden, and escape procedures went into effect.

At 5:15 p.m., the warden notified the state police barracks at Limerick. The radio operator transmitted the escape information, advising all police agencies to use extreme caution. The dispatcher said Bobby Nauss—now 31—was last seen wearing a blue jacket, with no prison markings. He was described as 5-foot-8, 195 pounds, of medium build, with brown eyes, short brown hair, and ruddy complexion and with tattoos on both arms, the most prominent one being a parrot and a wreath on his upper right bicep. The dispatcher described Hans Vorhauer as 5-foot-10, 150 pounds, of medium build, with red hair, fair complexion, and clean-shaven face. Vorhauer's upper tooth was conspicuously missing, the dispatcher said.

At that point, there were no physical signs that an escape had taken place. For the next four days, dozens of prison guards scoured the 62 acres inside the walls and the 1,700 acres of prison grounds outside the walls, trying to find the missing prisoners.

"They were not found," Captain Caison said. By then, the authorities theorized that the two convicts had submerged themselves into the biker underground, a nationwide network of state-to-state motorcycle-gang chapters with ties to organized crime.

"How effective are these ties?" a reporter asked.

A U.S. marshal told the reporter that Thomas Wellington, another Warlock, had escaped from the Delaware County prison five years earlier and was still at large.

Three years passed and it seemed as if the two fugitives had fallen into a huge black hole. State troopers working out of the Limerick Barracks were handling the pursuit and getting nowhere. Then, early in 1986, President Ronald Reagan appointed Tom Rapone as the U.S. Marshal for Pennsylvania's Eastern District. Rapone had known Bobby Nauss since high school and had overseen Nauss' stay at Delaware County Prison. Rapone induced the state police to turn the case over to the marshal's service.

"Rapone was the godfather of this case," said Bob Leschoron, the Chief of Domestic Operations at the marshal's headquarters in Alexandria, Virginia, "and of the twenty-eight thousand cases under my jurisdiction, Nauss was the toughest of the tough cases."

In the spring of '86, Rapone created the Motorcycle Gang Investigative Task Force to apprehend fugitive bikers. The special force was composed of federal marshals, state troopers, city and county detectives, and local cops. Rapone assigned Deputy-Marshal Hurley Trout to take charge of the Nauss-Vorhauer escape. In July, the Pennsylvania Crimestoppers offered a $1,000 reward for information leading to Nauss' capture, providing a toll-free line at 1-800-4PA-TIPS.

Starting three years after the escape, Deputy-Marshal Trout, working closely with Trooper Griscom and Detective Bill Marker of the Philadelphia PD, began re-creating the prison break. Trout interviewed bikers known to be acquainted with the fugitives and painstakingly gathered information. In time, Trout learned that Bobby Nauss had phoned an old biker girlfriend the day before his escape and instructed her to rent a truck and pick up a piece of furniture at Graterford the next morning. She had performed the task several times in the past and was familiar with the procedure. Nauss told her that he would call her the following day with delivery instructions.

365

On the morning of the escape, the two cons crawled inside a wooden cabinet that Bobby Nauss had constructed in the shop, and they waited. Before long, prison guards rolled the heavy piece of furniture into the prison wheel-lock and loaded it onto the waiting truck. Moments later, the unwitting accomplice drove the rented truck away from Graterford.

When the woman reached her home in Manayunk, a hilly section of Philadelphia about five miles outside of center city, she heard pounding coming from inside the truck. Nauss had never trusted her with the escape information, so she was surprised to see the two fugitives inside the van when she opened the truck's back door. With barely more than a hello and a goodbye, the two fugitives fled on foot.

Another female biker-connection was waiting a few blocks away with a getaway car and a change of clothes. She drove the two men to a nearby train station and dropped them off. But that was as far as Deputy-Marshal Trout could track the fugitives. Trout's only resort at the moment was to initiate surveillances on the fugitives' family members who were still living in the Philadelphia area.

"One of the problems in the investigation was that Vorhauer was in prison for about thirteen years," Marshal Tom Rapone recalled, "and we had no current photograph of him. We took his original mugshot to a local artist and sculptor and he actually aged the photo for us."

The artwork paid off when someone resembling the sketch of Vorhauer was sighted in Upper Darby three years later, during the summer of 1986.

"There were about six kids playing in the immediate vicinity of Vorhauer," said Detective Paul Schneider, a man who had hounded Bobby Nauss, for one transgression or another, for nearly 15 years. "We weren't about to move in that situation. We didn't want to jeopardize anyone's safety, including the fugitive."

The policemen decided against trying to capture Vorhauer that afternoon, but they believed another chance would be close at hand. Marshal Tom Rapone theorized that Bobby Nauss and Hans Vorhauer were most likely manufacturing methamphetamines in another state and distributing the drugs in the Pennsylvania and New Jersey areas. Rapone believed that wherever Vorhauer was, Nauss was close at hand and the marshal ordered the surveillance to be increased.

"Everyone remotely involved was deputized on detainers from the federal government," recalled Lieutenant Nicholas Bratsis of the Upper Darby PD. "Day and night we followed [Vorhauer's relative] from her residence to work, shopping, wherever she had to go, using five or six [unmarked] cars so she wouldn't spot the same car."

Criminal Investigator Michael Kenny and Patrolman Gerald Colvin, both of the Upper Darby PD, followed Vorhauer's relative to a South Philadelphia motel on a Monday afternoon in early September. When Vorhauer's relative went inside a motel room, the sleuths called for backup. U.S. marshals, state troopers, Delaware County detectives, and policemen from Upper Darby, Haverford, Philadelphia, and Springfield converged on the motel.

"Everything had to be perfect," Lieutenant Bratsis would say later, "and totally by surprise to avoid innocent bystanders. [Vorhauer and the woman] walked out of the room together and offered no resistance. We were thankful for the way it turned out, and nobody got hurt."

Task force officers found a Michigan driver's license, credit cards from a Michigan bank, and an airline ticket to Yale, Michigan, in Hans Vorhauer's possession, all under a fictitious name. But there were no signs that Bobby Nauss had been in Vorhauer's company.

"Vorhauer had changed considerably in appearance," Marshal Rapone said at the time of the arrest, "and [the artist's] drawings were invaluable helping investigators recognize him. His aging sketch was right on the money. When Vorhauer was taken into custody, he had a receding hairline, a mustache, and a hair length close to that of the sketch."

Once again, Rapone solicited the artist's help, certain that Nauss was living a yuppie lifestyle, supported by drug money. Correspondingly, the artist sculptured a full-color bust of Bobby Nauss, aged to look like a man in his mid-30s, wearing a short, contemporary hairstyle.

Marshals followed Vorhauer's trail to a home in Yale, Michigan. Inside the home, they found a sophisticated meth lab, $37,000 dollars in cash, and enough chemicals to manufacture 92 pounds of speed, which had a street value of $10,000 per pound at the time. But they found no trace of Bobby Nauss.

Marshal Rapone was obsessed with capturing Bobby Nauss, but the funding wasn't sufficient for the large-scale effort necessary to apprehend him. Rapone would have to convince the marshal's headquarters to elevate the case to a national priority if Bobby Nauss were ever to be caught. The problem was, Rapone wasn't sure if the feds still had jurisdiction on the case. He assigned Janet Doyle, a deputy-marshal fresh out of college, to research Bobby Nauss' sentences.

Deputy Doyle learned that Nauss' only federal rap was three years on a drug conspiracy charge back in 1977. But nine years had already passed and it looked as if Tom Rapone would have to give up his obsession.

"We double-checked to see if his sentences were consecutive or concurrent," Janet Doyle recalled, "and we learned that we still had a federal detainer on the narcotics case. He owed us two years." Armed with that fact, Tom Rapone pulled political strings and called in favors.

"We want this guy," Tom Rapone told a January 1987 press conference. With that announcement, Bobby Nauss had been elevated to the marshal's list of the 15 most wanted fugitives and, to boost awareness of the case, the federal government threw $3,000 into the reward kitty for information leading to Nauss' arrest.

In the meantime, unconfirmed sightings had placed Bobby Nauss in Michigan, New Jersey, California, Arizona, Maryland, Delaware, Florida, Washington State,

Canada, and Australia. Looking for a pattern, Deputy Janet Doyle analyzed the toll records of phone calls emanating from homes belonging to Nauss' relatives. But no patterns existed, either in the destinations of the relatives' phone calls or the times that the calls had been placed.

The marshals were ready to throw up their hands in exasperation when, suddenly, there appeared to be a break in the case. Re-coding a national computer program to search for Social Security numbers instead of fingerprints, Deputy-Marshal Rick Iannuci found a two-year-old armed robbery arrest in San Antonio, Texas, in which the perp's Social Security number matched the Social Security number of a local Warlock. (It was standard M.O. for fugitive bikers on the lam to assume another biker's ID.)

Janet Doyle phoned the San Antonio PD and learned, unfortunately, that the perp had served his time. But Doyle did obtain the serial numbers of the two guns used in the hold-up. So Doyle contacted a friend at Alcohol, Tobacco, and Firearms (ATF). The ATF friend traced one of the weapons to a California retailer who had sold the gun to a young woman. Doyle got the woman's name and address from the retailer, along with her Social Security number. Doyle knew that California driver's licenses, which contained the bearer's Social Security number, would have been required as proper ID in purchasing the firearm.

Next, Deputy Doyle called a friend who worked at the Social Security Administration (SSA). The SSA friend found out that the 17-year-old woman who had purchased the gun was collecting her husband's death benefits.

Doyle tracked the woman from California to Denver, Colorado, but learned only that the woman's husband was a biker who died in Orange County, California. The Orange County coroner told Hurley Trout, via telephone, that the man's body had been cremated. But the coroner had kept a detailed record of the deceased, which he recited over the phone.

In Philadelphia, Hurley Trout repeated the vital facts out loud while Janet Doyle jotted down the information: white male, mid-30s, medium build, medium height, brown hair, brown eyes, and assorted tattoos. Trout and Doyle were getting excited as Trout repeated the information to the California coroner for verification. Everything was right, the coroner confirmed, except the height. The deceased's height was 6-foot-6, not 5-foot-6. Janet Doyle glanced at the wanted posters on the bulletin board and compared the descriptions of the tattoos. The marshals had not succeeded in locating Bobby Nauss but, after 11 years on the lam, Thomas Wellington was no longer a fugitive.

But Hurley Trout felt as if he had reached a dead end. He called the marshal's headquarters to ask for help. Chief Bob Leschoron personally responded to Trout's call.

Bob Leschoron, one of the country's top-notch detectives, teamed up with Deputy Trout to pull out all the stops in an effort to get their man. Leschoron suggested that they start at square-one, by drawing linkage charts and time lines. Once that was done, they interviewed everyone remotely involved with the case, no matter how many times each person had already been seen. They enlisted the cooperation of the local police forces in the area to stop all known Warlocks for routine checks and minor traffic violations at every opportunity. Then they started walking the streets and knocking on doors.

"I don't know where the m------f----- is," a Warlock chapter president told Leschoron and Trout, when the two federal lawmen surprised him in his living room one evening. "If I did, I'd give him to you to get the heat off. You're killing us."

"I spent twenty years on the streets of New York as an investigator," Bob Leschoron would say later, "and, honestly, there isn't much about investigation that I don't know. I helped Hurley out, every way I could, but we didn't solve the case, and Hurley Trout died working this case."

Hurley Trout died of cancer in August 1988 and, not surprisingly, no one else wanted the case. But Deputy-Marshal Steve Quinn nailed a pair of bank robbers who had netted more than $6,000,000 in a series of cross-country stick-ups and his reward was the Bobby Nauss assignment.

"Reluctantly," was the word Steve Quinn used to describe how he accepted his new assignment. His partner would be Janet Doyle.

"We thought Bobby Nauss was a myth," Doyle recalled. "We only knew him from other people. None of us now on the case had ever seen him. No one had heard anything about him, or from him, in years. We honestly thought he was dead."

But Doyle's boss, Tom Rapone, refused to buy that, even though the television show *America's Most Wanted* twice ran segments featuring Bobby Nauss and failed to produce a single reliable lead."

"We get information several times a week as the result of wanted posters that are on display nationwide," Rapone said. "It is not unusual to have as many as fifteen queries in a single day from police in other states. Some have indicated that Nauss is dead, but I don't buy that. If he was dead, I would have heard about it from a Warlock.

"We are maintaining an intensive investigation with a high level of activity. If Nauss died, the Warlocks would tell us, in an attempt to get the pressure off of them."

Before he died, Hurley Trout had retraced Bobby Nauss's footsteps from Graterford Prison to a Manayunk train station on the day of their escape. What Hurley Trout never learned was that Nauss boarded a commuter train for a short ride to center city. From Philadelphia, Nauss hopped a cab to a New York airport and caught the first flight out of the Big Apple.

What Deputy-Marshals Steve Quinn and Janet Doyle

didn't know was that on May 16, 1984, four years before they inherited this case, a clean-shaved, short-haired man married a Toledo, Ohio, government worker he had met at the Detroit airport the previous November, shortly after his flight from New York touched down. On his Lucas County marriage license, the groom listed his name as Richard Ferrer, said he was born in South Carolina, lived in Redford, Michigan, and worked as a carpenter.

The newlyweds paid $35,000 cash for a campground in Brimly, in northern Michigan, in September 1986, the same month that the fugitive task force collared Hans Vorhauer outside a South Philadelphia motel. Two years later, the couple bought a second home, this one in Luna Pier, Michigan, a small town on the banks of Lake Erie, about an hour south of Detroit. They paid $70,000 for the sprawling lake-front home at a sheriff's sale, $14,000 in cash, the rest mortgaged in the wife's name. A short while later, Ferrer paid $30,000 cash for a 27-foot Sportcraft cabin cruiser, which he docked at a local marina about a mile from the new home.

In Luna Pier, the neighbors called him Rick. They saw him as a loving husband, a devoted father, and a good provider, although no one ever saw him work for a living.

"He told everyone he owned rental homes," one of his neighbors later recalled.

Stories circulated around Luna Pier that Rick Ferrer was the kind of guy who would do anything for anybody.

"He was a good friend to a lot of people," the marina's co-owner would later say. "Just last week he took a bunch of retirees out fishing. It was totally unplanned. They were just sitting on the bench kibitzing."

"I would have given him the keys to the city," said the mayor of Luna Pier, who met Rick Ferrer at the marina.

"You really must be a model citizen because I've never met you," said Sergeant Darryl Ansel of the Luna Pier PD when a mutual friend introduced the police officer to Rick Ferrer late in 1990.

"He always chewed gum," said Frank Jumper, a boater

372

who rented a boat slip at the marina, "and he never wore a short-sleeved shirt. He wore a gray-and-black plaid shirt or a green-and-black plaid shirt. In the summer he wore long-sleeved shirts, lighter weight. I never seen the man's arms. I never seen him in shorts."

Jumper figured Ferrar was a Vietnam vet who had suffered war injuries and was collecting disability benefits.

"He always complained about his back," Jumper said. "He walked horrible sometimes, like his back was twisted out of shape."

Jumper's wife observed Ferrer helping her husband construct a deck, which they added onto their home in April 1990.

"He was so methodical," the woman recalled. "I asked him if his dad was a carpenter. He said no. I asked him if his father was alive. He said no. He said his father was killed in a car accident; he was an orphan.

"He wanted to know what I thought about the school system. I told him the only thing he could do better would be to put his boys in the parochial school. He was worried about the little boys going to school in the fall. He didn't want them to be exposed to drugs, involved with hoodlums, in with a bunch of misfits and eight-balls."


A dentist pulled two of Deputy-Marshal Janet Doyle's wisdom teeth on Mischief Night day in October 1990. She was home recuperating, full of pain-killers, when her telephone rang.

"I think we just made Nauss," Steve Quinn told her,.

"Right," she said, "tell me another one."

"Seriously," Quinn said. "We're about eighty percent sure. You better come in."

While Janet Doyle, in no condition to drive, called a friend to arrange a ride to Sixth and Market Streets in Philadelphia, a small army of marshals, troopers, and policemen was mobilizing around Luna Pier.

373

More than a year after the last airing of Bobby Nauss' exploits on *America's Most Wanted,* the anonymous-tip line rang. A woman's voice said a man using the name Rick Ferrer was, in reality, Bobby Nauss. The operator recorded the tip in triplicate. One copy was retained in the television show's files, a second copy went to the marshal's offices in Michigan, the third copy to Jay Frey's desk at the marshal's headquarters in Alexandria. Frey faxed a copy to Steve Quinn in Philadelphia, who took one look at the tip-sheet and said, "Yeah, right."

Shortly after 6:00 p.m., Rick Ferrer—wearing a plaid long-sleeved shirt, green work pants, tan shoes, and a baseball cap—packed his family into a Chevy Suburban and pulled out of the driveway. Ferrer drove to the marina, where the family got out and boarded the cabin cruiser. An hour later, they stepped back ashore and headed home. Less than an eighth-mile from home, blue emergency lights started flashing and a policeman waved the Suburban over onto the shoulder.

"The children thought they were being pulled over because they didn't have their seat belts on," recalled Officer Jerald Winkelman of the Luna Pier PD.

Rick Ferrer denied being Bobby Nauss to the officers, but a large parrot tattoo on his right biceps convinced the officers to take him to the station. An NCIC and triple-I search verified Nauss' identity and instantly terminated Rick Ferrer's bogus life, after seven years on the lam.

On November 2, 1990, Steve Quinn, Janet Doyle, and Trooper Joe Yazvac flew to Michigan to transport the most-wanted fugitive back to Philadelphia. A security force of four marshals and four state troopers awaited Nauss' return at the Philadelphia airport. Meanwhile, on the second floor of the federal building, someone walked up to the bulletin board and stamped "APPRE-HENDED" on Nauss' most-wanted poster.

Around seven o'clock that night, District Justice Carroll Rosenberger added escape and criminal conspiracy to the list of Bobby Nauss' offenses. The following year, in

October 1991, — nearly 20 years after Bobby Nauss murdered Liz Lande — Judge Samuel Salus II found Nauss guilty of felony escape, but not criminal conspiracy. Bobby Nauss was sent to the state correctional facility in Pittsburgh to continue serving the remainder of his life term.

"Sometimes it takes longer than others," said Tom Rapone, who, by then, was a Delaware County commissioner, "but it's a case that was solved. The bottom line is: It is a sad, sad affair. So many people have been hurt by this whole escapade. That is really a crime in itself."

EDITOR'S NOTE:
*Roscoe Edwards, Ace Wiggins, Richie DiPaolo, Tanya Weston, Thomas Wellington, and Frank Jumper are not the real names of the persons so named in the foregoing story. Fictitious names have been used because there is no reason for public interest in the identities of these persons.*

# "FOUR VICTIMS TORTURED FIRST, THEN MURDERED!"

by Peggy Poor

**MIAMI, FLA.,**
**APRIL 25, 1980**

At 4:55 a.m. on a January morning, I-95, South Florida's main artery, which shortly would become bumper-to-bumper congested, is almost deserted. That hour is late even for late carousers, and early, with a few exceptions, for the early work force. Among such exceptions, by long tradition, are the milkmen.

Therefore, not surprisingly, it was a truck driver for Velda Farms Dairy who made the horrifying discovery, Tuesday, January 8, 1980, at 4:55 a.m. Headed for Fort Myers with a load of dairy products, the milkman turned his delivery truck up onto the northbound ramp of I-95 at Miami Gardens Drive, which is also NW 186th Street.

The dark shape of a two-door sedan hulked about 50 feet off the pavement by a utility pole. It was ringed in flames.

The milkman swung off the pavement and jerked his brake on. Snatching his fire extinguisher, he leaped out of the truck and ran toward the burning car. As he approached the fire, he saw that it was concentrated in the surrounding grass and was just reaching to lick at the vehicle. Squirting his extinguisher, the milkman doused an area sufficient to safely reach the car's door handle. Even in the fading darkness and the smoke he thought he had seen a pile of blankets and clothing inside.

The door was unlocked. As the milkman yanked it open, he saw a foot protruding from beneath an orange and black quilt in the front. A blue-fringed rug of oriental design was humped in back over a shape suggesting another body.

The milkman backed away in disbelieving horror. His eyes frantically swept the ramp and the access street. Another Velda truck was just making its entry turn. The milkman flagged his fellow worker down and yelled for him to call police.

Sheriff's deputies and firemen were there in minutes. The fire itself was swiftly controlled. Apparently, it had barely started, and the dew-damp grass had checked rapid spreading. But Lt. Charles F. Watterson of the Dade County Fire Department called it arson. Flammable liquid had been poured on the ground in the area of the vehicle and ignited in an obvious attempt to destroy the car and its contents. The attempt failed because of the milkman's arrival. The car's side windows were scorched, but not enough heat had been generated to cause much damage inside. Some of the vinyl ceiling had melted as well as the right visor and the right-hand portion of the left visor. Several plastic containers of flammable liquids were found inside the car and in the trunk. The odor around the car indicated that gasoline had been poured under and into the trunk, but still, it had escaped the flames.

The contents of the automobile, a 1975 white over blue Chevrolet Monte Carlo, were not burned. Dr. Donna Brown from the Medical Examiner's office confirmed that death of the human cargo had not been caused by the fire. These conclusions were reached after an investigation and autopsy.

Officer Ben Anjina, the first deputy from Dade Public Service Department (PSD) to reach the scene, at once called Homicide, which turned out a large team: Det. Steve McElveen, who would be lead investigator, Det. Sgt. Steve

Jackson, Det. John LeClaire, Det. Carl Callenberger, Det. A.D. Moore, Det. Lloyd Hough, among them. Gerald J. Reichart supervised the crime scene technicians which included John Lurvey who processed for latents, Al Kaplan who took photos at the site, and Dolly Ballard who shot aerials.

The first investigators noticed the corner of a blanket sticking out from under the closed lid of the trunk. With the car keys which were still in the ignition, they opened it. Inside were two bodies, one on top of the other. One was wrapped in a royal blue crushed velvet bedspread, the other in a pink comforter. Both were drenched with blood. These two plus the body in the front seat and the one on the floor in back made it a quadruple murder.

Near the death car were some scraps of cardboard trash which bore tire imprints from a skidding vehicle, quite different from the tires on the Monte Carlo. Shattered glass from a pop bottle also appeared to have been in the path of what police speculated was the getaway vehicle. Detectives further surmised that the culprits had abandoned the death car, believing that setting a fire would destroy the evidence. The milkman had probably arrived shortly after they sped away. This conjecture was supported by the report of a patrolman who had stopped another vehicle on a traffic violation close by. The Monte Carlo had not been there at that time the officer was handing out the ticket.

The death car was registered to Scott T. Bennett at an address on SW 107th Avenue. McElveen asked Callenberger to check it. The owner of the house said that Scott Bennett did not reside there but did sometimes receive mail at that address. At the present time, the owner informed detectives, Bennett might be located by inquiring at the Sun-Moon Lake Apartments on N. Kendall Drive.

Dets. Callenberger and Moore tried there, but the apartment manager was not in. They left word for her to phone PSD headquarters, which she did about 2 p.m. This provided the first link in an intricate chain of evidence.

Scott Bennett was not himself a resident of the Sun-Moon

Lake Apartments, the manager said, but he did frequently stay with two young women who were tenants.

Callenberger and Moore called on the young ladies who said they were hometown friends of Bennett from Rhode Island where the two girls and the victim had grown up. Bennett's father, now a traveling machinery salesman, had been a police officer in Pawtucket.

Bennett was an all-state football halfback at Tolman High School. But, because of poor grades, he switched to Moses Brown prep school in Providence where he set New England records for the 50 and 300 yard dashes. He enrolled in Pennsylvania's Slippery Rock College where he remained on campus just long enough to win recognition as a football punt-return star in 1974. Right after the football season, he dropped out of school and went to Florida. In 1976 he was readmitted to Slippery Rock on the solemn promise to the coach that he would attend classes conscientiously and finish school.

That football season, Bennett set a punt return record that still stands: 102 yards. But when the season ended, he broke his promise and dropped out again. This ruined any chance for readmittance to the college.

For a couple of years Bennett worked for a restaurant in South Attleboro, Mass. Then, in 1978, headed to South Florida again. On a visit home at Christmas, he admitted that he was using cocaine and had become a dealer. Warning that his life had been threatened by "people who believed him to be an informer," Bennett requested that if anything happened to him, his body be cremated, because he "didn't like waste."

The two girls, who were students at the University of Miami, told detectives that because he feared for his life, Bennett carried a .38 at all times. They said he was an active drug dealer. When the girls agreed to a search of their apartment, detectives found sophisticated druggist scales and a leather purse containing small plastic bags with a white powder residue. The girls, who agreed to come down to headquarters to give formal statements, said that the bags, when all filled, would hold a kilo of cocaine.

Meanwhile, the technical people had spent an intensely busy four or five hours. They lifted 73 latents from the death car which they turned over to George Hertel in the ID section. They took blood samples from inside and outside the car, including smears on the left door, in the rear below the trunk, and the rear bumper, which they turned over to PSD serologist George Borghi. They collected eight plastic evidence bags of nail scrapings, animal and human hairs, and other small bits carefully retrieved with a vacuum. They also troweled up soil specimens and impounded a milk jug, a bleach container, a jerry jug similar to those for pool chlorine, several oil cans all containing flammables, and some aerosol products. They also tagged a light brown brush and white dog hair in it, a small four-bladed wood handle knife which was in the glove compartment, the tire-imprinted scraps of cardboard and the crushed soda bottle.

On the floor by the victim in back was a tan-striped pillow case. A beige one was stuffed into the trunk with the two gory corpses. Both contained bloody clothing and the beige one had an eight-inch knife with a broken tip, a broken, blood-stained pool cue, and a bloody glove. The knife might have been heated and used to burn one of the victims.

Everything at the scene was photographed as it was found and as it was removed.

Photographing continued at the morgue after the bodies were removed there; this time movies as well as stills were taken. The camera recorded the gruesome sequence as a medical team peeled off the blood-soaked wrappings. Besides the oriental rug, the crushed blue velvet spread, and the pink comforter, the gory packages were cocooned in an Oleg Cassini spread, an orange spread, a white flowered sheet, a white and blue spread, a black-gold-white sheet, a red sheet and sections of carpeting. The outer covering of one corpse was a brown "bean bag" chair which had been split open and emptied of most of its stuffing. Still, as the doctors slid the victim out from this wrapping, a shower of white and orange "beans" scattered across the morgue floor.

380

A technician scrambled to gather them up and bag them for evidence.

All four victims were white males. All had been bound, beaten, stabbed, strangled, and one had also been shot. Police cameras focused on the horror show as doctors cut away the bindings: twine, electrical cord, gray duct tape, a black and white tie, a brown tie, strips of a white sheet with tulips and a piece of macrame with a light switch.

According to Dr. Brown, the one who had been shot in the head had also received an equally fatal blunt trauma to the skull. Another one had also died from a blunt blow to the head. The cause of death in the other two was stab wounds to the chest.

Preliminary blood tests showed three of the victims had been using cocaine. This finding, together with Callenberger and Moore's information obtained from the two college girls and the find at their apartment, tended to confirm the detectives' first hunch: the quadruple murder was drug related. Immediately, the ID section began checking prints in the narcotics file with those taken from the four victims.

The first victim to be identified was Scott Bennett. Identification of the other victims was facilitated by a list of his associates. By late afternoon, two other victims were identified as Rodolfo L. Ayan, 41, of Hialeah, and Nicomedes Hernandez, Jr., 46, of Miami.

Det. Izagguire accompanied Det. Callenberger to the home of Hernandez' parents who spoke no English. The dead man's father, who was prominent and respected in the Cuban exile community, said his son had not resided with him for more than a year. The family was shocked and bewildered.

"We don't have the slightest idea who could have done this," one family member told reporters. "He didn't have any enemies. He made his living honestly" as an independent tow-truck driver. Divorced, the murder victim had one son.

Izagguire also went with Callenberger to Hialeah where

they talked with Rudy Ayan's brother, who also was unable to offer any helpful information.

About 10 p.m., however, another brother of Rudy's telephoned police headquarters to say that he did know something that might aid the investigation and he would come down at once. He identified the fourth victim and, in a three hour interview with Sgt. Jackson and Dets. McElveen and Izagguire, contributed sufficient pieces of the puzzle.

The fourth victim, whom the brother identified from morgue pictures, was John Merino, 29, of Fort Lauderdale. Police were soon to learn he was a colorful character indeed and the key in winding up the case. Colombian-born Merino was a "Cocaine Cowboy," a wheeler-dealer in the multi-billion dollar narcotic trade.

Recently, somewhat mysteriously, and, according to Ayan's brother, most unethically, Merino was also an undercover informant for the U.S. Drug Enforcement Administration (DEA) and other law enforcement agencies. Facing federal narcotics charges in Baltimore, Md. in the spring of 1979, Merino agreed to work for DEA. Baltimore agent Patrick O'Connor confirmed this fact to reporters.

In July, 1979, Merino was arrested on cocaine charges by Pompano Beach police who told reporters Merino was suspected as a principal of three defendants who were taken in custody during a hand-to-hand sale of 1.5 pounds of cocaine to an undercover narc. Several police agencies were reported to have contacted him while he was in jail. On December 5, he withdrew a plea of innocent and had been scheduled for sentencing on January 25.

"He hadn't made any cases for us," Pompano Beach vice and narcotics Sgt. Kenneth Staab told reporters.

In August, 1979, Merino was in a Dade County jail on a U.S. Marshal's order to hold him as a witness "to testify in a case." The Marshal's Office told reporters "there was no criminal charge" against Merino, but refused to elaborate.

According to court records, during that same month, Merino pleaded guilty to one count of a multiple-count indictment, but had not been sentenced in that case at the time of his murder.

After Merino was identified as one of the four corpses in the burning Monte Carlo, Dade Homicide Commander Frank Marshall, in reply to questions from the media, said his men were "looking into" the possibility that all the victims may have been informants for various police agencies.

"Some of these guys may have been information sources to certain law enforcement people. We're exploring the possibility of all of them being known by other law enforcement agencies," Marshall said.

George Brosan, Agent in Charge at the Baltimore DEA, told reporters that Rodolfo Ayan was also "known to our office. We have heard the name before." But Brosan refused to comment further on this or on any cases in which Merino may have been providing information.

DEA agents, however, did disclose to reporters that Merino's brother Billy, now believed to be at a family home in Barranquilla, Colombia, was a fugitive in a 1974 case. According to DEA, Billy Merino was aboard a Cessna 210 Centurion loaded with cocaine when, presumably, he discovered a bugging tracking device aboard. He escaped arrest by landing in the Bahamas. The load was subsequently seized in Miami and four other men were arrested.

Reportedly John Merino phoned Colombia from Florida at Christmas time and told his family everything was "fine, with no problems."

Rudy Ayan's brother told detectives that he had known Merino about two years but had introduced him to Rudy just the day before. Merino had been living in Fort Lauderdale since he got out of jail. He had telephoned Rudy's brother early Monday morning, January 7, to set up a meeting at a Miami Springs motel.

There Merino told Rudy's brother that he was working as an undercover informant for DEA and that it was "almost like having a license to deal drugs." He wanted to let Rudy's brother in on a narcotics transaction about to come off. He was in contact, he said, with some Fort Lauderdale people named Sally, Bo and Paul or Paulie, who were heavy dealers.

But Rudy's brother was upset by the DEA connection and refused to be lured by promises of "lots of money." The two men did not quarrel, however, and Merino and his seven-year-old son accompanied the brother to Rudy's home in Hialeah. The brother left there about an hour later, thinking that Merino and his son were also about to go home.

That afternoon, Monday, January 7, when the brother tried to contact Rudy again, he learned that Merino, Bennett, Hernandez, and Rudy had struck an agreement for a drug deal. He was so upset he telephoned Merino's wife at Bo's residence, in Fort Lauderdale. She claimed to know nothing. Rudy's brother threatened that if Rudy was not home by 5 p.m., he was going to call the police.

Before that deadline, however, a friend called to say that he had heard from Rudy, who was in Pompano Beach. Later, the brother reached Rudy by phone at home and asked him to bring him $300. After Rudy came by with the money, the brother went to sleep.

Some time later during the night another friend called, looking for Rudy, and said he had been by Rudy's house and found the lights on and the door unlocked, which was unusual.

About 10 a.m. the next morning, Tuesday, January 8, Rudy's son telephoned to say that Scott Bennett's car had been found set afire. He wanted to know where his father was. Rudy's brother had been frantically phoning everywhere ever since the call came from the friend who said he found Rudy's door unlocked. Police finally confirmed the brother's fears. He told police that Bennett had approximately $5,000 and Rudy about $16,000 on the day before the murder.

Detectives now had two good leads: the names Bo, Sally, and Paulie, and an address on NE 34 Avenue in Fort Lauderdale, a lavish $1,600 a month spread in a posh neighborhood.

Callenberger accompanied by Det. June Fernandez, headed for Fort Lauderdale shortly before midnight.

Callenberger was now on almost two duty shifts.

At the luxury home, the two investigators found only three women and a small boy. One of the women and the boy were Merino's wife and son, also Colombians. One of the other girls turned out to be Sally who said she was Bo's girl friend. Bo, she explained, was Alexander Solo, who, according to the girl, was a partner in a concern that rented trained animals to TV and the movies.

Callenberger further was told that Bo had invited Merino to live at his home when he got out of jail, and Merino, his wife, and son had moved in on December 24, moved out on January 1, but moved back January 4 or 5. Merino had left the house about 11 or 11:30 p.m. on January 7. The girls identified Rudy and Scott from photos as having been at Bo's after dark January 7, maybe between 7 and 9 p.m.

By now, the case was into its second day, January 9. A check on Alexander Solo revealed he was also known as Bernard John "Bo" Bolander or Bolender. And he had a PSD identification number. Even better, the technical section which had been tediously eliminating prints from the many latents lifted from the death car and one footprint found on the body of one of the victims, made a positive match of a latent taken from the car's trunk with a standard of Bo's on file.

Encouraging, but not yet enough for a court case. Records showed Bolander was on probation for federal and state narcotics violations. Federal Parole Officer Richard Miklic told Det. McElveen that one of Bolander's close associates was Joseph T. Macker, 42, a former bail bondsman with a police rap sheet dating back to 1957. Miklic said Bolander had given him Macker's address as a possible contact point.

McElveen decided to put the Macker residence on NE 6th Ave, Miami, under surveillance. It was a single family, one story, concrete block dwelling with red trim. Detectives watched it round the clock in teams.

On January 10, McElveen and Sgt. Jackson visited Bolander's fancy home in Fort Lauderdale, but got nowhere.

385

Bolander told them he had only known Merino since he got out of jail in December. A mutual friend had asked that he give the Colombian refuge. "How about putting him up until he gets on his feet?"

Bolander denied that he was even acquainted with the other three victims and said he had never seen a vehicle like the white over blue Monte Carlo.

On Friday, January 11, the investigators got a break. A family of three — husband, wife and grown son, showed up at headquarters. All three worked different time schedules, but when they put their experiences together, they decided police would be interested. For three years they had been neighbors of Macker.

Some kind of party at Macker's the night of January 7-8, with much coming and going of vehicles and people was nothing unusual there. Around 4 a.m., the elder man said, he heard a moaning sound, which he described repeatedly as "a man's dying moan." He insisted that during World War II he had been in a foxhole next to a man who died making exactly the same sounds. He said the sound was distinctive and unforgettable.

This eerie noise was accompanied and followed by other noises of great activity. He peered through his window but his view was restricted by an intervening tool shed so that he could only see a part of the sidewalk and street. But he heard "much commotion," voices, a car trunk slam, a car door close, vehicles driving away.

McElveen listened attentively. The burning Monte Carlo had been found less than a half mile from the Macker house.

The next day, January 8, the former bail bondsman's neighbors reported, they saw loads of carpets in a van parked next door. Shown photos of various items of evidence which had been collected, in particular the wrapping found around the bloody corpses, the elderly man's wife identified the oriental rug which had covered the victim on the death car's back seat. She told police she was positive it was one she had seen displayed at a Macker garage sale about a year before.

McElveen swore out an affidavit and Judge Wilkie Ferguson granted a search warrant for the Macker residence. Detectives found $9,877 hidden above a kitchen closet, but they turned up less than a pound of cocaine, although the victims were supposed to have had two kilos of the white powder and $18,000 to $25,000 when they went to the Macker residence.

Gerald Reichart, heading the technical team, was more productive. He found photos taken in the Macker house at an earlier date which showed the crushed blue velvet spread that had wrapped one victim and the burnt orange spread which had been a winding sheet for another. A blue print sheet still in the house was similar to one that had bound a tortured body. A black-brown-white sheet that had been twisted around one corpse's waist matched a mattress still on a bed in Macker's house. Some gold carpeting remaining was consistent with that found in the death car. The mat was found to be a white sheet with tulips which had been knotted around one of the Monte Carlo's gory passengers. There were white and orange "beans" dribbled all over the Macker home, just like the ones that had spilled out on the morgue floor.

Reichart also turned up tablets stamped "Rorer" in a jacket pocket, presumably counterfeit Quaaludes.

Macker was arrested on charges of murder one and armed robbery the night of January 12, and Bolander was taken into custody the following day.

Through repeated conversations and return of the seized money in time to meet a mortgage threatened with foreclosure, McElveen managed to convince Macker's wife she should persuade her husband to make a statement. On January 18, he did.

The former bondsman told detectives that on January 7 he had been awakened by a phone call about 5 or 6 p.m. He had gone to Paulie's, returning home about 10 or 10:30 to find Bo, his wife, and Paulie at the house besides his own handyman. None of them had been expected, and Bo kept

387

muttering, "The man should be here."

Shortly after, a man he later recognized from news pictures as Rudy arrived carrying a "little shoe box."

Macker asked Bo, "What's this all about?"

"Don't worry," Bo replied. "It'll be good."

"In the back bedroom, Rudy, Merino, Bo and I were talking," Macker said. "I wasn't paying much attention until Bo said, 'Mr. Macker has the money.' I believed then they were talking about a cocaine deal. I heard Bo asking, 'Where is it?' They were all looking at each other. I left the room and Paulie left the room and went outside, and caught someone in the bushes."

From later news photos, Macker said he now realized the man skulking in the bushes was Bennett. Macker told detectives, "I asked, 'What's going on?' Paulie said, 'He's with them,' and walked Bennett in the house. I followed.

"In the bedroom, Bo had a gun on Merino. Bo said, 'It looks like they came to rip us.' I asked, 'Rip us from what?'

"And when we walked Bennett in, he said, 'I got the package.' He opened the little shoe box and showed a brown bag.

"Then Bo put them on the floor, all three with their clothes off . . . Now my words were, 'If these three are here, how many more are out there?' So Paulie and I went out. There was another man in a Chevrolet parked right across the street, driving back and forth in the Monte Carlo which to me it looked bluish, dark bluish or maroonish or bluish. At this junction, you know, it doesn't take an expert to figure out what's going on. I got very scared, because, you know, all these guns.

"Bo was yelling, 'Why you bring all these people over here? There's supposed to be one person coming over!' I saw him kick Rudy in the head. Rudy was trying to say something. Bo yelled, 'Shut up!'

'Bo,' I asked. 'What are we doing here? I got my wife in the other room!'

"So many people were coming in and out. I got a rag to wipe the guy's head. Bo pushed me out of the way. 'Leave him alone! This is what they would do to you. We got a deal going here and they disrespect you with your wife.'

"When Bo came in the house, he had two guns. He showed us. I was flipped. I mean I couldn't believe that this was happening in my house, you know what I mean?

"The guy in the auto had not come in. So with a gun on him, Bo gets John Merino up and dressed to go lure him in. Bo is kicking these people like a football game, you know what I mean? I had taken out a gun of my own and put it in my pocket."

The man in the automobile "a big fat guy"—was "lured" into the house. "Paulie took a knife out of the kitchen . . . He brought me another gun and some money, rolled up. It looked like hundreds. I laid it on the table . . . Paulie was saying, 'You know what we have to do.' I was flipped. Paulie said, 'Well, come on. We'll get it straightened out.'

"What flipped me was that we had to murder them or they were going to come back and murder me and my wife. Why? Because of what Bo done to them already, put them on the floor and started kicking them and things of that nature.

"In the bedroom, Bo was screaming up and down like a madman . . . He asked for tape and I gave him gray masking, air-conditioning tape. He taped them up while me and Paulie held the gun on them: mouth, hands, legs . . .

"This ain't something occurs every day. Bo says, 'Go get a bat.' My wife keeps a little bat in her car in case anybody bothers her . . .

"Bo told me to get sheets and blankets. I opened the closet door. He told me to hold the gun on them and he got the sheets and some type of oriental rug and wrapped them up . . .

"He told me to get him a knife. I'm very naive at certain things. I went and got a kitchen knife."

Macker told police he was sent from the bedroom at this point. "I heard like screams and yells," he said.

Macker related how he urged his other guests out of the house, explaining the noises as "nothing. Someone tried to come and kick my wife in the stomach." The guests left.

Back in the bedroom, "Bo gave Paulie the bat and told him to keep them quiet. Paulie hit them in the head. Bo handed me a pool stick. 'Keep Merino quiet,' he said. I hit him in the head.

"Bo kept saying, 'Where's the money, the cocaine?' He cut and stabbed them. I seen him shoot somebody in the leg. There was a big gush of blood. I never saw anything like it in my life. All over the rug.

"It had to go on for at least two hours. Bo kept asking each one, 'You got money at home?' . . . The noises never stopped . . .

"They used a bean bag (to wrap one victim in). Emptied all the stuff in the tub. Like from dolls, or stuffed animals, white, round. Bo stabbed them through the carpet."

When the Monte Carlo was backed into Macker's driveway, ready for loading, "they were still kicking. We put two in the trunk and two in the car. Their personal stuff was put in a bag with the bat and everything else, wallets, etc. I believe the bag was put in the car with the bodies . . .

"They cut up my hose and syphoned gas into a yellow plastic can. They got some perfume bottles belonging to a girl staying at the house. There was blood all over the place. They were dragging them, and wherever they dragged there was blood. They took two cars . . . Returned in eight or ten minutes, tops.

" 'What the hell did you do?' " I asked.

"Well, it's done. We murdered everybody.' Bo said.

"Paulie pulled all the rugs up. Bo laid on the bed like nothing happened . . . They had broke the tip of the knife off. They put that and the guns in my Cadillac . . . and we took (one victim's) Thunderbird to 187th Street and left it in a parking lot with the engine on. They said that knocks off prints . . .

" 'Are they still alive?' " I asked. Bo said, 'I don't know. I stabbed them. I shot one.' "

Macker showed detectives where the guns had been jettisoned into a small lake about 100 yards west of the crime scene. Sgt. Duckworth, head of PSD Underwater Recovery Unit, retrieved the bag of weapons.

On Monday, April 14, 1980, Joseph Macker pleaded guilty to second degree murder acceptable to Circuit Court Judge Richard Fuller on condition that a polygraph test be given to prove the testimony he gave was the truth. He received 12 concurrent life sentences.

On Friday, April 25, 1980, Bernard Bolander received four consecutive death sentences. Judge Fuller's decision was aimed at preventing a high court reversal of one sentence from nullifying the others. Eight concurrent life sentences were added for kidnapping and armed robbery of the four victims.

"It was one of the most brutal . . . most heinous torture slayings in Dade County history," remarked Asst. State Attorney Abe Laeser. "And it was the handiwork of only one man, Bernard Bolander, the ring-leader, who personally committed each of the drug-related murders."

Newspapers reported that Bolander offered to pay for cremation of one of his victims. Calling the widow the day after the murder, he asked, "How do you want him, regular or crispy?"

Paulie—Paul Thompson—prior to the quadruple murders had been judged insane by a federal court and declared incompetent to stand trial. Therefore, he must be considered innocent until a jury can decide otherwise. He has been committed to a mental institution.

EDITOR'S NOTE:
*The name Sally is fictitious and was used because there is no public interest in her true identity.*

# "DEATH WAS THE FINAL MERCY FOR LITTLE AMY!"

by Bruce Gibney

The call was a request for information about an abandoned car in Glacier National Park, Montana. But Illinois Detective Mike Anthis knew it was more than that. He knew he had solved a murder.

"I got a hunch," he admitted. "I don't know how to explain it. I just knew."

It was no ordinary murder.

It was perhaps the most shocking crime in Jefferson County history—nothing less than the kidnapping, rape and throat-slitting murder of a 10-year-old girl.

It was a brutal, wanton crime that sent this southern Illinois farming community reeling and put pressure on law enforcement agencies to solve it.

For a long time, however, that seemed a remote possibility.

Amy Rachelle Schulz was a fifth grader at Kell Consolidated Grade School. A member of the cheerleading squad and a straight-A student, the pretty youngster with the cheerful smile and easygoing disposition was one of the most likable kids at school.

Amy lived with her family in Kell, a hamlet so small that it isn't found on most maps.

On Wednesday, July 1, 1987, a relative of Amy's left the

house in search of the family dog, which had sneaked out through the fence gate and was busy exploring the neighborhood.

When the relative did not return within the hour, Amy volunteered to go find him. "He's probably down at the square skateboarding," Amy told her family.

That was a possibility; kids often gathered at the town square in the humid evenings to skateboard or simply hang out.

Amy's family told her okay, but instructed her not to dawdle. Twilight was over and darkness was falling; besides, they were getting ready for the Fourth of July.

"I won't be late," she promised.

With that, Amy bounded out the door.

The first to return to the Schulz home was the wayward dog, who slunk in through the open gate, tail wagging.

Next to appear was Amy's relative.

Amy, however, never made it home.

Fearing the worst, another Schulz relative contacted the sheriff's office. He told the deputy who arrived at the front door that Amy was a responsible youngster and was not in the habit of disobeying her family. After contacting friends she might have visited and conducting his own investigation, Amy's relative decided to call in the police.

The deputy searched around the house and drove along the road the pretty 10-year-old would have taken into town. He didn't find the girl, or evidence she had been there.

A search was begun for the missing youngster. Seventy-five lawmen and volunteers, under the direction of the Kell Fire Department, took part in the operation, one of the largest ever conducted in this small community.

The search was called off at 2:30 Thursday morning, then resumed at the crack of dawn. After the initial sweep failed to turn up the girl, searchers brought in bloodhounds to aid them in their work.

The bloodhounds followed a scent from the Schulz home and along the road leading into town to a point where they stopped and started barking and turning in circles.

393

Fearing the little girl had been kidnapped and taken from the area, searchers debated about using an infrared-equipped airplane. It had been put at their disposal by the state police and was capable of spotting a body from several hundred feet in the air.

The plane proved unnecessary.

At nine o'clock that morning, 12 hours after Amy Schulz was reported missing, an oil rigger in neighboring Jefferson County pulled off the road and made a grisly discovery — the dead body of a little girl.

Jefferson County deputies sped to the scene, followed by Captain Mike Anthis and a team of detectives.

The victim lay in the thick grass that grew alongside the edge of the road. She was about 10 years old, had light brown hair and was completely nude. Her throat was cut and blood had drained down the sides of her neck, forming a huge pool in the dirt.

Although Amy Schulz had disappeared from neighboring Marion County, Captain Anthis was aware of the search going on and was certain he had found the missing fifth grader.

He notified Marion County officials and a family friend, accompanied by a minister, arrived at the crime scene. They looked at the body and without hesitation identified her as Amy Schulz.

With this done, the body was photographed and measured, then taken to the coroner's office. Captain Anthis, meanwhile, ordered his men to conduct a canvass of the crime scene and both sides of the road.

Roadblocks were put up to turn back reporters and spectators who are routinely drawn to grisly, high-profile crimes.

Lawmen worked through the hot afternoon and into the early evening. Investigators not involved in the crime scene search questioned the victim's relatives and rounded up witnesses.

Police released few details about the crime. On Thursday evening, Jefferson County State's Attorney Kathleen Alling and Sheriff Bob Pitchford distributed a news release saying that the Illinois State Police, the Jefferson County State's

Attorney Office and the Marion and Jefferson County Sheriff's Offices were conducting a joint investigation.

The release declined to describe where the body was found and how the girl was killed.

"If all the details of the death are disclosed before potential witnesses are interviewed, it is difficult to determine if their evidence was gained independently," State's Attorney Alling said in the prepared statement. She added that police had no suspects.

More was known about the gruesome murder after the autopsy was conducted on Thursday evening. According to the preliminary report, Amy Schulz had been killed between 9:30 and 10:30 Wednesday evening—perhaps just minutes after she left the safety of her home to search for her relative. She had been stabbed five times in the throat, severing the carotid artery and jugular vein and making it almost impossible for her to scream. The girl's liver had also been ruptured, and there were signs of a sexual assault.

Reading the single-spaced coroner's report, Captain Anthis felt his stomach grind and lurch. He reasoned that the victim had been abducted shortly after she left the house, then strangled, raped and finally stabbed.

Judging from the amount of blood, the stabbing probably took place where the body was found. Very likely the girl, once kidnapped, never had a chance.

The murder of Amy Schulz was the third in Jefferson County that year. In April, the night manager of a grocery store was shot to death by a sniper as he drove along Interstate 64. The next month, a truck driver was slain and his rig stolen.

Investigators had arrested two suspects in the killing of the night manager. The other case was still unsolved.

Neither incident, however, had created the outrage that the Amy Schulz murder did.

On July 5th, an overflow crowd attended a memorial service for the slain girl at Donoho Prairie Christian Church. Later, a reward fund was established in Amy's name for information leading to the arrest and conviction of her killer.

At first there was no shortage of leads. Investigators checked out "suspicious-activity" reports, questioned paroled felons and administered polygraph exams to convicted sex offenders.

As the long, hot summer wore down, sleuths also investigated reports of other attempted abductions. In neighboring Franklin County, a teenager told police that a heavyset man with a beard tried to pull her into his car as she was walking home. A 16-year-old girl from Kell also reported that a man stopped to ask her for directions, then ordered her to get into his car. She ran and the motorist fled.

Investigators also received a number of reports about men exposing themselves and propositioning women.

Jefferson County Sheriff Bob Pitchford kept close tabs on the county's hottest murder case. He read the case file and conducted regular meetings with the investigation team.

Unfortunately, good news was hard to find. Although investigators had collected 3,500 clues and questioned 200 witnesses, they had been unable to come up with a suspect.

The last person to see Amy Schulz alive was a 16-year-old high school student who spotted Amy as she was walking through Kell at 9:10 on Wednesday evening. The witness said Amy was alone at the time and was apparently headed toward home.

Within 90 minutes, according to the autopsy report, the girl was dead, her body tossed by the roadside.

"We've canvassed just about everyone in town," Captain Anthis told Sheriff Pitchford. "But no one saw her after that."

Anthis said investigators had worked on the assumption that Amy was kidnapped after accepting a ride home. If so, that meant she possibly knew her killer, since Amy had been instructed not to talk to or accept rides from strangers.

But as the investigation progressed, lawmen admitted the possibility that Amy had been forced into the car and that the killer could have been anyone, including a complete stranger.

To learn more about the victim's killer, Anthis asked the FBI for psychiatric profiles of killers whose methods of operation matched the Schulz rape-slaying. He also sent hairs and other physical evidence discovered on the body to the Illinois Division of Criminal Investigation in Carbondale, which operates one of the top forensic labs in the country.

Anthis reported that the lab had typed and classified the hairs. They could be used for identification purposes — if police found a suspect.

What they desperately needed was a suspect. Then, 15 months later, they had one.

On October 11, 1988, a federal agent in Glacier National Park, Montana, contacted Illinois' Jefferson County Sheriff's Office for information about a man arrested for the shooting of a federal employee. Captain Anthis took the call.

A ranger at the national park had been driving through a camp area when he came under fire. He was wounded in the shoulder, but managed to elude the shooter and summon help.

According to the investigator, armed federal agents sealed off the campsite and began a search for the sniper. During the search, they discovered a 1977 Plymouth with Illinois plates parked illegally off the road. A note stuck on the inside of the windshield read, "Mom, car busted. You can have it."

The car was registered to a Cecil S. Sutherland, 33, of Dix, Illinois.

Sutherland was arrested the next day and booked into jail, charged with attempted murder.

"We ran a federal crime check, but he's clean," the investigator told Captain Anthis. "We thought you guys might have something on him."

"I'll check it out and get back to you," Anthis said. Before hanging up, he asked what color car Sutherland was driving.

"Mud brown," the investigator responded. "Why?"

"Curiosity," Anthis responded.

But it was more than that. In the canvass following Amy Schulz's murder, several witnesses had told detectives that they saw a dark brown, late model American car cruising downtown Kell in the early evening of July 1st.

No one recognized the car, and police initially believed it might belong to a mourner attending a funeral that was being conducted that Fourth of July weekend. But none of the mourners drove such a vehicle, and investigators had been unable to locate the owner.

In an attempt to locate the driver, Captain Anthis dispatched detectives to scour backroads in three neighboring counties and jot down the license numbers of cars matching the description of the wanted vehicle. Registered owners of the cars were then checked to see if any had criminal records and were recorded in a log.

Going to the log, Captain Anthis ran down the list — and stopped when he came to Sutherland.

A detective cruising Marion County had spotted Sutherland's car and duly recorded the license number. Sutherland had never been questioned because he did not have a prior criminal record.

But his car did match the mud-brown, late model car seen cruising around Kell at about the time Amy Schulz was looking for her relative. And Sutherland had been in town, because the officer had spotted his car and jotted down the license number.

And there was another link — although the Schulzes and Sutherland lived in different counties, their properties each backed up to the county line, making them neighbors. In fact, Sutherland's home was only a few hundred yards from Amy Schulz's.

Captain Anthis informed Sheriff Pitchford of these developments. Although the evidence was at best circumstantial, Anthis had a hunch that Amy's killer was the Glacier National Park sniper.

Sheriff Pitchford, who knew something about police hunches, agreed and encouraged his ace detective to vigorously pursue the lead.

Anthis got on the phone to the federal agent in Montana and informed him that Sutherland was a prime suspect in the child's rape-murder. He requested that Sutherland's car be sealed until they arrived in Montana.

The response: "You bet."

With expense money provided by the Illinois State Police, Captain Anthis and State Investigator Charles Parker flew to Billings, Montana. Their first stop was the federal impound lot where Sutherland's Plymouth had been towed. Much to their relief, they saw that the dusty car had been sealed and fitted with signs warning that it should not be touched.

Anthis and Parker went to the jail to question Cecil Sutherland. They waited in an interrogation room, and a few minutes later Sutherland was brought in.

Six feet seven inches tall and 270 pounds in weight, the bearded inmate glared at his two visitors and demanded, "What do you want?"

Coolly, Anthis informed him that they were detectives from Jefferson County and were investigating the murder of a 10-year-old girl who had been slain the previous summer.

"I didn't do it," Sutherland broke in. "I know exactly where I was July first."

Captain Anthis shot a surprised look at his partner. He had not said what case they were investigating, yet Sutherland knew the date.

Sutherland said he had spent the morning of July 1st at home and the afternoon with friends. That evening he went for a drive, and his car broke down at a gas station in Mount Vernon, Illinois.

He said he called a family member, who drove him home. On the way back, he said, they were stopped at a police roadblock, then continued home.

When asked if he knew Amy Schulz, Sutherland said he was finished answering questions and wanted to return to his cell.

The investigators left the jail and returned to the impound yard. The brown Plymouth was loaded into a truck trailer

399

and driven to the Jefferson County Fire Department station. There, criminalists broke the seals and searched the vehicle for evidence that might link Sutherland to the Schulz murder.

A few days later, the preliminary report was made available — and it was promising. In it, criminalists reported that they had found fibers and hairs in the car similar to those discovered on the victim's clothing and body.

Captain Anthis notified the Schulz family and told them a suspect was in custody. He cautioned, however, that the investigation was ongoing and that it might be weeks or months before charges were filed, if ever.

Cecil Sutherland stayed jailed in Montana on federal attempted-murder charges. At a preliminary hearing, the chained and handcuffed defendant angrily entered a plea of not guilty. A trial date was set for spring 1988.

With Sutherland in jail and the lab examining the physical evidence, the Schulz case was put on hold. But the Jefferson County detectives were not out of cases to solve.

Earlier, in November 1987, investigators were called to a home outside the small community of Ina. There they found the body of 30-year-old Ruby Elaine Dardeen, beaten to death inside her mobile home. Also murdered was her three-year-old son, Peter Sean.

During the vicious assault, the seven months pregnant housewife had given birth to a baby girl. The baby, born alive, was also bludgeoned to death.

Stunned, police began a search for Ruby's husband, Russell. Their search ended after hunters found his body in a field near Rend Lake College. He had died of head injuries after being dragged over some distance behind a car.

The horrifying murders struck fear into the community. A family physician told a reporter that his patients were intensely preoccupied with the murders. He said one patient was so worried that he had lost 14 pounds and developed insomnia.

Theories about the murders abounded: the Dardeens had been slain by devil worshippers; the killer was someone they

400

knew.

Police explored these angles and others. A suspect was brought in for questioning and released. Investigators looked for tie-ins to other murders, including the slaying of a junior college student.

"We got a lot of leads, but frankly we could use a lot more," Sheriff Pitchford said a month after the slayings.

By January 1988, the case was still unsolved.

Cecil Sutherland was scheduled to go on trial for the Glacier case in federal court in May, but in April 1988, he pleaded guilty to one count of assault on a federal officer with intent to kill. In exchange, eight additional assault charges were dropped. On June 10, 1988, he was sentenced to 10 years in federal prison.

Sutherland began serving his sentence at the federal penitentiary in Marion, Illinois.

That same month, a Jefferson County grand jury heard evidence in the Schulz murder case. On Friday, June 24th, jurors indicted Cecil Sutherland on charges that he abducted, raped and murdered Amy Schulz.

The indictment was made public on June 28th, nearly a year after the pretty 10-year-old went looking for her relative and never came back.

At a press conference, State's Attorney Kathleen M. Alling said that charges could have been filed months earlier, but that authorities intended to move slowly. "He has been in federal custody, so there was no chance he could run away or hurt anyone else," she said, adding that she would seek the death penalty on the murder charge.

The trial began early in May 1989 at the Richland County Courthouse in Olney, where the trial was moved after the defense argued successfully for a change of venue.

In testimony before the jury, the defense argued that Cecil Sutherland could not have committed the crime because he was far away from Kell when the abduction occurred.

In the conversation with Captain Anthis, Sutherland had said his car broke down on the way to Mount Vernon, Illinois, and he had called his family from a gas station.

A long-distance telephone bill indicated that a call had been placed from the gas station pay phone to Sutherland's home at 10:57 on the night of the murder.

But Sutherland was tripped up by a coroner who testified that the little girl was murdered earlier than that.

Dr. Steven Nuerenberger of Collinsville, who had performed more than 1,500 autopsies, said an examination of food in the dead girl's stomach indicated that she was killed between 9:30 and 10:30 p.m. — giving Sutherland plenty of time to abduct and murder her, then head for Mount Vernon.

In graphic and often shocking testimony, Nuerenberger said the autopsy also revealed that the child had been strangled to the point of unconsciousness or even death, with hemorrhaging to the larynx; had been beaten by a blunt instrument on the top and both sides of the head; had her liver torn away; and had bled so much that there was hardly enough blood left to take samples. The coroner also noted that the girl's genitals had been bruised and she had been sexually assaulted.

Illinois State Police crime lab technician David Brundage then testified that a "footprint" or inked impression of the right front tire on Sutherland's 1977 Plymouth and the tread pattern was the same as the impression taken at the crime scene where Amy Schulz's body was discovered.

Illinois forensic scientist Ken Knight then testified to finding 33 dog hairs from various articles of the girl's clothing and one from a sheet on which the crime scene technician placed the body before it was put into a body bag. Those hairs were consistent with dog hair samples taken from the defendant's black Labrador retriever, but were not consistent with samples from the four dogs owned by the Schulz family. Knight said he also found an upholstery fiber in the victim's shorts that appeared to be the same shape, color and nylon material as that of the defendant's car seat upholstery.

Knight had also concluded that 19 clothing fibers from the victim's car were similar, if not identical, to the fibers in

402

the girl's clothing.

He also testified that an examination of pubic hairs found near the child's rectum were consistent with samples taken from the defendant.

As witnesses took the stand, Cecil Sutherland squirmed and glared. Impressive in size, Sutherland, according to one lawman, was "the type of man you wouldn't want to cross. When he entered a doorway, he filled it."

But size and brute force were no match for the scientists and their microscopes.

After five days of testimony, two dozen witnesses and presentation of more than 130 exhibits, Cecil Sutherland was found guilty on all counts. On June 14, 1989, jurors voted that he be sentenced to death for his crimes.

Sutherland was quickly led from the courtroom. By law, the verdict will be appealed, a process that could easily take 10 years or more. In the meantime, Sutherland remains behind bars on Death Row.

As millions are spent on his appeal, observers say, Jefferson County lawmen work within a tightening budget to solve more cases. At the top of the list are the Dardeen murders. Although the case remains unsolved as of this writing, police say they are making progress.

# "WACKO WANTED TO WATCH THE BEAUTY BLEED!"

## by Tom Basinski

The typical murder mystery starts out with a dead body, sometimes identified and sometimes not. In the really good thrillers, there are either no suspects or too many suspects. English drawing-room mysteries have the entire guest list of a cocktail party as suspects until, one by one, each is eliminated and only the killer is left. The murder is usually committed off camera, often with poison or a single gunshot wound and no bleeding.

Such is not life, however, The men and women who work homicide investigations seldom have a "drawing-room" case, neat and clean with several suspects to eliminate before determining that "the butler did it." Real detectives have to confront lots of blood, grieving families, pushy newspaper reporters, and the roadblocks of the legal system.

At 4:30 p.m. on February 17, 1988, a warm and sunny Tuesday, Ron Peters, a construction foreman in San Marcos, California, received a call on his pager from a distraught relative.

The caller informed Peters that his two small stepchildren had not yet been picked up from school. Peters' wife, Anne Jenkins, always picked the children up, and the relative was worried.

Arrangements were made to have another relative pick up the children, and Peters drove home to the 1400 block of Leslie Court in San Marcos to see if anything was wrong.

When Peters arrived, he saw the family car in the driveway, partially washed. Dried soap residue covered half of the vehicle. A bucket was in the driveway. Water was coming from a hose attached to the faucet at the side of the house.

The front door was locked, and the garage door was closed. Ron Peters entered the house. In the back hallway, where the bedrooms and bathroom were, lay the body of Anne Jenkins.

There was a large pool of blood on the carpet and blood spots on the wall. A gaping wound in Anne's throat was the cause of all the blood.

Peters ran to a phone and dialed 911, summoning emergency medical help and law enforcement.

This wasn't the typical mystery, as far as Ron Peters was concerned. He informed the sheriff's dispatcher who he thought had killed Anne Jenkins.

The dispatcher attempted to calm Peters down until the patrol deputy arrived. Suddenly Peters said, "Oh my God, the baby."

Peters returned moments later carrying a crying child. It was Anne's 10-month-old child, hoarse from crying and wearing soiled diapers.

Within a minute, Patrol Deputy William Burmeister arrived. Burmeister hung up the phone and escorted Peters and the baby outside, allowing Peters to pick up a clean diaper on the way out.

Within seconds, medical help arrived. Burmeister met them at the curb. He informed a fireman/paramedic that a homicide had taken place and an obviously dead woman was inside.

Burmeister told the crew he would take one of them inside to confirm the death, but no one else would be allowed to enter.

The paramedic was a veteran, and he accepted this restriction. Many are the homicide scenes where the firemen and paramedics tromp through, carrying their lifesaving gear. The result is always the same: Not only is the victim unable to be saved, but to make matters worse, the scene is unnecessarily contaminated with footprints, body hairs, bandage wrappings, and sometimes even fingerprints, which only confuse the proceedings and sometimes even aid the guilty party.

Deputy Burmeister had dispatch contact the homicide division. Detectives Dave Decker and Bob Sams rolled out to the freeway from headquarters. This was rush hour and it took the veteran investigators over 40 minutes to get to San Marcos, a small city north of San Diego that contracts with the sheriff for police services.

Decker and Sams were not in a hurry to barge into the house and start to work. They knew others were on the way and that a game plan would be formulated.

While Deputy Burmeister spoke with Ron Peters, Detectives Sams and Decker made sure that yellow crime scene tape had been extended around the property.

Soon the other homicide specialists arrived. Sergeant Chuck Curtis headed up the crew along with Terry Wisniewski and Mark Parmely, the detectives who would eventually live with this case over the next two years. Crime Lab Deputy Sam Bove arrived. Nothing would happen without him. Deputy Coroner George Dickason was notified, but he was also told that it would be several hours before the body could be released. Lieutenant Bill Baxter, the head of homicide, was there to field questions from the media, which had already set up a small camp in the quiet neighborhood.

Before entering the house, the investigators talked to Deputy Burmeister, who briefed them on what Ron Peters had told him.

The front door had been locked. This was not normal for Anne Jenkins, sleuths were told. When Anne was in the front yard, she would leave the door unlocked so she could go inside if she heard the baby cry.

The garage door was closed. This too did not appear right since Anne would need to go inside the garage to get additional items for washing her car, including wheel cleaner and a chamois for drying.

The deputies were told that on January 13, 1988, four

weeks before, Anne Jenkins and Ron Peters had won $727,000 in the California Lottery. Detectives Mark Parmely and Terry Wisniewski exchanged silent glances at that bit of news.

The detectives wanted to talk with Peters in depth. However, the 10-month-old baby had to be dealt with. So the sleuths collected Peters' clothing to be checked later for blood spattering. Then they accompanied Peters into the house so he could point out anything unusual. Nothing had been taken or disturbed, he told them. On the mantle were plane tickets and reservations for accommodations at Disney World in Florida, the one extravagance the family had allowed itself since winning the lottery.

When Peters saw the tickets, he burst into tears. He told the investigators that Anne had wanted to visit Disney World for years. Now she never could.

Peters left after signing consent forms for the detectives to search and photograph the house, and the officers went to work.

The house was a typical single-family dwelling. It was neat and clean. Breakfast dishes had been done. A pound of ground beef, long since thawed, had been placed near the sink that morning.

In fact, the only thing that distinguished that particular house from any other in the 1400 block of Leslie Court was the presence of a body with a slashed throat in the hallway.

Anne Jenkins had been a homecoming queen in high school. She was beautiful and charming. Now she lay on her back in the hallway wearing a white T-shirt, gray sweatpants, and white high-top aerobic workout shoes. The victim's throat had been slashed down to the bone on the right side.

The entire house was photographed and dusted for fingerprints. While this was being done, Dave Decker and Bob Sams fanned out into the neighborhood, interviewing every neighbor they could find and leaving business cards on the doors of those people who were not home.

Anne's body was removed and the crime scene was secured at about 11:00 p.m. Terry Wisniewski and Mark Parmely contacted Ron Peters, who had found the body. The sleuths wanted him to explain why he thought Anne's ex-husband, David Harrison, was responsible for her death.

Peters alternately cried and was angry. Anne Jenkins and David Harrison had been high school sweethearts, Peters related. They married in 1976. Their first child was a girl. Shortly after the birth of their son in 1980, David Harrison divorced Anne.

Peters said Harrison preferred men to women. Once a male child was born, Harrison was gone. Harrison had a series of male lovers. Although slight of build, Harrison was no wimp. In fact, he was a black belt in karate.

Detective Wisniewski seemed confused. "If they were already divorced, why did he want Anne dead?"

Peters explained that Harrison wanted custody of the children, especially the boy. During the past year and a half, Anne Jenkins had been in court at least once a month to fight different kinds of motions and hearings that had been initiated by Harrison, most of them frivolous and all of them expensive.

Harrison was portrayed to the investigators as a master of harassment. He would have Anne served with legal papers for a court date; she would be forced to take time off from work to appear and then Harrison would not show up.

Harrison seldom won in court, but did not seem to mind. Each court appearance cost Anne several hundred dollars in legal fees, money she did not have.

Peters despondently sat there, talking to sleuths with his head in his hands, saying that Anne had quit her job only one week before.

Peters told probers that Harrison tried to get Anne to give up custody of the children and assured her he would not be a problem to them if she agreed. Anne refused.

Peters said Harrison was undoubtedly upset because the lottery winnings now gave Anne the resources to fight her ex-husband.

Detective Parmely asked Peters where Harrison got his

408

money for the legal battles. Peters seemed to get angry. "He had lots of money. He hid it in different bank accounts in another relative's name. That guy had real estate holdings in his relative's name. He wasn't rich, but he was very comfortable.

"His plan was to wear us out and dry up our money. That little creep could never wear us out, and after the lottery, our money was equal to his."

Bob Sams and Dave Decker interviewed David Harrison at his apartment. They were not accusatory, nor did they mention that he had been accused of being the killer by Ron Peters.

Harrison admitted that the relationship between him and Anne had been stormy and that he did not like Anne. Harrison inquired where the children were. He was told they were safe and with Ron Peters.

Harrison said he had not seen Anne since the last court appearance. His reaction was basically a non-reaction.

Harrison told the detectives he had been at his apartment all day on the day of the murder. In the morning he had driven his Cadillac to a relative's house to leave her the car for the day.

The relative had dropped Harrison off back at his place where he stayed all day, making several phone calls. Harrison said the Cadillac was the only vehicle he owned.

The detectives took notes, then left. All the detectives met back at the homicide office to compare notes. Criminalist Sam Bove found nothing unusual at the scene. He had obtained rolled fingerprint cards from Anne's relatives and other family members who had visited the house.

There were fiber and hair samples to compare. They also needed to get samples from David Harrison.

The officers who canvassed the neighborhood came up empty. There were rumors that some illegal Mexican aliens had been in the area knocking on doors looking for food or work. Northern San Diego County is rural in many places. Thousands of illegals live in homemade tents and communal campsites. It was not uncommon for them to be seen in neighborhoods.

One neighbor insisted the killing had to be the work of illegals bent on robbery. Her theory made no sense since Anne Jenkins was still wearing a gold chain and rings when she was found dead. No money was taken from the house, nor had the house been ransacked. Aliens who commit residential crimes often steal food as well as valuables, sometimes even leaving partially eaten food right at the crime scene. No food had been taken from the residence.

This neighbor knew and liked David Harrison and when asked if Harrison might be a suspect, she replied there was no way he could ever kill someone.

The interview of Ron Peters by Detectives Parmely and Wisniewski revealed even more eye-opening suspicions about David Harrison.

Various tricks had been pulled on Anne Jenkins and other members of her immediate family. These tricks were not funny, nor could they be categorized merely as "practical jokes."

The proper term would be "harassment," pure and simple. For example, numerous magazine subscriptions had been completed in Anne's name and sent in with instructions to "bill me later."

Anne and Peter began receiving a deluge of unwanted literature. They had to contact each magazine and cancel the subscriptions. No harm had been done, but it was a bother to them nonetheless.

Then, mail stopped arriving at Anne's house and at the house of another close relative in San Diego County. Someone had filled out change of address forms and submitted them to the U.S. Post Office. Anne's mail had been rerouted to a location in Hawaii and the other relative's mail went to Michigan. That prank was much worse than the magazine subscription gag.

Next, when Peters tried to phone Anne from work one day, a recording told him, "The number you have reached is no longer in service and there is no new number . . ."

When Anne called the phone company she could not get

any help because the new number was unlisted and could not be given out by the phone company, a Catch-22 if ever there was one. Anne could not even find out what number to cancel.

Anne's family went without phone service for nearly a week while this mess was untangled. Anne and Peters were sure David Harrison was behind the maliciously juvenile prank.

Two other pranks were pulled involving another male relative of Anne Jenkins. This man had given financial help to Anne in her protracted legal battles with Harrison.

One day the relative began receiving phone calls and letters from homosexual men and from swinging couples inviting him for some sexual encounters. It was soon learned that someone had placed an ad in *Swinger* magazine listing the relative's name, address, and phone number. In all, over 300 phone calls were received and numerous letters seeking sexual relations. There was no proof, but the one and only suspect was David Harrison.

Finally, letters were circulated in the neighborhood where the relative lived. The letters were entitled "Pervert Alert" and accused the relative of incest and a variety of sexual deviations. Again, there was only one suspect: David Harrison.

Ron Peters told Detectives Parmely and Wisniewski there was one violent act David had committed. Peters' ex-wife lived nearby. After their divorce, Peters and his ex maintained a civil relationship. One morning at about 2:00 a.m., the ex-wife's van, parked in her driveway in another city, suddenly exploded. Shrapnel went sky-high and even penetrated the ex-wife's house. David Harrison phoned Peters and demanded an immediate meeting with him or there would be more explosions. Peters hung up on him.

Of course, the police were notified and an investigation was conducted. However, no evidence was found linking Harrison to this crime, other than the phone call.

Another meeting was held at homicide headquarters on February 21st, four days after Anne Jenkins' murder. The evidence was summarized and a plan of attack was formulated.

Robbery was ruled out as a motive. Anne had not surprised a burglar, the probers agreed. The detectives felt Anne was chased into the house by the killer.

At the autopsy performed by Deputy Medical Examiner John Eisele, it was determined that Anne had not been sexually assaulted and that no sex crime had been attempted against her. She had been strangled to the point of unconsciousness, after which her throat was cut from the middle point to the right ear and back again to the middle. It was murder, pure and simple: killing for the sake of killing.

Ron Peters was ruled out as a suspect. He had an alibi that was rock-solid. True, he would inherit the remainder of Anne's $727,000 lottery money, but he seemed disinterested in that.

The finger pointed at only one person — David Harrison. He appeared to possess the requisite wicked mind and intentions. Yet there was no physical evidence pointing toward him.

The detectives decided to get subpoenas and the necessary warrants to examine the documents submitted to the magazine companies requesting the bogus subscriptions. Sleuths hoped they could get enough probable cause to provide the link between the acts and David Harrison. But they knew that even if they could prove Harrison planned all the tricks against Anne Jenkins and her family, they were still a long way from proving David Harrison guilty of murder.

That same day, February 21st, four days after the murder, Detectives Parmely and Wisniewski finally got a break in the case.

A man named Fred Webb reluctantly phoned homicide and asked to come in for an interview. Webb was a 22-year-old truck driver for a small delivery firm. The story he told sent a ray of hope, ever so slight, into the hearts of Detectives Parmely and Wisniewski.

First of all, Webb independently confirmed that David Harrison held a burning hatred for Anne Jenkins. That claim had not been exaggerated by Ron Peters at all.

Webb told the detectives he was at a party on Valentine's Day, three days before Anne's murder. Webb had gone to his car to get a book. When he returned he was about to walk past the open garage door at the residence. David Harrison was in the garage with another man named Cleve Bennett. Both men were friends with Webb. Neither was aware of Webb's presence. Harrison had just put down the last of three large duffel bags, which he had carried from another direction.

Webb overheard Harrison say, "Now take these and hide them. The police will probably be searching my house in a few days and there are some things I don't want them to see."

"Like what?" Bennett asked.

Harrison replied, "Never mind, just hide them. And don't call me or leave a message on my machine for thirty days."

Bennett was very curious. "What the hell is going on? Why all the secrecy?" he asked.

"Just watch the news Wednesday or Thursday," Harrison replied, "You'll find out."

Webb returned to the party without further contact with Bennett or Harrison.

That sounded good to the detectives. They would rather that Harrison said, "Watch the news, I'm going to cut her throat." But he didn't, and they had to work with what they had.

Fred Webb also told the detectives that David Harrison owned a motorcycle registered in Cleve Bennett's name. The detectives were puzzled at that. Webb told the detectives that the arrangement had to do with the bombing of Peters' ex-wife's van.

Webb explained that Harrison had examined court documents and learned that Ron Peters and his ex-wife were about to have a hearing on some financial matters. Harrison hoped he could spark some animosity between Peters and his ex-wife by making her think Peters had bombed the van. Harrison said everyone knew he owned a big white Ca-

413

dillac. He wanted a motorcycle to drive to and from the bombing. He thought registering it under someone else's name would deflect attention from himself if he was stopped or spotted near the scene of the crime.

The wheels were set in motion to get a search warrant for Cleve Bennett's house and garage. The lawmen thought they would tighten the screws on Bennett, while they were at it. They figured that anyone who was told what Bennett was told by David Harrison after Anne Jenkins' murder and didn't come forward to tell police was probably a punk with something to hide.

Search warrants were served at both Bennett's and Harrison's respective homes. Inside the duffel bags the officers found a strange collection of equipment. There was a revolver, of no use in this case. There was a hunting knife, which would be no help since it had been in the duffel bag before Anne Jenkins' throat was cut.

The books were the most interesting of all. There were books on how to commit perfect crimes, how to get revenge against people, how to manufacture and live under assumed names, how to build bombs, and best of all, how to commit and get away with murder. There was black powder and pipe and thread used to make a pipe bomb. Now maybe there was something to go on in the case involving Ron Peters' ex-wife.

There was nothing that actually proved David Harrison killed Anne Jenkins, but there were things that strongly pointed toward that fact.

The search of David Harrison's apartment was relatively unproductive. Sleuths did find a motorcycle helmet in Harrison's bedroom closet. The motorcycle was found parked a few hundred feet away. It was impounded as evidence.

Under questioning, Cleve Bennett caved in. He verified the things Fred Webb had said, without knowing Webb had even talked with the police. Bennett insisted he did not know the contents of the duffel bags. However, Bennett was not completely truthful, admitting to only what he thought the officers already knew. Bennett could not explain why he agreed to have Harrison register Harrison's motorcycle in his name.

Bennett downplayed the hatred David Harrison had for Anne Jenkins. Whereas others told police that Harrison was consumed by anger toward her, Bennett merely said he did not think they got along very well.

When the detectives directed Bennett to give a handwriting sample, he asked why. Parmely, who looks like a younger, more fit version of Nick Nolte, narrowed his eyes and responded, "Because we have some other documents we want to see if you filled out."

Bennett said, "Oh, the change of address forms for the post office. That was a joke, you know, a trick. I didn't sign that under penalty of perjury or nothin'."

Parmely said, "Maybe not, but whose name did you sign?"

Bennett lowered his head and exhaled. He had signed Ron Peters' name, and that was forgery.

Since Harrison was not home when the search warrant was executed, a list of the things the officers seized was left there with a request to have Harrison call the sheriff's department. He never called. Included in the list was Harrison's motorcycle parked down the street. The motorcycle was the one registered to Cleve Bennett.

The following day, February 23rd, a surveillance was set up on David Harrison. The officers hoped to catch him doing something suspicious. Harrison was cool, though. He did a few errands and drove into San Diego.

Finally, about 3:00 p.m., on a busy San Diego street, the surveillance officers made their move. David Harrison gave up without incident. A search of his Cadillac revealed a motorcycle ignition key thrown down in the space between the driver's door and the seat. The key fit the ignition of Harrison's secret motorcycle.

Some brown thread removed from Harrison's house was matched to thread used in the making of the pipe bomb from Peters' ex-wife's van. That was enough to book Harrison into the federal jail. It was enough to buy some time for

415

the murder investigation.

After the arrest of David Harrison, Federal Prosecutor Larry Burns was assigned to the case. Burns, a 35-year-old former basketball star from the University of San Diego, had been a prosecutor for the district attorney. Burns had not lost a case in five years with the U.S. Attorney's Office.

Detectives Parmely and Wisniewski were not accustomed to working with "the feds." It was hard enough working with the local D.A.s. They wondered who this hotshot was and what made him so special.

Burns, the son of a police officer, also has a sister who is a deputy district attorney in Los Angeles. Burns got right to work, reviewing what they had in the bombing case and mapping out what he hoped they would uncover in the murder case.

Fred Webb was re-interviewed and actually gave the investigators an arson case. Webb told them Harrison had firebombed a boat belonging to a man named Hal Costa on September 23, 1987. The investigators wondered how Webb knew about this. He said Harrison had told him about it.

Apparently, Harrison had a homosexual relationship with Costa. During the relationship Costa had told Harrison that Costa's homosexuality was a very sore subject between his parents and him. The boat was the family's one common ground.

Eventually Costa wanted to end his relationship with Harrison, but Harrison resisted. Costa prevailed and the relationship was over. However, at 2:30 a.m. on September 23rd, the Costa boat, a beautiful 25-footer parked in the driveway of Costa's parents' home, erupted in flames and was completely destroyed.

Still another crime involving Cleve Bennett and David Harrison surfaced. Officers learned Harrison had been a victim of auto theft about two years before. Harrison's Corvette had been stolen and never recovered.

Webb informed them that Bennett had "stolen" the car at Harrison's direction. After the requisite waiting period, the insurance company paid Harrison $17,000. Meanwhile, the

416

car was dismantled and sold for parts with the profits going to Bennett and Harrison.

Since the insurance company check paid to Harrison originated in another state, Prosecutor Burns felt he could get Harrison for interstate fraud.

Burns assembled the three federal crimes: the bombing of Peters' ex-wife's van, the burning of Hal Costa's boat, and the insurance fraud of Harrison's phony car theft report.

Burns said, "These cases are solid. We'll prosecute him for these and keep working on Anne Jenkins' murder. There is no statute of limitations on murder."

However, the murder investigation did not go very far. People were interviewed and re-interviewed. Larry Burns set up his home computer to keep the people and evidence straight.

Neighbors of Anne Jenkins told of a witness who vanished after telling them he saw Anne arguing with "a guy" in her front yard. This witness vanished for over a year. He had outstanding traffic warrants and told his father he did not want to get involved. Burns wanted to talk to this witness to see who it was Anne was arguing with. But the man could not be located.

One more witness, Bob Karl, was located in Oregon. He too had a sexual relationship with David Harrison. Harrison had told Karl he would love to cut Anne Jenkins' throat and "watch her bleed." This would not blow the case wide open, but it was another brick in the foundation.

Karl also gave the officers a photograph depicting him with his throat being cut by David Harrison, who was clad only in underwear. It was a staged photograph with ketchup as blood. Still, it was a chillingly bizarre photo.

By now it was February 1989, one year after Anne Jenkins had been murdered. David Harrison was still in federal custody. He had contacted inmates and tried to arrange for harm to come to Fred Webb because of his part in Harrison's jailing. Every time he tried to get his bail lowered, Larry Burns paraded witnesses in front of the federal magistrate showing what a dangerous person Harrison was. So

Harrison remained behind bars.

Harrison had contacted family members by phone and tried to decide who to blame for Anne's murder. The phone calls were monitored. (There were signs above all the phones in jail, informing inmates their calls were being listened to.) Recordings were made of Harrison's strategy sessions on shifting the blame.

Prosecutor Larry Burns was set to go ahead with the federal charges. Harrison surprised them by pleading guilty and accepting a 20-year sentence, 10 for burning the boat and 10 for bombing the van. He was given probation for insurance fraud on his "stolen." Corvette.

David Harrison was hoping he would be shipped out of state to a federal prison and be forgotten by the likes of Prosecutor Burns and Detectives Parmely and Wisniewski. He underestimated these dedicated law enforcement officers. They had seen Anne Jenkins' body and seen what her murder had done to her family members. A 20-year-sentence for bombing and arson was not enough.

Burns suggested they go with what they had on the murder. The maximum amount of evidence had been accumulated. If it was not enough, so be it. David Harrison would have committed the "perfect crime" that he so dearly loved.

Burns had thoroughly reviewed the books in the duffel bag. There was *The Joy of Cold Revenge*. In this book were chapters instructing the reader to subscribe his enemies to scores of magazines the enemy did not want. It detailed the other "pranks" David Harrison had pulled on Anne Jenkins and her family.

One of the books had a chapter on murder. It told how to avoid leaving evidence the crime lab could find. It told of the value of secrecy, of not telling *anyone* about the crime. And the most incriminating part of the book actually told how to cut someone's throat. The chapter detailed exactly how Anne Jenkins died. She was strangled unconscious, then stabbed in the middle of the throat, slashed to her right ear and back to the middle. This would make interesting reading for the jury.

Prosecutor Larry Burns had mountains of documents and police reports. Detectives Terry Wisniewski and Mark Parmely had literally been all over the United States tracking down leads, some good, some useless. They had been as far away as New England and Oregon. At first, the two sleuths were cautious in their appraisal of Burns. Parmely was stubborn and untrusting, only because he had invested so much of himself in the Anne Jenkins case. Parmely approached his job as a seeker of scientific truth. In fact, Parmely had a bachelor's degree in biology.

Eventually the detectives came around. They finally perceived Larry Burns as being an ally instead of just another lawyer. Many cops believe "a lawyer is a lawyer," with the district attorneys only a little bit better than a defense attorney. Detectives Parmely and Wisniewski soon regarded Burns as a cop with a law degree. Burns thought like a cop and had a slightly twisted sense of humor like a cop. Best of all, Burns was not the least bit impressed with the fact that he was an attorney, as so many are.

The prosecution had a solid team. Since Larry Burns was cross-designated as a state prosecutor and a federal prosecutor, District Attorney Edwin L. Miller Jr., in conjunction with Assistant U.S. Attorney William Braniff, appointed Larry Burns to prosecute the case in state court, a move which surprised no one with an interest in the case.

Meanwhile, David Harrison had been through two defense attorneys and was now on his third, Alan May.

May often paraded the prosecutor's expected case before the press. May said the prosecution investigated the case carelessly. He said the police never even considered anyone else as a suspect. May conceded it was true that Harrison "did not like Anne Jenkins." This was a little more tame than what other witnesses had said: "He was consumed with anger. He was obsessed with hatred for her. He wanted to cut her throat and watch her bleed."

Lastly, May said there was no physical evidence, not one shred or particle that linked David Harrison to Anne Jenkins' murder. Larry Burns agreed with May's final point.

But Burns was also sure Harrison had killed his ex-wife.

On February 27, 1990, David Harrison surprised court watchers by waiving a jury trial. Instead, Judge David Moon Jr. alone would hear the evidence and decide Harrison's fate.

May and Harrison reasoned Harrison was a character too easy to dislike. He was a homosexual. He was vengeful. He admitted blowing up a van and fire-bombing a boat of two of his enemies. There were the "pranks" committed against Anne and her family. Harrison was dishonest. He committed fraud on an insurance company on a phony theft case.

In short, David Harrison was a despicable person. May and Harrison were afraid jurors would say, "There's no evidence he killed Anne Jenkins. But since he's such a creep, let's find him guilty anyway."

That was an oversimplification of the situation, but it was generally true. Judge Moon was highly respected by both sides and would make fair rulings and a good decision.

Larry Burns prepared for the trial in an impeccable manner. He knew court cases were not won by theatrics or "thinking on your feet." Cases were won by preparation, preparation, and more preparation.

The case proceeded right down the line. The evidence was circumstantial, but there was so much of it. Harrison had an alibi on the day of the murder, but there was a one-hour-and-18-minute "window" when Harrison could have ridden his secret motorcycle to Anne Jenkins' neighborhood, killed her, and ridden back home.

Prosecutor Burns presented testimony from a police officer who had made two trial runs from Harrison's apartment to Jenkins' home and back. Both were done while obeying posted speed limits. One of the trial runs allowed at least 26 minutes of latitude. Burns said Harrison could have used the 26 minutes to kill Anne Jenkins.

After Larry Burns completed the prosecution case, Alan May began the defense by calling David Harrison to the stand. The first question asked by May was, "Did you kill Anne Jenkins?" Harrison replied, "No." May said, "No further questions. Your witness."

This is what Larry Burns had hoped for, had dreamed about, had prepared for. It was no secret that Burns' feelings for David Harrison went beyond the hundreds of defendants he had prosecuted for murder and violent sex crimes. Burns believed Harrison was an evil, manipulative, dishonest, and violent person. Burns took Harrison apart for the next three hours.

Harrison was intelligent, to be sure. But he was no match for Larry Burns. Burns made Harrison go over in detail all the evidence in the case relating to the pranks, the bombing, and the arson. Burns spent a long time going over the "how to" crime books and the proper way to cut someone's throat as outlined in the book.

Burns made Harrison admit how Harrison had perjured himself in previous court appearances; how Harrison had discussed over the prison phone how to point the finger of guilt at someone else; and how he planned to carry a picture of his children into court to elicit sympathy from the jury before he decided to waive the jury.

Both attorneys presented their final arguments on Friday, March 16th. Everyone expected Judge Moon to mull over the evidence for a while.

Instead, Judge David Moon immediately found David Harrison guilty of first-degree murder. On April 25, 1990, Harrison was sentenced to 25 years to life in prison, a sentence that will run consecutively with the 20 years he is now serving for bombing and arson.

EDITOR'S NOTE:
*Ron Peters, Fred Webb, Cleve Bennett, Hal Costa, and Bob Karl are not the real names of the persons so named in the foregoing story. Fictitious names have been used because there is no reason for public interest in the identities of these persons.*

# "BOUND, GAGGED, AND RAPED WITH STICKS!"

## by Brian Malloy

Ronda Cayford carefully checked to find the right baby-sitter for her infant. She wanted someone she could trust, someone she knew who could handle the busy job of feeding and caring for the newest, most dependent member of her family while she went to work. Sarah Cherry, 15, had the right combination of trustworthiness and maturity. Ronda offered the job to Sarah and the teenager was more than happy to make some pocket change. It was summer vacation, and young Sarah hoped to make enough money to buy school clothes and maybe a high school ring.

On the Wednesday morning of July 6, 1988, Sarah Cherry arrived at the Cayford residence ready to begin her first day of babysitting. As Ronda hurried out to her car to go to work, she gave Sarah last minute instructions. Sarah seemed to understand exactly what Ronda wanted her to do, so when Ronda drove away from her home in Bowdoin, Maine, she was sure that her baby was in good hands.

Ronda almost never left her baby, so at lunchtime, around noon, she called Sarah to find out how things were going. Sarah told the anxious mother she was pleased with the way she and the baby were getting along. Ronda learned that Sarah had just fed the baby and was now making a sandwich for herself. Satisfied with the situation, Ronda said goodbye and went back to work.

Ronda didn't bother to make any other phone calls to the competent young babysitter for the rest of the work day. She drove back to her home and pulled into the driveway around 3:20 p.m. It was then that Ronda immediately sensed something was wrong. The front door of the house was ajar and several pieces of paper were littering her driveway. Ronda picked up the papers and then walked into the house, not knowing what she would find.

Ronda's first concern was for her child, whom she found safe and secure in the living room. The babysitter, however, was nowhere to be found. Ronda called out for Sarah, but there was no response. With her baby in her arms, Ronda checked each room of the house. Nothing appeared to be disturbed in the rooms and nothing had been stolen. Only Sarah Cherry was missing. It was as if the babysitter had simply walked off the job and left the infant to fend for itself.

Ronda was confident that Sarah would never leave the baby unattended. Something must have happened to take Sarah away, Ronda thought. As soon as she was sure Sarah was not on her property, Ronda called the sheriff's department.

Sagadahoc County Deputy Sheriff Daniel Reed took the orders from the dispatcher and drove his cruiser out to the Cayford residence to investigate the matter. He arrived at the scene at approximately 4:30 in the afternoon and was met in the driveway by Ronda Cayford.

Ronda gave Deputy Reed a quick summary of her story and handed him the papers she had found in the driveway. This was no ordinary missing person's case, Deputy Reed quickly concluded. He called for an all-out search for the missing babysitter.

While help was on the way, Deputy Reed looked over the papers Ronda had found in her driveway. He asked Ronda if she was certain that they weren't from her house. There was no way the papers were from her house, Ronda said. She suspected they had something to do with Sarah's disappearance.

Deputy Reed discovered that one of the papers was a sales receipt from a local garage for work done on a vehicle. The deputy called into headquarters the information contained on the receipt and asked that it be investigated further. Although the receipt did not give a license number, it did give information on the make and color of the vehicle that had been repaired: a red Toyota pickup. The recent date on the receipt suggested to Deputy Reed that the owner of the garage would probably remember whose vehicle the receipt was for.

The second paper found in the driveway was some type of business note, the deputy concluded. As soon as the business was identified, the law officers would have a cross-reference. Deputy Reed and the rest of the searchers hoped the papers would point directly to the missing babysitter's whereabouts.

As night began to fall, a large contingency from the sheriff's department and the Maine State Police were involved in a ground search for Sarah Cherry and the red pickup truck. As some officers searched by foot with the aid of trained K9 police dogs, other detectives were calling upon Sarah's friends and family. One by one, possible locations where Sarah might be were checked out and scratched off the list until it seemed that the only place Sarah might be was somewhere deep in the Maine woods.

The town of Bowdoin is located in southern Maine, where 75 percent of the state's one million residents live. This concentration of people is still spread out over a huge area of land, leaving vast parcels of thick second-growth forest. The searchers were faced with nightfall and countless miles of backcountry roads to search. Each of these country roads was intersected by numerous unpaved private roads leading to camps or secluded homes. Sarah Cherry and the red pickup truck could be anywhere, and the search proceeded slowly.

Residents noticed the large number of law enforcement vehicles in the area. Neighbors learned through the grapevine that Sarah Cherry was missing. In the small rural town of Bowdoin, Maine, neighbors watch out for each other. It was exactly this watchfulness that led to the first report of an unidentified man spotted wandering through the backyard of a home near Ronda Cayford's residence.

The call was logged at approximately 8:30 p.m., and a team of lawmen were immediately assigned to that area. While living in a small community does instill a sense of unity between people during times of tragedy, it also means that some people live so far apart from others that they are cut off from local news. That was the case for an elderly couple who saw a young man wandering through their backyard later that evening.

The couple knew nothing about the search for Sarah Cherry. They approached the man in their backyard without any reason to fear him. When the man said he had gotten lost while he was out fishing that day, the couple offered him their assistance. He was looking for his truck, he told them, so the couple decided to drive the man around the countryside until he found his pickup truck. It was a red Toyota, the man said.

As the couple drove the stranger down one of the back roads, they came upon a sheriff's patrol car. The elderly man pulled up beside the official. He explained that the young man sitting in the backseat of his car had lost his truck and asked the sheriff if he had seen a red Toyota pickup. The law officer, without mentioning the massive search for just such a vehicle, told the young man that he could help him find the truck. The lost fisherman, who said his name was Dennis Dechaine, then voluntarily entered the sheriff's car.

Dennis Dechaine was immediately taken to the search control center, where Detective Al Hensbee of the Maine State Police interviewed him. By this time, sleuths had identified the papers found in the Cayford driveway as relating to a vehicle owned by one Dennis Dechaine. Also, the business papers were discovered to be from a local enterprise that was managed by the same Dennis Dechaine.

Detective Hensbee had quite a few questions for Dechaine, and, as an incredible stroke of luck would have it, Dechaine had virtually walked in on his own. Dechaine was read his rights and shortly thereafter, the detective began a long grilling.

Dechaine appeared completely surprised by the situation he found himself in. He told Detective Hensbee exactly what he had told the elderly couple: He was out fishing on the stream beyond the road and had gotten lost. He said he didn't know Sarah Cherry, had never seen Sarah Cherry, and didn't know where she was.

Hensbee showed Dechaine a picture of the Cayford house and asked Dechaine if he had been there that day. No, Dechaine said. Then how did the receipt for the pickup truck and the other papers get in the Cayford driveway? the detective wanted to know. Dechaine's answer was that someone must have put them there.

This was a totally unsatisfactory answer, as far as Detective Hensbee was concerned. He continued to grill Dechaine, hoping to get a better answer. Surely, people had been framed before. Yet it seemed unlikely in this case. Detective Hensbee believed that Dennis Dechaine was the one and only person who knew what had happened to Sarah Cherry. With skillful questioning, a suspect can often be led into revealing the details of a crime merely by being allowed to talk. At that point in the investigation, this was all Detective Hensbee could do. After all, Sarah Cherry was still missing. There was no crime to charge Dechaine with, only one that was suspected.

As the night wore on, Dechaine began to change his story. He decided that he had seen the Cayford residence, after all. While searching for a place to start fishing, Dechaine said, he had used the Cayford driveway to turn around in. When he was asked again how that accounted for the papers coming out of his truck, Dechaine suddenly remembered that he had also stopped to urinate in the yard. Detective Hensbee decided to detain the suspect a while longer to see what else he would say.

A search of Dechaine's body revealed that he had a bruise

on his left biceps. That, Dechaine explained, came from a fall he had taken while wandering lost through the woods. As for Dechaine's clothes, no blood was found on them. Dechaine felt that was enough to stop the questioning. It wasn't.

While Dechaine was being questioned, sleuths found his red pickup truck. It was parked off the road and locked. Detectives took imprints of the vehicle's tires to see if they matched those taken from the Cayford driveway. The area around the truck was scoured for evidence, and a few cigarette butts were gathered from the ground by the driver's side door. When it was time to examine the truck's interior, the detectives decided to call over Dechaine to unlock the truck, rather than jimmy the door and risk ruining any evidence that might possibly be present.

Dechaine identified the truck as his and used his key to unlock the door. When asked if this was the place where he had parked the truck to go fishing, Dechaine claimed that the darkness made it impossible for him to be sure. None of the police officers were surprised at that response.

Once the truck was opened for examination, a team of sleuths descended on it in search of evidence. They found a rope behind the passenger's seat but little else. Nothing could be identified at that moment. The detectives at the scene found nothing, such as an article of clothing, to automatically link Dennis Dechaine to Sarah Cherry.

Throughout the night, Dechaine appeared confused by what was happening to him and repeatedly told the detectives that he was being framed. All he had done, he repeated, was go to fishing and be unfortunate enough to get lost. Everything was circumstantial, he said, and he asked to be released. At 4:30 on the morning of July 7th, since detectives had nothing concrete to hold him on, Dechaine was driven to his home and released from police custody.

The detectives assigned to the case were sure that something, somewhere, would break the case of the missing babysitter, even though their prime suspect was free. Throughout the day of July 7, 1988, more and more lawmen were assigned the task of finding Sarah Cherry. The main thrust of the search was in the area surrounding Dechaine's parked pickup. In addition to units already involved in the search, a special task force from the naval air base in nearby Brunswick was bused to the site to search the woods a square foot at a time.

It was the unit from the navy base that came upon Sarah Cherry's body a few hundred yards from where Dechaine's truck was parked. The 15-year-old girl, naked and with her hands tied, was found in a shallow grave. A red bandanna that had apparently been used to gag her was still in her mouth. A number of stab wounds perforated her neck and throat, and sticks were found inserted in her vagina and anus.

The grisly crime scene was thoroughly combed and every piece of evidence was catalogued. Sleuths found a fiber of red cloth clinging to a tree near where the body was found. After bagging the evidence and photographing the scene, the probers backtracked from the body to the location of the pickup truck. As the lawmen worked to determine the most likely route the murderer had taken with Sarah, they found another bit of evidence, a piece of rope, lying on the ground. While these bits of evidence were significant; the detectives never found the knife that had inflicted the fatal wounds or any other object that might help identify the murderer.

A team of law enforcement officials drove out to Dennis Dechaine's house and placed him under arrest. This time there was no need to play cat and mouse, waiting for Dechaine to make an incriminating remark. This time sleuths had a body and a murder charge. The detectives, confident they had the right man, led Dechaine away in handcuffs.

The town of Bowdoin was shocked by both the crime and by the identity of the accused murderer. The very nature of the crime was enough to get the blood boiling in any human being with a conscience. The murder of a 15-year-old baby-sitter was in itself unconscionable, but coupled with that was the horrifying idea that the abduction took place while a helpless infant watched. The crime was totally out of the bounds of humanity. And who had committed such a crime? The residents of Bowdoin were shocked, saddened, and confused to hear that it was lifelong resident and neighbor Dennis Dechaine.

Dechaine had graduated at the top of his high school class. The mild-mannered Dechaine was a nonviolent man, his friends were quick to point out. At age 23, he had already settled down with a wife and a secure job as a much-seen manager of a local business. Did the police have the right man? some of the residents wondered.

Other residents were confident the police had the right man behind bars, yet they had another question: What had caused the apparently peaceful man to snap?

The police could not answer the question why Dennis Dechaine chose to murder. Even if a psychologist could have uncovered a dark spot in Dechaine's personality, the discovery of evil is not an explanation of evil. And police officers are not psychologists or philosophers. If anything, they're more like scientists. They deal in facts and evidence. Though the probers could not answer the questions of why Dechaine did what he did, they could prove he was the guilty man.

To accomplish this task, chemist Judith Brinkman was asked to analyze the evidence. From the outside, the case against Dechaine seemed good. He was caught wandering through the area of the crime only a few hours after Sarah Cherry was reported missing. It was his papers that were found in the Cayford driveway where Sarah was babysitting. It was his truck that was found only a few hundred yards from the body. Yet Dechaine could, as he claimed, have been the victim of circumstances. Without an eyewitness, without any blood found on his body or his possessions, a good defense lawyer could prove to a jury that the police had nabbed the wrong man. Somewhere in the few bits of evidence found at the scene was a physical link between Dennis Dechaine and Sarah Cherry, and the chemist was the only one who could uncover it.

Brinkman had three fields of evidence to study. First was the Cayford house, where Dechaine's papers were found. The papers themselves, it turned out, showed nothing in the way of fingerprints because they had been handled by Ronda Cayford and subsequent police officers. Inside the Cayford house, there were no fingerprints that belonged to Dechaine. For that matter, no fingerprints belonging to any person other than the residents of the house and Sarah Cherry were discovered.

The truck had the potential of yielding a great deal of evidence, since it appeared that Sarah was transported to her death in it. Brinkman paid special attention to finding solid evidence establishing that Sarah had been in the truck. When all the tests were run, however, no physical evidence was found to indicate Sarah's presence in the truck. Only one spot of blood was found, and that was old and of Dechaine's type.

What the chemist Brinkman could and did do was examine the rope found in the truck and look for a match between it and the rope used to tie the victim. This rope, under analysis, proved that there was a physical link between Dennis Dechaine and Sarah Cherry. When placed under a microscope, the chemist was able to match the tiny braids of rope. This evidence disproved Dechaine's claim that the case against him was purely circumstantial.

To help beef up the case, detectives were issued a search warrant of Dechaine's home in hopes of finding more links. In the barn on his property, sleuths uncovered more rope of the same type and make. This, too, was sent to the chemist for testing.

In her report to the court, Brinkman confirmed that the rope found on Dechaine's property and that used to tie up Sarah Cherry was significantly similar. Because of the rope's age, however, Brinkman could not prove conclusively that both pieces were from the same coil.

Since the first two fields of evidence were turning up little hard evidence, the chemist had but one chance left to determine if Dechaine was Sarah's murderer. The detectives had discovered hairs on Sarah's body that were not her own, which, due to the violent nature of the crime, was to be expected. The hairs were placed under a microscope by the chemist for study. The prospect of making an exact match was not good because hair follicles are not like fingerprints. The chemist could note the color and qualities of the hair and seek similar qualities in Dechaine's hair. Judith Brinkman found that Dechaine's hair was extremely similar to the hair found on Sarah's body. As for a perfect match, the chemist had to admit that the samples could not be proven beyond a shadow of a doubt to belong to Dechaine. These hairs, while not proving that Dechaine was guilty, could not be used to prove he was innocent, either. If hairs of a totally different color had been found, then the case against Dechaine would have never taken a new twist. But the overall evidence continued to point directly at Dennis Dechaine.

With all the evidence in, Assistant Attorney General Eric E. Wright was assigned as state prosecutor for the murder trial. So little hard evidence was found that a guilty verdict was far from certain. The defense was highly critical of the way police handled Dechaine's arrest. The heart of the defense revolved around what Dechaine considered suppressed evidence. He stated on the witness stand that he had immediately asked for DNA samples of his hair but was never granted his request. He also claimed that cigarette butts found outside his parked truck were of a different brand from those he smoked. He was totally innocent, he maintained. Instead of considering all the possible suspects, his defense lawyer said, the police were myopic and closed minded once they had Dechaine's papers identified. Instead of assuming Dechaine was innocent until proven guilty, the defense asserted, the police had focused only on him and had chosen not to investigate any other possibilities.

The judge and jury heard both sides of the case during the spring of 1989. They listened to the testimony of neighbors who stated that they had seen a red pickup truck cruising near the Cayford residence. Some of Dechaine's friends took the stand to say on record that he was a nonviolent person. Another friend of Dechaine's told the jury that earlier that summer he had mentioned to Dechaine that the stream behind the Cayford house was full of trout. Dechaine told him that some day he would take a whole day and fish it. The chemist's testimony was looked at carefully, as was the testimony of all the police officers involved in the investigation.

During the course of the trial, Dennis Dechaine's carefully constructed persona as a misunderstood "nice guy" came unraveled when it was revealed that he had an expensive drug habit. Prosecutor Wright established that Dechaine frequently drove to Boston to purchase exotic drugs in the men's room of the bus station. It also came out that on the afternoon of July 6, 1988, Dechaine was not fishing in the woods near the Cayford residence but was taking a variety of potent drugs. This, Wright argued, would more than sufficiently explain Dechaine's sudden snapping that fateful afternoon.

After deliberating, the jury returned to the courtroom and told Justice Carl O. Bradford that they had found Dennis Dechaine guilty as charged. He was charged with two counts of murder: intentional or knowing murder, which assumes a degree of premeditation, and depraved indifference murder, which assumes a particularly heinous quality to the crime. The judge sentenced Dechaine to two life terms at the Maine State Prison in Thomaston, the maximum sentence allowable for his crimes.

Even after the sentencing, many people still wondered if Dechaine had been framed. Dechaine later mounted an appeal, based on disproving the circumstantial nature of most of the evidence. In an odd, Hollywood-like twist, Dechaine also claimed he had evidence that would finger the "real" murderer. Through a private investigator, Dechaine and his lawyers were able to find another resident of Bowdoin who owned the same type of red truck involved in the murder. The resident did not have a good alibi on the day of Sarah Cherry's murder.

Another witness came forward in Dechaine's defense, stating that prior to the murder, Dechaine had mentioned that some of his private possessions had been stolen out of his truck. This witness, the defense believed, would give substance to Dechaine's claim that he had been framed.

The appeal was never granted. The judge decided that, if anything, Dechaine had tried to frame himself. The appeal never made clear how the same rope used to tie the victim had been found in the truck. There was also no way anyone would have known he was going fishing, since Dechaine had already stated that his decision to go to the stream that day had been on the spur of the moment.

One possible conclusion to draw from the baffling case is that Dechaine had, for some unfathomable reason, planned to commit a random murder months in advance. He may have "stolen" his own possessions, placed them in the Cayford's driveway to appear that he had been framed, and hoped that his case would be dismissed for lack of evidence. To further throw police off his track, Dechaine might have washed up in the stream and buried his bloodstained clothes along with the murder weapon in the deep woods where they would never be found. Then he would have returned to his truck and smoked several cigarettes of a different brand from the one he ordinarily smoked, thinking that would further point to some killer other than himself.

But if that were his plan, it failed dismally, and Dennis Dechaine now smokes his cigarettes behind bars.

EDITOR'S NOTE:
*Ronda Cayford is not the real name of the person so named in the foregoing story. A fictitious name has been used because there is no reason for public interest in the identity of this person.*

# APPENDIX

"A Fire Poker Pierced His Brain!" *Master Detective*, July, 1992

"Alive and Thrashing as They Cut Off Her Head!" *Official Detective*, January, 1992

"Gruesome Foursome Prescribed Death for 41" *True Detective*, January, 1993

"Gary Heidnik's House of Horrors . . . His Sex Slaves Were Shackled, Nude and Fed Dog Food!" *True Detective*, January, 1993

"Unnatural Acts with a Red-Hot Knife!" *Master Detective*, February, 1993

"Beaten, Tortured, Degraded: A Ten-Year-Old's Ordeal!" *Front Page Detective*, August, 1993

"Pedophile Trolled for Young Boys . . . He Used 3 As Experiments in Torture!" *True Detective*, October, 1991

"Stuck Salt into His Dying Victims' Wounds!" *Official Detective*, June, 1993

"Torture Killing of the Wealthy Stockbroker" *Front Page Detective*, March, 1981

"48 Hours of Rape and Torture!" *Front Page Detective*, October, 1986

"Beheaded and Castrated Alive!" *Official Detective*, October, 1991

"He Won't Talk? Torture Him!" *Official Detective*, December, 1989

"Ghoul Killers Took Turns Stabbing Her 120 Times!" *Front Page Detective*, December, 1983

"He Dropped Her in a Vat of Acid!" *Master Detective*, February, 1993

"Bible-Clutching Gang-Raped Teen!" *True Detective*, January, 1993

"Twisted Torture Tools of the Rush-Seeking Sickos" *True Detective*, January, 1992

"Rabbi Suffocated with His Skullcap!" *Front Page Detective*, September, 1985

"Bound Sex Slave Had Her Throat Slit!" *Master Detective*, April, 1993

"He Raped Her, Bashed Her, and Buried A Compass in Her Arm!" *Master Detective*, April, 1993

"Ravaged, Then Burned Alive!" *True Detective*, January, 1991

"Hanged Her, Then Yanked Out Her Teeth!" *Official Detective*, June, 1992

"Four Victims Tortured First, Then Murdered!" *Front Page Detective*, December, 1980

"Death Was the Final Mercy for Little Amy!" *Official Detective*, January, 1991

"Wacko Wanted to Watch the Beauty Bleed!" *Master Detective*, April, 1992

"Bound, Gagged, and Raped with Sticks!" *Master Detective*, July, 1992